Testing the Limits

Testing the Limits

George W. Bush and the Imperial Presidency

Mark J. Rozell and Gleaves Whitney

ROWMAN & LITTLEFIELD PUBLISHERS, INC.
Lanham • Boulder • New York • Toronto • Plymouth, UK

ROWMAN & LITTLEFIELD PUBLISHERS, INC.

Published in the United States of America
by Rowman & Littlefield Publishers, Inc.
A wholly owned subsidiary of The Rowman & Littlefield Publishing Group, Inc.
4501 Forbes Boulevard, Suite 200, Lanham, Maryland 20706
www.rowmanlittlefield.com

Estover Road
Plymouth PL6 7PY
United Kingdom

British Library Cataloguing in Publication Information Available

Library of Congress Cataloging-in-Publication Data

Testing the limits : George W. Bush and the imperial presidency / edited by Mark J.
  Rozell and Gleaves Whitney.
    p. cm.
  Includes bibliographical references and index.
  ISBN 978-1-4422-0039-5 (cloth : alk. paper) — ISBN 978-1-4422-0040-1 (paper :
alk. paper) — ISBN 978-1-4422-0041-8 (electronic)
  1. Bush, George W. (George Walker), 1946– —Political and social views. 2. Bush,
George W. (George Walker), 1946– —Influence. 3. United States—Politics and
government—2001–2009. 4. United States—Foreign relations—2001–2009.
5. Political leadership—United States—Case studies. 6. Executive power—United
States—Case studies. 7. Imperialism—Case studies. I. Rozell, Mark J. II. Whitney,
Gleaves.
  E903.3.T46 2009
  973.931092—dc22   2009021172

Printed in the United States of America

∞ ™ The paper used in this publication meets the minimum requirements of
American National Standard for Information Sciences—Permanence of Paper
for Printed Library Materials, ANSI/NISO Z39.48-1992.

Contents

Acknowledgments   vii

Introduction   ix
Gleaves Whitney

Part I: Analyzing the Bush Presidency

Chapter 1   The Evolution of the George W. Bush Presidency   3
             John P. Burke

Chapter 2   The Bush Staff and Cabinet System   23
             Charles E. Walcott and Karen M. Hult

Chapter 3   George W. Bush's Domestic Policy Agenda   45
             Andrew E. Busch

Chapter 4   How George W. Bush Remade American
             Foreign Policy   73
             Ryan J. Barilleaux and David Zellers

Chapter 5   The Deficit Redux: Budget Politics during the
             Bush Administration   91
             Iwan Morgan

Chapter 6   The Anatomy of a Divorce: Conservatives versus
             George W. Bush   117
             Gleaves Whitney

Part II: Presidential Powers and the Bush Presidency

Chapter 7   War Powers in the Bush Administration   131
John Yoo

Chapter 8   Bush and the War Power: A Critique from Outside   157
Louis Fisher

Chapter 9   George Bush as Commander in Chief   177
Dale R. Herspring

Chapter 10   Executive Privilege: The Bush Record and Legacy   199
Mark J. Rozell and Mitchel A. Sollenberger

Chapter 11   Bush's Greatest Legacy? The Federal Courts and
the Republican Regime   219
Thomas M. Keck

Chapter 12   George W. Bush and the Imperial Presidency   243
Andrew Rudalevige

Index   269

About the Authors   281

~

Acknowledgements

We incurred many debts in organizing, writing, and editing this volume. Our gratitude to the very distinguished group of contributors who agreed to write the chapters of this volume and to then also present their findings at two academic conferences on the Bush presidency. We especially thank the Hauenstein Center for Presidential Studies at Grand Valley State University for its sponsorship and support for the November 2008 conference in Grand Rapids, Michigan and for the December 2009 program at the Library of Congress in Washington, DC. The Library of Congress and the George Mason University School of Public Policy cosponsored the Washington, DC conference. GVSU vice presidents Maribeth Wardrop and Matt McLogan provided substantial support for this project. Working hard but cheerfully in the trenches were Mary Eilleen Lyon, Brian Flanagan, Mandi Bird, Kathy Rent, Austin Knuppe, Heather Landis, and a bevy of interns. In addition, John Sisk, Melissa Wilks, and the capable staff at Rowman & Littlefield provided expert editorial direction and advice. To all who made this book possible, the editors convey their gratitude.

Mark J. Rozell
Gleaves Whitney
April 2009

~

Introduction

Gleaves Whitney

The presidency of George W. Bush brimmed with paradox. Critics on the Left and Right have teased out many of the ironies. They stress that in 2000, Bush received a half million fewer votes than Al Gore, yet gained the White House. His approval numbers were the highest ever polled (89 percent in 2001)—but also the lowest ever polled (22 percent in 2008). He championed tax cuts, yet ended up presiding over a dramatic expansion of the federal government. A self-styled "compassionate conservative," Bush did not effectively mobilize the federal government to help poor residents on the Gulf Coast ravaged by Hurricane Katrina.

Bush was the longest serving commander in chief in U.S. history, yet the Global War on Terror he did so much to define and prosecute got bogged down in Iraq—a state peripheral to the September 11 attacks. He advanced the idea of spreading freedom abroad even while he was lambasted for the Patriot Act that eroded freedom at home. In 2004 Bush's chief political strategist, Karl Rove, believed a durable Republican majority was taking shape—until just two years later when the Republican Party lost both houses of Congress. Bush trumpeted the ownership society, yet more Americans foreclosed on their homes than ever before during his eight years in office. How ironic that our first president with a master's degree in business administration presided over the near collapse of Wall Street.

Paradoxes indeed. Yet as this volume will demonstrate, one can also search out many positive formulations of the Bush presidency. Upon entering the Oval Office, the 43rd president lacked substantial military experience, yet learned quickly how to be a decisive commander in chief. Although the nation experienced its worst attack since Pearl Harbor and braced for more, no further attacks occurred on his watch—that dog did not bark. As a result, his successor Barack Obama campaigned on a message of change, but actually continued many of Bush's policies in national security and foreign affairs (including wiretaps and the troop surge in Afghanistan). When a long-awaited vacancy on the Supreme Court opened up, his hapless initial choice of Harriet Miers gave way to a much higher caliber nominee in John Roberts. The president who was regarded as a reckless cowboy in foreign affairs was the same president who saved an estimated 1.1 million Africans in their fight against AIDS. And while the war in Iraq made Bush extremely unpopular, it may yet prove to be one of the president's enduring legacies if popular government takes root in the heart of the Middle East.

Plumbing the tensions, ironies, and paradoxes of the Bush administration are fifteen scholars whose work is gathered in these pages. The book is divided in two parts. Part I looks at the administration from various analytical angles, beginning with John Burke's overview in chapter 1. Burke traces the evolution of the Bush presidency from 2001 to 2009. He points out that "Bush 43" began his transition in office well, laying the groundwork for a reasonably successful early presidency. Indeed, his leadership and decision-making processes enabled the White House to respond vigorously to September 11 and then to the war against the Taliban in Afghanistan. Partisanship, however, asserted itself as the mid-term 2002 elections approached. Decision making and information gathering proved problematic in the decision to go to war against Iraq and also in the postwar reconstruction of that divided nation. Although Bush won re-election in 2004, his campaign themes failed to lay the foundation for a successful second term. Moreover, the administration failed to make much needed personnel changes. As a result, mistakes piled up, the most notable being the response to Hurricane Katrina. The loss of Republican control of Congress in 2006 effectively made Bush a lame duck president. Bush experienced significant success by ordering the troop "surge" in Iraq. But when the economic crisis hit—unprecedented since the Great Depression—the president's stimulus package, bank bailout plan, and aid to the U.S. auto industry were met with strong criticism on both sides of the aisle. Time had run out for this president. Devising an effective response was now a problem that fell to his successor.

In chapter 2, Charles Walcott and Karen Hult look closely at how the Bush presidency handled staff and cabinet processes. They argue that the Bush administration inherited several trends in White House-executive branch relations—among them, centralization of decision making in the

White House; politicization of policy; formal structuring of White House management; a "permanent campaign" approach to governing; and a powerful vice presidency. These trends were not only embraced, but were often amplified. In the aftermath of September 11, Vice President Richard Cheney and his allies especially came to dominate many policy areas. Although more inclusive decision making eventually reemerged, it came relatively late in the second term, making policy innovation unlikely.

Andrew Busch focuses on domestic policy in chapter 3. During his campaign for office, Bush set out to change the political landscape through a domestic policy agenda that would satisfy conservative Republicans, while simultaneously softening the party's image it had inherited from the Bill Clinton years. In some areas of domestic policy, Bush enjoyed surprising successes; and in other areas, embarrassing failures. Observers of the Bush White House have been quick to argue not only over whether Bush's initiatives were good or bad, but also even how to characterize them. For some, Bush was at least as conservative as Ronald Reagan, an ideologue who sought to turn narrow electoral victories into a conservative mandate for public policy. Others argue that Bush's efforts were an ambitious and commendable attempt to turn big government to conservative ends for the first time in decades. Tax cuts, education reform, and Supreme Court appointments were among some of the domestic successes of the Bush administration.

Ryan J. Barilleaux and David Zellers in chapter 4 set their sights on foreign policy. Like many of the men who came to the Oval Office, Bush had little background in foreign policy. In the end, he remade foreign policy in ways that will be difficult to revise and committed the nation to policies that will continue into the foreseeable future. The Bush revolution in foreign affairs included the Global War on Terror and U.S. intervention in Iraq. But other aspects of the Bush transformation will not outlive his administration—for example, the use of U.S. military might for purposes of regime change, nation-building, unilateral diplomacy (which tended to alienate close allies), and a cavalier attitude toward the public's concerns with the Patriot Act and domestic wiretaps.

In chapter 5, Iwan Morgan turns to budget matters in the Bush administration. Despite a tendency to tolerate large budget deficits inherited from previous administrations, Bush did not prioritize debt reduction as part of his ambitious economic agenda. The 43rd president subordinated fiscal responsibility to other elements of his governing agenda—most importantly, tax cuts, defense expansion after September 11, and the growth of domestic programs such as the No Child Left Behind Act. Morgan also considers Bush's reversion to deficit control in dealing with a Democratic Congress in 2007 and how the economic crisis in his final year in office undid that agenda.

Gleaves Whitney, in chapter 6, looks at why numerous conservatives at first supported, then opposed, the 43rd president. Many fiscal conservatives were appalled by the dramatic growth of the federal budget and federal government, especially during the six years Bush had allies in the Republican-controlled Congress. A number of foreign policy realists thought the president was not well served by neoconservatives who imprudently championed a neo-Wilsonian foreign policy that involved grandiose plans to spread democracy and freedom abroad—at not an inconsiderable cost to U.S. blood and treasure. And several cultural conservatives criticized Bush's embrace of the religious right as dangerous and even un-American.

Part II examines the highly controversial topic of presidential powers vis-à-vis the Bush administration. In chapter 7, John Yoo takes an inside look at presidential war powers. Yoo argues that, "It is often said that the 43rd president advanced claims of executive authority farther than any other president—but this argument is an exaggeration." Several Bush administration policies—including signing statements, executive privilege, and national security wiretaps—followed presidential precedent. "Bush's exercise of war powers may have differed in number, but not in kind," Yoo says. Many believed that war was an unnecessary scourge and that our constitutional processes should be designed to discourage resorting to it. But weapons of mass destruction (WMD) proliferation, the rise of international terrorism, and the persistence of non-state actors have made the use of force more necessary and the prospects for worldwide peace and prosperity more problematic. Yoo surmises, "Balanced institutional participation and greater deliberation may do a better job than sole presidential initiative in committing the nation to a war today that shows no sign of disappearing." Yoo concludes that the Constitution permits, but does not compel, this choice.

Louis Fisher, who in chapter 8 critiques the president's war powers from the "outside," provides a very different perspective. In previous times, presidents exercised broad authority both unilaterally and on the basis of statutory grants by Congress during national emergencies. "President George W. Bush exceeded their grasp for power by claiming he could invoke 'inherent' powers under Article II that could not be limited by Congress or the courts," writes Fisher. More than other presidents, Bush worked on the basis of confidential legal memos and the state secrets doctrine to violate many statutes, treaties, and most importantly, the Constitution. The damage to constitutional government, individual rights, national security, and the rule of law has been profound. Fisher concludes that "the Bush record is one of executive fiat over democracy and representative government."

In chapter 9, Dale Herspring assesses the role of Bush as a commander in chief. Herspring notes that one important factor that characterized the 43rd president was his background as a chief executive officer (CEO). In fact, Bush was the first CEO to assume the presidency. Because of this background in business, Bush attempted to stay above the normal tug-of-war in the federal bureaucracy. He let his subordinates, especially cabinet-level secretaries, deal with everyday policy making. Once a policy recommendation was ready, he discussed it with the relevant officials and made a decision. Herspring argues that from the viewpoint of the bureaucracy, "this meant that Bush was dependent on whom he chose to lead a department, in this case the Department of Defense." His first choice, Donald Rumsfeld (a former CEO as well), treated the Defense Department as if it were a multinational corporation, refusing to recognize military protocol and procedure. The result was continuous battle between Rumsfeld and the rest of the military brass. Finally, the situation improved dramatically when Robert Gates was appointed to take Rumsfeld's place in December 2006. Gates provided the Pentagon with clear leadership, and he also respected military culture. Thus, the Rumsfeld-to-Gates transition restored civil-military relations both in the Department of Defense and the Bush administration.

Mark J. Rozell and Mitchel A. Sollenberger, in chapter 10, describe and analyze Bush's controversial penchant for secrecy. The 43rd president engaged in a number of battles over executive privilege—the constitutional principle that recognizes the right of presidents and high-level staff to withhold information from Congress, the courts, and ultimately the public. (The phrase "executive privilege" itself was never used by any president until the 1950s, but the same power effectively has existed since the Washington administration.) Bush's use of executive privilege did not rise to the level of protecting the general national interest. Many of his claims appeared to be attempts to conceal department and agency decision-making processes, not high-level presidential deliberations on issues of national importance. The authors maintain that one should be mindful not to leave the executive branch unprotected by weakening executive privilege to the point where all presidential deliberations become public almost instantly. "Executive privilege, when taken too far, can hinder congressional investigations into policymaking endeavors, corruption cases, and other important matters," they argue. Throughout Bush's presidency, the executive branch prevented Congress from viewing documents and material that related to key aspects of the bureaucracy. Creating a closed-door policy, where the executive branch alone decides these important issues, removes Congress from the process and handicaps the constitutional framework of U.S. government.

In chapter 11, Thomas Moylan Keck examines Bush's federal court appointments. Aggressively employing his powers to nominate federal judges and direct the litigation efforts of the Department of Justice, the 43rd president aimed to construct a reliable institutional ally that would "facilitate his policy and political goals in the short term and remain in place long after he had left the White House." Bush's lasting mark on the courts is clear—sixty federal appellate judge appointments and two Supreme Court justices are two of the strongest pieces of evidence. However, given the scope of Republican ambitions—a thorough makeover of the judicial branch—Bush's efforts ultimately fell short.

Chapter 12 concludes our work with Andrew Rudalevige examining Bush in light of the imperial presidency. Political pundits of all persuasions originally expected Bush to be a "post-imperial" president. Bush—and history—had different plans. Seeking to reverse what he and Vice President Cheney saw as "the crippling limits Congress had placed on the executive branch in response to the Watergate/Vietnam era," the president laid out expansive claims to exclusive authority grounded in a newly broad theory of the "unitary executive." This held true even before September 11, but those attacks moved the nation to a war footing and enhanced the president's position as commander in chief. This potent combination justified wide-ranging diplomatic and military policies in the Global War on Terror. Congress and courts were told not to intervene; and any of their attempts to put executive power on a short leash were criticized as unconstitutional. The most extreme of these claims were moderated during Bush's eight years in office. As a lasting legacy to future presidents, the Bush administration's executive strategies are likely to remain in the presidential playbook for many years to come. The "imperial presidency" will thus continue to be a phrase with currency.

PART ONE

ANALYZING THE BUSH PRESIDENCY

CHAPTER ONE

~

The Evolution of the
George W. Bush Presidency

John P. Burke

How to understand and account for the presidency of George W. Bush? There are a number of what might be termed "lenses of analysis" that are useful in making sense of the U.S. presidency or the administration of a particular president. Many of the other chapters in this volume exemplify this, whether it is attention to the use of the cabinet and the organization of the White House staff, reliance on the bully pulpit, the politics of a foreign or domestic agenda, the president's leadership style, or the administration's conception of war-time prerogatives and other constitutional powers.

Stephen Skowronek has argued, quite persuasively, that the broader "political time" of a presidency especially matters in understanding its success or failure. In his view, the place of a presidency within a broader historical cycle of political regimes defines its challenges, sets forth its resources and opportunities, and establishes the parameters for evaluating its performance.[1] Much can be learned from Skowronek's perspective. However, I would like to focus on a more internal lens of analysis, one composed of three interrelated parts.

The first part is what might be termed the "internal time" of the Bush presidency. By that I mean the internal rhythms *within* a presidential administration that set down challenges and call for an effective response. As I and others have argued, for example, transitions to office can be highly consequential for new presidencies, not just in putting an administration in place but also in charting the course for its future success. Next, as administrations progress through time, electoral cycles within a presidency become important: first the consequences of the mid-term congressional races, followed by the ramping up for re-election. For presidents who are successful at re-election, the prospect of a "lame duck" presidency looms. It might arise, first, in terms of the "sixth-year itch" that often brings losses in congressional seats. Difficulties are then compounded, as the election of a successor approaches, by a significant deflection of attention away from the policy initiatives and actions of the incumbent administration. In fact, the situation is increasingly debilitating for a sitting president as attention now focuses on the upcoming presidency earlier and earlier each election cycle.

The second part of my analytic lens is crises; they too must be factored in. They punctuate those internal rhythms, interrupting the routine, and putting presidents and their advisers to the test. They mark key moments in a presidency. Sometimes crises are external in source and unexpected: the invasion of South Korea for Harry Truman, the Suez crisis and Sputnik for Dwight Eisenhower, the Cuban missile crisis for John Kennedy, and the Iranian seizure of U.S. hostages for Jimmy Carter. Sometimes events are of an administration's own making: the Bay of Pigs invasion for Kennedy, Watergate for Richard M. Nixon, Iran-Contra for Ronald Reagan, and the Lewinsky affair and the subsequent impeachment effort for Bill Clinton.

Third, internal time and crisis call for response. Here we come to individual presidents and the deliberative apparatus that has been created to assist their decision making. Some presidents have recognized the opportunities presented and made decisions leading to success. Others have failed to do so and suffered the negative consequences. Moreover, presidential decision and response loom large in Bush's presidency—both early and thereafter. While the imprint of the individual president on his or her presidency must clearly be factored in for all incumbents to the office, for this president that impact was clearly significant in its own ways. He was the first president to hold a master's degree in business administration. He had seen how his father's presidency had unfolded. During his governorship, he developed a decision-making and managerial style that he carried over to his presidency. As he told reporters late in the 2000 campaign, "I'm the kind of person who trusts people. And I empower people. I am firm with people. On the other hand, I am a decider. I do not agonize. I think. I listen, and I trust my instincts and I trust the advisers I get. And I am an accessible person."[2] It was a decision-making coda that bode well, but also at times ill for his presidency, particularly as he charted a course for dealing with a war on terror in the aftermath of September 11. We shall revisit Bush's words.

Internal Time: A Successful Transition

One of the forgotten aspects of the Bush presidency is that he and his associates—despite the uncertainty of the electoral outcome in the 2000 election—did a remarkable job of "hitting the ground running." Whatever one might think of their ensuing policies, they were prepared to take office. They planned and then unfolded a transition to the presidency under the most difficult circumstances any modern president has faced. Indeed, one must go as far back as the Rutherford Hayes-Samuel Tilden contested election of 1876 to find a situation as unsettling.

What did Bush do? His political and organizational situation could have been a disaster in the making, but it was not. While Vice President Al Gore was largely busy contesting the election results, Bush and his team quietly put together a presidential administration. Most notable was attention to the White House staff. They recognized that these were crucial appointments in crafting their program—especially given the likely delays in securing Senate approval of sub-cabinet appointments.

Andrew Card, Jr., was quietly tapped as White House chief of staff before Election Day. And while the public and pundits focused on Florida, Card, a former deputy chief of staff and secretary of transportation under Bush, Sr., effectively organized the new White House staff. His efforts were quite unlike what transpired in the contextually tranquil Clinton transition eight years previously. During the latter, it was not until December 12, 1992—roughly the half-way point between Election and Inauguration Day—that a chief of staff was finally selected, effectively delaying the appointment of most of the rest of the Clinton White House staff. In addition, during the 2000 transition, cabinet nominations were also rolled out relatively quickly. The initial set of cabinet appointees was set by January 2, 2001, ahead of Reagan and Bush, Sr., and only slightly behind Carter and Clinton.

But it was not all about appointments to office. Meetings were held with key members of Congress as well as important constituency groups. More importantly, Karl Rove—soon to become the White House "senior adviser" with a robust portfolio—devised a narrowly tailored presidential agenda. There would be no confusing laundry list of presidential initiatives of the sort that Carter had pursued in 1977. Still more importantly, key initiatives were targeted to build a new Republican electoral majority: tax cuts, education reform, "faith-based" initiatives, and new proposals for Social Security and Medicare. In Rove's view, they would create the sort of party realignment that his political hero, William McKinley, had achieved in 1896 for the Republicans.

Rove's work was complemented by the role of Karen Hughes, a long-time Bush media adviser, now with the title "counselor to the president." Hughes was in charge of orchestrating and communicating the White House message. The remainder of the White House staff was an interesting blend of Bush loyalists from Austin, Texas, but also one where a significant number had served in his father's and Reagan's presidency. Most notable in the latter group, besides Card, was National Security Council (NSC) adviser Condoleezza Rice and her deputy Stephen Hadley. Bush was thus able to meld personal allegiance to his policy agenda with "inside the Washington Beltway"—if not prior White House—experience. It seemed as if there would be no steep learning curve that other political outsiders have faced in assuming office by bringing a large cadre of novice loyalists from back home into the White House.

The cabinet was likewise a seemingly experienced one. Its members were diverse by race and gender. Its principal members—Colin Powell at State, Donald Rumsfeld at Defense, and John Ashcroft at Justice—brought a wealth of prior governmental experience. So, too, did Richard Cheney, who quickly became the most influential vice president in U.S. history, surpassing even the strong role that Gore had occupied during the Clinton years. Much looked promising. But also recall Bush's words: "I empower people," "I trust people," but "I am firm with people." Would he be able to match empowerment and trust with the firmness needed to manage such a core group of experienced heavyweights, especially Cheney and Rumsfeld? The White House staff was seemingly strong on strategy (Rove) and communications (Hughes); an organizational design with a heavy emphasis on something resembling a permanent campaign, as noted in chapter 2. But would it prove adaptable to governing and to hard analysis, especially as the policy agenda shifted from the key issues of the campaign and as the political context changed over time?

Internal Time: A Reasonably Successful Honeymoon

For the most part, President Bush was successful in his initial legislative efforts, largely following the playbook Rove had laid out. Democrats had pushed for a "coalition government" in the aftermath of a divisive election in which Bush had lost the popular vote and won in the Electoral College by the narrowest of margins. But Bush resisted their invitation; in fact, he took office as if he had been elected by a substantial margin.

Across-the-board tax cuts, whether well advised or not, were the centerpiece of the legislative push; they passed the Congress with a rather small degree of compromise (a $1.35 trillion cut rather than the $1.6 trillion Bush initially proposed). The "No Child Left Behind" education bill eventually passed into law at the end of the year, although without the voucher program for students in failing public schools that the administration desired. "Faith-based initiatives" did encounter congressional resistance, but the administration turned to executive orders to secure their implementation. A more controversial campaign proposal to reform social security by privatizing individual accounts was put on the back burner.

The first seven months of the Bush presidency seemed to portend relative success. Bush was the first Republican president since Eisenhower to enjoy a Congress controlled by his party. But that proved short lived. In May 2001, politically Bush was weakened with the defection of Senator Jim Jeffords from the Republican caucus and the subsequent loss of Senate control.

There were also warning signs as time passed. Rove's operation was regarded as too restricted by some.[3] According to one report, "There is a danger that the lack of competing views in the famously tight White House could cause Bush advisers to become stale and insular." As one Bush official said, "with satisfaction," there "isn't a lot of competition in the policy arena."[4] Tailoring a campaign agenda into a more limited policy agenda to be pursued once in office served this White House well, at least initially. But was there too much reliance on it over time? Did it overwhelm pursuit of further initiatives down the line?

Also, some were not impressed by the intellectual caliber of Bush's White House advisers. In the view of David Frum, who had been a chief White House speechwriter, "there was a dearth of really high-powered brains. . . . Conspicuous intelligence seemed actively unwelcome.[5] According to John DiIulio—a professor of political science at the University of Pennsylvania who headed the White House's faith-based initiatives effort—both the political strategy of Rove's shop and the communications efforts of Hughes's operation sometimes swamped policy analysis and deliberation. In the eight months DiIulio served, he heard "not three meaningful, substantive policy discussions. . . . [T]hey could stand ways of inserting more serious policy fiber into the West Wing diet. . . . [T]hey have been for whatever reasons, organized in ways that make it difficult for policy-minded staff . . . to get much West Wing traction, or even to get a non-trivial hearing."[6] Bush's operational code—"I trust the advisers I get"—began to belie the seeming quality of his decision making and his proclamation that "I am an accessible person."

A final point on this early period: much of the attention of the White House focused on its domestic policy agenda. Could it adjust to a context in which foreign affairs and national security issues, particularly a war against terror, occupied the top of the president's agenda?

Crisis: September 11 and Its Aftermath

September 11, 2001, fundamentally altered the national consciousness and the agenda of this presidency. Bush's initial public pronouncements on the day of the attack were a bit wobbly in performance, yet he quickly rallied the public and Congress to wage war on the terrorists and those who harbored them. The war on terror would, for the remainder of his presidency, force an administration that valued discipline, order, and preparation to deal with an environment that was constantly in flux—whether dealing with the catastrophes and consequences of the attack, homeland security, war in Afghanistan, treatment of enemy detainees, or finally, war in Iraq and its aftermath.

Although Bush was a president prone to delegate, in the period after September 11, he clearly took charge. It was Bush who made key decisions and was willing to stick to them. Within hours, he made two crucial decisions, according to Frum. The first was that "This war *was* a war." The second was "to hold responsible for those acts of war not merely the terrorists who committed them, but also the governments that aided, abetted, financed, and shielded terrorism."[7] Both decisions marked a profound change in U.S. foreign policy.

After September 11, Bush's own leadership was more firmly entrenched. His day would begin not just with the normal Central Intelligence Agency (CIA) briefing but, now, with a "threat assessment," followed by a briefing by the Federal Bureau of Investigation (FBI) and Attorney General John Ashcroft.

He met frequently with what came to be known as his "war cabinet." Full meetings of the NSC were convened more frequently. Those meetings were especially crucial in Bush's decision to focus on Al Qaeda rather than to go after a range of terrorist organizations and (at the time) Iraq, which some of the president's more hawkish advisers were pressing for. According to journalist Frank Bruni, during this early period, aides observed that Bush "was asking more questions in . . . meetings, grilling his advisers with more requests for explanation and often demanding to talk not only to the deputy from an administration agency who was giving him a briefing but to the head of the agency."[8]

NSC adviser Rice acted as an honest broker of the process, at least as war in Afghanistan unfolded. As James Pfiffner observes, "Rice's role as NSC adviser had expanded during the months after 9/11. Beginning the administration as junior to the other principals in age and experience, she demonstrated skill in her role as neutral broker as well as enforcer of the president's wishes."[9]

Rice was especially useful in curbing a president impatient to act and desirous of quick results. As Bush later reflected to journalist Bob Woodward, "I'm ready to go." But Rice's braking was welcomed by the president: "Sometimes that's the way I am—fiery. On the other hand, her job is to bear the brunt of some of the fire, so that it—takes the edge off a little bit. And she's good at that. I was growing a little impatient. I can be an impatient person."[10]

To return to Bush's self-description of his decision-making and managerial style, at this point in time—and it was a crucial one—the parts worked, the process served him well. Crisis punctuated normal internal rhythms, but the president's decision making rose to the challenges.

Internal Time: A Return to Partisan Politics

In the aftermath of September 11, Bush, for a time, rallied bipartisan support in Congress and was willing to compromise to achieve most of his legislative goals. An aviation security bill passed Congress within months, as did the USA Patriot Act. However, by early 2002, bipartisanship began to diminish, whether due to Bush's own instincts, Rove's political calculations, or Democrats in Congress emboldened to oppose the administration as the immediacy of September 11 began to fade.

In the short term, developments worked to the White House's advantage. In the 2002 mid-term elections, the Republicans regained control of the Senate. That achievement should not be gainsaid. This was the first presidency since Franklin D. Roosevelt (FDR) in 1934 where there was a pick-up in seats for a president's party in *both* houses of Congress in a *first* mid-term cycle.[11] Bush was also the first president since popular election of the Senate began in 1914 to have his party regain control in a mid-term election.

Bush had campaigned aggressively. Yet the legislative results were mixed. On the plus side, with Democrats smarting from the 2002 election results, the administration successfully pushed through a bill creating a new Department of Homeland Security in the lame duck session. In the next session of Congress, the 108th, the White House successfully pressed for another round of tax cuts. It also secured approval of a new Medicare prescription drug benefit for seniors, a bill banning partial birth abortions, and in late 2004, a major reorganization of the intelligence agencies.

But other key proposals remained stymied, particularly limits on class action lawsuits and a patients' bill of rights. The bipartisan approach to

Congress in the months after September 11 also evaporated. With strong Republican majorities (although not a filibuster-proof Senate), hostile legislation could be blocked, but a more inclusive approach to tackle more difficult issues became increasingly harder to muster. White House determination prevailed over compromise, the old agenda continued to be pursued, and relations with congressional Democrats became increasingly bitter. The Bush operational formula was showing strain: "empowerment," "trust" in the president's own instincts or those around him, and "firmness" lacked presidential adaptation as conditions changed.

Crisis: War in Iraq

Analysis of Bush's decision to go to war against Saddam Hussein's regime in Iraq requires a volume in its own right (indeed, Bob Woodward has produced four to date). But suffice it to say here, whereas the decision-making process served Bush reasonably well in the immediate aftermath of September 11 and during the early part of the war in Afghanistan, the deliberations that led up to the Iraq War were another matter. So too were Bush's inclinations and style as a decision maker, as well as the mindsets—if not machinations—of key principals such as Cheney and Rumsfeld. The end result was that much of the case for war—as we now know—proved to be based on faulty evidence and questionable intelligence. As well, the post-war reconstruction of Iraq was poorly planned and executed. Although a free, democratic, and politically stable Iraq may yet emerge, few major decisions made by a modern president were so defective in terms of *process*.

There were a number of sources of problems; not all of the blame can be laid upon this president and his decision making. Yet President Bush's words are again revealing. "I trust people," Bush tells us. Yet one repository of that trust—the formal structure of decision making—was not permeable enough so that dissenting views and dissonant information percolated upward. This may not have been a problem early in the administration when the policy agenda was driven by key campaign proposals. But in the more complex case of war with Iraq, difficulties were surely there. Errors, faulty inferences, misplaced assumptions, and public exaggerations ranged across the administration's case for war: purported links between Iraq and Al Qaeda; claims about Iraq's nuclear capabilities; its attempts to acquire "yellowcake" uranium ore in Niger; its efforts to purchase aluminum tubes for centrifuges used in uranium enrichment; its use of mobile weapons labs; its continued possession of chemical and biological weapons; and its presumed fleet of manned and unmanned aerial vehicles to deliver them.[12]

Difficulties also beset the planning and implementation of Iraq's post-war stabilization and reconstruction. To take but one example: the crucial decision to disband the Iraqi army. The latter is still the subject of some controversy, and it remains unclear who was the final authority issuing that order. But a number of reports indicate that Powell, Rice, the Joint Chiefs of Staff, and even President Bush learned of it only after it had been made.[13] This is surely an impressive roster of the uninformed.

"I am an accessible person," Bush tells us. Yet as James Risen notes in his book, *State of War*, there was dissent concerning the intelligence underlying the case for war: "If someone had spoken up clearly and forcefully, the entire house of cards might have collapsed. A little bit of digging might have revealed the truth."[14]

"I listen," Bush tells us. Yet, while he might have asked questions at times, Bush did not engage his principals on the most fundamental questions. As Woodward relates, he never directly asked Rumsfeld whether he recommended going to war against Iraq. Nor had Bush asked Powell or Cheney: "I could tell what they thought. I didn't need to ask. . . ."[15] Nor did Bush heed the advice of a number in the military and other professionals who thought too few troops were being committed to the effort.

"I trust the advisers I get," Bush tells us. Yet, during deliberations on war with Iraq, NSC adviser Rice now failed to act as an honest broker, as she had done during Afghanistan.[16] In fact, the case for war against Iraq may have been a closed issue for her.[17] In Powell's view, "she tended to echo back to the president what she thought he wanted to hear rather than what he needed to know."[18]

"I am firm with people," Bush tells us. Yet part of Rice's difficulties was a failure of cooperation from Defense and particularly Rumsfeld. The interagency vetting process became broken as a result. Especially with respect to planning for and then executing Iraq's postwar stability and reconstruction, intramural disputes broke out. Yet Bush was unwilling to bring order and discipline to the process, ride herd on some of his principals, or reach out for alternative sources of counsel.

"I am a decider," Bush tells us. But what was the quality of the information and advice at the foundation of those decisions? What had served Bush well in the aftermath of September 11 now served him poorly.

Internal Time: Re-Election and the Second "Transition"

Bush was able to elude his father's electoral fate and somewhat narrowly achieve re-election. The campaign skills of the Bush team, especially those of

Rove, were able to make the election as much about Senator John Kerry (D-MA) and his record as that of the administration. Yet campaign skills are not the same as governing skills. Most importantly, the campaign did not success-fully lay the groundwork for the domestic priorities of a Bush second term.

With respect to his deliberative apparatus in the White House, Bush did not take advantage of the opportunity re-election offered to take stock of his team and perhaps make some needed changes. In the aftermath of the 2004 election, many of the major White House players remained in place: chief of staff Card, communications chief Dan Bartlett (who had replaced Hughes in 2002), Office of Management and Budget director Josh Bolten, and Rove. Indeed, Rove's responsibilities markedly increased as he was given greater control over policy development.

The role of the White House staff in the second term promised continuity. But was an opportunity missed to inject fresh blood into the mix and perhaps shake things up a bit, especially in enlisting a counter-weight to Rove's po-litical calculus?[19] Was there, again to return to Bush words, too much "trust," too much "delegation"?

Change in the cabinet was more significant: nine out of now fifteen new faces.[20] Yet the cabinet at the start of the second term was also more con-servative than in the first. As Shirley Anne Warshaw notes, this may have led to "a narrower focus in the decision maker structure" and "reduced the number of differing opinions in the policy-making process."[21] Also notable is who was kept on. Rumsfeld, the most controversial of cabinet members, continued as secretary of defense until the mid-term elections of 2006, and it may have been another missed opportunity for change. One wonders what the administration's strategies—and fortune—in Iraq might have been had Rumsfeld been replaced two years previously.

Internal Time: A Lame Duck Second Term

As a chief executive and decision maker known for delegation and for promo-tion from within, Bush increasingly relied upon a more parochial team. Many on the White House staff now drew their experience from service within the limited confines of this one presidency, unlike at the start when many of their elders had broken their political and administrative teeth working for the president's father or even Ronald Reagan. Subsequent reports of internal debates, especially within the White House staff, suggested a lack of "reality testing," increasing insularity, and a "Bush bubble."

There were also problems over time in President Bush's abilities as a deci-sion maker and manager. The victories of the early first term developed from a coherent strategy derived from a few key election themes. But as new challenges emerged, the old approach seemed shop worn. Interestingly, there was no mention of adaptation or of learning behavior in the Bush operational code, with which we began.

Although Bush's 53 percent approval rating right after re-election was the lowest of any re-elected president since Gallup began polling, Bush seemed to assume that all the cards were in his favor. In a press conference right after the election, he spoke about his new "political capital" and his willingness to "spend it." As Grossman, Kumar, and Rourke note, however, such expansive hopes may be doomed to failure. During the second term, the "energy" to be drawn from the election is lessened: "The administration must make more concessions to other political actors, who soon decide that it may be both safe and profitable to defy the president. Presidents who refuse to bow to this necessity, and go it alone, such as Truman and Nixon, only aggravate their appearance of weakness."[22]

For Bush, however, that potential loss of energy and increasingly negative political fortune were hardly factored in. Largely under Rove's crafting and strategic direction, the administration pursued an ambitious agenda, often in a highly partisan, White House-directed way. This approach may have served them well at the start of his presidency (although even then the No Child Left Behind Act was *highly* bipartisan), but it was a recipe for disappointment in the second. There was a failure to adjust and to learn lessons, not only from what had transpired in this presidency but also from the experience of past administrations. As Joshua Green observes, "Throughout his presidency, Roosevelt had large Democratic majorities in Congress but operated in a nonpartisan fashion, as though he didn't. Bush, with razor-thin majorities . . . operated as though his margins were insurmountable, and sowed interparty divisions as an electoral strategy."[23] According to Gary Jacobson, "Nothing in George W. Bush's second-term policies, objectives, or strategies promises any significant narrowing of the wide partisan divisions generated by his first administration—on the contrary. His domestic agenda is largely a conservative Republican wish-list with little cross-party appeal."[24] And through the remainder of his presidency, it would be such. In terms of evolution through internal time, there was a failure to adapt strategies and tactics to a changed and increasingly hostile political context.

Bush claimed a mandate.[25] Yet it was an assertion that fell on deaf ears. The same was largely true for Rove's second-term legislative agenda and the highly partisan way in which it was pursued. Social security and immigration reform were moved to the front burner, but opposition prevailed.[26] Both proposals also sparked resistance among some Republicans in Congress; White

House efforts to enforce party discipline, which had worked in the first term, could no longer be counted on. Renewal of the No Child Left Behind Act was mired in disagreement and its reauthorization was left to Bush's successor. As Steven Schier observes, "Pushing big policy changes costs political capital. It's important not to overestimate one's political capital and thus spend it too freely, as Bush did regarding Social Security."[27]

Three strategic mistakes made in the fall of 2005 were especially notable. The first was the response to Hurricane Katrina and the devastation it particularly caused to New Orleans on August 29. Bush cut short a trip to California, but he returned to his ranch in Texas, and it was another two days before he saw the devastation, and that by air as he returned to the White House. Given the magnitude of the disaster, response was slow at the outset. Subsequent federal disaster relief was hampered by poor coordination with state and local officials (and their own lack of cooperation) and by a hapless director of Federal Emergency Management Agency (FEMA) with slim credentials for the job. Both the White House's political antennae and its bureaucracy for emergency management had failed the president. But the episode also signaled slippage in Bush's own abilities as a decision maker, a manager, and, most important of all, a leader in times of a critical national crisis.[28]

A second major misstep occurred weeks later with the nomination of Harriet Miers, a long-time Bush friend from Texas now serving as White House legal counsel, to a Supreme Court vacancy. Although the White House had made a successful pick previously with John Roberts' nomination to replace Chief Justice William Rehnquist, Miers' lack of judicial experience and her unclear record on abortion rights roused opposition from both liberals and conservatives; her nomination was eventually withdrawn. Many attributed her ill-fated pick to the insularity of the Bush White House.

The third error was a controversial deal allowing a Dubai state-owned company to run six U.S. ports. Bush was not informed until a month after the deal was approved by federal bureaucrats, and it raised a storm of controversy, particularly among conservative Republicans, once it was publicized. But Bush stuck to his guns and initially threatened to veto any attempts to block the sale. Opposition was intense, however, even among Republican congressional leaders. In a face-saving measure, Dubai agreed to transfer control to a U.S. company. Closely grouped together in the first year of Bush's second term, the three episodes might have been another chance for the administration to take stock of its deliberative effectiveness, but that did not occur.

On the positive side—and let us remember that there was a positive side, at least from the administration's perspective—Bush did succeed in gaining an extension to some of his tax cuts, although not the permanent ones he wanted. Roberts and Samuel Alito were confirmed to the Supreme Court, the latter replacing the more moderate Sandra Day O'Connor. Congress eventually passed a compromise bill on warrantless monitoring of international phone calls, and it gave the administration what it wanted in a bill responding to the Court objections to the military tribunals proposed for trying detainees. The Supreme Court, however, had a different and final say in the *Boumediene* decision in 2008, when it ruled against that legislation.[29]

Democratic control of the House and the Senate after 2006, however, clearly dealt Bush a weaker hand. In *Congressional Quarterly*'s measure of presidential legislative success (a calculation of the number of times a president wins on roll call votes in which he took a clear position), the first six years registered percentages ranging from a high of 88 percent in 2002 to a low of 72.5 percent in 2004. Bush's six-year average was 81 percent, higher than Eisenhower (77%), Reagan (67.3%), and Clinton (61.5%). But in 2007, after the Republicans lost control of Congress, Bush's support dropped to 38 percent. By contrast, in the seventh year of their presidencies, Eisenhower stood at 52 percent and Reagan at 44 percent (the lowest scores for each), while Clinton also stood at 38 percent. Only Clinton registered a lower score (36% in 1995, right after his party's loss of Congress) since *Congressional Quarterly* began measuring in 1953.[30] In 2008, Bush recovered a bit (47.8%), but his score was lower than Eisenhower (65%) and Clinton (55%) and roughly the same as Reagan (47%); Bush's score was also the eighth-lowest in the 56-year history of the *Congressional Quarterly* survey.[31]

There were some successes from Bush's vantage point: the administration was especially successful in thwarting Democratic efforts to set a deadline for troop withdrawals in Iraq. Bush also had his constitutional powers. During his first term, Bush was the first president since John Quincy Adams not to have used his veto power.[32] However, Bush increasingly exercised it in the second term, especially following the Democratic takeover of Congress.[33] It proved a useful weapon for blocking Democratic initiatives. But it was at most defensive armament, not one useful in resuscitating a lame duck presidency.

Perhaps the best that can be said is that if the broader Bush agenda had limited positive traction toward the end of his presidency, the White House was adept enough at forestalling the emergence of a Democratic alternative. But the White House's hope at the start of the second term to secure approval of an ambitious legislative agenda in order to avoid the negative fate of most second-term presidencies had largely failed. Indeed, Bush was in a seemingly worse position in securing a successful second-term legacy than any of his post–World War II, second-term predecessors, whether Eisenhower, Reagan, or even Clinton. Ironically, he also had a greater degree of freedom in focusing on his legacy because, unlike them, he did not have to factor in any effects on his vice president running to succeed him.

The Judgment of Time: The Bush Legacy

How then to understand the Bush presidency? Bush's words, with which we began, provide one set of clues. Let us recall them: "I'm the kind of person who trusts people. And I empower people. I am firm with people. On the other hand, I am a decider. I do not agonize. I think. I listen, and I trust my instincts and I trust the advisers I get. And I am an accessible person." They surely worked—at times—as a decision-making and managerial coda. The transition, the early presidency, and the response to September 11 most notably attest to this. More generally, the president had his defenders. According to NSC adviser Hadley, "This notion that somehow the president didn't know what was going on, information was withheld from him in some way, he didn't have a picture of what was going on: He got that picture." In the view of chief of staff Bolten, Bush told him when discussing his appointment that "he neither wanted nor needed a prime minister. Our job is to make sure he's well positioned to make good decisions." Moreover, according to Bolten, Bush is "very good about hearing and wanting contrary advice."[34]

But tested against the full measure of internal time, the crises besetting the Bush presidency as the Iraq War unfolded and after Katrina occurred and the pressures of the more mundane politics of his second term more seems likely needed than what perhaps the president comprehended or practiced. The Bush decision-making and leadership coda needs to be filled out, adjusted, and fine-tuned:

- The need for adaptation must be recognized as internal time moves forward and political conditions change, especially in dealing with Congress.
- Learning behavior, particularly from mistakes, is required.
- Accountability must accompany "trust."
- Presidential steps—to make sure that those "empowered" are up to the task—must be taken, both in the form of more attentive management on the president's part and a greater willingness to take stock of the team and make more timely adjustments in personnel.
- Presidential "firmness" is part of this managerial task, but it should be more than just laying down the game plan all are expected to follow;

it also requires deliberative openness and a reasonable toleration of dissent.

- Resoluteness is advantageous—"I am a decider"—but the presidential choice underlying resolute decisions must be based on good analysis and sound information: telling the president what he needs to know not what he may want to hear.
- Presidential "instincts" may be right in the end, but they must be examined, at least, by the reality testing of others.
- Presidential "accessibility" must be real—no bubbles, no insularity, and no echo chambers.

Likewise, crises needed better handling. For Eisenhower, mundane decision making was a useful prelude and learning experience for when the unexpected occurred. In a paper produced by his former NSC adviser, Robert Cutler, in March 1968 and circulated to Eisenhower, the former president noted in the margins that "through this practice [of continuous planning], the members of the NSC became familiar *not only with each other but with the basic factors of problems* that might, on some future date, face the president." Furthermore, as Cutler notes in the paper, "Thus in time of sudden, explosive crisis, these men would gather to work with and for the president, not as strangers, but as men intimately made familiar, through continuing association with the character, abilities, and understandings of each colleague at the Council table. Such training and familiarity enabled them to act in an emergency, not as ciphers and not as yes-men for the president, but as men accustomed to express their own views. . . ."[35] Absent well-organized routine decision making, Eisenhower and Cutler imply, decisions during crises are likely to suffer. For Bush, there was an odd and counter-intuitive degeneration in the quality of decision making over time, once a war against Iraq was on the table. Neither the mundane or crises deliberations functioned effectively.

But in the long run, is it perhaps too bold or simplistic to suggest that presidencies ultimately stand or fall on two things: the economy and war. Here decision, crises, and time may count for the most. As for war, immediate political time is often unkind to even the best of war leaders. Although not a U.S. president, the greatest of all—Winston Churchill and his political fate in 1945—is the best testimony here. But history takes in a broader sweep and ultimately judges by results, not by the character of deliberative process nor immediate popularity.

For Bush it would be Iraq, in the end. And here we come perhaps full circle. Bush's own stubbornness in seeking something approximating victory, rather than a stalemate or the sort of face-saving exit recommended by the bipartisan Baker-Hamilton Commission, led him to significantly increase the size of U.S. forces in Iraq and direct it toward a more aggressive counter-insurgency strategy—the so-called surge of 2007 and 2008.

Largely devised by NSC adviser Hadley and his staff rather than by the generals at the Pentagon (who mostly preferred the status quo), the change in strategy was the result of a more careful vetting process than had occurred in the previous decision to go to war. Discontent with the progress of the war led to greater consultation with outside experts on counter-insurgency, with retired military officers, as well as a more thorough interagency review process.[36] Although advice was at times mixed, in the end, the president decided a change in strategy was needed and a major effort was called for.

The effort was also undoubtedly aided by the appointment of Major General David Petraeus, an expert on counter-insurgency and an advocate for a new strategy, as the new field commander in Iraq. Petraeus' efforts paid off. Increased cooperation with Sunnis and their increasing hostility to local Al Qaeda forces—the so-called Sunni Awakening—boded well. The surge proved politically controversial. Yet as months passed, violence decreased in Iraq.

Whether the surge will lead to a peaceful and democratic Iraq still remains an open question. But if the surge does mark a turn toward success, it will in all likelihood be judged a significant point in the evolution of this presidency, and one of the most important legacies of a most determined wartime president. In the end, did the Bush operational coda once again begin to serve him well?

As for the economy, severe difficulties clearly developed at the end of this presidency. As 2008 wore on, the administration faced a serious crisis with declining home values and a substantial increase in defaulting home mortgages. The latter led to instability in the financial sector unprecedented since the Great Depression. The country also faced the onset of a severe recession. The stock market registered historic declines: the NASDAQ index lost 40 percent of its value in 2008; the Dow Jones industrials dropped 34 percent, its largest decline since 1931, while the Standard and Poor's 500 sank 39.5 percent, matching its decline in 1937. Deficits skyrocketed from $162 billion in 2007 to $485 billion in 2008 to a projected deficit of over $1 trillion for 2009—and that may be a conservative estimate since it does not include any amounts for a stimulus package under the Barack Obama administration (potentially an additional $700 billion to $1 trillion).

It was a context that called for renewed presidential leadership, but were the White House and Bush equipped to provide it? Did Bush decide and lead well or did he do poorly? There was a stimulus package, and the White House accepted a compromise proposal on the bailout of banks and other financial institutions. Bush also arranged for temporary federal aid to General Motors and Chrysler to avoid their impending bankruptcy.

But was it enough? Was it even the right course? One thing is sure, however. Time remained important: It had simply run out for this president. Time, crises, and presidential response now passed to his successor.

Notes

1. Stephen Skowronek, *The Politics Presidents Make: Leadership from John Adams to George Bush* (Cambridge, MA: Harvard University Press, 1993); also see *Presidential Leadership in Political Time: Reprise and Reappraisal* (Lawrence: University Press of Kansas, 2008).

2. Dan Balz and Terry Neal, "For Bush, Questions, Clues, and Contradiction," *Washington Post* October 22, 2000.

3. Dana Milbank, "Serious Strategery," *Washington Post* April 22, 2001.

4. Dana Milbank and Ellen Nakashima, "Bush Team Has 'Right' Credentials," *Washington Post* March 25, 2001.

5. David Frum, *The Right Man: The Surprise Presidency of George W. Bush* (New York: Random House, 2003), 20.

6. John DiIulio to Ron Suskind, "Your Next Essay on the Bush Administration," October 24, 2002; Drudge Report, "Bush Aides Letter to Esquire Reporter Revealed," December 2, 2002, www.drudgereport.com, accessed December 2, 2002.

7. Frum, *The Right Man*, 141–42.

8. Frank Bruni, *Ambling into History: The Unlikely Odyssey of George W. Bush* (New York: HarperCollins, 2002), 248.

9. James Pfiffner, "National Security Policymaking and the Bush War Cabinet," in Richard S. Conley ed., *Transforming the American Polity: The Presidency of George W. Bush and the War on Terrorism* (Upper Saddle River, NJ: Pearson Prentice Hall, 2005), 86.

10. Bob Woodward, *Bush at War* (New York: Simon & Schuster), 158.

11. The Democrats picked up seats in 1998 in the mid-term elections during Clinton's second term. However, the Democrats lost control of both the Senate and the House during the 1994 mid-terms in his first term.

12. See, for example, David Barstow, William Broad, and Jeff Gerth, "How the White House Embraced Disputed Arms Intelligence," *New York Times* October 3, 2004; James P. Pfiffner, "Did President Bush Mislead the Country in His Arguments for War with Iraq?" *Presidential Studies Quarterly* 34 (1): 25–46; Kenneth M. Pollack, "Spies, Lies, and Weapons: What Went Wrong?" *Atlantic Monthly* January/February 2004, 78–92. Among the better lengthier accounts of war deliberations that have appeared are James Bamford, *A Pretext for War: 9/11, Iraq, and the Abuse of America's Intelligence Agencies* (New York: Doubleday, 2004); Michael R. Gordon and Bernard

E. Trainor, *Cobra II: The Inside Story of the Invasion and Occupation of Iraq* (New York: Pantheon, 2006); and Thomas Ricks, *Fiasco: The American Military Adventure in Iraq* (New York: Penguin, 2006).

13. See John P. Burke, "From Success to Failure? Iraq and the Organization of George W. Bush's Decision Making," in *The Polarized Presidency of George W. Bush*, edited by George C. Edwards III and Desmond King (New York: Oxford University Press, 2007), 173–212; Gordon and Trainor, *Cobra II*, 476, 482–85.

14. James Risen, *State of War* (New York: Free Press, 2006), 121–22. Colin Powell later noted that in preparing for his key February 2003 speech before the United Nations laying out the case for war with Iraq, although "Nothing was spun to me. What really upset me more than anything else was that there were people in the intelligence community that had doubts about some of this sourcing, *but those doubts never surfaced up to us*" (Richard Leiby, "Breaking Ranks," *Washington Post* January 19, 2006, emphasis added). Others were skeptical about the case for war, yet their dissent for a variety of reasons, never surfaced or had impact on deliberations. According to Bob Woodward, "Well-placed officials in the administration were skeptical about the WMD intelligence on Iraq—among them [Richard] Armitage [Powell's chief deputy at State], some senior military officials and even the CIA spokesman Bill Harlow. . . . This skepticism apparently did not make it in any convincing form to the president" (Bob Woodward, *Plan of Attack* [New York: Simon & Schuster, 2004], 295).

15. Woodward, *Plan of Attack*, 272, 416.

16. On the shifts in Rice's role as NSC adviser, see John P. Burke, *Honest Broker? The National Security Advisor and Presidential Decision Making* (College Station: Texas A&M University Press, 2009), 238–78; and Burke, "Condoleezza Rice as NSC Advisor: A Case Study of the Honest Broker Role," *Presidential Studies Quarterly* 35 (3): 554–75.

17. Assistant Secretary of State for Policy Planning Richard Haass later recalled a meeting with Rice in the first week of July 2002 when he raised the issue of whether Iraq should be the focus of concern in the war on terrorism: "she said, essentially, that the decision's been made, don't waste your breath" (Nicholas Lemann, "How It Came to War," *New Yorker* March 31, 2003, 39; also see Frum, *The Right Man*, 197–201).

18. Karen DeYoung, *Soldier: The Life of Colin Powell* (New York: Knopf, 2006), 417.

19. Changes in the White House staff came later in the second term. Almost all of the major players departed, except for NSC adviser Hadley and Bolten, who succeeded Card as chief of staff in April 2006. Turnover in other positions was notable: five individuals would end up serving as chairs of the Council of Economic Advisers, four as directors of the National Economic Council. Even Rove left in August 2007.

20. By comparison, change in *both* the cabinet and staff was significant for Reagan and Clinton. Both had new chiefs of staff and NSC advisers (Reagan later in 1985); seven of the thirteen cabinet members were new under Reagan, eight of fourteen for Clinton.

21. Shirley Anne Warshaw, "Choices for the President: Structuring the Second-Term Cabinet of President George W. Bush," in *The Second Term of George W. Bush: Prospects and Perils*, edited by Robert Maranto, Douglas Brattebo, and Tom Lansford (New York: Palgrave Macmillan, 2006), 77.

22. Michael B. Grossman, Martha Joynt Kumar, Francis E. Rourke, "Second-Term Presidencies: The Aging of Administrations," in *The Presidency and the Political System*, 3rd ed., edited by Michael Nelson (Washington, DC: CQ Press, 1990), 230.

23. Joshua Green, "The Rove Presidency," *Atlantic Monthly* September 2007, 60.

24. Gary C. Jacobson, *A Divider, Not a Uniter: George W. Bush and the American People* (New York: PearsonLongman, 2007), 236–37.

25. The Bush win over Sen. Kerry was not as narrow as in 2000. In 2004, he won 50.7 percent of the popular vote (Kerry took 48.2%), certainly an improvement over his loss of the popular vote to Gore in 2000. Bush's electoral vote was 286; it was a slight increase from the 271 he had garnered in 2000—one more than the 270 electoral votes needed to elect. Bush's popular vote win was not as impressive as the second-term victories of FDR (60.8%), Eisenhower (57.4%), Nixon (60.7%), or Reagan (58.8%). But it was slightly larger—and over the 50 percent mark—than the re-election victories of Wilson (49.2%) and Clinton (49.2%). However, there was a bright spot: since 1900, Bush could claim—only along with FDR in 1936—an increase in his party's strength in *both* houses of Congress: a net gain of three seats in the House and four in the Senate.

26. For a fuller analysis of social security reform, see George C. Edwards III, *Governing by Campaigning: The Politics of the Bush Presidency* (New York: Pearson-Longman, 2008), 247–312; Jason D. Mycoff and Joseph A. Pika, *Confrontation and Compromise: Presidential and Congressional Leadership, 2001–2006* (Lanham, MD: Rowman & Littlefield, 2008), 213–26.

27. Steven E. Schier, *Panorama of a Presidency: How George W. Bush Acquired and Spent His Political Capital* (Armonk, NY: M. E. Sharpe, 2009), 160.

28. For further analysis of Bush's errors during the Katrina disaster, see James P. Pfiffner, "The First MBA President: George W. Bush as Public Administrator," *Public Administration Review* 67 (1): 15–17. According to Pfiffner, Bush's "public image as a competent, MBA-type manager of the executive branch probably suffered most from the disaster" (15).

29. *Boumediene v. Bush* (2008). The Court ruled, 5–4, that Lakhdar Boumediene and the other detainees at the U.S. military base at Guantanamo, Cuba, had a right to habeas corpus not adequately provided for in the Military Commissions Act of 2006.

30. Clea Benson, "The Power of No," *CQ Weekly* January 14, 2008, 132–33. It should be noted that the CQ measure is of limited value. It does not measure passage of the *president's* agenda, only floor votes on issues where the president has taken a position. It does not distinguish the importance of pieces of legislation: each vote is given equal weight. It also relies on public statements about a president's position, and it does not take account of what might be substantial differences between

a president's initial position and a final compromise that the White House might reluctantly support.

31. Richard Rubin, "An Unpopular Lame Duck Prevails," *CQ Weekly* December 15, 2008, 3322–25.

32. The presidential veto was especially important after 2006. Prior to the Democratic takeover, Bush had used the veto only once (in 2006 on the stem cell research bill). In the last two years of his presidency he began to use it more. In 2007, he vetoed seven times; only one—a pork-laden water resources bill—was overridden. In 2008, he vetoed five times; three were overridden—two pork-laden farm bills and a bill dealing with Medicare improvements for patients and providers. Although the number of vetoes was not large by comparison, the percentage of overrides (33%) was the third highest on record—after Andrew Johnson (52%) and Franklin Pierce (56%)—hardly good historical company.

33. Republicans lost control of both houses of Congress, losing 30 seats in the House and 6 in the Senate, well above the mid-term average (since 1954) of 22 in the House and 3 in the Senate. In their sixth-year mid-terms, Eisenhower lost 48 seats in the House and 13 in the Senate in 1958, Reagan lost 5 in the House and (including Republican control) in the Senate in 1986, while Clinton picked up 5 in the House and none in the Senate in 1998. For an extensive analysis of the 2006 mid-term elections, see Larry J. Sabato, ed., *The Sixth Year Itch: The Rise and Fall of the George W. Bush Presidency* (New York: PearsonLongman, 2008).

34. Michael Abramowitz, "Two Advisers Reflect on Eight Years with Bush," *Washington Post* January 2, 2009.

35. R. C. Cutler, "The Use of the NSC Mechanism: Korea, Vietnam, Lebanon," March 1968, Gordon Gray Papers, Box 1, Eisenhower Library, emphasis added.

36. See: Fred Barnes, "How Bush Decided on the Surge," *Weekly Standard* February 4, 2008, 24–25.

CHAPTER TWO

~

The Bush Staff and Cabinet System

Charles E. Walcott and Karen M. Hult

Each new presidency differs from its predecessors because each president brings his or her own background, talents, preferences, and agendas to the office. Recognition of this homely truth has sometimes made it convenient to imagine that new presidents effectively reinvent the office, imposing their personal stamps and styles on it. This view gave rise to what political scientists sometimes referred to as the "n of one" problem: the idea that generalizing across presidencies would be frustrated by the uniqueness of each one. More recent scholarship, however, has taken a different tack. Presidents may come and go, but the office of the presidency remains, adapting and being shaped to each new incumbent, but maintaining its basic form and functions while evolving in ways that are only partly due to the efforts of presidents themselves.

Thus, when George W. Bush became the 43rd president in 2001, he inherited a developed institution from those who had come before him—a "standard model" of the organization and operation of the presidential institution.[1] He embraced this, and thus found himself carried along by five continuing patterns in presidential politics and organization: (1) the centralization of policy control in the White House and the Office of Management and Budget (OMB), (2) politicization of the executive branch, (3) a hierarchically structured White House, (4) an emphasis on public outreach and responsiveness often labeled the "permanent campaign,"[2] and (5) the delegation of significant power and responsibility to vice presidents. Despite his declared determination to handle the presidency differently from his predecessors, Bill Clinton and George H. W. Bush, the junior Bush found himself embracing all of these tendencies, with consequences that were important for his administration and for the governance of the United States.

Here, however, we will argue that the operation and performance of the Bush administration's White House and cabinet structures, although initially shaped by and consistent with trends that have emerged over decades, became something different in the intense crisis atmosphere that followed the terrorist attacks of September 11, 2001. Personalities and power relations that had been latent grew dominant, and governmental decision making was shaped accordingly. At the same time, some of the noticeable tendencies of the Bush administration, such as centralization, discipline, and information control, became exaggerated, sometimes to the point of pathology. What is more, the aftermath of the attacks was lengthy enough that it fundamentally shaped the character and legacy of the Bush administration.

Our discussion begins with examination of the five patterns of presidential structuring and administrative politics, highlighting the similarities and differences in their appearance in the Bush administration. Then attention turns to tracing the evolution of these arrangements. We conclude with brief musings on some of their implications for Bush's legacy.

The "Administrative Presidency": Strategies of Centralization and Politicization

At least since the presidency of Richard Nixon, presidents have sought to increase their control over the massive and unwieldy executive branch by following more or less systematic administrative strategies, a pursuit Richard Nathan first labeled the "administrative presidency."[3] Those departments and agencies are crucial to achieving many presidential policy priorities. And, as the Federal Emergency Management Agency's (FEMA) sluggish response to Hurricane Katrina illustrated, the performance of executive branch organizations can be important to how citizens evaluate presidents.

Presidents, then, desire that their immediate aides in the White House and Executive Office of the President (EOP) as well as those in the far-flung executive branch exhibit *responsive competence*.[4] At the same that presidents have incentives to seek staff expertise, they also demand responsiveness to presidential priorities. In pursuing responsive competence, recent presidents have followed two general kinds of strategies: centralization and politicization. *Centralization* involves moving political and policy decisions closer to the president, placing them in the White House Office or the larger EOP; there, presidential aides are more likely to act based on the president's priorities and values. Meanwhile, *politicization* aims at fostering greater congruence with presidential goals by placing appointees who share those goals in key positions in the cabinet, sub-cabinet, and elsewhere in executive branch departments and agencies. President Bush followed his predecessors, especially Ronald Reagan, as he instituted his own versions of centralization and politicization.

Centralization

The idea that modern presidents have been centralizing policy control in the White House is hardly new. In the realm of national defense, it is not new at all, at a minimum tracing back to efforts at strategic coordination during World War II. In the domestic and economic policy areas it can be traced at least to Lyndon Johnson, and especially Nixon, who created formal staff units to oversee the policy process. Nonetheless, centralization qualifies as a trend because, although its impact has varied across policy areas, it generally has been on the rise over recent decades and presidencies.

Centralization has several components. The first and most common in contemporary White Houses is the establishment of staff offices to explore and recommend policy ideas, prepare legislation, draft executive orders, and oversee the implementation of laws within their areas of policy responsibility. In the 1960s, President Johnson set up a domestic policy staff under Joseph Califano that focused on projects relevant to his Great Society initiative. Nixon took this idea even farther, creating a Domestic Council modeled on the National Security Council (NSC) and establishing units to oversee domestic and international economic policy. Subsequent White Houses have demonstrated variations on these themes but have generally followed the pattern. Bush was no exception.

The Bush White House's organization for the "policy side" of the presidency closely mirrored that of recent presidents, especially that of Clinton. Bush continued Clinton's National Economic Council (NEC), a structure modeled after the NSC, with cabinet members and agency heads serving on the council, supported by a professional staff. The NEC's principal functions have been "to coordinate policy-making for domestic and international economic issues, to coordinate economic policy advice for the President, to ensure that policy decisions and programs are consistent with the President's economic goals, and to monitor implementation of the President's economic policy agenda."[5] Along the same lines, Bush retained a cabinet council to oversee domestic policy and to translate Bush's promise of "compassionate conservatism" into actual programs. As during the Clinton years, the staffs of both the NEC and the Domestic Policy Council were lodged in the Office of Policy Development in the EOP and directed by senior presidential aides.

The office of cabinet secretary, a staple of most recent administrations, also was a part of the Bush system. As a conduit for cabinet members and departments to the White House, this unit might seem to have occupied a policy nexus, as it had in some previous administrations. In the Bush scheme of things, however, it was intended more as a two-way communications channel, at least as valuable for allowing the White House to inform cabinet members about policy as for influence flowing in the other direction. The intended effect of these organizational efforts was to ensure central guidance of policy across the board, granting departments and agencies input, but also insuring that they would remain responsive to the president's purposes.

The Bush administration continued the process of reviewing the rules and regulations proposed by department and agencies, performed by the Office of Information and Regulatory Affairs (OIRA), a unit in OMB. Initially, regulatory review "kept the mechanical features" of Clinton process, with the "only notable change . . . the complete removal of the vice president from the review process."[6] Later in the administration, changes required that proposed rules identify "the specific market failure" they were intended to address, and adding a hint of explicit politicization, mandated that officers working with OIRA on regulatory review be political appointees.[7] An illustration of how this process operated to ensure that agency actions were consistent with presidential priorities is OIRA's handling of a rule proposed by the National Oceanic and Atmospheric Administration (NOAA) that was designed to limit the fishing of krill, an important food source for whales and other animals; OIRA rejected the rule on the grounds that the supporting scientific findings were too "uncertain."[8] Such decisions have led scholar William West to term regulatory review a "politicized mode of centralization."[9]

The organizational structuring of the White House and cabinet was designed to counter the centrifugal forces that always push and pull policy debate in Washington: Congress and its constituencies, organized interests, bureaucratic turf struggles, and even the mass media. Bush, widely touted as the first president with a master's degree in business administration,[10] understood the need to seize control of policy processes. His administration was primed to "hit the ground running" with policy proposals such as tax cuts and the "No Child Left Behind" education reform, and it organized accordingly. As we will elaborate, concerns arose as the administration continued, however, that the control sometimes grew too tight, screening out alternate and competing views and people.

Politicization

The second broad approach, politicization, has been called the "core" of strategies exercised by administrative presidencies, in which appointees are selected "strategically, based on their ideological policy congruence with the president."[11] Although most of the contemporary focus has been on politicization aimed at aiding electing officials in achieving their policy priorities, patronage concerns with finding jobs for campaign supporters and party loyalists also continue to influence appointments. Thus, David Lewis usefully distinguishes between policy and patronage politicization and notes that both have appeared throughout U.S. history.[12] Both forms are evident as well in the Bush administration.

It may be helpful to begin by placing the discussion in a somewhat broader context. If one defines politicization as the percentage of department and agency managers who are political appointees, politicization reached its peak in 1980; it declined thereafter, dropping through the 1990s.[13] Bush named approximately 350 more political appointees than did Clinton in his second term; the levels, however, remain well below those of the late 1970s and early 1980s. Like other presidents serving in times of unified government, where more policy congruence can be expected between the branches, Bush had somewhat higher numbers and proportions of political appointees than his Republican predecessors who faced Democratic Congresses.[14]

The Nixon administration conceived of a strategy of policy politicization of necessity when facing a hostile Congress controlled by opposition Democrats, and the Reagan presidency had brought it to full fruition. President Bush's father, a relatively non-ideological politician, had not pursued this strategy as aggressively, in part because it is hard for a more moderate president to find "militant moderates" to impose his views on the bureaucracy. This was not a problem for the second President Bush, a committed conservative who was easily able to identify and attract true-believing loyalists. Although the need to govern by working around Congress was not evident at the outset of the Bush administration in 2001, preparations were in place nonetheless.

From the start, the White House personnel office worked to screen applicants and attract loyalists to serve in the administration.[15] It "wasn't enough for White House job seekers to be Republicans, or even friends of the Bushes—they had to agree with George W. Bush's ideology."[16] Although the definition of loyalty had a stronger ideological component than was the case with Clinton or the first Bush, there was nothing unusual about this, especially in light of a polarized Washington politics that left little room for fence-sitters. The White House exercised control over sub-cabinet personnel, as well as the cabinet departments and heads of agencies, offering cabinet members "a choice of subordinates already vetted by the White House personnel and political teams."[17] These efforts typically targeted particular parts of the federal executive: appointees requiring Senate confirmation increased more in apparently "liberal" agencies (e.g., Consumer Product Safety Commission, Department of Health and Human Services, or Environmental Protection Agency [EPA]) than in more "conservative" ones (e.g., Small Business Administration, Department of Defense).[18] Like its predecessors, the administration also left some positions vacant or filled with "actings" (i.e., interim personnel, sometimes placed as recess appointments) as ways of slowing or halting undesired action or of avoiding Senate confirmation fights. Beyond trying to secure bureaucratic responsiveness through appointments, the Bush team continued in the Clinton-Gore practice of reducing the size of the permanent bureaucracy by outsourcing government functions to contractors. The highly visible role played by such private firms as Halliburton and Blackwater in Iraq was only exemplary of such contracting, which was practiced throughout the executive branch.

Such policy politicization had clear effects, frequently helping guide agency activities in directions consistent with the president's priorities. In its first year in office, for example, officials "rebuked Clinton-era environmental policies by easing wetlands rules affecting developers; reducing energy-saving standards for air conditioners; allowing more road-building and power lines in national parks; and easing restrictions on mining on public lands."[19] More generally, in enforcing clear air laws, the emphasis of the EPA worked to streamline, revise, and in some cases abolish rules to give businesses more time to comply and to reduce compliance costs.[20]

Over time it began to appear that some of Bush's appointees had taken the idea of responsive bureaucracy to extremes. In 2004, for instance, the Congressional Research Service reported that the administrator of Medicare, political appointee Thomas A. Scully, violated federal law by directing Medicare's chief actuary, Richard Foster, to withhold information from Congress that indicated that the new Medicare prescription drug benefit would cost far more than the administration had stated.[21] Another high-profile example occurred in the Justice Department. Triggered by the backlash from an apparently politically motivated firing of several federal prosecutors, a commission found that not only was the White House screening and punishing these political appointees for political reasons, but it was also imposing ideological litmus tests on candidates for career positions as federal prosecutors.[22] The latter was especially egregious, and in fact, illegal. Congressional committees also held hearings highlighting a range of alleged Justice Department abuses, including its handling of national security letters and interference in tobacco and redistricting litigation.[23] It also is worth noting, as an indication of how deeply committed the administration was to policy politicization, that this continued well into President Bush's second term, refuting the conventional wisdom that administrations run out of steam and ideological enthusiasm (and appropriate job candidates) during the second four years.

In some ways, some of the centralization of the first term produced more visible policy politicization in the second term. Reminiscent of the Nixon administration's efforts to repopulate the executive branch with presidential loyalists following his 1972 re-election, several top Bush aides were elevated to cabinet positions. For example, National Security Advisor (NSA) Condoleezza Rice replaced Colin Powell as Secretary of State (and was herself replaced by Deputy NSA Stephen Hadley), and White House domestic policy advisor Margaret Spellings (who had shepherded No Child Left Behind through Congress and into implementation) became Secretary of Education. Later in the term, senior Richard Cheney advisor F. Chase Hutto ("who played a prominent behind-the-scenes role in shaping the administration's environmental policy") was a leading contender for assistant secretary for policy and international affairs at the Department of Energy.[24]

In addition, as under previous presidents, *patronage* politicization was apparent. Typically, patronage appointments tend to cluster in more liberal locations for Democratic presidents and more conservative ones for Republican chief executives, reflecting the background and interests in the pool of available appointees. President Bush's actions were consistent with this expectation, with less policy relevant "Schedule C" appointees placed in relatively conservative-friendly settings such as the Small Business Administration and the Department of Commerce.[25]

The White House Office

In most respects, the Bush White House staff was organized along familiar lines, led by a chief of staff, supported by a staff secretariat, and comprised of units found in all recent presidencies, such as congressional relations, personnel, press, communications, public (i.e., interest group) liaison, and the counsel's office. To these, Bush added an Office of Faith-Based and Community Initiatives, reflecting one of the administration's particular domestic priorities.

This conventional approach evidently was responsive to the Washington community's horror at the disorganization of the early Clinton White House. As 2000 approached, think tank and academic energies were bent toward advising on effective presidential transitions, seeking to create a body of wisdom, a kind of surrogate "organizational memory," that was deemed lacking in 1992–1993.[26] Although the Clinton White House had largely brought its problems under control by the midpoint of its second year, the early less-than-capable White House operation shared in the blame for the Democrats' debacle in the 1994 elections. Bush, like Clinton, a former governor with relatively modest Washington experience, would not make the same mistake. He signaled this clearly with his selection of Cheney as his running mate; Cheney, a former White House chief of staff under Gerald Ford, was a member in good standing of "the establishment." Cabinet posts were filled with White House and executive office veterans like Paul O'Neill (Treasury) and Donald Rumsfeld (Defense). Indeed, it was more than a bit ironic that the scholarly community's heroic efforts to compensate for presidential inexperience were rendered largely unnecessary by the election of a president determined to tap many of those same sources himself.[27]

In adopting the hierarchical organizational model favored especially by Republican presidents,[28] Bush and his advisors were not attempting to stifle the free flow of information or debate. Indeed, one of the tasks of the chief of staff and staff secretary in such a White House is to assure that all relevant opinions on important issues or situations are collected and forwarded to the president. Of course, such a process has dangers, especially since staff members charged with collecting information must exercise judgment when deciding from whom to collect it and what is important enough to send to the president. Here the conventional wisdom is clear: the chief of staff (as well as his or her subordinates) must play the role of "honest broker," making sure that the president is amply informed and that the information he gets is presented in an unbiased manner.[29] Only in this way can the chief maintain the confidence of the rest of the administration. A similar challenge faces the president's special assistant for national security affairs (usually called the NSA) in "staffing out" foreign and military policy issues.

Chief of Staff Andrew Card, Jr., a veteran of the Reagan administration and deputy White House chief under the first President Bush, was fully familiar with the now-standard ways of structuring and managing the White House. Card was a chief in the honest broker tradition: seldom if ever an advocate for a personal policy agenda and trusted to give all relevant views a hearing before the president. Card was a ubiquitous presence, in the room during virtually all significant policy discussion, including those relating to foreign policy and national security, an area avoided by some of his predecessors. If Card's approach differed from most precedents, it was because a large number—more than a dozen—administration figures had access to

Bush without Card's clearance. This was Bush's preference, reflecting his philosophy of trusting and empowering loyal subordinates. Perhaps in response, Card tended to hold some issues rather closely, creating "stovepipes" that could leave potentially relevant participants in the dark about certain decision processes.[30]

On the national security side, Bush chose a confidante, Stanford provost and international relations scholar Rice, who had advised him during his campaign, as NSA. Although Rice previously had served on the NSC staff, she was nonetheless relatively inexperienced in the job. Her close relationship with the president was a plus, but she would be challenged in her job of coordinating such powerful personalities as the Secretaries of Defense and State, Rumsfeld and Powell. Former presidential press secretary Scott McClellan went even further, commenting that his experience with her "led me to believe she was more interested in figuring out where the president stood and just carrying out his wishes while expending only cursory effort in helping him understand all the considerations and potential consequences."[31] Ultimately, once President Bush decided, in effect, which side he was on, there was little Rice could do to respond to the complaints of Powell and his staff that they were not being heard.

Governing as Campaigning

In an administration with a substantial population of veterans of the Reagan years, it was not surprising to find something like a "troika" at the top of the initial White House staff. Certainly, counselors Karl Rove, Karen Hughes, and chief of staff Card were the three obvious luminaries at the outset, inviting comparison to Reagan's trio of James Baker, Edwin Meese, and Michael Deaver. But there were important differences. First, there was not the (sometimes creative) tension among Bush's three that had existed between Baker and Meese. Both Meese and Deaver were longtime Reagan associates and campaign veterans who had long since learned to work together. Perhaps more important was the substantive expertise each brought. In the Reagan case, Meese's focus was on policy, Deaver's on image and public relations, and Baker's on White House and cabinet management, although the latter had strong policy influence as well. Overall, they reflected the balance one expects in the White House, which conventionally is described as the place where policy and politics come together. By contrast, Bush's threesome reflected a heavy bias toward the public side of the presidency. Hughes' specialty was communications, Rove's was political strategy, and Card's process. Although none of the three was oblivious to policy concerns, those were not why they were there. The White House had policy shops, but Hughes was not central to their activities and Rove's job was to assess and promote policy in the context of overall political strategy.[32]

George Edwards and others have characterized the Bush approach (and Clinton's as well) as "governing by campaigning." The phrase has more than one meaning. It refers to the use of campaign techniques to govern through appeals to the people and the polls rather than, or in addition to, the institutions of government. But it also refers to shaping the purposes and proposals of the administration toward gaining partisan advantage, emphasizing policies that will "sell," and spinning their presentation to achieve that end. In the latter sense, this suggests a tilting of priorities toward "politics" and away from "policy." Given the interests of the top White House advisers, especially Rove, this was at least a plausible suspicion.

Wild Card: Vice President Cheney

Another trend the Bush administration continued was the growing importance of the vice presidency. Since at least Walter Mondale—and arguably, Mondale's predecessor, Nelson Rockefeller—vice presidents increasingly have been called upon to go beyond the traditional ceremonial and representational (in the sense of ticket balancing) responsibilities of the job. Vice presidents in recent administrations have been domestic policy advisors (Rockefeller), foreign policy advisors (G. H. W. Bush), political savants (Mondale), regulatory overseers (Dan Quayle), and government reformers (Al Gore), among other things. Bush's selection of Cheney, whose long government experience included stints as White House chief of staff, U.S. Representative from Wyoming, and Secretary of Defense, presaged another strong, active vice presidency. Cheney proved to be all of that and more. Like Gore before him, Cheney was furnished with a strong staff that included policy and legal advisors who came to play key roles in formulating and overseeing administration policy. Moreover, the top Cheney staff were fully integrated into White House operations and thus participated in the full range of policy decisions. Jack Goldsmith, director of the Justice Department's Office of Legal Counsel in 2003–2004, observes, for example, that no previous administration had fully "integrated" the vice president's legal counsel into the White House counsel's office. Goldsmith recalls that Cheney's counsel David Addington "received all the important governmental documents that that went to the Attorney General, and [he was] always in the room when [White House Counsel Alberto] Gonzales was discussing an important legal issue"; Goldsmith remembers only one of close to 100 meetings he had with Gonzales to discuss national security issues when Addington was absent.[33]

From the outset of the administration, Cheney had a broad portfolio limited only by his own interests coupled with walk-in privileges to the Oval Office. Initially, the vice president was asked to take the lead in formulating the Bush energy program, an appropriate assignment in view of his experience in the petroleum business. This background also extended his involvement into environmental policy. There, oversight investigations by the U.S. House Select Committee on Energy Independence and Global Warming uncovered evidence that the opposition of the vice president's office to a finding that greenhouse gases are dangerous and should be regulated under clean-air laws led to regulatory initiatives being rejected.[34] Cheney also took a lively interest in national security policy, allying himself with the aims of his old friend and mentor, Secretary of Defense Rumsfeld.

After September 11, 2001, Cheney's focus became sharper and his influence arguably even greater. Not only did he weigh in heavily on the side of overthrowing Saddam Hussein in Iraq, but Addington was a key member of the administration group that drafted White House positions on the treatment of enemy combatants at facilities such as Guantanamo.

Cheney's office has been described as "one side of a continuing information cleavage, with its own direct line to the president"; it contributed as well to the administration's policy politicization, "ensuring that only ideologically vetted civilians were allowed to serve in the Iraqi reconstruction effort, even where that meant passing over more qualified personnel."[35]

Evolution of the Administration

Among the intriguing unknowns about the Bush presidency is what it might have been like had the terrorist attacks of September 11 not taken place. Some might imagine opportunities would have been present for sustained pursuit of initiatives in education and faith-based and community activities, while needed attention could have focused on pressing needs in health care, social security, immigration, and physical infrastructure. Others would be more cautious, pointing to emerging early difficulties, such as drops in the president's public approval levels in summer 2001, the unexpected loss of party control in the Senate, and continuing Democratic bitterness about the 2000 election; these as well as other factors loomed as constraints on presidential achievement. Meanwhile, by the late summer of 2001, the systematic efforts at centralization and politicization were beginning to bear fruit. This section explores the seeming impact of September 11 on the administrative structuring and dynamics of the Bush presidency.

The Early Months

In its initial months, the Bush White House functioned relatively well, avoiding the stumbles of the early Clinton staff. The primary complaint about the administration was that it was brusque in its dealings with Congress, engaged in more demanding and less consulting than even Republican members expected. Although the early Bush legislative record was solid, including the passage of tax cuts and the arrival of different versions of the signature "No Child Left Behind" education reforms at a congressional conference committee, the administration suffered a major setback when Republican Senator James Jeffords of Vermont abruptly quit the party to become an independent and caucus with Senate Democrats. His central complaint was the "my way or the highway" attitude of the White House. This defection gave the Democrats an operating majority in the closely divided Senate. Beyond the perception of arrogance, the White House had also begun to develop a reputation for secretiveness that went beyond the usual concern with "leaks" to the media. Emblematic of this was the vice president's refusal to turn over documents from his energy task force to the Government Accountability Office, resulting in a legal battle that for the first time established that the principle of executive privilege applied to the vice president as well as to the president.

As for Bush, so impressive were the credentials of the staff and much of the cabinet that, prior to the attacks of September 11, there was some concern that the president himself might be overshadowed by the talented, experienced, and aggressive group of people with whom he had surrounded himself. Bush's initial cabinet, for example, perhaps was most notable for its deep experience. Among the "inner" cabinet members were Rumsfeld, undertaking his second tour as head of the Defense Department, former NSA General Powell at the State Department, and former OMB executive and corporate CEO Paul O'Neill at Treasury. At Justice, in a move that pleased the socially conservative segment element of the Republican Party base, Bush appointed the recently defeated Senator from Missouri, John Ashcroft. The "outer" cabinet posts were filled by the sort of people Washington was accustomed to. For the most part, they were tied to or on good terms with Republican interest groups, and all but one, holdover Transportation Secretary Norman Mineta, were Republicans. Jokes about the revival of the Ford administration (in which Cheney, Rumsfeld, and O'Neill had served) aside, the cabinet was reassuring to those who worried about the new president's experience or questioned his policy commitments.

Changes

The terrorist attacks of September 11 fundamentally changed the governing priorities of the Bush administration. At the same time, they also altered the dynamics of process and power within the White House, the cabinet, and beyond. Perhaps the first thing to change was the public perception of President Bush. After a shaky beginning, he famously found his voice through a megaphone in New York City, rallying emergency workers and through them the country, with strength, resolve, and the promise of revenge. In the public eye, at least, the president was at last clearly "presidential" and the specter of overshadowing forgotten.

Inside the White House, the Pentagon, and Foggy Bottom things were different, if no less hectic and improvised. An administration notable for careful, hierarchical control of decision processes became, in Paul Light's oft-quoted words, "an organized anarchy or an organized adhocracy. . . . [T]here's more dotted lines here than on a dress pattern."[36] In time, the emphasis on fighting terrorism, then engaging in war with Iraq, would inevitably expand the influence of those in the White House who were responsible for homeland and national security affairs.

Homeland Security

The most obvious such consequence was the creation of the post of White House homeland security advisor, a position occupied by former Pennsylvania governor Tom Ridge. The sense that intelligence failures helped lead to the success of the September 11 attacks made it clear that better communication and coordination among the responsible agencies were urgently needed, all the more so in an atmosphere where further attacks were considered possible or even likely. Ridge's position was modeled on that of the NSA. Thus, he was not only a presidential advisor but also head of a council with representatives of the key executive branch units charged with any aspect of domestic security (e.g., the Federal Bureau of Investigation [FBI], FEMA, the Army). From that position Ridge, aided by a modest staff, a small budget, and minimal legal authority was asked to effect significant changes in the way that these agencies worked, and especially, related to one another. To the surprise of nobody who understood government bureaucracies, Ridge was unable to accomplish this feat. Many voices, led in the Senate by then-Democrat Joe Lieberman of Connecticut, began to call for the creation of a cabinet department to be responsible for homeland security.

Bush initially opposed a new department, partly because he and his advisors saw the obvious difficulty involved in merging diverse agencies with established cultures and conflicting missions into a single unit. The federal government's prior experience with the old Department of Health, Education and Welfare, and before that, the Defense Department would give anyone pause. However, the White House solution was not working, and the departmental option appeared to be the only feasible alternative. Thus, was born the Department of Homeland Security (DHS) under Ridge as secretary, an administrative entity whose growing pains fulfilled the most pessimistic prognostications without really addressing the full problem of integrating bureaucratic functions. Due essentially to their political clout in Congress, key actors such as the Central Intelligence Agency (CIA) and FBI were not brought under the umbrella of the new department. Rather, they were left to work out, under congressional scrutiny and prodding, their own improved relationships.[37] Meanwhile, internal politics in the new DHS were blamed in part for the dismal performance of one of its elements, FEMA, in the aftermath of Hurricane Katrina, which devastated an underprepared New Orleans.[38]

The DHS under Secretary Michael Chertoff ultimately redeemed itself in 2008 with a strong performance during another terrible hurricane season.[39] Nonetheless, its struggles seemed to embody the lesson that simply sticking organizations together in a "garbage can" reorganization will mostly produce confusion, inefficiency, and ineffective performance.[40] Perhaps if Bush had been willing to try to muscle the FBI and CIA into the new department it would at least have had a better chance to coordinate anti-terrorist intelligence activities. On other fronts, however, such as the performance of FEMA, things might actually have gotten worse.

The War on Terror(ism)

As the Bush presidency strove to make administrative adjustments in the face of the heightened threat, Bush's rhetoric became simultaneously soaring and belligerent, as he declared a "war" on terrorism (usually abbreviated to "war on terror," as if terror itself could be expunged from the human experience) and vowed revenge on those who had perpetrated the September 11 attacks. Initially, this led to a decision to launch military action against the Taliban in Afghanistan. The move received broad domestic and international support, since the Taliban clearly had given Al Qaeda the training bases and logistical support that its terrorist ambitions required. At the same time, however, in Rumsfeld's Defense Department and especially in the office of Vice President Cheney, further plans were afoot to extend the "war" to an attack on Iraq. The rationale for this and the means of decision have been discussed exhaustively elsewhere. Here it is sufficient to note that this revealed two key characteristics of the Bush system. The first underscores the pervasive influence of the vice president, whose sway mounted as the administration focused on the threat of terrorism. The second was the partial breakdown of the carefully managed "multiple advocacy" decision system that aimed to compel consideration of a wide range of options before crucial choices were made.

Decision making concerning the Iraq invasion exposed sharp differences between Rumsfeld, Cheney, and their allies, on the one hand, and the State Department under Powell, on the other. In the middle, asked in effect to referee the contest, was NSA Rice. Hers was an impossible position after it became clear that the Rumsfeld-Cheney axis had the ear of the president (and unmediated access to him) in ways that Powell did not. If the president at some point was not hearing all the possible data and options, it was because he had made up his mind already.

At the same time, domestic security efforts as well as the military actions abroad led to the capture of large numbers of individuals suspected of involvement in anti-U.S. terrorist activity, including but not limited to the hijackings. Dealing with these people forced the administration to make difficult decisions, including the determination that such possible terrorists were not enemy combatants and thus not entitled to protection under the Geneva conventions. This and other decisions, including a broadening of the accepted definition of torture and a generous interpretation of the government's power to conduct electronic surveillance, brought Vice President Cheney, his aide Addington, White House Counsel Gonzales, and Attorney General Ashcroft into the vortex of post-9/11 policy making. As frequently happens, such unanticipated issues produce ad hoc groupings of advisors and sometimes key exclusions; it is not yet clear whether a full and fair survey of available options ensued. Most important was the strong sway of the hardliners, especially the vice president, with President Bush.

Discussion of some decisions evidently did include only those with similar values and objectives. For example, Jack Goldsmith (who worked in the counsel's office at the Defense Department before becoming director of the Office of Legal Counsel) describes a "self-styled 'War Council'" composed of White House counsel Gonzales, Cheney Counsel Addington, Department of Defense Counsel William Haynes, Timothy Flanigan (a Gonzales deputy), and John Yoo (from the Office of Legal Counsel). The group met:

> every few weeks in Gonzales's office . . . or behind closed doors in Haynes's Defense Department office. It would ploy legal strategy in the war on terror, sometimes as a prelude to dealing with lawyers from the State Department, the National Security Council and the Joint Chiefs of Staff who would ordinarily

be involved in war-related interagency legal decisions, and sometimes to the exclusion of the interagency process altogether.[41]

Overall, national security decision making after September 11 did not generally conform to the "multiple advocacy" formula or the recommendation for thorough staffing found in the literature supporting the standard model. Under the pressures of secrecy and intense advocacy within the administration, the process broke down in ways reminiscent of the symptoms of "groupthink" outlined by Irving Janis and observed when decision-making groups come under intense pressure. NSA Rice was unable to balance the inputs of the Cheney-Rumsfeld faction with those of Powell's State Department, largely because of the access President Bush had granted Cheney (and not Powell) and the trust Bush had in his vice president.[42] This was accentuated by the [resident's much-remarked proclivity for making decisions early in a process, after which he would become uninterested in alternatives to the choices already made. Thus, the preferences or "style" of the central decision maker shaped the decision process, an outcome particularly noteworthy in the area of policy that most engaged this president and his advisers.

No set of decisions exemplified these tendencies more than those surrounding the invasion of Iraq and overthrow of Hussein, in which warnings and reports from the State Department were ignored in favor of optimistic scenarios presented by Rumsfeld and his aides. In the second term, with Robert Gates replacing Rumsfeld at Defense (following the Republican losses in 2006), Rice moving to the State Department, and a new White House chief staff (OMB Director and former deputy chief of staff Joshua Bolten), national security decision processes appeared to be somewhat more inclusive, with less conflict between the principals in Defense and State. Moreover, Bush's resistance to expert advice can be overstated. In 2007, for example, with the situation in Iraq seemingly deteriorating, he acquiesced in the advice of his military commanders—and rejected the counsel of others in the administration—in approving a troop "surge" that appeared to at least bring the military situation under better control.[43]

Domestic and Economic Policy

President Bush received positive reviews for his decision to continue the NEC, and he appointed highly regarded people to key economic policy positions, but seemingly the economic team never quite jelled. O'Neill, the first Secretary of the Treasury, left the administration early, largely as a result of his disagreement with the Bush tax cuts and his unwillingness to suppress his views in public. This was just the beginning of a story of turnover and difficulty at the top, while the economy struggled, first in the wake of the bursting of the dot-com bubble in the early 2000s and then the mortgage lending and oil crises of the latter part of the decade. The treatment of O'Neill and Lawrence Lindsey, the first NEC chair, was revealing. Lindsey's crime was to suggest that the Iraq War might cost as much as $200 billion (less than half of what it in fact cost as of mid-2008). For that, essentially, he was dismissed. Early on, the administration demonstrated a "circle the wagons" mentality and intolerance for dissent, even from Republicans in Congress.

O'Neill's replacement, John Snow, largely avoided such missteps and dutifully defended the administration's positions. He departed, and as the economy struggled in the mid-to-late 2000s, beset by high oil prices and a crisis in real estate lending, Treasury Secretary Henry Paulson emerged as the administration's strongest voice, and indeed, its first really imposing leader in the area of economic policy. Indeed, as the *New York Times* reported,

> For a president like Mr. Bush, who holds a master's degree in business administration from Harvard and has strong economic views of his own, Mr. Paulson's emergence as the administration's primary voice on economic policy is striking. But time and again in recent months, Mr. Paulson has taken Mr. Bush where he instinctively would not ordinarily go: into the realm of government intervention in the markets.[44]

At least in the face of persistent economic problems, President Bush showed a capacity to listen and heed advice that he would not have agreed with previously. His reliance upon Paulson echoed his eventual willingness to rely on his field commanders in Iraq.

Meanwhile, on the domestic policy front the White House seemed to lack strong leadership from the beginning, at least once the No Child Left Behind education reform was approved and much of the "Faith-Based Initiatives" program was put in place by executive order (but not necessarily adequately funded[45]). Throughout the second term, though, Education Secretary Spellings worked relentlessly to ease some of the opposition at the state and local levels raised by initial implementation of No Child Left Behind and to advocate its reauthorization.

When political strategist Rove was moved to deputy chief of staff for policy in 2005, much was expected, but little was delivered. In the midst of the 2006 loss of Congress, the scandal surrounding the revelation of CIA operative Valerie Plame, and rising dissatisfaction with the economy and the war in Iraq, Rove left the White House in 2007. In any case, with a Democratic Congress in place that had a voracious appetite for wide-ranging oversight, little would be accomplished in domestic policy.

Conclusion

Although President Bush has remarked that he pays scant attention to what his legacy might be, the same cannot be said for many others—pundits, political scientists, and citizens among them. Bert Rockman usefully cautions, though, that "legacy implies something durable," which with future administrations and others will have to cope.[46]

In the broad sphere of White House staff and executive branch governance, the Bush presidency leaves several inheritances. Whether his successor embraces, avoids, or changes them remains to be seen, as does whether any may constitute part of a positive or a more negative legacy.

As we have suggested, each of the five patterns of presidential politics and organization has persisted. Among the Bush presidency's signal contributions to the nature of such continuities are the breadth and depth of its centralizing and politicizing tendencies, often personified and infused by Vice President Cheney and his staff and by senior aides like Rove. Meanwhile, the searing experience of September 11 had a powerful, pervasive, and long-lasting impact on the administration. It further empowered those with claims to national and homeland security expertise, and it amplified preexisting tendencies toward secrecy and centralized control. In the process, until relatively late in the administration, key players in the Defense and Justice departments and in the White House dominated ad hoc decision groupings and contributed to narrowing the flow and diversity of information apparently reaching President Bush; he, himself, complicit in these arrangements.

Like his predecessors, the next president will enter a White House with little physical evidence of its former occupants. He will have to confront, however, the staffing and administrative inheritances left by Bush.

Notes

1. Charles E. Walcott and Karen M. Hult, "White House Structure and Decision Making: Elaborating the Standard Model," *Presidential Studies Quarterly* 35 (June 2005): 303–18.

2. See, e.g., Norman Ornstein and Thomas Mann, eds., *The Permanent Campaign* (Washington, D.C.: Brookings Institution Press, 2000).

3. Richard P. Nathan, *The Plot That Failed: Nixon and the Administrative Presidency* (New York: John Wiley and Sons, 1975); see too Richard P. Nathan, *The Administrative Presidency* (New York: John Wiley and Sons, 1983).

4. Terry M. Moe, "The Politicized Presidency," in *The New Direction in American Politics*, edited by John E. Chubb and Paul E. Peterson (Washington, D.C.: Brookings Institution Press, 1985).

5. Description of the National Economic Council is available at www .whitehouse.gov/nec/. See also Alexis Simendinger, "Administration: The Broker's Burden," *National Journal* (April 26, 2003): 1306–8. More generally, see Kenneth I. Juster and Simon Lazurus, *Making Economic Policy: An Assessment of the National Economic Council* (Washington, D.C.: Brookings Institution Press, 1997).

6. William West, "The Institutionalization of Regulatory Review: Organizational Stability and Responsive Competence at OIRA," *Presidential Studies Quarterly* 35 (March 2005): 82.

7. Executive Order 13422, January 18, 2007, *Federal Register* 72 (14), (January 23, 2007): 2763–65.

8. Anne Joseph O'Connell, "Well-Regulated," *Democracy: A Journal of Ideas* 8 (Spring 2008): 112.

9. West, "The Institutionalization of Regulatory Review: Organizational Stability and Responsive Competence at OIRA," 88.

10. James P. Pfiffner, "The First MBA President: George W. Bush as Public Administrator," *Public Administration Review* 67 (January/February 2007): 6–20.

11. Marissa Martino Golden, *What Motivates Bureaucrats?: Politics and Administration during the Reagan Years* (New York : Columbia University Press, 2000), 5; Robert F. Durant and Adam L. Warber have labeled it an indirect, "contextual" approach, compared to more direct, "unilateral" approaches ("Networking in the Shadow of Hierarchy: Public Policy, the Administrative Presidency, and the Neoadministrative State," *Presidential Studies Quarterly* 31 (June 2001): 221–44.

12. David E. Lewis, *The Politics of Presidential Appointments: Political Control and Bureaucratic Performance* (Princeton, NJ: Princeton University Press, 2008).

13. Lewis, *The Politics of Presidential Appointments*, 98. Lewis includes three types of appointees in his examination: those requiring Senate confirmation (PAS), Schedule C appointments (jobs that are policy determining or confidential), and noncareer members of the Senior Executive Service.

14. Lewis, *The Politics of Appointments*, 118–19.

15. See, for example, Joel D. Aberbach, "The State of the Contemporary American Presidency: Or, Is Bush II Actually Ronald Reagan's Heir?" in *The George W. Bush Presidency: Appraisals and Prospects*, edited by Colin Campbell and Bert A. Rockman (Washington, D.C.: CQ Press, 2004).

16. Robert Draper, *Dead Certain: The Presidency of George W. Bush* (New York: Free Press, 2007), 105.

17. Andrew Rudalevige, "'The Decider': Issue Management and the Bush White House," in *The George W. Bush Legacy*, edited by Colin Campbell, Bert A. Rockman, and Andrew Rudalevige (Washington, D.C.: CQ Press), 140.

18. Lewis, *The Politics of Appointments*, 116, 127. See too John J. DiIulio, Jr., "The Hyper-Rhetorical Presidency," *Critical Review* 19 (2–3): 315–24.

19. "White House: How Bush Flexes His Executive Muscles," *National Journal* (January 26, 2002), 235.

20. For example, Christopher Drew and Richard A. Oppel, Jr., "How Industry Won the Battle of Pollution Control at EPA," *New York Times* March 6, 2004.

21. Robert Pear, "Agency Sees Withholding of Medicare Data from Congress as Illegal," *New York Times* May 4, 2004. See too Amy Goldstein, "Probe Starts in Medicare Drug Cost Estimates," *Washington Post* March 17, 2004.

22. See, for example, Eric Lipton and David Johnson, "For Gonzales, More Records, and Questions," *New York Times* March 25, 2007. For the reflections of one of the fired U.S. attorneys, David Iglesias, see *In Justice: Inside the Scandal that Rocked the Bush Administration* (Hoboken, NJ: John Wiley and Sons).

23. For example, Carl Hulse and Scott Shane, "Congress Expands Scope of Inquiries into Justice Department Practices and Politics," *New York Times* March 25, 2007.

24. Juliet Eilperin, "Anti-Regulation Aide to Cheney Up for Energy Post," *Washington Post* August 19, 2008.

25. Lewis, *The Politics of Appointments*, 136, and *passim*.

26. One example is the memos collected and delivered to each candidate's transition teams in Fall 2000 by the White House Transition Project. They appear in edited form in *The White House World: Transitions, Organization, and Office Operations*, edited by Martha Joynt Kumar and Terry Sullivan (College Station: Texas A & M University Press, 2003). See too http://whitehousetransitionproject.org/.

27. Nor would this have been different, of course, had Gore been president.

28. Walcott and Hult, "White House Structure and Decision Making."

29. Charles E. Walcott, Shirley Warshaw, and Stephen Wayne, "Office of the Chief of Staff," in *The White House World: Transitions, Organization, and Office Operations*, edited by Martha Joynt Kumar and Terry Sullivan (College Station: Texas A & M University Press, 2003).

30. Scott McClellan, *What Happened: Inside the Bush White House and Washington's Culture of Deception* (New York: PublicAffairs, 2008).

31. McClellan, *What Happened*, 145.

32. See too Lawrence R. Jacobs and Robert Shapiro, "Bush's Democratic Ambivalence: Responsiveness and Policy Promotion in Republican Government," in *The George W. Bush Legacy*, edited by Colin Campbell, Bert A. Rockman, and Andrew Rudalevige (Washington, D.C.: CQ Press)

33. Jack Goldsmith, *The Terror Presidency: Law and Judgment Inside the Bush Administration* (New York: Norton, 2007), 76.

34. See, for example, Siobhan Hughes, "Climate Report Cites Cheney's Office," *Wall Street Journal* July 21, 2008.

35. Rudalevige, "'The Decider,'" 151.

36. Quoted in Dana Milbank and Bradley Graham, "With Crisis, More Fluid Style at White House," *Washington Post* October 10, 2001.

37. Their continuing difficulties at doing so are described, for example, by Amy B. Zegart, *Spying Blind: The CIA, the FBI, and the Origins of 9/11* (Princeton, NJ: Princeton University, 2007).

38. See, for example, Lewis, *The Politics of Appointments*, ch. 6.

39. For example, Eric Lipton, "FEMA Is Eager to Show It Learned from Katrina," *New York Times* September 1, 2008.

40. Karen Hult, *Agency Merger and Bureaucratic Redesign* (Pittsburgh, PA: University of Pittsburgh Press, 1987).

41. Goldsmith, *The Terror Presidency*, 22.

42. See, for instance, Murray Waas, "What Bush Was Told about Iraq," *National Journal* March 4, 2006, 40–42; James Fallows, "Blind into Baghdad," *Atlantic Monthly* January 2004.

43. See, for example, Bob Woodward, *The War Within: A Secret White House History, 2006–2008* (New York: Simon & Schuster, 2008).

44. Sheryl Gay Stolberg, "Rescue of Mortgage Giants Displays Paulson's Clout," *New York Times* September 9, 2008.

45. See J. David Kuo, *Tempting Faith: An Inside Story of Political Seduction* (New York: Free Press, 2006.)

46. Bert A. Rockman, "The Legacy of the George W. Bush Presidency–A Revolutionary Presidency?" in *The George W. Bush Legacy*, edited by Colin Campbell, Bert A. Rockman, and Andrew Rudalevige (Washington, D.C.: CQ Press), 325.

~

CHAPTER THREE

George W. Bush's Domestic Policy Agenda

Andrew E. Busch

From the moment he announced his bid for the presidency in 1999, George W. Bush sought to recast U.S. electoral politics by recasting the Republican Party's domestic policy approach. While Bush's foreign policy agenda has received more attention, the character and implications of his domestic policy agenda are arguably more difficult to disentangle. In some areas of domestic policy, Bush enjoyed surprising successes; in others, embarrassing failures. And observers have been quick to disagree not only about whether Bush's initiatives were good or bad, but also how to characterize them. For some, Bush was at least as conservative as Ronald Reagan, an ideological president who sought to turn narrow electoral victories into a broad shift to the right in public policy. "George W. Bush's administration," one such critic noted, offered a good example of "adroitly managed plutocracy."[1] For others, his domestic policy represented a lamentable betrayal of Reagan, a shift away from limited government conservatism that bloated the federal government and sundered the Republican coalition.[2] Yet others argued that Bush's efforts were a bold and commendable attempt to turn big government to conservative ends for the first time.[3]

Political Background and Philosophical Foundations

Bush's domestic policy agenda sprang from the national political and policy environment of the mid- to late 1990s, which was characterized by intense and growing partisanship, a close balance between the parties, and a drive by Republican conservatives to significantly downsize the role of the federal government. Republicans gained a new majority in the 1994 mid-term elections calling for a balanced budget, limited government, decentralization, and a variety of political reforms epitomized by congressional term limits. In 1995–1996, the Republican Congress confronted President Bill Clinton on a number of fronts, especially appropriations and federal regulation. Republicans sought, among other things, to close four federal departments, the departments of Education, Energy, Commerce, and Housing and Urban Development. This struggle culminated in two partial federal government shutdowns that, in the long run, damaged Congress more than Clinton. Although they gained short-term spending cuts in a number of programs, Republicans failed to achieve the sweeping changes for which they had hoped. The president then ran a successful re-election campaign in 1996 against the alleged extremism of Newt Gingrich and the 104th Congress.

Although Clinton won a second term, Republicans held on to control of Congress, and the stage was set for a period of policy stalemate and escalating political partisanship. After a balanced budget agreement was reached in 1997, there was little policy movement in either direction for the remainder of Clinton's term. Instead, much of the president's second term was consumed in scandal, particularly the Monica Lewinsky scandal that led to Clinton's impeachment by the House of Representatives and his trial by the Senate. Though Clinton was spared removal by the Senate, the whole episode fed the already high levels of partisanship. In the midst of the impeachment imbroglio, House Republicans lost five seats in the 1998 mid-term elections, the first time since 1934 that the president's party had gained House seats in a mid-term election.

Into this environment stepped Bush. Elected Governor of Texas in the 1994 Republican sweep, Bush was elevated to the status of Republican presidential front-runner almost immediately after the disappointing congressional elections of 1998. While his copartisans were losing ground in Washington, Bush was reelected in Texas by a large majority and seemed to promise a different approach.

Bush's new approach was known as "compassionate conservatism" (or, as it came to be known in some quarters, "big government conservatism"). It was always an open question whether compassionate conservatism was a political philosophy, a policy departure, an electoral tactic, or a bit of all three.

As an electoral matter, it promised to supply the need of the moment for national Republicans, who were struggling against an image of harshness and ideological rigidity. When Bush openly scolded House Republicans in the fall of 1999 for trying to "balance the budget on the backs of the poor," many observers concluded that compassionate conservatism was Bush's center-right version of Clinton's center-left "third way," to be likewise defined by triangulation against elements of his own party.[4] In general, Bush sought to soften the hard edges of the Republican image, making the party more acceptable to women and racial minorities, especially Hispanics but also blacks.

However, it would be a mistake to treat compassionate conservatism as nothing more than a tactical maneuver. As a policy matter, compassionate conservatism was a term drawn from the work of academic Marvin Olasky, who argued for an active conservative approach to the problems of the poor.[5] Bush's own convictions led him in this direction, as well. His evangelical Christianity and his own previous struggles against alcohol contributed to his views.[6] "We have a responsibility that when somebody hurts," Bush would later summarize his philosophy, "government has got to move."[7] He often seemed instinctively driven more by the social gospel than by Friedrich Hayek or Milton Friedman. The same evangelical strain impelled Bush in the direction of social conservatism—and the same political calculations. Far from clashing with the premise of compassionate conservatism, social conservatism was an integral component of it. It was one of the strongest attractions toward Republicans for blacks and Hispanics, who were typically economically liberal but culturally conservative.

By whatever combination of conviction and calculation, Bush entered the 2000 campaign with a mix of domestic policy commitments. On the "conservative" side of the ledger was his promise of a $1.6 trillion, 10-year across-the-board tax cut. On the "compassion" side of the ledger was a pledge to support a new Medicare prescription drug entitlement and immigration liberalization, a call for federal resources for "faith-based initiatives," and a de-emphasis on a discourse of limited government and federalism. (In one respect at least, Bush was drawing from the same well as his father, who had famously called for "a thousand points of light" and "a kinder, gentler nation" in 1988.) Bush clearly saw education as a linchpin for his project. He abandoned the call, heard in Republican platforms since 1980, to abolish the federal Department of Education. Instead, he touted a plan of increased federal education funding combined with a state-by-state system of testing for accountability.[8]

In his July 2000 nomination acceptance speech, Bush called for Americans to meet the challenges posed by prosperity. Calling for a new "era of responsibility," Bush defined compassionate conservatism by promising to "put conservative values and conservative ideas into the thick of the fight for justice and opportunity." Although he expressed concern with the deterioration of the U.S. armed forces and called for effective missile defense, the bulk of Bush's remarks dwelled on domestic matters, starting with education. Decrying the "soft bigotry of low expectations," he declared that "When a school district receives federal funds to teach poor children, we expect them to learn. And if they don't, parents should get the money to make a different choice." Bush also promised to repair Medicare, strengthen Social Security by offering private accounts to young workers, and cut taxes for all Americans, elucidating the principle driving his tax cut proposal: "The surplus is not the government's money. The surplus is the people's money." He called for greater charity and for promoting "a culture that values life" by supporting adoption and a partial birth abortion ban. Throughout, Bush promised a change in tone in Washington—greater bipartisanship on behalf of a "party of reform."[9]

The highly controversial endgame of the 2000 election, involving a 36-day political and legal battle, finally ended with Bush the winner. According to Gallup polls, four in five Americans accepted Bush's victory as legitimate, but there is little question that the controversy colored the next eight years. Most immediately, the election results meant that Bush entered office with a shallower reservoir of goodwill than any president since perhaps Rutherford B. Hayes in 1876. Bush's lack of a plurality in the nationally aggregated popular vote made it impossible for him to claim a "mandate" for his policies as modern presidents typically do. Not least, Republicans had also lost ground in Congress, losing four seats in the House and another four in the Senate, leaving a 50-50 tie in the upper chamber. Bush was about to enter the first of several stages of his domestic presidency.[10]

The Honeymoon

The circumstances of his election led some observers (mostly Democrats) to argue that Bush should abandon his domestic policy agenda and preside over a "unity government" that would split the difference between Bush's and Gore's proposals. Bush rejected this notion decisively, pledging to press forward with his campaign promises. As Bush expressed days after taking office, "I told the American people if I had the honor of being the President, I would submit these positions I was campaigning on to the legislative branch, and that's exactly what I've done."[11]

In his January 2001 inaugural address, Bush reiterated the themes of his campaign, extolling responsibility and compassion ("the work of a nation, not just a government") and calling on Americans to "reclaim our schools . . . reform Social Security and Medicare . . . reduce taxes."[12] At the same time, he made a number of lesser gestures of bipartisanship. In the first few months of his presidency, he frequently invited Democratic leaders like Senator Edward Kennedy (MA) to the White House and kept in place some Clinton appointees like Central Intelligence Agency Director George Tenet and Secretary of Transportation Norman Mineta. Against the odds, Bush managed to enjoy a "honeymoon."

At the outset of his presidency, Bush made clear that he, like Reagan, would focus on a limited number of big objectives. Specifically, he advanced two key agenda items that represented the balance he sought in compassionate conservatism: the tax cut he had promised during the campaign and the education overhaul he had made the centerpiece of his effort to forge a new image for Republicans. Although the education bill, dubbed the "No Child Left Behind Act," was given the number H.R. 1 to symbolize its priority to the president, the tax cut was enacted first.

Bush's proposal—what became the "Economic Growth and Tax Relief Reconciliation Act"—envisioned cuts in every tax bracket of individual income tax, the creation of a new lowest rate of 10 percent (replacing the existing 15 percent low rate), doubling of the per child tax credit from $500 to $1,000 per child, and the establishment of a new tax credit of up to $10,000 per child for adoption expenses. The president also advocated a reduction in the "marriage penalty" and a gradual phase out of the estate tax (or "death tax," as Republicans liked to call it). Although the tax cut was originally proposed as a means of returning to taxpayers a large part of the projected federal budget surplus, added urgency was given to the proposal by the obvious deterioration of economic indicators in late 2000 and early 2001. (The economic commission charged with defining the beginning and end of recessions later determined that the nation entered recession by March 2001.)

Critics of the tax cut argued, correctly, that most of the aggregate dollar savings would accrue to taxpayers in the upper tax brackets.[13] Bush and other defenders of the tax cuts countered, equally correctly, that it was taxpayers at the lower end who would get the largest percentage cuts, with many lower-middle class taxpayers (especially those with families) relieved from federal income tax altogether. As a palliative to Senate Democrats, Bush agreed to a proposal by Senate Democratic leader Tom Daschle to add a "stimulus" component to the tax cuts, consisting of a flat $300 per person check mailed from the Treasury as an "advance" on the next year's tax cut. In the end, a $1.35 trillion tax cut passed 240 to 154 in the House (with 28 House Democrats in support) and 58 to 33 in the Senate (with 12 Senate Democrats voting yes). When it passed, it was one part supply-side tax cut, one part Keynesian tax cut, and at least one part tax cut for reasons of political economy, including relieving families and draining away the putative surplus so it could not be spent by ambitious politicians. Senate rules required that the tax cut be effective for only a 10-year period, meaning it would expire in 2011 unless renewed. As a proportion of the economy, the 2001 Bush tax cut was the third largest tax cut since 1960, with only the 1964 Kennedy-Johnson tax cut and the 1981 Reagan tax cut larger.[14] When he signed the tax cut bill, Bush predicted the victory would be "the first major achievement in a new era, an era of steady cooperation."[15]

While the tax cut was making its very noisy way through Congress, No Child Left Behind was moving more quietly. The heart of Bush's notion, with which he had already experimented in Texas, was that federal education funding should be increased, but states should be required to adopt some form of standardized assessment of schools that could then be shared with parents and the community. Schools that were consistently graded as "failing" would lose funds and children would receive aid to move to another school (including vouchers to a private school). No Child Left Behind provoked the creation of unusual coalitions both for and against. Opposition to No Child Left Behind included some liberals and a major portion of the education establishment, who did not approve of the accountability provisions, and a large number of conservatives, who saw No Child Left Behind as an unprecedented intrusion of the federal government into state and local education matters. To secure passage, Bush had to make a believer out of Kennedy, who held a powerful seat on the Senate Health, Education, and Labor Committee. Kennedy rallied Democrats and forced the administration to back away from elements of the original bill, including the voucher provision and provisions giving substantial autonomy to states. The Massachusetts Senator then endorsed the testing and accountability provisions and helped assure passage. No Child Left Behind passed both the House and Senate by the middle of June, but for a time was bogged down in conference committee.

With these two top priorities either passed or on the road to victory, Bush basked in the glow of media commentary that expressed surprise at his successes. Troubles began at the end of May when Vermont Republican Senator James Jeffords announced he was leaving the Republican Party and would caucus as an independent with Senate Democrats, giving the opposition party a slim edge in the chamber.

A few items attracted Bush's attention for the remainder of the summer. In 2000, energy had made a comeback as an issue due to rising oil prices, and upon taking office Bush had appointed a task force headed by Vice President Richard Cheney to make recommendations. In late summer, the House passed a controversial provision, supported by Bush, allowing for oil exploration in the Arctic National Wildlife Refuge. The House also pressed forward with legislation enabling faith-based social service organizations to receive federal money, another key focus of compassionate conservatism. (In the end, neither Arctic National Wildlife Refuge nor the faith-based initiative became law.) Health care made a brief appearance as the Senate and House passed dueling versions of a bill reforming health maintenance organization practices, a big issue during the 2000 campaign. The administration floated a trial balloon for a new and more liberal immigration policy establishing a guest worker program for illegal immigrants. Not least, Bush made a notable speech discussing the issue of embryonic stem cell research. In his speech, which aimed to thread the needle between scientific advocates and social conservatives who had deep moral misgivings, Bush agreed to allow federal funding of embryonic stem cell research for the first time, but only along limited lines. When Congress returned back from Labor Day recess, it began a debate on the budget question of the moment: how best to create a "lock box" for Social Security to protect it from raids on the federal surplus.

September 11 and Domestic Policy

When terrorists struck the United States on September 11, 2001, they instantly transformed the Bush presidency from a domestic presidency into a national security presidency. Some of the items attracting concern in the late summer of 2001 went away entirely (health maintenance organization reform and the budget surplus "lock box," which sank without a trace), while others simmered and occasionally surfaced (e.g., stem cells, energy, and immigration), but the whole focus of the administration, and indeed the nation, was radically altered.

In terms of domestic policy, one issue was immediately eclipsed by September 11, and three others emerged. First, budget constraint was immediately lost. Within days, Congress passed a $40 billion bill for war and New York reconstruction without regard to budgetary impact. Not only was the lock box gone, the surplus itself was soon gone.

Second, the September 11 attack pushed the economy into deeper trouble. The stock market shuddered, losing 13 percent of its value within one week, and within four months a million jobs had been lost. The Federal Reserve Board took the lead in responding by slashing interest rates, but Bush also responded. The administration's first reaction was to urge Americans to go shopping, an approach that later brought Bush considerable criticism from those who thought the moment was ripe to call on Americans to sacrifice for their country. Congress also quickly passed, with presidential support, a $15 billion bailout of airlines, which were hard-hit by the effects of September 11.[16]

In 2002, some small business tax cuts were pushed through Congress in the "Job Creation and Worker Assistance Act," but economic recovery was hampered by a series of accounting scandals in major firms such as Enron, Global Crossing, and Adelphia Cable, which took a serious toll on the stock market well into 2002. Democrats thought Enron might help them retake control of Congress, but Bush co-opted the issue by embracing the Sarbanes-Oxley regulatory bill, which then passed 97 to 0 in the Senate.

Finally, September 11 directly stimulated a whole new area of domestic policy that quickly became known as "homeland security." This area contained two main branches and a side issue. One main branch consisted of new laws and policies aimed at mitigating terrorism near the point of impact, such as the USA PATRIOT Act, which aimed to facilitate information-gathering about terrorist suspects and information-sharing among intelligence and law enforcement agencies. The other was structural reform of government to create new organizations and reconfigure old ones. In the first, Bush was consistently on the offensive. In October 2001, the USA PATRIOT Act passed 98 to 1 in the Senate and 357 to 66 in the House, though it was soon under fire from civil libertarians. In the second, Democrats led, with Bush often accepting their recommendations only after some resistance. In the immediate aftermath of September 11, Democrats proposed the federalization of baggage security through creation of the Transportation Security Administration (TSA); Bush initially resisted calls for a new bureaucracy but ultimately gave in. It was also Democrats who originally proposed creation of a Department of Homeland Security, though Bush effectively made the issue his own during the 2002 elections.

The side issue related to homeland security was the high priority Bush placed on tamping down any anger Americans might have felt against Muslims in their midst in the weeks after September 11. He had already been the first president to include mention of mosques in the familiar rhetorical litany of church and synagogue; immediately after September 11 he met with U.S. Islamic leaders in an effort to shield Muslims from the sort of backlash that struck Japanese Americans after Pearl Harbor or the German Americans in 1917.

One important but indirect domestic effect of September 11 was the push that it gave to the leadership in both parties to finish up work on No Child Left Behind.[17] To grease the wheels, Bush agreed to a major increase in federal education spending. No Child Left Behind reached final passage in December with large bipartisan majorities (381 to 41 in the House and 87 to 10 in the Senate). In the end, there were more Republicans than Democrats in the "no" column. Nevertheless, Bush's education strategy erased the Democratic lead on the issue among the public, although the effect seems to have been temporary.[18]

Aside from domestic issues flowing out of September 11, a handful of other (mostly) domestic issue shone through the otherwise dense fog of war. One issue was the farm economy, which many saw as crucial to Republican prospects for success in the upcoming elections. Here, Bush endorsed a farm bill that undid much of the free market approach of the 1996 Freedom to Farm Act and instead raised federal farm subsidies by $90 billion over the previous farm bill. Likewise, a major increase in steel tariffs was imposed by Bush in 2002, perhaps with the key industrial states of Pennsylvania, Ohio, and West Virginia in mind (by 2004, the tariffs were repealed amid a brewing trade war with Europe). The president's energy bill, faith-based initiatives program, human cloning ban, and tort reform stalled in the Democratic Senate.

Senate Control

The 2002 elections gave control of the Senate back to the Republican Party. Although only a net of two seats shifted, it was enough to ensure that Republicans would control both houses of Congress again, and Bush made the most of his narrow majorities.[19] Indeed, before the new Senate was even sworn in, Democrats reversed course and agreed to the president's version of the Homeland Security Department. However, Democrats were also embittered by the 2002 campaign, in which they believed Bush and Republicans had unfairly tarred them as soft on national security. Overall, the return of the Republican Senate majority turned Bush toward a more partisan approach.

In early 2003, in hopes of bolstering the tepid economic recovery then underway, Bush won passage of a large new tax cut measure, the "Jobs and Growth Tax Relief Reconciliation Act of 2003." The measure cut the top tax rate on capital gains by 25 percent and cut taxes on dividends by applying the lower capital gains rates (rather than ordinary income tax rates) to them. Important elements of the 2001 tax cut, including the per-child tax credit and the across-the-board reduction of income tax rates, were accelerated. Tax incentives were also included to encourage investment by small businesses. Concerns about the federal deficit among Senate Republicans like George Voinovich of Ohio led the Senate to cut the proposal in half, but the final version still offered an estimated $350 billion in tax relief over 10 years. Unlike the 2001 tax cut, the 2003 tax cut was enthusiastically received by supply-siders. Opponents, including a cohort of 450 economists, argued that the bill would skew the nation's distribution of wealth.[20] In contrast with the 2001 tax cut, the 2003 tax cut was a highly partisan affair. Only seven House Democrats and two Senate Democrats voted for it; Vice President Cheney had to cast the tie-breaking vote in the U.S. Senate to assure passage.

At the other end of the spectrum, Bush also succeeded in pushing through Congress a prescription drug entitlement for seniors. In keeping with the principle of channeling rather than resisting big government, Bush agreed to a program that, at the time of passage in December 2003, was publicly estimated to cost $400 billion over 19 years. Within a short time, that estimate rose to $534 billion and then again to $800 billion; controversy later erupted when it became clear that the administration had suppressed a higher estimate prior to the vote. The program was designed to foster consumer choice and hold down costs by promoting competition among private insurance plans. The legislation also included a provision allowing taxpayers to establish Health Savings Accounts (HSAs), tax-free savings for medical expenses. Democrats largely opposed the bill, which they thought should be more expansive and less dependent on private companies. They also objected to HSAs and to provisions prohibiting direct negotiation between the federal government and pharmaceutical companies. Republicans balked at the price tag and at creating a new entitlement program. For his part, Bush brushed aside suggestions by some Senate Republicans that the benefit should be means-tested (i.e., limited to those in need) or that the program should be paid for in higher taxes or spending cuts elsewhere. In the end, the congressional majority swallowed its philosophical objections and Medicare Part D passed in the House by a 220 to 215 margin after Republican leaders held open the vote for three hours and strong-armed several doubters.[21]

The 2002 elections also opened the road for another policy initiative. Since the late 1990s, conservatives in Congress had tried to secure passage of a federal act banning the late-term practice widely known as partial birth abortion. Indeed, the pro-life movement, shifting to a more incremental strategy, had long made a partial birth abortion ban one of its central aims. Such a measure had twice passed Congress in the 1990s and 27 states had enacted laws at the state level, but the federal law was vetoed by President Clinton and state laws were overturned in a 5 to 4 Supreme Court decision in 2000 (*Nebraska v. Carhart*).[22] In 2003, public opinion polls consistently showed a substantial majority of Americans wanted to make the practice illegal.[23] Once Republicans regained control of the Senate, they and the administration made passage of a federal act a high priority. The Partial Birth Abortion Ban Act was enacted in 2003, winning support from nearly all

Republicans and about one-third of Democrats in the House and Senate.[24] It marked perhaps the most important victory of the Bush administration in its agenda of social conservatism.

Re-election

As Bush geared up for re-election, it was clear that national security would play the predominant role in his campaign, as it had in his presidency since September 11. Nevertheless, some domestic issues intruded, at times against Bush's inclinations. Most notably, in November 2003 the Supreme Judicial Court of Massachusetts struck down the state's marriage law, holding it to violate the state constitution because it did not recognize same-sex unions. This decision immediately pushed same-sex marriage into the forefront of national debate, sparking a fierce negative reaction among social conservatives and advocates of judicial restraint. Bush immediately came under enormous pressure to endorse a federal constitutional amendment establishing that marriage is reserved for one man and one woman.

He hesitated for some months before devoting two paragraphs to the issue buried deep in his 2004 State of the Union address. A constitutional amendment received only conditional support: "If judges insist on forcing their arbitrary will on the people, the only alternative left to the people would be the constitutional process."[25] However, support of traditional marriage became a refrain of his campaign, and he did encourage Congress to vote on a federal marriage amendment in the summer. It received a majority, but fell short of the two-thirds vote necessary to send the measure to the states for ratification. (This scene was reenacted in identical fashion in the summer of 2005.) Bush also gave verbal support to ballot measures banning same-sex marriage in 13 states, all of which passed convincingly. Throughout, Bush walked a tightrope. On one hand, his social conservative base demanded action, and most Americans declared themselves opposed to same-sex marriage. On the other hand, he did not want to alienate the significant number of voters who opposed same-sex marriage but were repelled by politicians who made the issue a high priority.

Compassionate conservatism never fell away completely—the faith-based initiative, for example, funneled large amounts of federal money to black pastors in 2004—but as Election Day drew closer, Bush shifted from open touting of compassionate conservatism to another manifestation of big government conservatism, the "ownership society." Bush had been developing the notion of the ownership society for some time.[26] Again, government would act positively, using conservative values to facilitate greater self-reliance and "empowerment." In his nomination acceptance speech at the Republican National Convention, Bush said "Another priority for a new term is to build an ownership society, because ownership brings security, and dignity, and independence." He then enumerated goals necessary to achieve the ownership society, particularly rising home ownership and individual ownership of health plans and retirement. He specifically pointed to Social Security as a program that could be updated by giving citizens personal accounts.[27] Overall, Bush's 2004 nomination acceptance speech featured a long laundry list of domestic proposals before turning to the central issue of national security.

These themes were repeated in debates and advertisements throughout the fall campaign. However, there is no question that, in the campaign as in the speech, the domestic themes were submerged beneath national security. Exit polls showed that 34 percent of voters picked terrorism or Iraq as their most important issue. Another 22 percent of voters chose moral values, 80 percent of whom voted for Bush. The economy placed close behind, with health care, taxes, and education trailing badly.[28]

Political Capital

Bush's 2004 victory was, in certain ways, quite notable. He was the first presidential winner since 1988 to win a majority of the popular votes cast, and the first Republican winner since Dwight D. Eisenhower in 1952 to get a popular vote majority at the same time as a majority of seats in both houses of Congress. His biggest vote gains came in Democratic states and among Democratic-leaning voting groups. And he won in a year when turnout surged, defying expert predictions that high turnout would benefit Democrats. As a result, Bush declared "I earned capital in the campaign, political capital, and now I intend to spend it." Here he took a cautionary look back to Reagan, who won a 49-state landslide in 1984 but converted his win into few major policy innovations in his second term, or perhaps to his own father, who squandered astronomical approval ratings in the aftermath of the Gulf War.

Bush came into his second term with two overarching domestic policy goals: Social Security reform, grounded in the ownership society, and broad tax simplification. To initiate the latter, he appointed a tax reform commission, headed by former Democratic Senator John Breaux (LA) and former Republican Senator Connie Mack (FL). Breaux began his work in February saying "The ever increasing complexity of our tax laws imposes an unnecessary burden on Americans," encouraging cynicism and noncompliance and harming the United States' global competitiveness. "Over the next six months," Breaux promised, "we will have a real discussion about what kind of tax system we want in this country."[29] Breaux also believed that Bush should tackle taxes first to build momentum for the tougher task of Social Security.[30] Instead, the president opted to start with Social Security.

There is always an opportunity cost to establishing such priorities, and Bush's case was no exception. Bush might have chosen to tackle immigration first. He might have taken Breaux's advice and approached taxes before entitlements. He might even have laid low on domestic policy altogether, focusing instead on the spiraling difficulties in Iraq.[31] The second term of the Bush presidency might have looked very different had the president selected any of these options.

Instead, Bush threw the dice on Social Security, the legendary electric "third rail" of U.S. politics. He launched the effort to recast Social Security in his 2005 State of the Union address. Bush contended that "Social Security was created decades ago, for a very different era. . . . Our society has changed in ways the founders of Social Security could not have foreseen." He argued that by 2018 the program would be paying out more than it brings in, and "By the year 2042, the entire system would be exhausted and bankrupt." Bush proceeded to lay out several key principles, including no increase in the payroll tax, and offered to listen to "anyone who has a good idea to offer." Part of the solution, he proposed, was to allow workers to divert a portion of their payroll tax into voluntary personal retirement accounts that would be their property.[32] The State of the Union address kicked off an intense presidential campaign to drum up support for reform.[33] However, Bush's speaking tour was accompanied by falling, rather than rising, support for his approach.[34] Attempts to revive discussions with Democrats by agreeing to "progressive indexing" of benefits—a formula that would increase benefits faster for those at the bottom of the income scale—failed. When Bush and Republican congressional leaders threw up their hands eight months later, he had not even come close to getting a floor vote.

In retrospect, Bush's reform effort went aground on several rocks. Perhaps most important, it is clear that Bush severely miscalculated the extent and character of his political capital. He had, after all, won only 51 percent of the vote, the narrowest re-election of a sitting president since 1916, had drawn an electoral map almost identical to the one seen in 2000, and had won with a campaign that spent far more effort on national security than on the owner-ship society or any other domestic issue. Arguably, if Bush had a mandate for anything, it was to defend the nation as he had done since September 2001.

Second, in contrast with the Iraq War, where in 2005 a solid phalanx of Republicans faced off against divided Democrats, the Social Security battle-field was exactly the reverse. A few years before, Democrats like Bob Kerrey,

Daniel Patrick Moynihan, and Joseph Lieberman had considered supporting personal accounts. In 2005, however, Democrats made a strategic decision to give no ground, consciously mimicking the unified Republican drive against Clinton's health care proposal in 1994. Bush's efforts to reach out to Democrats were almost uniformly rebuffed, and early on Senate Minority Leader Harry Reid claimed he had enough votes to filibuster personal accounts. Bush stoked the partisan fires by running a public campaign to pressure moderate Democratic senators in Republican states.[35] While the Social Security push may have exacerbated polarization, it was almost certainly the case that it was hurt more by existing polarization than it contributed to new polarization.[36]

At the same time, Republicans themselves were divided. They were, of course, fearful of the political potential of allowing oneself to be painted as threatening Social Security. Beyond electoral calculation, any move to personal accounts would incur substantial "transition costs," perhaps as great as $2 trillion over 10 years. Many fiscal conservatives were wary of any plan that would incur such large short-term deficits and began pushing the administration for plans to pay for the transition costs. Bush himself ultimately allowed that the personal accounts would only save Social Security if coupled with limits on future benefits, an admission which gave opponents an even bigger target.

Finally, some suggested that Bush hurt his own cause by failing to put forward a concrete proposal to assure Social Security solvency. Rather, he pushed personal accounts and hoped that Congress would fill in the details through deliberation and compromise. As a result, opponents of the president's concept were free to define it in negative terms while his supporters were uncertain exactly what it was they were supporting.[37]

In one respect Bush's public campaign was successful; polls showed that he convinced Americans of the long-term gravity of the crisis facing Social Security. However, he was never able to convince Americans to embrace his solution, let alone to press Congress for it. The powerful American Association of Retired Persons (AARP), which had swung behind Bush's Medicare prescription drug plan, just as decisively allied with Democrats to stop Social Security reform.

When Hurricane Katrina battered New Orleans in August 2005, the disaster gave a handy excuse to Republican leaders to pull Social Security off the table. When Katrina finished off Social Security reform, she killed tax reform with it. Breaux and Mack issued a report on November 1 calling for elimination of the Alternative Minimum Tax, reduction of investment taxes and the marriage penalty, and change or elimination of a number of deductions, but Breaux's "national discussion" never materialized.[38] The bulk of Bush's big second-term domestic agenda had been washed out to sea.

In the short term, hurricane reconstruction took center stage. Not only did Katrina's aftermath undercut Bush's image as a decisive leader and put a halt to a major part of his domestic agenda, it also unraveled the difficult compromise necessary to make compassionate conservatism work politically. Pieces remained, but as a coherent package, the concept was finished. The inadequate response of the federal government to Katrina undermined much of the work Bush had done to reach out to black voters, especially the black churches that he had cultivated with the faith-based initiatives.[39] On the other side of the equation, Bush's extravagant promise to spend "whatever it takes" to rebuild New Orleans—up to or beyond $200 billion—might well have been the key moment that crystallized a full-fledged rebellion against Bush's promiscuous fiscal record by fiscal conservatives, who had already grown restive throughout 2005.

Largely hidden from public view, however, Bush also had considerable congressional success in 2005 on a hodgepodge of secondary issues. For example, he enjoyed early legislative victories making it more difficult to file bankruptcy and initiate class action lawsuits. Bush's transportation bill was approved by Congress, albeit with a price tag $30 billion higher than he had said was his upper limit a year before.[40] The administration's comprehensive energy bill was enacted, including heavy tax incentives and subsidies for energy production, consumer conservation, and alternative fuels, as well as tighter energy efficiency standards for appliances.[41] Not least, Bush worked with Congress in 2005 to quietly secure reauthorization of the landmark 1996 welfare reform legislation, strengthening work requirements and child support enforcement, increasing funding for child care, and launching a $150 million annual program to encourage healthy marriages and two-parent families.[42]

Not until the spring of 2006, though, did Bush regain his post-Katrina footing well enough to take up a third major domestic (or perhaps "intermestic") issue: immigration. What Bush liked to call "comprehensive immigration reform" had been on his compassionate conservatism agenda in the summer of 2001, before it was sidetracked by September 11. As the former governor of a border state, there is no question that Bush believed in immigration liberalization as a matter of principle, but it was also clearly part of his strategy of making Republicans more competitive among Hispanic voters. Nevertheless, Bush had more allies among Democrats than among Republicans. Indeed, signs had been building that Republican voters were particularly exercised about illegal immigration for both security and cultural reasons. While Republicans still controlled Congress and hence the timing and structure of the debate, Bush could have sought sequential bills that would have addressed border security first and some sort of guest worker program second. Instead, he insisted on a comprehensive bill that many Republicans could not swallow. By May 2006, at the height of the debate over immigration, Bush's average approval ratings had sunk below 30 percent for the first time in his presidency. He had already lost Democrats and liberal independents to the Iraq War; now many Republicans and conservative independents deserted him over immigration. The comprehensive immigration bill failed, and in the end Bush had nothing to sign but a border security bill establishing a 700-mile fence just weeks before the November 2006 mid-term elections. At that point, he may have wished that he had secured a stand-alone fence bill in March and then been able to move on to the aspects of immigration reform he found more congenial.

Playing Defense

When the votes were counted in November 2006, Democrats had gained 31 seats in the House and 6 in the Senate, enough to take control of both chambers. The war in Iraq played a major role in the results, as did congressional corruption, and perhaps, a sense that Republicans had lost their sense of purpose as a party. Whatever the cause, at that point, Bush's presidency as an exercise in domestic policy innovation was almost over.

One exception came in spring of 2007, when Bush hoped to take advantage of Democrats' liberal views on immigration to revive his comprehensive immigration measure. Again, there was intense congressional debate over the bill; again, Republicans proved Bush's staunchest adversaries; again, the president's average approval ratings fell below 30 percent; and again, the measure failed, this time to die for the remainder of Bush's presidency.

Another exception came in a new energy bill, fashioned more to the liking of congressional Democrats but also supported by Bush. The "Energy Independence and Security Act of 2007" (EISA) was devoid of new incentives for producers. Instead, it mandated a 500 percent increase in use of alternative fuels by 2022, an increase in automobile fuel efficiency standards, a phase out of incandescent light bulbs by 2014, higher appliance efficiency standards, and a carbon-neutral standard for federal buildings by 2030.[43] While EISA was clearly an attempt by the new Democratic Congress to put its own stamp on energy policy, it was of a piece with Bush's previous funding of hydrogen car research and portions of the 2005 energy bill. By the end of 2007, it could be said that Bush's energy approach had more in common with Jimmy Carter's than with Reagan's.

Outside of immigration and energy, Bush engaged in trench warfare with the new Democratic majority. For the first time in his presidency, he began vetoing bills for fiscal extravagance, and he was able to make the vetoes stick. The most notable of his dozen vetoes were two vetoes of a bill designed to expand access to the State Children's Health Plan (SCHIP). Democrats claimed to be helping the working poor, while Bush attacked the bill for giving federally funded health care to families with incomes up to 300 percent of the poverty line. Bush also began to heavily criticize the Democrats' use of appropriations "earmarks." Conservatives applauded and liberals deplored Bush's newfound fiscal discipline, but both asked why it had taken so long to appear. The president also remained caught up in long-running disputes with Democrats over wiretapping provisions in the Foreign Intelligence Surveillance Act (FISA)—Bush finally won—and a variety of separation of powers questions.

In his final State of the Union address, Bush put on a brave face and called for action on a variety of priorities, including making permanent the 2001 tax cut, expanding HSAs, increasing funding for scientific research, and providing educational grants to poor children.[44] Realistically, he knew, as did congressional Democrats, that little would come of his entreaties.

Confronting Crisis

Just when it looked that Bush would run the clock out, the nation was confronted with a deteriorating economy and ultimately a major financial crisis traceable to bad mortgages, rising foreclosures, and collapsing liquidity. In early 2008, Bush and Congress came to a quick compromise on an economic stimulus package that sent rebate checks of $600 to most taxpayers. As in 2001, Bush was not averse to Keynesian pump-priming. The president and his Secretary of the Treasury Henry Paulson increasingly struggled with the question of how to prevent the burgeoning home mortgage crisis from turning into a full-scale collapse of the financial system. After a series of ad hoc rescues of troubled financial firms, the administration proposed the creation of an unprecedented $700 billion fund to salvage financial firms and restore liquidity. Despite the resistance of most House Republicans and the evident unpopularity of the "Wall Street bailout" around the country, Congress ultimately voted to approve an $800 billion package. Both major party nominees were among the Senate supporters of the plan.

The Bush Domestic Agenda in the Scales

Bush set out to change the political landscape through a domestic policy agenda that would mollify the conservative base of the Republican Party while softening the edges of the party's image acquired in the rough-and-tumble 1990s. His domestic successes ebbed and flowed with his standing and leverage. In the end, however, big government conservatism, whether in its original form of compassionate conservatism or its outgrowth like the ownership society, clearly fell short of Bush's hopes.

Bush was not without significant domestic policy accomplishments, most notably the tax cuts, education reform, and a significant reformulation of Medicare. One might add an incremental but significant redirection of the nation's energy policy. (Of course, analysts will long debate whether these departures were good or bad for the country.) Nevertheless, the overall political/policy structure of compassionate conservatism and its successor, the ownership society, did not hold together. Key components like Social Security reform and immigration reform simply died on the vine; Hurricane Katrina unraveled much of Bush's outreach to black Americans; after a promising start in 2001, faith-based initiatives hit a wall in Congress and were relegated to a program subsisting on easily reversible executive orders; and financial crisis called into question the rush, embraced by Republicans and Democrats alike, to expand home ownership by lowering lending standards.

Bush's record on compassionate conservatism was ambiguous enough that commentators debated whether he had even acted on it. *Slate* editor Jacob Weisberg argued in the pages of the *New York Times* that Bush as the Compassionate Conservative "remains an appealing figure, but a largely fictional one" whose preoccupation with war and tendency toward polarization came to dominate his presidency.[45] For his part, former Bush speechwriter Michael Gerson countered that "by any fair historical measure, Bush's achievements on social justice at least equal those of Bill Clinton," although "Bush has received little attention or thanks for his compassionate reforms." In the end, Gerson conceded, compassionate conservatism was "a cause without a constituency"—except for Bush himself. Traditional conservatives disliked Bush's departures, while liberals gave Bush no credit for political reasons.[46]

Consequently, it is an open question whether even Bush's successes will prove enduring. In particular, analysts are divided about whether Medicare Part D and No Child Left Behind would remain essentially intact, though most analysts seemed to believe so.[47] The 2001 tax cuts, set to expire after 10 years, are highly vulnerable as well, though in 2008 Barack Obama vowed to repeal the tax cuts for only the highest-income taxpayers.

Table 3.1. Major Domestic Policy Initiatives during the George W. Bush Presidency

2001
Economic Growth and Tax Relief Reconciliation Act
No Child Left Behind Act
Embryonic stem cell research policy (executive order)
USA PATRIOT Act

2002
Job Creation and Worker Assistance Act
Sarbanes-Oxley Act
Department of Homeland Security

2003
Jobs and Growth Tax Relief Reconciliation Act
Medicare Part D/Health savings accounts
Partial-birth abortion ban

2005
Energy bill
Bankruptcy limits
Class action lawsuit limits
Welfare reform reauthorization
Transportation bill

2006
USA PATRIOT Act reauthorization
Border security bill

2007
Energy Independence and Security Act

2008
Economic stimulus plan
Rescue of financial institutions

Major domestic initiatives not enacted (as of December 2008)
Social Security reform
Tax reform (Breaux commission)
Comprehensive immigration reform
Faith-based initiative legislation (implemented by executive order)
ANWR oil exploration
Federal Marriage Amendment

Some critics such as John DiIulio, former head of the White House Office of Faith-Based and Community Initiatives, argued that Bush's domestic agenda consisted of too much politics and too little policy. In this view, rigorous policy analysis was sacrificed to the perceived political expediencies of coalition-building.[48] On the other hand, as his presidency drew to a close, the jury was still out on the actual effectiveness of many of Bush's departures. The national debt grew tremendously, but the nation enjoyed economic growth from late 2001 through the end of 2007, an outcome that could hardly have been taken for granted in the aftermath of September 11. It was unclear whether historians would end up blaming Bush for the financial meltdown in late 2008, crediting him for preventing a depression, or both. There were conflicting interpretations of how much No Child Left Behind was responsible for pulling up academic achievement for low-income students, but test scores of black and Hispanic students rose. After a rocky start, most seniors seemed satisfied with the prescription drug plan. Disaster preparedness fell down badly after Katrina, but homeland security measures did not fail against terrorism from September 11 through January 2009. As in foreign policy, much will depend on how things turn out after Bush leaves office.

Politically, it was notable that in the 2008 race for the presidency no Republican contender of appreciable strength openly attached himself to the label compassionate conservatism. Senator Sam Brownback of Kansas explicitly called himself a compassionate conservative (along with an economic, fiscal, and social conservative) and sought many of the same voters as Mike Huckabee, but he left the race by October 2007, unable to attract a sizeable following. Former Arkansas governor Huckabee adopted much of Bush's evangelical approach—downplaying limited government, supporting liberal immigration, and embracing social conservatism—without admitting so. Huckabee won the Iowa caucuses and a few southern states on February 5 but was arguably not a serious threat to win the nomination. In this respect, compassionate conservatives might be lumped together with Eisenhower's "Modern Republicans" and Clinton's "New Democrats" as bearers of similarly short-lived experiments in third-way triangulation. However, compassionate conservatism arose from real strategic dilemmas faced by Republicans, and some elements of it will undoubtedly survive. John McCain was nominated despite his embrace of Bush's immigration strategy in 2006–2007, and Huckabee's persistent strength demonstrated that a substantial (though much reduced) constituency still existed in 2008 for something resembling compassionate conservatism. It is possible to imagine the Republican Party embracing a hybrid that includes some components of Bush's strategy.[49]

Bush's domestic presidency leaves Republicans with a number of political challenges. Not least, compassionate conservatism entailed a change in the balance between social conservatism and limited government economic conservatism, tilting toward the former and away from the latter. This had both policy and political consequences. Bush embraced the partial birth abortion ban (enthusiastically) and the Federal Marriage Amendment (reluctantly), flew home to sign a bill supported by social conservatives trying to save the life of Terri Schiavo, and cast his first veto as president against a 2006 bill funding embryonic stem cell research. At the same time, Bush's domestic agenda seriously downplayed limited government and constitutionalism as general themes in either rhetoric or policy. For example, Republicans under Bush's leadership talked less and did less about federalism than they did even a few years before, and the shift was very likely intentional, part of Bush's drive to soften Republican ideology.[50] Overall, Bush's drive may have contributed significantly to the breakdown of the Republican coalition in 2006, 2008, and perhaps beyond. Bush's problem may have been, as some analysts have contended, that he was too socially conservative. Alternatively, his social conservatism may have stood out too singularly because it was not balanced by the party's traditional themes of fiscal or limited government conservatism.

A good argument can be made that political polarization grew during Bush's presidency, although the evidence on this score is not unmixed.[51] In any event, he undoubtedly failed in his promise to be "a uniter, not a divider."[52] However, the polarization of the Bush years is not primarily explainable by domestic policy. More plausible explanations start with the simple momentum of partisanship flowing from the Clinton years, and—as in the Clinton years—a visceral distaste by his opponents for the cultural stereotype represented by the president.[53] Others include the bitterness surrounding the 2000 election controversies; the very close partisan division of the country and Congress; Bush's aggressive approach to national security, including the Iraq War and homeland security measures, and the Democratic response, which tended to oscillate between timid acquiescence at the moment policy was made and harsh criticism after the fact; and sharp-elbowed campaigning by Republicans in the 2002 and 2004 elections coupled with the rise of the uncompromising and often vituperative left-wing blogosphere.[54] Presidential scholar George Edwards points to Bush's tactical tendency to "govern by campaigning," an extension of an approach utilized by most recent presidents, as a factor contributing to the polarization of the era (and to Bush's limited success on a number of issues).[55] Gary C. Jacobson likewise indicts Bush for being A Divider, Not a Uniter, but he assigns primary blame for that fact to the Iraq War, rather than to domestic issues.[56]

On some key issues, such as the 2003 tax cuts, Bush clearly relied on a partisan strategy, but on many he did not. Even when he did, as when pushing the prescription drug entitlement or the Department of Homeland Security, he sometimes paradoxically used a highly partisan strategy to impose policies that were in substance more naturally Democratic than Republican and that had been initially proposed by Democrats. Sometimes, as on Social

Security reform, his approach appeared partisan largely because Democrats made a strategic decision not to participate in meaningful negotiations. And sometimes, as with the partial birth abortion ban and opposition to same-sex marriage, Bush may have struck liberals as divisive, but he was also representing a position held by upwards of two-thirds of the American people; even the Schiavo bill garnered the support of nearly half of House Democrats and passed the Senate on a voice vote.

Substantively, claims that Bush simply betrayed the conservatism of Reagan founder on his tax cuts and social conservatism, but arguments that he was a right-wing ideologue are even harder to sustain. Bush was responsible for the most significant expansion of federal authority into state and local K–12 education since the Elementary and Secondary Education Act of 1965; the biggest new entitlement program since Medicare in 1965; two Keynesian stimulus packages; restoration of a big government approach to farm subsidies; a consistent preference for national energy "plans" rather than reliance on market forces; unsuccessful promotion of what would have been the greatest liberalization of immigration policy since the Immigration Act of 1965; and sponsorship of a massive taxpayer-funded bailout of the

Table 2. Partisanship and Key Elements of the Bush Domestic Agenda in Congress

High partisanship	Modest partisanship	Low partisanship
Homeland Security Dept. 2002	**Tax cut** 2001	**USA PATRIOT Act** 2001
Tax cut 2003	**Tax cut** 2002	**No Child Left Behind** 2001
Medicare Part D 2003	**Partial birth abortion ban** 2003	**Sarbanes-Oxley Act** 2002
Social Security reform (failed) 2005		**Tax reform** (failed) 2005
		Energy bill 2005
		Immigration reform (failed) 2006/2007
		Economic stimulus 2008
		Financial rescue 2008

financial sector. When Democrats urged sizeable new federal bureaucracies to guard homeland security or a big new regulatory scheme to prevent future Enron scandals, Bush almost uniformly gave in, as he did (despite his stated constitutional misgivings) when Congress passed a measure promising the most substantial tightening of campaign finance laws since 1974. And Bush's fiscal record was characterized by a 21.4 percent real increase in discretionary nondefense spending (including a 126.6 percent real increase in Department of Education funding) from 2001 to 2006, when spending finally leveled off due to pressure from congressional conservatives. Relative to the size of the economy, discretionary nondefense spending rose from 3.3 percent of gross domestic product in 2000 to 3.6 percent in 2007.[57] Although Bush notably restrained the Environmental Protection Agency from some regulatory initiatives, his overall regulatory record was similar. In his first seven years in office, pages in the *Federal Register* averaged more than 75,000, compared with 72,000 under Clinton and 55,000 under Reagan.[58] Given this balance sheet, Bush appears closer to Nixon than to Reagan.[59]

Bush entered the presidency expecting to be a domestic president. When the world intruded, domestic policy took a back seat to foreign policy and national security. In the end, while not devoid of significant victories, compassionate conservatism failed to fundamentally transform the nation's domestic policy or its politics as Bush had hoped. Instead, Bush appears fated to have served as merely a transitional president. A transition to what will be the next big question of U.S. domestic policy.

Notes

1. Walter Williams, *Reaganism and the Death of Representative Democracy* (Washington, D.C.: Georgetown University Press, 2003), 229. Long-time conservative activist Grover Norquist also saw Bush as "more conservative than Reagan," though he meant the appraisal as a compliment. For an early assessment of Bush as "Reagan's Son," see Bill Keller, "Reagan's Son," *New York Times Magazine* January 26, 2003, 26–31, 42–44, 62.

2. Bruce Bartlett, *Imposter: How George W. Bush Bankrupted America and Betrayed the Reagan Legacy* (New York: Doubleday, 2006).

3. Fred Barnes, *Rebel in Chief: Inside the Bold and Controversial Presidency of George W. Bush* (New York: Crown Forum, 2006).

4. For a later comparison of Bush's strategy with the strategy Dick Morris designed for Bill Clinton, see Richard Lowry, "Slow and Steady, But Will It Win W the Race?," *National Review* July 3, 2000.

5. Marvin N. Olasky, *Compassionate Conservatism: What It Is, What It Does, and How It Can Transform America* (New York: Simon & Schuster, 2000); Marvin N.

Olasky, *The Tragedy of American Compassion* (New York: Free Press, 1996). In a similar vein, see also Myron Magnet, *The Dream and the Nightmare: The Sixties' Legacy to the Underclass* (New York: W. Morrow, 1993); Myron Magnet, "What Is Compassionate Conservatism?," *Wall Street Journal* February 5, 1999, available at www.manhattan-institute.org/html/_wsj-what_is_compassionate_con.htm, accessed May 13, 2008.

6. For an extended discussion of this influence, see Barnes, *Rebel-in-Chief*, 141–47; Paul Kengor, *God and George W. Bush* (New York: Harper Perennial, 2005).

7. "President's Remarks on Labor Day," September 1, 2004, available at www.whitehouse.gov.

8. For a discussion of the role of education in Bush's new political package, see Patrick J. McGuinn, *No Child Left Behind and the Transformation of Federal Education Policy, 1965–2005* (Lawrence: University Press of Kansas, 2006), 151–58.

9. "Governor George W. Bush—Acceptance Speech," Philadelphia, Pennsylvania, August 3, 2000, available at www.4president.org/speeches/bushcheney2000convention.htm, accessed October 13, 2003.

10. For other reviews of the Bush presidency, see Michael Nelson, "George W. Bush and Congress: The Electoral Connection," in *Considering the Bush Presidency*, edited by Gary L. Gregg II and Mark J. Rozell (New York: Oxford Press, 2004), 141–59; Charles O. Jones, "Bush's Paradoxical Governing Style," in *Second-Term Blues: How George W. Bush Has Governed*, edited by John C. Fortier and Norman J. Ornstein (Washington, D.C.: Brookings Institution and American Enterprise Institute, 2007), 121–22.

11. "Remarks Prior to a Meeting with Bipartisan Congressional Leaders and an Exchange with Reporters, January 24, 2001," *Public Papers of the President: Administration of George W. Bush*, 15, available at http://frwebgate.access.gpo.gov/cgi-bin/getpage.cgi?position=all&dbname=2001_public_papers_vol1_misc, accessed May 9, 2008.

12. "Inaugural Address of George W. Bush, January 20, 2001, available at www.yale.edu/lawweb/avalon/presiden/inaug/gbush1.htm, accessed January 6, 2004.

13. For an example of such analysis, see "Final Version of Bush Tax Plan Keeps High-End Tax Cuts, Adds to Long-Term Cost," *Citizens for Tax Justice* May 26, 2001, available at www.ctj.org/html/gwbfinal.htm, accessed May 9, 2008.

14. The Bush tax cut was estimated to be 0.8 percent, the Reagan tax cut 1.4 percent, and the Kennedy tax cut 1.9 percent of national income. See William Ahern, "Comparing the Kennedy, Reagan, and Bush Tax Cuts," *Tax Foundation* August 24, 2004, available at www.taxfoundation.org/news/printer/323.html, accessed May 14, 2008.

15. "Remarks by the President in Tax Cut Bill Signing Ceremony," June 7, 2001, available at www.whitehouse.gov/news/releases/2001/06/20010607.html, accessed May 9, 2008

16. The legislation provided for $5 billion in cash grants and $10 billion in federally guaranteed loans. "Congress approves $15 billion airline bailout," http://archives.cnn.com/2001/US/09/21/rec.congress.airline.deal/. Accessed June 10, 2009.

17. See McGuinn, *No Child Left Behind*, 176.

18. See McGuinn, *No Child Left Behind*, 157–58. In 1996, Bill Clinton enjoyed a 33 percentage point edge over Bob Dole on the education issue; in 2004, George W. Bush and John Kerry were tied. By 2008, however, Democrats had reopened an advantage on education.

19. It should be pointed out that some observers, including disaffected former Bush advisor Matthew Dowd, hold that the Republican takeover of the Senate actually harmed Bush in the long run by allowing him to move away from a more bipartisan model of governing. Comments by Matthew Dowd at Annual Forum on the State of the Presidency, Institute for Governmental Affairs, University of California–Berkeley, April 2, 2008.

20. Preliminary analyses of the 2001 and 2003 tax cuts, however, called these predictions into question. The percentage of total income tax paid by the top 1 percent of earners has continued rising. See Michael D. Stroup, "Tax Code Became More Progressive after the Bush Tax Cuts," *Brief Analysis*, National Center for Policy Analysis, No. 606 (January 21, 2008); Ahern, "Comparing the Kennedy, Reagan, and Bush Tax Cuts."

21. See Barbara Sinclair, "Living (and Dying?) by the Sword: George W. Bush as Legislative Leader," in *The George W. Bush Legacy*, edited by Colin Campbell, Bert A. Rockman, and Andrew Rudalevige (Washington, D.C.: CQ Press, 2008), 177–79.

22. *Nebraska v. Carhart*, 530 U.S. 914 (2000).

23. Six major national polls from January through November 2003 showed an average margin of 60 percent to 31 percent. The polls were Gallup/CNN/USA *Today* (January 2003), *Los Angeles Times* (January 2003), ABC News (July 2003), Gallup/CNN/USA *Today* (October 2003), NBC News/*Wall Street Journal* (November 2003), and *Los Angeles Times* (November 2003). Data provided by Roper Center for Public Opinion Research, University of Connecticut.

24. The final vote saw 218 Republicans and 63 Democrats vote yes in the House, and 47 Republicans and 17 Democrats in the Senate.

25. George W. Bush, "State of the Union Address, January 20, 2004," available at www.presidency.ucsb.

26. Barnes, *Rebel-in-Chief*, 125–31.

27. "In Acceptance Speech, President Bush Shares His Plan for a Safer World and More Hopeful America," Republican National Convention, September 2, 2004, available at www.4president.org/speeches/georgewbush2004convention.htm, accessed May 9, 2008.

28. See James W. Ceaser and Andrew E. Busch, *Red Over Blue: The 2004 Elections and American Politics* (Lanham, MD: Rowman & Littlefield, 2005), 135–40.

29. "Opening Statement by Senator John Breaux," President's Advisory Panel on Tax Reform, February 16, 2005, available at www.treas.gov/press/releases/reports/breauxopeningstatement.pdf.

30. Dan Balz, "Bush's Second Term Agenda Hits Reality," in *Second-Term Blues: How George W. Bush Has Governed*, edited by John C. Fortier and Norman

J. Ornstein (Washington, D.C.: Brookings Institute and American Enterprise Institute, 2007), 31–32.

31. For a critique of Bush's decision to focus on Social Security instead of Iraq in 2005, see Balz, "Bush's Second Term Agenda Hits Reality," 26–27. Whether the Iraq troop surge executed in 2005 instead of 2007 might have saved Bush's second term is an intriguing question, but unknowable.

32. "State of the Union Address 2005," available at www.whitehouse.gov/news/releases/2005/02/20050202-11.html.

33. Christopher H. Foreman, Jr., "The Braking of the President: Shifting Context and the Bush Domestic Agenda," *The George W. Bush Legacy*, edited by Colin Campbell, Bert A. Rockman, and Andrew Rudalevige (Washington, D.C.: CQ Press, 2008), 273; Sinclair, "Living (and Dying?) by the Sword," 182.

34. See Balz, "Bush's Second Term Agenda Hits Reality," 33–34.

35. See Balz, "Bush's Second Term Agenda Hits Reality," 32–33.

36. For example, Bush's proposals did significantly better in polls when his name was not attached than when his name was attached.

37. See, for example, Gary C. Jacobson, *A Divider, Not a Uniter: George W. Bush and the American People* (New York: Longman, 2007). Jacobson argues that reform failed partly because "the administration could not control the terms of debate. Critics . . . harped on Bush's refusal, for several months, to propose any concrete changes in the system that actually addressed the 'bankruptcy' threat," 210.

38. For a summary of the commission's recommendations, see "Proposal: Kill AMT, some breaks and fat," CNNMoney.com, November 1, 2005, available at http://money.cnn.com/2005/11/01/pf/taxes/tax_proposals/index.htm, accessed May 13, 2008.

39. It was at least somewhat ironic that this was the case, insofar as the first responsibility for response to Katrina was held by Ray Nagin, the black Democratic Mayor of New Orleans, and Kathleen Blanco, the Democratic governor of Louisiana.

40. Foreman, "The Braking of the President," 271.

41. "Fact Sheet: The Energy Bill: Good for Consumers, the Economy, and the Environment," The White House, July 29, 2005, available at www.whitehouse.gov/news/releases/2005/07/print/20050729-9.html, accessed May 12, 2008.

42. "The Next Phase of Welfare Reform: Implementing the Deficit Reduction Act of 2005," United States Department of Health and Human Services, available at www.hhs.gov/news/press/2002pres/welfare.html.

43. "Energy Security for the 21st Century," The White House, available at www.whitehouse.gov/infocus/energy/, accessed May 12, 2008.

44. "President Bush Delivers State of the Union Message," The White House, January 28, 2008, available at www.whitehouse.gov/news/releases/2008/01/print/20080128-13.html, accessed May 13, 2008.

45. Jacob Weisberg, "The Bush Who Got Away," *New York Times* January 28, 2008, available at www.nytimes.com/2008/01/28/opinion/28weisberg.html, accessed May 13, 2008.

46. Michael Gerson, "Compassionate to the End," *Washington Post* January 30, 2008, A15.

47. For a view emphasizing the vulnerability of the Bush departures, see Sinclair, "Living (and Dying?) by the Sword," 184–85; for a view emphasizing their durability, see Foreman, "Braking the President," 281; McGuinn, *No Child Left Behind*, 188–90; Kenneth Wong and Gail Sunderman, "Education Accountability as a Presidential Priority: No Child Left Behind and the Bush Presidency," *Publius: The Journal of Federalism* 37 (3) (Summer 2007): 346–48.

48. Ron Suskind, "Why Are These Men Laughing?," *Esquire* January 2003, 96–105.

49. Andrew E. Busch, "The Republicans' Strategy for the Future," in *The Future of America's Political Parties*, edited by Andrew E. Busch (Lanham, MD: Lexington Books, 2007), 49–61.

50. See Andrew E. Busch, *The Constitution on the Campaign Trail: The Surprising Political Career of America's Founding Document* (Lanham, MD: Rowman & Littlefield, 2007); U.S. Federalism and the Bush Administration, Special Issue of *Publius: The Journal of Federalism*, 37 (3) (Summer 2007). In 2003, a dust-up occurred when Republican National Committee chair Ed Gillespie was reported by the Manchester Union-Leader to have indicated that "the days of Reaganesque railing against the expansion of federal government are over." Gillespie disavowed the comments, but in retrospect they seem to have accurately reflected the administration's approach. Ramesh Ponnoru, "The Reaganite RNC," September 4, 2003, available at www .nationalreview.com/ponnoru/ponnoru090403.asp.

51. For example, in the election of 2004, Bush improved his standing compared with 2000 more among women than among men, more among Jews and Catholics than among Protestants, more among the urban than the suburban, more among Hispanics than among whites, more among non-gun owners than among gun owners, and more among liberals than among conservatives. See also Morris P. Fiorina, Samuel J. Abrams, and Jeremy C. Pope, *Culture War? The Myth of a Polarized America* (New York: Sourcebooks, 2005).

52. See Gary C. Jacobson, *A Divider, Not a Uniter* (New York: Longman, 2006).

53. In Bush's case, opponents saw a cocky, Bible-thumping Texan, where Clinton's opponents saw a draft-dodging, pot-smoking hippie from the 1960s.

54. See Jones, "Bush's Paradoxical Governing Style." Jacobson, *A Divider, Not a Uniter*, argued that "Anyone elected president in 2000 would have faced a Congress and a public predisposed to respond in sharply partisan terms with even the gentlest provocation" (21).

55. George C. Edwards III, *Governing by Campaigning: The Politics of the Bush Presidency* (New York: Longman, 2007).

56. Jacobson, *A Divider, Not a Uniter*, 240. Jacobson identifies a number of secondary factors driving political polarization besides Iraq, including the election of 2000, religious polarization, some domestic issues, and like Edwards, the administration's strategy of "going public."

57. By way of comparison, this category of spending fell under both Reagan (from 5.2% in 1980 to 3.5% in 1987) and Clinton (from 3.7% in 1992 to 3.2% in 1999). Table 8.4, available at www.whitehouse.gov/omb/budget/fy2009/pdf/hist.pdf.

58. Available at http://angrybear.blogspot.com/2008/08/president-bush-and-federal-registery.html; Available at http://www.llsdc.org/sourcebook/docs/fed-reg-pages.pdf.

59. This point is also made by Bruce Bartlett, *Imposter*, 141–56.

~

CHAPTER FOUR

How George W. Bush Remade American Foreign Policy

Ryan J. Barilleaux and David Zellers

Like most U.S. presidents since World War II, George W. Bush came to the office with little background in foreign policy. In the first several months of his term, international affairs played a modest role in administration concerns. All of this changed in September 2001, when a new era for the United States and for this president began. Bush became a war-time commander in chief and there was a palpable shift in his priorities toward security, defense, and foreign policy. In the wake of Bush's presidency and the election of 2008, one of the major issues confronting President Barack Obama is the future direction of U.S. foreign policy. Obama has found that Bush remade the foreign policy agenda in ways that will be difficult to alter and that he committed the nation to policies and missions that will continue into the foreseeable future.

The Prehistory of Bush's Foreign Policy

The U.S. presidential election of 2000 will be remembered mostly for its dramatic and drawn-out conclusion. The nation sat by for weeks as both candidates planned for the transition without knowing if such planning was for naught, while a controversial legal battle ensued. The eight years of Bill Clinton's administration was marked by limited presidential interest in foreign affairs and a handful of military operations including Somalia, Haiti, and Serbia.[1] There were also several acts of international and domestic terrorism against the United States. Despite these developments, the public's focus in the final years of the Clinton administration was dominated by a number of high-profile White House scandals that ultimately led to the drama of an impeachment trial.

As a result, much of the candidates' attention in the 2000 campaign was focused on domestic policy issues. Both Al Gore and Bush were viewed by the electorate as not differing much on the great issues of the day and as being political centrists.[2] The Bush strategy for much of the campaign was to focus on a few key issues: welfare reform, military overhaul, Social Security, Medicare, and tax cuts.[3] The foreign policy goals established in the campaign were primarily those expressed in the 2000 Republican Party platform. On the subject of military overhaul, the platform called for an expansion of active duty personnel, modernization of techniques and equipment, and a need for a military force that could react and reach anywhere in the world through high levels of readiness.[4] The platform and the campaign were critical of the Clinton administration's use of the military: "At the same time, the current administration has casually sent American armed forces on dozens of missions without clear goals, realizable objectives, favorable rules of engagement, or defined exit strategies."[5] The criticism leveled at the Clinton administration did not stop with only questions of military deployments. Further criticism was also leveled at diplomatic efforts, specifically the courting of China and Latin America policy.[6]

As one example of the relatively small engagement of foreign policy in the 2000 campaign, Bush's acceptance speech at the Republican convention devoted one paragraph to foreign policy:

> The world needs America's strength and leadership, and America's armed forces need better equipment, better training, and better pay. We will give our military the means to keep the peace, and we will give it one thing more . . . a commander-in-chief who respects our men and women in uniform, and a commander-in-chief who earns their respect. A generation shaped by Vietnam must remember the lessons of Vietnam. When America uses force in the world, the cause must be just, the goal must be clear, and the victory must be overwhelming. I will work to reduce nuclear weapons and nuclear tension in the world—to turn these years of influence into decades of peace. And, at the earliest possible date, my administration will deploy missile defenses to guard against attack and blackmail. Now is the time, not to defend outdated treaties, but to defend the American people.[7]

The final weeks of the 2000 campaign were focused on a back-and-forth barrage of attacks leveling charges of inexperience and ignorance against Governor Bush and charges of aloofness and complicity in corruption and vice against Vice President Gore. Foreign policy was all but lost in this struggle as the competition became increasingly bitter and carried on past Election Day and into the courts.[8]

Once the election was resolved, the quasi-transition period ended and President-elect Bush began putting together his foreign policy team.[9] The key foreign policy players put in place during transition were Secretary of State Colin Powell, Secretary of Defense Donald Rumsfeld, and National Security Advisor Condoleezza Rice. Perhaps no member of the group had a more distinguished record of national service than Powell. Powell's record of service made him a national hero—service in Vietnam as a young Army commander, National Security Advisor under Ronald Reagan, and Chairman of the Joint Chiefs of Staff who waged the successful Persian Gulf War for President George H. W. Bush.[10] Upon introducing the press to Powell on December 16, 2000, in Crawford, Texas, Bush spoke of Powell being the "finest of the United States" and compared him to former Secretary of State George Marshall for his common sense, directness, and his integrity.[11] Powell went on to make remarks identifying several important issues that he saw as being the coming challenges for the administration. Among these were the consequences of the global information revolution, the continuing fallout of the Cold War, and evolving relationships with Russia and China.[12] Powell concluded his remarks by stating his support for a national missile defense system and making it clear that it would be a topic of discussion with allies and other nations as well.[13]

The next day, Bush introduced Rice as his National Security Advisor. Like Powell, Rice was a veteran of the White House, having previously served in the Reagan administration.[14] Rice had worked with the Bush campaign well before the primaries and became the architect of the national security and foreign policy rhetoric of the campaign. As an example of this role, Rice penned an essay in Foreign Affairs early in 2000 that sought to redefine the role of the United States in the new century. The key themes outlined in the article included the need to reshape the U.S. military, creating relationships with allies that allowed the United States to carry fewer burdens, reforming the United States' relationship with Moscow and Beijing, and addressing the proliferation of weapons of mass destruction and rogue regimes.[15] The article also made it clear that U.S. foreign policy would stem from national interests and not from the "illusory international community";[16] this type of strong statement of national interest would become the cornerstone of the challenges the United States would come to face.

The last member of the national security triumvirate was introduced near the end of December 2000. Rumsfeld was well known within Washington, having already served in Congress, several administrative and White House posts in the Richard Nixon and Gerald Ford administrations, and a number of national security posts (including Secretary of Defense) before entering the private sector.[17] Rumsfeld's prior experience with the Department of Defense made him a logical choice for Bush, who had received considerable criticism for his lack of experience in foreign and security matters.[18] In his introductory remarks the president-elect stated that Rumsfeld's priorities would be to work with the Congress to build a military force for the 21st century and to challenge the status quo at the Pentagon.[19] Bush also noted that he selected Rumsfeld because of his experience with missile defense.[20]

Once Bush assumed office, foreign policy activity was of the sort that has become common for a new president. There were the standard meetings with the president of Mexico and the prime minister of Canada (although Bush's first foreign trip was to Mexico rather than Canada) and other world leaders.[21] The incident that received the greatest attention in the early months of the Bush administration involved the collision of a U.S. Navy surveillance aircraft with a Chinese fighter patrol on April 1, 2001. The president soon demanded the safe return of both the crew and the aircraft and called for the Chinese government to make a quick and diplomatic response to the incident.[22] He reiterated this demand on April 3. The incident concluded peacefully on April 12 with the return of the crew, but meetings and investigations between the two governments continued for some time thereafter.

Ultimately, in the short time span prior to September 11, 2001, the administration was not able to move very far forward with any agenda, whether foreign or domestic. The extended election deadlock and the indecisive transition process it produced contributed to a slow start for the administration. International terrorism was an issue that had been discussed during the 2000 presidential campaign, but it had not possessed the urgency it would acquire in the fall of 2001. Osama bin Laden, the Taliban, and other rogue foreign elements were well known in the U.S. intelligence community, but they tended to be overshadowed by other foreign policy concerns. This would be dramatically changed by events in the late summer and early fall of 2001.[23]

The Transformation of Bush and His Foreign Policy

It has become a cliché of U.S. politics to say that everything changed on September 11, 2001.[24] Indeed, Secretary of State Rice made exactly this point in a valedictory essay for Foreign Affairs in 2008, in which she provided a defense of Bush's foreign policy as he approached the end of his presidency:

And then came the attacks of September 11, 2001. As in the aftermath of the attack on Pearl Harbor in 1941, the United States was swept into a fundamentally different world. We were called to lead with a new urgency and with a new perspective on what constituted threats and what might emerge as opportunities. And as with previous strategic shocks, one can cite elements of both continuity and change in our foreign policy since the attacks of September 11.[25]

The words of Secretary Rice provide a summary of what happened to President Bush's foreign policy following the "strategic shock" of September 11: a "new urgency," "new perspective," and "continuity and change."

The impact of September 11 can be overstated, but it did have a real effect on the president and his policies.[26] As Michael Hirsch put it, "George W. Bush experienced this terrible new reality as directly and emotionally as any American. The difference was that he could do something about it . . . in Bush, the man seemed to meet the moment."[27] When he addressed Congress and the nation on September 20, 2001, his new policy was unequivocal: "Every nation, in every region, now has a decision to make. Either you are with us, or you are with the terrorists. From this day forward, any nation that continues to harbor or support terrorism will be regarded by the United States as a hostile regime."[28] Henceforth, a "war on terror" would define U.S. foreign policy under Bush.

The president gave fuller voice to his new approach to foreign policy in his State of the Union Address in January 2002, as he articulated what came to be called the "Bush Doctrine." As Ivo Daalder and James Lindsay have put it, the Bush Doctrine identified the "combination of terror, tyrants, and technologies of mass destruction" as the core threats to the United States and the most pressing priorities of American foreign policy.[29]

He asserted that the nation is threatened by terrorist organizations and rogue states that possess or covet weapons of mass destruction. As he told legislators, "A terrorist underworld—including groups like Hamas, Hezbollah, Islamic Jihad, Jaish-i-Mohammed—operates in remote jungles and deserts, and hides in the centers of large cities."[30] Moreover, the hostile regimes of Iran, Iraq, and North Korea—all anti-American in their orientation and possessing or seeking weapons of mass destruction—are special threats: "States like these, and their terrorist allies, constitute an axis of evil. . . . By seeking weapons of mass destruction, these regimes pose a grave and growing danger."[31]

Bush's response to these threats—the Bush Doctrine—was marked by a war on terrorism, preemptive and even preventive war to promote U.S.

security, and regime change to promote democracy in hostile countries. A man of action, the president made clear what he understood to be his own responsibility to meet these threats: "I will not wait on events, while dangers gather. I will not stand by, as peril draws closer and closer. The United States of America will not permit the world's most dangerous regimes to threaten us with the world's most destructive weapons."[32]

The war against "terror, tyrants, and technologies of mass destruction" is the central organizing idea of what Daalder and Lindsay came to call the "Bush revolution" in foreign policy.[33] This revolution was primarily a change in the means for promoting the nation's foreign policy goals, and a new perspective on how to order their ends. The Bush Doctrine and the Bush revolution in foreign policy are two sides of the same coin; the Bush Doctrine is the set of principles that underlie the revolution that occurred in Bush's conduct of U.S. policy.

The Bush Doctrine/Bush revolution led to a new emphasis on unilateral exercises of U.S. power, rather than on international organizations and international law. In December 2001, the president informed Congress that he intended to withdraw the United States from the Anti-Ballistic Missile (ABM) Treaty because it limited the nation's flexibility to develop a missile defense system. Likewise, despite support from a "coalition of the willing" in the Iraq War, the invasion and occupation of Iraq has been primarily a U.S. effort. This unilateralism has been the source of complaints from the United State's North Atlantic Treaty Organization (NATO) allies and others.

Another tenet of the Bush Doctrine/Bush revolution was the necessity of preemptive and preventive war as instruments for protecting U.S. security. This was particularly relevant with regard to Iraq, where the president waged war to remove the threat embodied in the regime of Saddam Hussein. In the *National Security Strategy of the United States* (released in the fall of 2002), the Bush administration made its position clear:

> The United States has long maintained the option of preemptive actions to counter a sufficient threat to our national security. The greater the threat, the greater is the risk of inaction—and the more compelling the case for taking anticipatory action to defend ourselves, even if uncertainty remains as to the time and place of the enemy's attack. To forestall or prevent such hostile acts by our adversaries, the United States will, if necessary, act preemptively.[34]

The Bush Doctrine also supported regime change rather than negotiations to deal with foreign governments who are threats to U.S. and international security. A U.S.-led invasion of Afghanistan in the fall of 2001 removed the Taliban government that had harbored bin Laden and

Al Qaeda, and the president pressed Congress and the United Nations on the need to remove the Hussein regime in Iraq. He sought, and in October 20002 received, congressional approval for the use of force to employ force to affect regime change in Iraq.[35] In March 2003, U.S. forces led an invasion that toppled Hussein's government and began a long-term occupation of the country as the United States tried to shepherd the creation of a democratic regime.

Concomitant with regime change, the Bush administration adopted a "freedom agenda" to promote the spread of democratic government around the world.[36] This agenda meant at least three things for U.S. foreign policy. First, the United States would abandon its previous practice—common during the Cold War—of supporting nondemocratic regimes in exchange for military cooperation and access to resources. Such support was blamed for fueling anti-U.S. terrorism in the Middle East and elsewhere. Henceforth, the United States would more aggressively promote democracy and democratic reform movements around the world.[37]

Next, the freedom agenda, combined with the war on terror, tyrants, and technologies of mass destruction, meant that the United States would use force to remove authoritarian governments it saw as threatening U.S. security. Building on the assumptions of "democratic peace" theory (the idea, first proposed by Immanuel Kant, that democracies rarely go to war against each other), the Bush administration made the case that more democracy around the world was not only a good idea, but also in the nation's security interests. In March 2006, for example, President Bush told reporters that "history has proven that democracies don't war with each other. Again, I kind of glossed over this, but particularly for the students here, look at what happened in Europe over a hundred-year period, from the early 1900s to today."[38] This idea helped undergird the case for using force to remove Hussein.

The freedom agenda meant more than toppling authoritarian governments. It also meant spending money on projects to promote democracy through support for local reform efforts and nongovernmental organizations in the Middle East and North Africa, support for democracy and human rights activists trying to reform nondemocratic political systems, and awarding democracy fellowships to political dissidents from around the world to study and speak in the United States.[39]

While the Clinton administration had previously endorsed the concept of democratic "enlargement" (i.e., enlarging the number of democracies in the world) as a theme in its foreign policy, it did not aggressively pursue that idea. Bush made the "freedom agenda" more central to his revolution in the conduct foreign policy.[40]

The transformation of Bush and his foreign policy was undeniable. In his first Inaugural Address (2001), Bush devoted less than 100 words to foreign policy and world affairs.[41] Then came the events of September 11, and Bush changed the direction and focus of his presidency. In his Second Inaugural (2005), Bush devoted about two-thirds of his text to world affairs, the role of the United States in the world, and the demand of world leadership.[42] He had become a foreign policy president and he had staked his presidency on his conduct of U.S. foreign policy.

The Bush Foreign Policy Record

To the casual observer, the defining piece of the Bush foreign policy record is the war on terror and its central front in Iraq and Afghanistan. However, this conflict alone must be taken as part of a larger context. Circumstances forced the administration to react to terrorism and rogue states in a much more proactive and unilateral approach than one may have expected based upon campaign rhetoric. The challenge in understanding the administration's foreign policy record is deciding if the Bush Doctrine extends beyond those actions it directly relates to. U.S. efforts to strengthen ties to NATO and other allies would suggest that the Bush doctrine is the driving force behind such overtures as a means of sharing the burden of global conflict. However, actions in nonsecurity and military matters are an important part of the Bush record and should not be ignored when considering to what extent the Bush Doctrine is influencing the total sphere of foreign policy.

Relations with global powers such as Russia and China saw a dramatic reshaping during the Bush administration. The Chinese have taken considerable steps in the last decade to begin to assert a presence beyond the Pacific. Russia has been transformed by Vladimir Putin's leadership and has seen better economic times as oil and natural gas prices have risen. Neither of these countries can be handled by military means alone. In particular, China presents a special challenge because of its complexity. It is a country of both great wealth and tremendous poverty; it has a large military but one with limited technology; and it has experienced both impressive economic liberalization and the continuation of authoritarian rule. Multilateral pressure on China to reform its political and human rights situation has seen marginal success; therefore, it is unlikely that the United States will have much success if it exerts unilateral economic, diplomatic, or military pressure on China.[43]

The economic position of the United States in the world has changed drastically. The global financial crisis that began in 2008 is likely to last for

several years, and it presents enormous challenges for the president that will
be at the center of U.S. foreign policy and also act as a constraint on U.S.
power.[44] Like the Bush administration before it, the Obama administration
has grappled with this crisis and is still trying to develop policies that will
shore up the U.S. economy and not hobble the United States in world affairs. But the challenges are grave, and the United States and other Western
industrial democracies have been seriously threatened by the economic
downturn.[45] As former U.S. Treasury official Robert Altman has observed,
the global crisis has diminished U.S. and Western influence in the world:

> There could hardly be more constraining conditions for the United States
> and Europe. First, the severe recession will prompt governments there to focus
> inward as their citizens demand that national resources be concentrated on
> domestic recovery. The priorities of Obama, as expressed in his campaign,
> fit this mold. . . . European leaders will also be focusing on the home front.
> They, too, will be implementing stimulus programs and trying to manage the
> financial damage. . . . Second, unprecedented fiscal deficits and difficulties in
> the financial systems will also preclude the West from embarking on major in-
> ternational initiatives. If Obama inherits a $1 trillion deficit, and temporarily
> enlarges it to $1.3 trillion with a stimulus program, there will not be much of a
> constituency calling for increased U.S. spending on endeavors abroad. Indeed,
> the country may be entering a period of forced restraint not seen since the
> 1930s. Should a crisis like the 1994 collapse of the Mexican economy present
> itself again, it is doubtful that the United States would intervene. And even in
> the event of economic crises in strategically important areas, such as Pakistan,
> major economic assistance from the United States or key European nations is
> unlikely. Instead, the IMF will have to be the primary intervenor.[46]

The prospect is for an international financial environment unlike that in
which U.S. presidents have been accustomed to operate. While financial
distress has made it possible for President Obama to win passage of an unprecedented stimulus package, it has not widened the president's freedom of
action in the world.

The Bush Doctrine informed U.S. foreign policy for most of a decade, but
it cannot control it completely. While the Bush Doctrine presented a cogent
and coordinated plan for aggressively pursuing terrorists and rogue states, it
lacked the comprehensive feel of the Truman Doctrine.[47] The foreign policy
of the United States has also evolved considerably since the days of the Truman Doctrine; the world is no longer a bipolar place, trade treaties are far
more complex, and humanitarian and environmental issues are no longer
framed in a communist versus noncommunist context. The next administration will be challenged to address not just the legacy of the Bush Doctrine

but also find its own way to put a stamp on those areas of foreign policy not directly affected by the enormous changes that have taken place.

The Bush Legacy for U.S. Foreign Policy

To what extent has the Bush revolution in foreign policy left a permanent impression on U.S. politics? There is considerable controversy over this question, just as there has been over Bush's policies. The central disagreements surround the war in Iraq, whether Bush has institutionalized his freedom agenda and whether the Bush Doctrine is the new paradigm for U.S. foreign policy.

The War in Iraq

The war in Iraq has elicited criticism from different elements of the U.S. political spectrum—many conservatives see it as a costly digression from the real challenges to national security,[48] while those on the left see it as an imperialistic war driven by hubris and greed[49]—but there is also broad agreement among most serious observers that the war cannot be ended precipitously. No matter what promises some candidates might make, the United States will remain in Iraq for several years.

As early as February 2008, Jim Hoagland of the *Washington Post* observed that the leading Democratic presidential candidates had "issued promises to withdraw from Iraq that are impossibly vague, unrealistic or worse."[50] As Hoagland explained himself, he argued that the United States cannot begin rapidly withdrawing from Iraq without endangering remaining U.S. troops: "It strains credulity to think that the Iraqis would—after being told that they are not worth protecting or working with—allow U.S. troops to stay on and hunt Al Qaeda and company or protect the huge U.S. Embassy in Baghdad."[51] Not long after Obama's victory in the 2008 election, his transition team began telling reporters that withdrawal from Iraq would be quite complicated.

Soon after taking office, President Obama ordered the Defense Department to prepare a plan for withdrawing most U.S. forces from Iraq in 16 months. Within a month, the administration had made that time frame—one of Obama's campaign promises—only one of three possible options. The other two were a 19-month withdrawal and even a 23-month withdrawal.[52] Whatever the time frame, the pullout would not be a complete one; some U.S. troops would remain beyond this pullout—perhaps indefinitely.[53] The upshot is that President Obama will be tied to an U.S. presence in Iraq for several years. This reality restricts his freedom of action and is a legacy of the overthrow of Hussein.

Institutionalizing the Freedom Agenda

While Bush's freedom agenda did not always lead him to abandon non-democratic regimes (e.g., Saudi Arabia), the Bush administration did make a number of strides to institutionalize its pro-democracy approach in what one observer called the "democracy bureaucracy."[54] Over the course of two terms, the administration spent over $6 billion on democracy projects and by 2007 had doubled its budget for these projects since 2001. The administration created a Middle East Partnership Initiative in the Department of State, expanded the democracy fellowship program at the National Endowment for Democracy (over 100 since 2001, compared to about 5 per year in the previous decade), and created the post of special envoy to North Korea on human rights. Moreover, in 2002 President Bush signed a law mandating an annual federal government progress report on the freedom agenda.[55] It is unlikely that the democracy bureaucracy will be dismantled soon.

Indeed, President Obama is not likely to abandon the freedom agenda.[56] As scholar Amy Zegart pointed out about candidate Obama during the 2008 campaign, there is considerable similarity between the positions Obama articulated and those of Bush regarding making the spread of democracy a goal of U.S. foreign policy:

> Obama also advocates democratization, the spreading of American values and American moral leadership. . . . His is a kinder, gentler freedom agenda, but a freedom agenda nonetheless. . . . The task of American foreign policy, he argued, was to change how those desperate faces saw America. "We can hold true to our values, and in doing so advance those values abroad," Obama declared. "And we can be what that child looking up at a helicopter needs us to be: the relentless opponent of terror and tyranny, and the light of hope to the world." It was vintage Bush, suffused with the same ambitions for American moral leadership and the same belief that freedom builds the surest road to peace.[57]

Obama's critics on the left have feared that his views on democracy promotion put him uncomfortably close to Bush and will lead to an institutionalization of the freedom agenda. As one of these critics put it,

> One thing is clear: The Bush administration's institutionalization of the "freedom agenda" as a core pillar of U.S. foreign policy, combined with Obama's

apparent commitment to democracy promotion and the new counterinsurgency paradigm suggests that, despite appearances that may emerge to the contrary, we are likely to see more continuity than change in U.S. foreign policy.[58]

Perhaps this will be the most enduring aspects of the Bush foreign policy legacy.

Is the Bush Doctrine the New Paradigm for U.S. Foreign Policy?

Many observers have concluded that the prolonged and costly occupation of Iraq has dealt a death blow to the Bush Doctrine because it is unlikely that the United States will engage in any attempt at regime change abroad for a long time. But there was more to the Bush Doctrine than just regime change; it also included greater unilateralism in foreign policy, the war on terrorism, the freedom agenda, and preventive war. Will any or all of these elements disappear?

The answer is that the Iraq War has discredited the notion of preventive war and regime change by force, but it has not undercut support for the war on terror. While President Obama was a firm critic of the Iraq War during the 2008 presidential campaign, nevertheless he expressed support for a military war on terror:

> When I am President, we will wage the war that has to be won, with a comprehensive strategy with five elements: getting out of Iraq and on to the right battlefield in Afghanistan and Pakistan; developing the capabilities and partnerships we need to take out the terrorists and the world's most deadly weapons; engaging the world to dry up support for terror and extremism; restoring our values; and securing a more resilient homeland. . . . The first step must be getting off the wrong battlefield in Iraq, and taking the fight to the terrorists in Afghanistan and Pakistan.[59]

In his Inaugural Address, Obama continued in this vein, again employing language that embraced the idea of a war on terror: "We will not apologize for our way of life, nor will we waver in its defense, and for those who seek to advance their aims by inducing terror and slaughtering innocents, we say to you now that our spirit is stronger and cannot be broken; you cannot outlast us, and we will defeat you."[60]

Conclusion

The historian Robert Divine once observed that a curious pattern marks the U.S. presidency in the period since World War II: we elect presidents whose background and experience is in domestic politics and policy, but they occupy an office that has large responsibilities for national security and which demands that they spend much (if not most) of their time on foreign affairs.[61] There have been significant differences in how these presidents have responded to the challenges imposed by the responsibilities of the office: some, like Truman or Reagan, came to shape U.S. foreign policy in significant ways; others, like Johnson, were overwhelmed by foreign affairs. Bush is another chief executive in this mold: his political education and experience was largely in the realm of Texas politics, yet he was called to be a war president and world leader at one of the most difficult times in modern U.S. history.

Bush redefined himself as a foreign policy president and in the process reshaped U.S. foreign policy. Some of his revolution in foreign policy will last long after him, including the war on terror, the U.S. presence in Iraq, and aspects of the freedom agenda. The option of unilateralism will remain available to subsequent presidents, as it was to prior ones, although few are likely to take as unilateralist an approach to world affairs as he did. But other aspects of the Bush revolution will not last his departure from office: the use of U.S. military power to affect regime change in other countries (without direct provocation, such as the Taliban's harboring and support for Al Qaeda), nation-building by U.S. troops, a unilateralist style of diplomacy that seemed to alienate allies unnecessarily, and (whatever the reality) an air of paying too little attention to concerns about excesses in pursuit of information about terrorists.

For better or worse, Bush committed the United States to a new course of action for dealing with the challenges of world politics in the 21st century. His freedom agenda and the war on terrorism will likely be his long-term legacy for U.S. foreign policy.

Notes

1. For a review and analysis of U.S. foreign policy under Bill Clinton, see United States Congress, Senate, Committee on Foreign Relations, *A Review of U.S. Foreign Policy at the End of the Clinton Administration: Hearing and Public Meeting Before the Committee on Foreign Relations, United States Senate, One Hundred Sixth Congress, 2nd Session, September 26, 2000* (Washington, D.C.: Government Printing Office, 2001), as well as Donald A. Nuechterlein, *America Recommitted: A Superpower Assesses Its Role in a Turbulent World* (Lexington: University Press of Kentucky, 2001).

2. See Ivo Daalder and James Lindsay, *America Unbound: The Bush Revolution in Foreign Policy* (Washington, D.C.: Brookings Institution, 2003), especially chapter 3;

and Richard A. Melanson, *American Foreign Policy since the Vietnam War*, 4th edition (Armonk, NY: M. E. Sharpe, 2005), 291–98.

3. See Andrew Busch and James Ceaser, *The Perfect Tie: The True Story of the 2000 Presidential Election* (Lanham, MD: Rowman & Littlefield, 2001).

4. www.presidency.ucsb.edu/ws/index.php?pid=25849, accessed July 15, 2008.

5. www.presidency.ucsb.edu/ws/index.php?pid=25849, accessed July 15, 2008.

6. www.presidency.ucsb.edu/ws/index.php?pid=25849, accessed July 15, 2008.

7. http://www.presidency.ucsb.edu/ws/index.php?pid=25954, accessed July 15, 2008.

8. See Busch and Ceaser, *The Perfect Tie*.

9. See Daalder and Lindsay, *America Unbound*, ch. 4.

10. Bob Woodward, *Bush at War* (New York: Simon & Schuster, 2002), 11–12.

11. www.presidency.ucsb.edu/showtransition2001.php?fileid=bush_news12-16, accessed July 15, 2008.

12. www.presidency.ucsb.edu/showtransition2001.php?fileid=bush_news12-16, accessed July 15, 2008.

13. www.presidency.ucsb.edu/showtransition2001.php?fileid=bush_news12-16, accessed July 15, 2008.

14. For more on Rice, see Jim Mann, *The Rise of the Vulcans* (New York: Viking, 2004).

15. Mann, *Rise of the Vulcans*, 46–47.

16. Mann, *Rise of the Vulcans*, 62.

17. Woodward, *Bush at War*, 20–22.

18. For a sympathetic portrait, see Midge Decter, *Rumsfeld: A Portrait* (New York: Regan Books, 2003); for a critical view, see Alexander Cockburn, *Rumsfeld: His Rise, Fall, and Catastrophic Legacy* (New York: Scribner, 2007).

19. www.presidency.ucsb.edu/showtransition2001.php?fileid=bush_rumsfeld_1228, accessed July 15, 2008.

20. www.presidency.ucsb.edu/showtransition2001.php?fileid=bush_rumsfeld_1228, accessed July 15, 2008.

21. See Daalder and Lindsay, *America Unbound*, ch. 5; Melanson, *American Foreign Policy since the Vietnam War*, 292–99; and Robert Swansbrough, *Test by Fire: The War Presidency of George W. Bush* (New York: Palgrave Macmillan, 2008), ch. 5.

22. www.presidency.ucsb.edu/ws/index.php?pid=45667&st=China&st1=, accessed July 15, 2008; and www.presidency.ucsb.edu/showtransition2001.php?fileid=bush_rumsfeld_1228, accessed July 15, 2008.

23. See Daalder and Lindsay, *America Unbound*, ch. 5; Swansbrough, *Test by Fire*, ch. 5; and, James M. McCormick, "The Foreign Policy of the George W. Bush Administration," in *High Risk and Big Ambition: The Presidency of George W. Bush*, edited by Steven E. Schier (Pittsburgh, PA: University of Pittsburgh Press, 2004), 189–223, especially 193–97.

24. For an examination of this issue, see Robert Jervis, *American Foreign Policy in a New Era* (New York: Routledge, 2005), ch. 2.

25. Condoleezza Rice, "Rethinking the National Interest," *Foreign Affairs* (July/ August 2008), available at www.realclearpolitics.com, accessed June 10, 2008.

26. See Jervis, *American Foreign Policy in a New Era*, ch. 2, and Melanson, *American Foreign Policy since the Vietnam War*, 299–308.

27. Michael Hirsch, "Bush and the World," *Foreign Affairs* 81 (September/ October 2002): 18.

28. George W. Bush, "Address before a Joint Session of the Congress on the United States Response to the Terrorist Attacks of September 11, September 20th, 2001," available at www.presidency.ucsb.edu/ws/index.php?pid=64731&st=&st1=, accessed June 11, 2008.

29. Ivo H. Daalder and James M. Lindsay, "Bush's Revolution," *Current History*, November 2003, 367. See also Daalder and Lindsay, *America Unbound*.

30. George W. Bush, "Address before a Joint Session of the Congress on the State of the Union, January 29th, 2002," available at www.presidency.ucsb.edu/ws/index. php?pid=29644, accessed June 11, 2008.

31. Bush, "Address before a Joint Session of the Congress on the State of the Union, January 29th, 2002."

32. Bush, "Address before a Joint Session of the Congress on the State of the Union, January 29th, 2002."

33. Bush, "Address before a Joint Session of the Congress on the State of the Union, January 29th, 2002."

34. *National Security Strategy of the United States*, available at www.whitehouse.gov/ nsc/nss.html, accessed June 11, 2008. See also John Lewis Gaddis, "A Grand Strategy of Transformation," *Foreign Policy* 133 (November/December 2007): 50–57.

35. "Authorization for Use of Military Force against Iraq Resolution of 2002 (PL 107-243)," October 16, 2002, available at www.c-span.org/resources/pdf/hjres114 .pdf, accessed June 11, 2008.

36. See James Traub, *The Freedom Agenda* (New York: Farrar, Straus and Giroux, 2008), 3–10.

37. For an examination of the rationale underlying Bush foreign policy, see Robert G. Kaufman, *In Defense of the Bush Doctrine* (Lexington: University Press of Kentucky, 2007), especially ch. 7.

38. "President Discusses War on Terror and Operation Iraqi Freedom," March 20, 2006, available at www.whitehouse.gov/news/releases/2006/03/20060320-7.html, accessed June 12, 2008.

39. Paulette Chu Miniter, "Why George Bush's 'Freedom Agenda' Is Here to Stay," available at www.foreignpolicy.com/story/cms.php?story_id=3959, accessed September 27, 2007.

40. See Daalder and Lindsay, *America Unbound*, ch. 7.

41. George W. Bush, "Inaugural Address, January 20, 2001," available at www .presidency.ucsb.edu/ws/index.php?pid=25853, accessed June 11, 2008.

42. George W. Bush, "Inaugural Address, January 20, 2005," available at www .presidency.ucsb.edu/ws/index.php?pid=58745, accessed June 11, 2008.

43. For a discussion of the challenges presented by Russia and China, see Daniel Deudney and G. John Ikenberry, "The Myth of the Autocratic Revival," *Foreign Affairs* 88 (January/February 2009), 77–93; Steven Sestanovich, "What Has Moscow Done?" *Foreign Affairs* 87 (November/December 2008), 12–28; and, Yoichi Funabashi, "Keeping Up with Asia," *Foreign Affairs* 87 (September/October 2008), 110–25.

44. For coverage of the global financial crisis, see "Global Recession," a special report on the BBC website, available at http://news.bbc.co.uk/2/hi/in_depth/business/2007/creditcrunch/default.stm, accessed February 18, 2009; and, "The World Financial Crisis," a special report on the *New York Times* website, available at www.nytimes.com/library/financial/index-global-fin-crisis.html, accessed February 18, 2009. For a discussion and analysis of its origins, see "Inside the Meltdown," on the website of the PBS program *Frontline*, available at www.pbs.org/wgbh/pages/frontline/meltdown/, accessed February 18, 2009.

45. See Roger C. Altman, "The Great Crash, 2008: A Geopolitical Setback for the West," *Foreign Affairs* 88 (January/February 2009), 2–14.

46. Altman, "The Great Crash, 2008."

47. For a comparison between the Bush Doctrine and the Truman Doctrine, see Mel Gurtov, *Superpower on Crusade: The Bush Doctrine in U.S. Foreign Policy* (Boulder, CO: Lynne Reiner, 2006), 3; and Robert Jervis, "Understanding the Bush Doctrine," *Political Science Quarterly* 118 (Summer 2003): 365–88.

48. Martin Durham, "The American Right and the Iraq War," *Political Quarterly* 75 (3) (2004): 257–65.

49. See, for example, Gurtov, *Superpower on Crusade*, 3, and John B. Judis, *The Folly of Empire* (New York: Scribner, 2004).

50. Jim Hoagland, "Promises They Can't Keep," *Washington Post* February 10, 2008.

51. Hoagland, "Promises They Can't Keep."

52. "White House Weighing 23-Month Iraq Withdrawal Plan," *FoxNews.com*, February 6, 2009, available at www.foxnews.com/politics/first100days/2009/02/06/white-house-weighs-month-iraq-withdrawal-plan-sources-say/, accessed February 18, 2009.

53. "White House Weighing 23-Month Iraq Withdrawal Plan."

54. See Miniter, "Why George Bush's 'Freedom Agenda' Is Here to Stay."

55. Miniter, "Why George Bush's 'Freedom Agenda' Is Here to Stay."

56. For a liberal case for the freedom agenda, see Traub, *The Freedom Agenda*, 3–10.

57. Amy Zegart, "The Legend of a Democracy Promoter," *National Interest Online*, September 16, 2008, available at www.nationalinterest.org/Article.aspx?id=19688, accessed February 18, 2009.

58. Anthony Fenton, "Bush, Obama, and the 'Freedom Agenda,'" *Foreign Policy in Focus*, January 27, 2009, available at www.fpif.org/fpiftxt/5818, accessed February 18, 2009.

59. "Security Address on Counter-Terrorism by the Honorable Barack Obama, United States Senator from Illinois," August 1, 2007, available at www.wilsoncenter .org/index.cfm?event_id=269510&fuseaction=events.event_summary, accessed June 12, 2008.

60. Barack Obama, "Inaugural Address," January 20, 2009, John T. Woolley and Gerhard Peters, *The American Presidency Project* [online]. Santa Barbara: University of California (hosted), Gerhard Peters (database). Available at www .presidency.ucsb.edu/ws/?pid=44, accessed February 18, 2009.

61. See Robert A. Divine, *Eisenhower and the Cold War* (New York: Oxford University Press, 1981), 3.

CHAPTER FIVE

~

The Deficit Redux:
Budget Politics during the
Bush Administration

Iwan Morgan

Budget politics took a new turn in George W. Bush's presidency, but not the one anticipated at its outset. In 2001, it was widely assumed that the United States had entered a new fiscal era. The large budget deficits of the 1980s and first half of the 1990s had given way to budget surpluses in Bill Clinton's second term. As Bush's presidency began, the Congressional Budget Office (CBO) calculated that the federal government would run up aggregate surpluses of $4.6 trillion in the next 10 years and pay off the reducible public debt in 2006.[1] What occurred instead was a new cycle of deficits that metamorphosed into historically unprecedented peace-time imbalances as a result of the economic crisis that blighted Bush's final months in office. However, the budget politics of his presidency were quite different to those of the late 20th century. The deficit had dominated the policy agenda from its explosion during Ronald Reagan's presidency until its elimination in Clinton's. In the words of Senator Daniel Patrick Moynihan (D-NY), it was "the first fact of national government."[2] During Bush's presidency, by contrast, the deficit never acquired the same political significance, and control of it was secondary to his other fiscal goals.

This chapter seeks to explain, first, why the Bush administration did not prioritize deficit reduction. It then analyses the politics of Bush's fiscal agenda that featured huge tax cuts and significant increases in defense and domestic expenditure. It also assesses the effect of divided party control of

This is an abridgement of a chapter in Iwan Morgan, *The Age of Deficits: Presidents and Unbalanced Budgets from Jimmy Carter to George W. Bush*, University Press of Kansas, 2009.

government on budget politics in 2007–2008. Finally, it evaluates the fiscal legacy of the Bush presidency.

Downgrading the Deficit

Unveiling his fiscal year (FY) 2005 budget plan when the FY 2004 deficit was heading toward a record current-dollar level, Bush declared that it met his "three highest priorities." These were to ensure that the United States prevailed in the Global War on Terror, to strengthen homeland security after the September 11 terrorist attacks on New York and Washington D.C., and to restore the economy after the downturn of 2001.[3] The president subordinated deficit control to these ends. When it first became evident that the budget was sinking back into the red, he often reminded audiences of a statement he supposedly made in the election campaign that deficits were acceptable in the event of recession, national emergency, or war. "Little did I realize," he would add, "we'd get the trifecta."[4]

Bush's contention that unbalanced budgets were the product of recession and war did not explain their persistence throughout his presidency. In reality, the principal cause of the chronic deficits was the cost of his 2001 and 2003 tax cuts. Though Bush claimed their enactment would boost the economy, traditional Republican hostility to high taxes was their main rationale. The complex phase-in rules of the 2001 tax cut benefits over 10 years and the distributional skew of both measures in favor of the wealthy limited their compensatory utility. In contrast, their effect on the deficit was long lasting. The congressional Joint Committee on Taxation put the total cost of tax cuts enacted since 2001 at $251 billion (including interest on higher government borrowing necessitated by revenue loss) in FY 2006, when the deficit itself amounted to $248 billion. In other words, had the tax cuts not been enacted, the FY 2006 budget would have been in balance, even with the costs of the Iraq and Afghanistan wars and the emergency response to the Hurricane Katrina disaster.[5]

Unlike Reagan, Bush gave no thought to reversing any of his tax cuts to control the deficit. Instead he expected them to generate economic recovery that would in time yield a harvest of revenues to close the fiscal gap. The surge in tax receipts that brought the deficit down from $412 billion (3.6 percent gross domestic product [GDP]) in FY 2004 to $162 billion (1.2 percent GDP) in FY 2007 seemingly vindicated such confidence. In July 2006, Bush declared: "Some in Washington say we had to choose between cutting taxes and cutting the deficit. . . . [These budget] numbers show that that was a false choice. The economic growth fueled by tax relief has helped to send our tax revenues soaring."[6]

In fact, economic growth was not unusually strong in 2005–2007 in comparison with equivalent stages of previous business cycles. Moreover, interest rate reductions were far more significant than tax cuts in bringing about economic improvement. According to conservative economist Bruce Bartlett, "Much revenue was sacrificed to achieve not very much in terms of improving the tax code or stimulating economic growth."[7] Buoyed by the surge in receipts, however, Bush stepped up his campaign to extend the 2001 and 2003 tax cuts beyond their scheduled expiry as necessary for sustained economic growth and fiscal recovery. His rhetoric on this score was reminiscent of Reagan's advocacy of the "Laffer curve" rationale for tax reduction in 1981 and just as spurious. According to Treasury Department data, extending the tax cuts would at best only increase annual economic output by 0.7 percent over 10 years. Meanwhile, the CBO calculated that the total cost of doing so would add $143 billion to the aggregate deficit through FY 2010 and $1.5 trillion in FY 2011–FY 2015.[8]

The benign nature of monetary policy for most of Bush's presidency facilitated his determination not to sacrifice any part of his tax program. The Federal Reserve had habitually tightened credit as a safeguard against the inflationary consequences of large fiscal deficits.[9] Reagan (in 1982), George H. W. Bush (in 1990), and Bill Clinton (in 1993) had each raised taxes for deficit-control purposes in the hope of bringing about interest rate reductions. However, the federal funds rate, which determines short-term lending rates in the U.S. banking system, remained remarkably low for most of Bush's presidency because deflation, not inflation, was the primary economic concern.

In contrast to his recent predecessors, Bush did not tailor his fiscal policies to meet the anti-deficit preferences of Federal Reserve chair Alan Greenspan, who grew openly critical of the administration's lack of fiscal restraint. Greenspan supported tax reduction in 2001 out of concern that the projected surplus would otherwise fuel new government spending once the public debt was paid off. Nevertheless, he advocated the introduction of "trigger" provisions in the enabling legislation to rescind or reduce the tax cuts automatically if the anticipated surplus did not materialize, an idea the Bush White House would not countenance.[10] In addition to criticizing domestic spending initiatives promoted by the administration and congressional Republicans, Greenspan opposed new tax cuts in 2003. Testifying before the Senate Banking Committee on February 11, he warned that "faster economic growth alone is not likely to be the full solution to the currently projected long-term deficits."[11]

Despite his disdain for administration fiscal policy, Greenspan did not tighten the monetary screws because there was no sign of general economic overheating. Instead, the Federal Reserve aggressively lowered interest rates from 6.5 percent in late 2000 to a historic low of 1 percent in mid-2003 to counter the uncertainty generated by stock market decline, recession, and the September 11 attacks. Cheap credit fueled a boom in residential real estate and home improvement that drove the recovery of the entire economy. The monetary authorities eventually changed course in mid-2004 for fear that house price inflation would feed into the rest of the economy. They raised the federal fund rate over the next two years to a peak of 5.25 percent, where it stayed for a year, but then reversed course in September 2007 to counter the decline in house prices and the credit crunch precipitated by the collapse of the sub-prime mortgage market. By the end of April 2008, the Federal Reserve had cut short-term interest rates to 2 percent, which was low by the standards of the late 20th century, if not by those of recent years.[12]

As federal finances sank deep into the red, the suspicion grew that the White House did not care. "As a drunk is to alcohol," declared Princeton economist and *New York Times* columnist Paul Krugman, "the Bush administration is to budget deficits."[13] Private and public comments by administration officials fueled this concern. When Treasury Secretary Paul O'Neill warned Vice President Richard Cheney of imminent fiscal crisis in late 2002, the latter responded, "Reagan proved deficits don't matter." Around the same time, Council of Economic Advisers chair Glenn Hubbard and Office of Management and Budget (OMB) director Mitch Daniels disputed that there was any connection between big deficits and high interest rates. "That's Rubinomics," Hubbard declared in reference to Clinton administration Treasury Secretary Robert Rubin, "and we think it's completely wrong."[14]

Seeking to provide reassurance that he would not tolerate growing deficits indefinitely, Bush declared in his FY 2004 budget message, "My administration firmly believes in controlling the deficit and reducing it as the economy strengthens and our national security needs are met."[15] In the same statement, however, he proposed a new round of tax cuts that would send the deficit still higher. A year later the president declared that he wanted to reduce the deficit by half in his second term. Nevertheless, he intended to measure success against the projected FY 2004 deficit of $521 billion (instead of the eventual level of $413 billion).[16] It was also evident that he would rely mainly on economic growth rather than fiscal actions to achieve this goal. If judged on the basis of his administration's policies rather than his rhetoric, Bush was the least deficit-conscious president since the Budget and Accounting Act of 1921 had endowed the office with responsibility for budget planning.

The Politics of Tax Reduction

The clearest issue difference in any policy domain between the Republican and Democratic candidates in the 2000 presidential election centered on what to do with the projected budget surplus. Bush advocated an across-the-board $1.6 trillion tax cut to sustain economic growth and boost investment. In contrast, Al Gore promised a $400 billion tax cut targeted at middle-income families but wanted the remaining surplus set aside in a "lockbox" to guarantee future Social Security and Medicare funding when the baby-boom generation reached retirement.

Honoring his pledge to cut taxes was for Bush a demonstration of the legitimacy of his presidency after the controversial circumstances of his election. As he told reporters at the end of his first hundred days in office, "You spend [political] capital on what you campaigned on . . . and you earn capital by doing that."[17] Promotion of tax reduction also sent out a powerful signal to his party that he would not compromise on its core belief in low taxes as his father had done in 1990.[18] Furthermore, it signified his determination to pursue a bold agenda in spite of the narrow Republican majorities in both houses of Congress and was an essential step to the achievement of other legislative goals. As Mitch Daniels asserted when the tax bill approached enactment, "It's not going to be a presidency of miniature gestures."[19]

Despite presidential determination to press ahead, the political climate was less favorable to tax reduction than when Reagan made it his legislative priority 20 years previously. In the 2000 campaign, Bush had presented his tax cut as a populist measure to give taxpayers their due. "See, I don't think the surplus is the government's money," he declared in the third presidential debate, "I think it's the people's money." Even aside from its questionable nature, however, his victory hardly constituted a mandate for tax reduction. A scholarly analysis of 2000 election survey data found a low level of issue voting on the tax cut/lockbox tradeoff because only a small segment of the public grasped the complex policy choice involved.[20]

Opinion polls taken early in 2001 similarly offered the new president no reassurance that his fiscal agenda had strong support among the public. These generally found that between 50 and 60 percent of respondents voiced approval when asked if they favored "the Bush tax cuts." On the other hand, the polls revealed that when given a choice between tax cuts and higher spending on specified domestic programs, respondents generally opted for the latter by two-to-one or better. Those that asked respondents about the kind of tax cuts they preferred also recorded overwhelming support for ones that provided greater benefits to middle-income families than the rich.[21]

In this context, congressional Democrats were not under the kind of pressure to yield on tax reduction that they had faced after Reagan's election. Consequently, they were broadly united in condemning the Bush tax proposal on grounds of its affordability, economic soundness, and equity.[22] Some Southern "Blue Dog" conservatives in the House of Representatives dissented from this party line like their "Boll Weevil" predecessors of 1981, but most of this group were more concerned to bring down the public debt. Meanwhile, moderate Republicans, particularly in the Senate, shared some of the opposition's concerns about the administration proposal. With the parties evenly divided in the upper chamber, where the GOP was dependent on the vice president's casting vote for its majority, the Democrats appeared to have a good chance of defeating Bush in the Senate. To circumvent this danger, the White House adopted a legislative strategy that combined boldness, compromise, and stealth.

Bush put the $1.6 trillion tax cut at the top of his agenda by sending its component measures early to Congress before he had even submitted a revised budget for FY 2002. This ensured that his proposal dominated the tax agenda. Abandoning Gore's idea of targeted tax cuts, congressional Democrats quickly countered with their own proposal for a $750 billion across-the-board reduction. The House of Representatives, where the Republican majority was unified in support of tax reduction, quickly enacted most of Bush's program. Republican Party leaders adopted a partisan strategy to give the president most of what he wanted. They did not modify its terms to win over Blue Dog Democrats, only 10 of whom consequently voted for it.[23]

To facilitate Senate enactment, the administration had resisted conservative House Republican demands for bigger tax relief and persuaded the business community not to press for inclusion of corporate tax cuts. As further insurance, Republican Senate leaders secured a budget resolution that included provision for tax cuts. Under congressional budget rules, this safeguarded any tax bill that emerged from the committee against floor amendment and filibuster but limited its duration to the period covered by the resolution. While the Balanced Budget Act of 1997 set a 5-year minimum for budget resolutions, it allowed the House and Senate Budget Committees to recommend a longer duration. In collaboration with the White House, Republican congressional leaders exploited surplus projections to set a 10-year target in the FY 2002 budget resolution. In his FY 2003 budget plan, the president announced that the administration would henceforth confine its budget planning to 5 years because the experience of 2001 demonstrated 10-year year fiscal forecasting to be "unreliable and ultimately futile." By then, of course, he had achieved a tax cut on a scale that would not have been possible without spreading the costs over 10 years.[24]

The administration also widened the scope of its original tax cut proposals through addition of a $100 billion tax rebate for FY 2001 to counter signs of economic decline. This preempted the danger of moderate Republican senators joining with the Democrats to enact the rebate as a substitute for the Bush program. Finally, the White House accepted a compromise proposal for a smaller tax cut of $1.25 billion for FY 2002–FY 2012 brokered within the Senate Finance Committee by chairman Charles Grassley (R-IA) and ranking minority member Max Baucus (D-MT). The committee bill gained the support of 12 moderate and conservative Democrats when it came to a floor vote. Bush then put pressure on Republican House members of the conference committee to accept the Senate version of the measure.[25]

The Economic Growth and Tax Relief Reconciliation Act (EGTRRA) of 2001 was the largest tax relief measure since the Economic Recovery Tax Act of 1981. It reduced marginal rates on individual income taxes, notably from 15 percent to 10 percent on the first $6,000 of income ($12,000 for families) and from 39.6 percent to 35 percent on income in excess of $297,350 (Bush compromised on his initial proposal to cut the latter to 33 percent). In addition to the rebate, its other provisions included child tax credits, estate and gift tax reductions, and important changes in tax law relating to married couples, retirement savings, and education expenses.

Other than its size, the most significant characteristic of EGTRRA was its distributional skew. The question of who benefited most from tax reduction was a bone of contention between the administration and the Democrats. As finally enacted, EGTRRA spread its benefits more widely than the original Bush proposal. According to CBO estimates, the new 10-percent bracket rate accounted for one-third of its revenue costs.[26] Nevertheless, this estimate implicitly inflated the progressive nature of the Bush tax cut, which significantly widened the disparity of income in the United States.

Under the terms of EGTRRA, individual taxpayers in descending order of income quintiles would respectively gain $46,243, $10,453, $6,516, $4,037, and $827 in after-tax income over the course of calendar 2001–2010. Even this set of statistics understates the bias toward the wealthy because of the disregard of those not paying income tax. Just over a quarter of returns in 2001 showed no income tax owed. Measuring EGTRRA's benefits across the whole of U.S. society, the Citizens for Tax Justice, a liberal think tank, calculated that 40 percent flowed to the richest 1 percent, virtually the same as went to the bottom 80 percent on the income ladder.[27]

The White House and the Republican congressional leadership crafted the tax cuts in a way that masked their distributional skew. The complex phase-in rules meant that relief for top-band taxpayers was disproportionately weighted in the latter half of EGTRRA's duration. This made little economic sense because it reduced the stimulus effects of tax reduction as the economy recovered from recession. In political terms, however, the phase-ins made EGTRRA appear more progressive than it actually was and blurred the long-term costs. The sunset rules were also expected to shape the political environment to the Republican's ultimate advantage because of the probable impetus to extend the tax cuts prior to expiry. Finally, EGTRRA's credit and deduction provisions made it likely that the proportion of taxpayers obliged to pay the Alternative Minimum Tax (AMT), initially designed to penalize use of tax shelters by the wealthy but not indexed to inflation, would mushroom from 2 percent in 2002 to about a third by 2010. This made it almost certain that further tax relief would be required to fix the AMT problem at an estimated 10-year cost of $800 billion in FY 2005–FY 2014.[28]

The slow pace of recovery from the recession prompted the Bush administration to propose a further tax cut in 2003 at a 5-year cost of $726 billion as estimated by the CBO. This reserved its new benefits almost exclusively for wealthier Americans and only accelerated tax cuts already scheduled to take place for the less affluent.[29] As in 2001, the House of Representatives quickly approved a bill in line with what the president asked. However, with the budget now deep in the red and war against Iraq imminent, moderate Republicans in the Senate would only support a measure with a $350 billion price tag. Bush eventually accepted this for fear of losing the tax cut in its entirety. In addition to accelerating some of the 2001 tax cuts, the Job Growth and Tax Relief Reconciliation Act (JGTRRA) of 2003 reduced the maximum tax rates on capital gains and dividends to 15 percent (from 20 and 38.6 percent, respectively). Supporters applauded this as an overdue correction of the excessive taxing of dividends dating from the New Deal. Critics dubbed it a charter for the rich because 46 percent of the capital gains and dividend tax cuts would flow to the 0.2 percent of households with annual incomes over $1 million and nearly three-quarters would go to the 3.1 percent of households making more than $200,000 a year.[30]

With JGTRRA's enactment, House Majority Leader Tom DeLay (R-TX) warned, "This ain't the end of it—we're coming back for more."[31] A further round of tax cuts duly followed in 2004. The $146 billion Working Families Tax Relief Act (WFTRA) renewed EGTRRA benefits scheduled for expiry at the end of 2004. It extended the $1,000 child tax credit, the $6,000 income level for the 10-percent tax rate, and the tax break for married couples to 2009. Additional provisions included postponement of new application of the AMT for one year. WFTRA won approval by 339 votes to 65 in the House and 92 votes to 3 in the Senate on September 23.

Framing the terms of debate, Representative Jim McCrery (R-LA) warned, "Anyone voting 'no' is voting for a tax increase for the American people, especially the middle class." With elections in the offing, most Democrats deemed it expedient to support renewal of the EGTRRA provisions that provided most benefit to nonaffluent taxpayers.[32] Lauding its bounty to middle-income families, Bush went to Des Moines to sign the bill on October 7. Despite its populist title, the wealthy still did best from the measure. According to one estimate, households in the top income quintile would receive 70 percent of WFTRA tax cuts, while those in the middle income quintile got just 9 percent.[33] Shortly afterward and with considerably less fanfare, the president signed another measure providing corporate tax breaks to manufacturers, energy producers, and agricultural producers at a cost of $136 billion.[34]

Analysts are divided regarding the political strategy that drove Bush's first-term tax-cutting extravaganza. According to Jacob Hacker and Paul Pierson, it was designed to please the Republicans' base—"the partisans, activists, and moneyed interests that are their first line of support"—in a highly competitive political environment rather than to broaden the foundations of party support among middle-income Americans in the manner of Reagan.[35] The Bush tax cuts were particularly successful in mobilizing business in support of the Republican Party. The Business Roundtable, a CEO organization, lobbied strongly on behalf of the 2003 tax cuts regardless of their effect on federal revenues. "We're always concerned about the budget deficit," it declared, "but for us that's a spending issue."[36]

Other commentators regard Bush's tax program as part of a base-broadening strategy for the long-term benefit of his party. In the opinion of Grover Norquist, president of Americans for Tax Reform, "The President got out ahead and laid claim to the growing investor class."[37] For this school of thought, the 2001, and in particular, the 2003 tax cuts paralleled administration efforts to expand Individual Retirement Accounts and create private Social Security Accounts in seeking to increase the number of people with a pool of private capital. Pollster John Zogby saw immediate payoff for this strategy in the president's re-election. According to his data, 46 percent of voters in 2004 were self-identified investors and this group went for Bush by 61 percent to 39 percent, whereas noninvestors voted for John Kerry by 57 percent to 42 percent.[38]

This theory undoubtedly conforms better with Bush's penchant for boldness and his ambition of creating a lasting Republican majority. If creation of a new investor class was truly his intention, the failure of Social Security reform in 2005 was a serious setback. The downturn of the economy in the last year of his presidency dealt it the final blow. In Norquist's opinion, the defining characteristic of the investor class was that it did not need anything from government, hence its natural tendency to be Republican.[39] As Bush left office, however, many Americans in the "ownership society" he had looked to expand now saw renewed cause for activist government to safeguard their jobs, homes, and futures.

Republican Big Spenders

Reversing "tax and spend" liberalism had been a Republican Party goal since the days of the New Deal. Achieving majority status in the Bush era for the first time since the 1920s, Republicans hewed to party tradition in cutting taxes but departed from it in their willingness to increase domestic as well as defense spending. Their commitment to enact a balanced-budget constitutional amendment as a means of spending control, which was party gospel in the 1980s and 1990s, disappeared from their agenda. They also allowed the Budget Enforcement Act pay-go rules controlling discretionary spending, initially enacted as part of the Omnibus Budget Reconciliation Act of 1990 and renewed in the Balanced Budget Act of 1997, to expire in 2002.[40] By the end of his first term in office, those on the right who still believed in fiscal orthodoxy denounced Bush as a "big government conservative" and the congressional Republicans as the "Grand Old Spending Party" for their mutual lack of expenditure restraint and expansion of domestic programs.[41] Some even admitted to a sentiment unthinkable a few years previously. "On the budget," declared Bruce Bartlett, "Clinton was better."[42]

What was not unexpected was that defense spending would grow under Bush. Republicans generally believed that the balanced budgets of the late 1990s had been purchased in part at the cost of unwise military retrenchment. Defense outlays had declined from 5.6 percent GDP in the final Reagan budget of FY 1989 to 3.0 percent GDP in the final Clinton budgets. Bush's first budget planned for defense growth with corollary domestic spending restraint, but the terrorist attacks of September 11 upset its calculations. The White House could not win congressional support for new domestic cutbacks to compensate for increased spending on defense and homeland security. Even though the Republican-led House and the now Democrat-controlled Senate could not agree an overall FY 2003 budget, they both wanted significantly higher domestic spending than the administration proposed.[43]

The congressional Republican Party had lost the revolutionary fervor that it had exhibited for domestic retrenchment during the 104th Congress of 1995–1997. In the estimate of Dick Armey, former Texan congressman and Contract with America coarchitect, it had sacrificed principle to the desire to hold on to power.[44] Perhaps nothing better demonstrated the Republicans' growing preference to serve their districts and states instead of retrenching domestic programs than the Farm Security Act of 2002. It not only resurrected subsidies that the expiring Freedom to Farm Act of 1996 had slashed but also created new ones at a total 10-year cost of $190 billion, an increase of $83 billion over scheduled payments. A group of conservative Republicans allied with liberal Democrats to block the bill but a counter-coalition of fellow Republicans and farm-state Democrats defeated them.[45]

Congressional Republicans were also enthusiastic practitioners of pork barrel politics, one of the most wasteful forms of federal outlays. They were instrumental in delaying a periodic review of military base capacity until 2005 to prevent closures in advance of the 2002 and 2004 elections. According to Defense Secretary Donald Rumsfeld, this necessitated maintenance of something like 20 to 25 percent more bases than needed.[46] Even more controversially, the Republicans made liberal use of "earmarks" to direct federal spending toward pet projects. According to one estimate, there were over 15,000 earmarks in FY 2006 appropriations, compared to 1,439 in FY 1995, the last budget of the Democrat-led Congress, and their cost amounted to 4.5 percent of total discretionary outlays. Congressional leaders frequently tacked them onto spending bills to broaden support for measures that might not otherwise have passed. However, a series of bribery and conspiracy scandals associated with earmarks eventually led to bipartisan enactment of the Pork Barrel Reduction Act of 2006 to strengthen regulation of their use.[47]

Bush did not implement the threat, oft repeated during his first year in office, to veto budget-busting spending bills. Party-building strategy was partly responsible for staying his hand. Without doubt the No Child Left Behind Act of 2002 embodied a personal commitment to educational reform on the president's part, but it also reflected White House intent to win Republican votes from the "soccer mom" target group on an issue that usually favored the Democrats. To the despair of many on the right, the budget of the Department of Education consequently doubled in real terms by FY 2006, the largest increase since the 1960s.[48] Bush also supported the farm bill to boost the Republican Party's support in farm states that were crucial to its prospects of regaining control of the Senate in the 2002 mid-term elections. Justifying agricultural subsidies as necessary to safeguard food supplies, he told the

Cattleman's Beef Association, "It's in our national security interests that we be able to feed ourselves."[49]

Bush's costliest domestic initiative honored his 2000 campaign commitment to provide prescription benefits for senior citizens. Enacted in 2003 as an extension to Medicare, this created a new entitlement that constituted "the biggest expansion in government since the Great Society" in the opinion of one irate conservative. House Republican leaders put huge pressure on their mostly unenthusiastic rank-and-file to back it. Medicare's chief administrator also threatened to fire its chief actuary if he released numbers showing that the 10-year cost would be $534 billion rather than $400 billion as the CBO estimated. Many Republicans later claimed that they would not have supported the bill had they known the real figure. Within 2 years of its enactment, however, the 10-year cost estimates had skyrocketed to $700 billion.[50]

Bush also wanted to avoid confrontation with the congressional Republican Party over domestic spending because he needed its support for defense expansion. As House Defense Appropriations Subcommittee chair Jerry Lewis (R-CA) observed, "There's no doubt we can get our house in order outside of defense. . . . But this Congress is not willing to bite the bullet and control the rate of [domestic] spending."[51] In constant (FY 2000) terms, outlays on national defense rose by 43 percent from $297 billion (3 percent GDP) in the final Clinton budget of FY 2001 to $426 billion in FY 2007 (4 percent GDP). If projections for Bush's final budgets were accurate, his military expansion looked set to overtake the scale of Reagan's. However, there was a corollary decline rather than increase in discretionary domestic outlays in the 1980s.[52]

The Bush defense program built in a long-term expansion of military costs. According to some experts, its procurement estimates significantly underestimated the costs of developing new weapons systems, which have a historical tendency to overrun, at a possible additional cost of $1.1 trillion from FY 2005 through FY 2014. Existing weaponry and military bases also need expensive maintenance and upgrades from FY 2010 onward just as the costs of pay and benefit increases needed to recruit and retain military personnel are set to hit their peak. In the words of Robert Bixby, director of the bipartisan Concord Coalition that advocates balanced budgets, "Defense is going to be a deficit driver for the foreseeable future."[53]

The costs of military operations in Afghanistan and Iraq put further pressure on the defense budget. Refusing to put a time limit on these commitments, the Bush administration would not provide an estimate of their likely costs. Any official who broke ranks was quick to feel the White House's displeasure. Larry Lindsey's public estimate that war in Iraq would probably cost $100 billion a year was thought to have been instrumental in his firing as National Economic Council chair in December 2002. Two years later, Harvard economist Gregory Mankiw resigned as Council of Economic Advisers (CEA) chair after White House staffers excised sections dealing with the Iraq War from the 2005 *Economic Report of the President*.[54]

The Bush administration funded military operations in Iraq and Afghanistan through emergency supplemental appropriations that regularly accounted for one-fifth or more of total defense spending. According to one estimate, this form of spending annually amounted in Bush's first term to more than eight times the yearly average in the final quarter of the twentieth century.[55] The practice did not make for efficient fiscal planning because it circumvented the requirement for 5-year cost estimates under budget resolution rules. According to some critics, the administration's reliance on supplemental appropriations was deliberately intended to hide the true costs of military operations in case of domestic reaction against their prolongation. As Loren Thompson of the Lexington Institute commented, "It looks as though they want a bigger defense budget without admitting it."[56]

In economic terms, the United States could afford to spend more money on national security than it did in the Bush era. Even with the costs of Iraq and Afghanistan, annual defense spending was lower as a share of GDP than at any time in the Cold War era (1950 to 1990). Whether Americans wanted to spend more or less was a political decision that could only be made on the basis of better information about the costs of military operations in Iraq and Afghanistan than the Bush administration provided. Others who attempted to make good the deficiency agreed that the price tag would be significant but differed about the sums involved. In 2005, for example, the independent Congressional Research Service estimated that 10-year costs could run to $458 billion. Former Clinton CEA chair Joseph Stiglitz and Harvard scholar Linda Bilmes put them much higher by taking into account not only military outlays but also veterans' benefits (including health and disability costs), other hidden extras, and interest payments. They calculated that costs of foreign military operations would amount from 2008 through 2017 to $1.68 trillion on a best case and to $2.85 trillion on a "realistic-moderate" (i.e., still conservative) one.[57]

The Hurricane Katrina disaster that hit New Orleans and the Gulf Coast in August 2005 also generated a surge of emergency spending. In response to Bush's request, Congress quickly passed two emergency bills totaling $62 billion to fund relief and reconstruction but made no provision for how this aid was to be financed and how it should be spent. Legislators consequently took the opportunity to channel money to any state that took in refugees rather than targeting it at areas of greatest need.[58] Fiscal conservatives in the Republican Study Group (RSG) countered with demands for offsetting economies in other programs, particularly the pork-laden Highway Act of 2005. Among its approximately 6,500 earmarks was Alaska's notorious "bridge to nowhere" that was to connect the city of Ketchikan to Gravina Island (population 50) at a cost of $231 million.[59]

Bush had signed the $295 billion highway legislation despite previously insisting that he would veto any bill costing more than $284 billion. Having stood up to the president, the congressional leadership initially refused to yield ground to the RSG. The tide of bad press for wasteful spending amidst the human tragedy of Gulf coast residents eventually persuaded it to eliminate funding for the "bridge to nowhere." True to the prerogatives of pork, however, the money saved went to another Alaska project rather than to New Orleans.[60] Piggybacking on the growing rebellion against spending in Republican Party ranks, Bush called for entitlement savings to offset some Katrina costs. The resultant Deficit Reduction Act of 2005, enacted largely on party lines, provided $40 billion savings over 5 years from the Medicare, Medicaid, student loan, and welfare programs in the main. However, the president had also called for a massive reconstruction package of long-term aid to Gulf Coast residents in addition to the original appropriations. He refused to put a price tag on this, but some analysts calculated that the total cost could run to $300 billion.[61]

The Budget Politics of Divided Government

Based on the examples of the Dwight D. Eisenhower and Clinton presidencies, some conservative analysts came to believe that divided party control of government offered the best hope of fiscal restraint. The 107th Congress of 2001–2003, for all but four months of which the Democrats controlled the Senate, did not offer much encouragement for this view. It increased Bush's nondefense spending requests by an aggregate of $29 billion, which only looked good in comparison with the 108th Congress's record of adding $62 billion.[62] The record of the 111th Congress in 2007 furnished stronger evidence that the presidency and legislature could check each other's fiscal ambitions in circumstances of divided party control. Nevertheless, the two branches cooperated in the rebirth of fiscal activism in 2008 in response to the worst economic downturn since the Great Depression.

In the new environment, each side sought to claim the mantle of fiscal responsibility. Believing they had won the mid-terms in part because of popular disillusion with Bush's budgetary recklessness, Democrats wanted to prove they were capable of fiscal discipline. On the second day of the new

Congress, the House enacted new rules requiring offsets for tax cuts or spending increases and disclosure of earmark sponsorship. Senate Democrats also promoted a budget plan with pay-as-you go provisions but had little chance of enforcing these through new regulations because of opposition from the sizeable Republican Party minority. Meanwhile, the president became a born-again budget-balancer by offering a FY 2008 budget plan that claimed to erase the deficit by FY 2012. This enabled him to attack Democratic policies that diverged from his priorities as a threat to fiscal responsibility.[63]

The fiscal battles between the president and the congressional Democrats over the course of 2007 fundamentally centered on three issues: domestic spending, Iraq funding, and tax-relief offsets. The Democrats proposed a $2.9 trillion budget plan that was $23 billion above what Bush had requested because of higher allocations for education, health care, and veterans' services. Defending the legitimacy of what was a very small increase in proportional terms, House Appropriations Committee chair Dave Obey (D-WI) declared, "It's that 2 percent difference that makes him a president, not a king, and I don't plan on crowning him."[64] The Democrats also sought to attach timelines to Iraq supplementary appropriations in a bid to secure the withdrawal of U.S. troops by the end of 2008.[65] Finally, the Democrats offered their own plan to balance the budget by FY 2012 on the basis of unspecified revenue enhancement. This raised Republican Party suspicions that their opponents were hiding plans to raise taxes. A later Democratic proposal to fund AMT relief and tax breaks for middle-income homeowners and low-income parents through closure of tax loopholes that benefited wealthy Wall Street financiers added grist to the Republican mill.[66]

The budget battles of 2007 ended in a messy draw that pleased Bush more than the Democrats. The president won two supplemental appropriations totaling $190 billion to fund Iraq operations without any conditions about eventual withdrawal. A majority of House Democrats—respectively 140 and 141—voted against both measures. To secure approval of the first supplemental, Bush accepted its inclusion of a set of 18 benchmarks that the Iraqi government had to meet in return for continuing U.S. support. In theory this was a significant assertion of congressional authority over operations in Iraq, but antiwar Democrats condemned it as a fig leaf for an abject surrender.[67]

The Democrats broke the president's domestic spending limit by $11 billion but only by designating funding for border security, veterans' care, and nutrition assistance as "emergency" provision. The Republicans still claimed this as a victory for the president's determination to hold the line. Implicitly acknowledging that it was easier for Bush to stand up to the opposition than to his own party, House Minority Leader John Boehner (R-OH) pronounced the omnibus domestic spending bill the best of his presidency. To Republican Party satisfaction, Congress also enacted AMT relief without offsetting tax increases. In the House 64 Democrats, predominantly Blue Dog conservatives, voted against the measure because it broke pay-go rules.[68]

The president's veto, or its threat, gave him considerable leverage in his jousting with the Democrats. Having been reluctant to use his pen against a Republican-led Congress, Bush vetoed in short order the expansion of the children's health insurance program, a water resource authorization, and the education, health, and labor bill—all on cost grounds. He was overridden on the water bill that had broad support because of its pork benefits, but it was vulnerable to retrenchment in the appropriations process.[69] Bush also used his bully pulpit to tar the Democrats as irresponsible spenders, on one occasion accusing them of behaving "like a teenager with a new credit card." Earmarks, on which he had said little when the Republicans controlled Congress, now came under his sustained attack. The Democrats also shot themselves in the foot by disregarding their own rules. Having stripped earmarks from FY 2007 bills that were still outstanding when they took power, they permitted a new round in FY 2008. According to Taxpayers for Common Sense, spending on them hit a new record in excess of $18 billion in this budget.[70]

Frustrated at being unable to best Bush, House Democrats accused their Senate counterparts of lacking the stomach to fight. They had twice enacted Iraq supplemental appropriations conditional on scheduled withdrawal of troops, but the Senate had not followed suit. The pattern was repeated on AMT offsets. Senate Democrats saw no alternative to compromise because not only did they lack the votes to override Bush but also the Republican Party had the numbers to filibuster bills under institutional rules. House Financial Services Committee chair Barney Frank (D-MA) accused them of a gutless "hold and fold" approach—the GOP put a "hold" on Democratic bills, and the Democrats promptly "fold" their tents. In their own defense, Senate Democrats rejected gesture politics as useless. "I understand the frustration; we're frustrated too," Evan Bayh (D-IN) declared. "But holding a bunch of Kabuki theater doesn't get anything done."[71]

As the Bush presidency entered its final year, the economic downturn changed the context of budgetary politics. While the White House still battled with the Democrats over the issues that divided them in 2007, both sides cooperated on a stimulus measure to avert recession. Treasury Secretary Henry Paulson, John Boehner, and Speaker Nancy Pelosi (D-CA) crafted a proposal for an immediate rebate for taxpayers scaled according to income (maximum $600 for individuals and $1,200 for joint filers). To reach a deal, the White House allowed income caps on full rebates to be set at $75,000 for individuals ($150,000 for joint filers) and did not press for the package to include renewal of the 2001 and 2003 tax cuts. In turn Pelosi accepted tax breaks to encourage business spending and did not demand extension of unemployment benefits and food stamp increases. Senate Democrats tried to load the bill with more benefits for low-income citizens but only secured Republican agreement to extend the rebates to Social Security recipients and disabled veterans who paid no income taxes.[72]

Enacted without offsetting savings, the $168 billion stimulus bill marked a return to bipartisan fiscal stimulus last seen in the 1970s. However, it proved a drop in the ocean in comparison to the bailout of the financial system in the late summer. The landscape of Wall Street changed forever as the sub-prime crisis entered a new phase with the collapse of Lehman Brothers in September. To preempt financial meltdown, the federal government between September 7 and October 3 nationalized the two semipublic mortgage securitization agencies, Freddie Mac and Fannie May, providing each with $100 billion additional capital, effectively took over AIG—the world's largest insurer, and enacted the $700 billion Troubled Assets Recovery Program that committed the treasury to take private mortgage-related assets onto its books. What all this meant in budgetary terms was that the federal government in less than one month had expanded its gross liabilities by more than $1 trillion, which was vastly greater than the cost to date of military operations in Iraq.[73]

Bush resisted demands for a spending-based stimulus measure to restore consumer demand in the wake of the confidence-sapping financial crisis. Not even the belated recognition that the economy had been in recession since late 2007 swayed him to cooperate with the Democrats in developing such an initiative. Nevertheless the election of 2008 ensured that the pendulum swung toward this form of fiscal activism. According to Lawrence Summers, newly appointed National Economic Council chair in the incoming administration of Barack Obama, the economy needed a spending stimulus that was "speedy, substantial and sustained over a several-year period."[74]

Bush's Budgetary Legacy

"I inherited a recession, I'm ending on a recession," Bush noted in his last press conference. This was a disclaimer of responsibility for both downturns and a plea for his economic and budgetary record to be judged on what happened in the interim, but there was little to recommend it therein. His fiscal policies did much to keep the budget in the red after the economy recovered from the 2001 recession, the financial hole in the United States' retiree programs had grown hugely during his stewardship, the tax system he bequeathed to his successor was an unstable, patched-up mess, and the transparency of the budget process had been undermined. The Bush legacy, according to a critical assessment that did not come from left field, "is littered with wasted opportunity, bad judgments and politicized policy."[75]

Bush had hoped through his economic and budget policy to build an enduring Republican majority to complete the process of political transformation started by Reagan but his presidency looked instead to have marked the end of the Age of Reagan. The Reaganite formula for economic growth had not delivered the goods for Bush's United States and the renewal of massive budget deficits had exacerbated the structural economic problems associated with low national saving that had first manifested in the 1980s.

As he departed the White House, Bush trumpeted enduring belief in the core element of his fiscal strategy: "Sound economic policy begins with keeping taxes low." Nevertheless, Mark Zandi, a Wall Street economist and John McCain campaign adviser, characterized his period in office as "almost a lost decade," a term conventionally used to describe Japan's economic experience in the 1990s. Bush's promotion of the largest tax cuts since 1981 had generated meager returns in the form of anemic economic growth. The annual average rate of 2.6 percent GDP during the 24 quarters of consecutive expansion between recessions compared to 3.7 percent GDP in the previous 38-quarter expansion cycle from 1991 through 2000. Moreover, job growth of 6.6 percent between the recessions compared poorly with the 15.5 percent expansion under Clinton.[76]

Bush may also prove to be the last president in the antistatist Age of Reagan. The economic crisis that engulfed the United States at the end of his tenure raised fundamental questions about the role of government in the economy and the relationship of budget deficits to this. In his Inaugural Address during an era of unprecedented stagflation, Reagan had proclaimed, "In the present crisis, government is not the solution to our problems; government is the problem." In his final *Economic Report* as president, Bush appeared to repudiate this antistatist credo by acknowledging that in the current "extraordinary circumstances . . . a systemic, aggressive, and unprecedented Government response was the only responsible policy action." Nevertheless, he was not throwing in the towel to declare the Age of Reagan over. Insisting that federal anti-recession initiatives should be a temporary response to crisis, he also called for his tax cuts to be made permanent as the best way to strengthen recovery and lay the foundations for sustained growth.[77]

The tax cuts that Bush had promoted in his first 6 years as president were instrumental in keeping the budget in the red long after recovery from the 2001 recession, but he considered their long-term benefits vastly more important than their short-term effect on federal finances. With his departure from office, however, the United States' fiscal history was about to take a new turn. The era of deficits looked set to continue for years to come, but it had entered a new phase. No longer the price for conservative tax reduction, unbalanced budgets were to become once more an instrument of liberal purpose. Signaling this, Bush's successor repudiated the ethos of his political economy and its Reaganite inspiration in avowing, "[A]s we've learned very clearly and conclusively over the last eight years, tax cuts alone can't solve all of our economic problems—especially tax cuts that are targeted to the wealthiest few Americans. We have tried that strategy, time and time again. And it's only helped lead us to the crisis we face right now."[78]

Notes

1. Congressional Budget Office, *The Budget and Economic Outlook: Fiscal Years 2002–2011* (Washington, D.C.: Congressional Budget Office, 2001), 1; Alan Greenspan, *The Age of Turbulence: Adventures in a New World* (New York: Penguin Press, 2007), 217.

2. Daniel Patrick Moynihan, *Miles to Go: A Personal History of Social Policy* (Cambridge, MA: Harvard University Press, 1996), 95. See, too, Joseph White and Aaron Wildavsky, *The Deficit and the Public Interest: The Search for Responsible Budgeting in the 1980s* (Berkeley: University of California Press, 1989).

3. "The Budget Message of the President," February 11, 2004, available at www .whitehouse.gov/omb/budget/fy2005/message.html.

4. "Remarks at a Fundraiser for Senatorial Candidate Elizabeth Dole and Congressional Candidate Robin Hayes in Charlotte," February 27, 2002 [Bush statements—unless otherwise indicated—are from John T. Woolley and Gerhard Peters, *American Presidency Project* University of California at Santa Barbara, www.presidency.ucsb .edu]. There is some dispute whether Bush ever made these campaign remarks. See Paul Begala, *It's Still the Economy, Stupid: George W. Bush, the GOP's CEO* (New York: Simon & Schuster, 2002), 22–23.

5. Richard Kogan and James Horney, "Deficit Announcement Masks Bigger Story: Long-Term Outlook Remains Bleak," *Center on Budget and Policy Priorities*, October 11, 2006.

6. George W. Bush, "Remarks on the Office of Management and Budget Mid-Session Review," July 11, 2006, *American Presidency Project* on www.presidency.ucsb .edu.

7. Bruce Bartlett, *Impostor: How George W. Bush Bankrupted America and Betrayed the Reagan Legacy* (New York: Doubleday, 2006), 62.

8. U.S. Treasury "A Dynamic Analysis of Permanent Extension of the President's Tax Relief," July 25, 2006, available at www.treas.gov/press/releases/reports/treasurydynamicanalysisreporjuly2520006.pdf; Congressional Research Service, *The Budget for FY 2006*, August 30, 2006. For commentary, see, James Horney, "A Smoking Gun: President's Claim That Tax Cuts Pay for Themselves Refuted by New Treasury Analysis," *Center on Budget and Policy Priorities*, July 27, 2006; and Lori Montgomery, "Lower Deficits Spark Debate over Tax Cuts' Role," *Washington Post* October 17, 2006.

9. John T. Woolley, *Monetary Politics: The Federal Reserve and the Politics of Monetary Policy* (Cambridge, MA: Harvard University Press, 1984); Donald Kettl, *Leadership at the Fed* (New Haven, CT: Yale University Press, 1986); Bob Woodward, *Maestro: Greenspan's Fed and the American Boom* (New York: Simon & Schuster, 2000).

10. Richard Stevenson, "In Policy Change, Greenspan Backs a Broad Tax Cut," *New York Times* January 26, 2001; Greenspan, *The Age of Turbulence*, 214–24.

11. Edmund Andrews, "Greenspan Throws Cold Water on Bush Argument for Tax Cut," *New York Times* February 12, 2003; Greenspan, *The Age of Turbulence*, 238–40.

12. Ashley Seager, "Solid foundations or dangerous house of cards? America Awaits Greenspan's Legacy," *Guardian* January 31, 2006; Steven R. Weisman, "Fed Cuts Rate but Hints about a Pause," *New York Times* May 1, 2008.

13. Paul Krugman, "Off the Wagon," *New York Times* January 17, 2003. See, too, Michael Kinsley, "How Reaganomics became Rubinomics," *Slate* December 19, 2003, available at www.slate.com/?id=2075796.

14. Ron Suskind, *The Price of Loyalty: George W. Bush, the White House and the Education of Paul O'Neill* (New York: Simon & Schuster, 2004), 291; Greenspan, *The Age of Turbulence*, 236; "Press Briefing on the Budget by OMB Director Mitch Daniels," February 3, 2003, available at www.whitehouse.gov/omb/speeches/daniels_04budget.

15. "The President's Fiscal Year 2004 Budget Message," February 3, 2003, available at www.whitehouse/gov/news/releases/2003/02/20030203-7.html.

16. George W. Bush, "The Budget Message of the President," February 11, 2004, *American Presidency Project* on www.presidency.ucsb.edu; Edmund Andrews, "In Plan to Reduce the Deficit, White House Turns to Old Projections," *New York Times* January 2, 2005.

17. John Harris and Dan Balz, "First 100 Days Go By in a Blur," *Washington Post* April 29, 2001. See, too, Dick Cheney's remarks to Paul O'Neill and Alan Greenspan as recounted in Alan Greenspan, *The Age of Turbulence*, 216.

18. Jeff Madrick, "Plans to Cut Taxes May Be Clever Politics, but They're Not Wise Fiscal Policy," *New York Times* February 15, 2001; Frank Bruni, "Bush's Tax Cut Triumph Is a Political Bouquet, Complete with Thorns," *New York Times* May 27, 2001.

19. David Frum, *The Right Man: The Surprise Presidency of George W. Bush* (New York: Random House, 2003), 29; Mitchell quoted in Dan Balz, "Next on Bush's Agenda: Bigger Policy Changes," *Washington Post* May 6, 2001.

20. "The 2000 Campaign: Exchanges between the Candidates in the Third Presidential Debate," *New York Times* October 18, 2000; Martin P. Wattenberg, "Elections: Tax Cuts Versus Lockbox: Did the Voters Grasp the Tradeoff in 2000?" *Presidential Studies Quarterly* 34 (December 2004), 838–48.

21. Karlyn H. Bowman, *Public Opinion on Taxes* (Washington, D.C.: American Enterprise Institute, 2004), 10; Jacob S. Hacker and Paul Pierson, "Abandoning the Middle: The Bush Tax Cuts and the Limits of Democratic Control," *Perspectives on Politics* 3 (March 2005): 39.

22. Alice Rivlin, "Why Fight the Surplus?" *New York Times* January 30, 2001; Richard Freeman and Eileen Appelbaum, "Instead of a Tax Cut, Send Out Dividends," *New York Times* February 1, 2001.

23. Barbara Sinclair, "Context, Strategy and Chance: George W. Bush and the 107th Congress," in *The George W. Bush Presidency: Appraisals and Prospects*, edited by Colin Campbell and Bert A. Rockman (Washington, D.C.: CQ Press, 2004), 112–13.

24. *Budget of the United States Government, Fiscal Year 2003* (Washington, D.C.: Government Printing Office, 2002), 6; Dennis Ippolito, *Why Budgets Matter: Budget Policy and American Politics* (University Park: Pennsylvania State University Press, 2003), 295.

25. John P. Burke, *Becoming President: The Bush Transition 2000–2003* (Boulder, CO: Lynne Rienner, 2003), 136–37, 154; Sinclair, "Context, Strategy and Chance," 111–15; Suskind, *The Price of Loyalty*, 131–37, 149–50, 161–62.

26. David Rosenbaum, "Doing the Math on Bush's Tax Cut," *New York Times* February 15, 2001; Congressional Budget Office, *The Budget and Economic Outlook: An Update* (Washington, D.C.: Congressional Budget Office, 2001), 8.

27. Daniel Altman, *Neoconomy: George Bush's Revolutionary Gamble with America's Future* (New York: PublicAffairs, 2004), 73, 237; Citizens for Tax Justice, "Year-by-Year Analysis of the Bush Tax Cuts Growing Tilt to the Very Rich," 2002, available at www.ctj.org/html/gwb0602.htm.

28. Jacob S. Hacker and Paul Pierson, *Off Center: The Republican Revolution and the Erosion of Democracy* (New Haven, CT: Yale University Press, 2005), 55–62. For similar criticism of EGTRRA's bias toward the rich, see Altman, *Neoconomy*, 74–88.

29. Richard Stevenson, "Bush Unveils Plan to Cut Tax Rates and Spur Economy," *New York Times* January 8, 2003, and Elizabeth Bumiller, "A Bold Plan with Risks," *New York Times* January 8, 2003. More than 450 liberal economists, including 10 Nobel laureates, signed a statement that appeared as a full-page ad in the *New York Times* declaring the measure inequitable, unhelpful to economic recovery, and harmful to the deficit. See, "Nobel Laureates, 450 Other Economists Fault Bush Tax Cut Plan," *Economic Policy Institute Press Release*, February 10, 2003, available at www.epi.org/newsroom/releases/o3/02/030210-econltr-pr.pdf.

30. Chris Edwards, "Options for Tax Reform," *Cato Institute Policy Analysis*, No. 536, February 24, 2005; Joel Friedman, "Dividend and Capital Gains Tax Cuts Unlikely to Yield Touted Economic Gains," *Center on Budget and Policy Priorities*, March 10, 2003, available at www.cbpp/cms/index.cfm?fa=view+id=1008.

31. David Firestone, "With Tax Bill Passed, Republicans Call for More," *New York Times* May 24, 2003.

32. In the Senate, the only nays were the retiring Ernest Hollings (D-SC), Olympia Snowe (R-ME), and Lincoln Chafee (R-RI). Though not present for the vote because of presidential campaign commitments, John Kerry (D-MA) and John Edwards (D-SC) voiced their support. See Jonathan Weisman, "Congress Votes to Extend Tax Cuts," *Washington Post* September 24, 2004.

33. George W. Bush, "Remarks on Signing the Working Families Tax Relief Act in Des Moines, Iowa," October 4, 2004, *American Presidency Project* on www .presidency.ucsb.edu; Robert Greenstein, "New 'Middle-Class' Tax Cut Bill Represents Cynical Policymaking," *Center on Budget and Policy Priorities*, September 24, 2004, available at www.policyarchive.org/handle/10207/7845.

34. Associated Press, "Bush Quietly Signs Corporate Tax-Cut Bill," October 22, 2004, available at www.msnbc.msn.com/id/6307293/.

35. Hacker and Pierson, *Off Center*, 48–49.

36. Quoted in "U.S. Economy: Bush Deficits May Raise Borrowing Costs," January 9, 2003, available at www.forexhsi.com/forexnews/news0103/news_231989.php. See, too, Alan K. Ota, "Business Newly Tolerant of 'Manageable' Deficit," *Congressional Quarterly Weekly* January 17, 2004, 162–64.

37. Quoted in Thomas B. Edsall, *Building Red America: The New Conservative Coalition and the Drive for Permanent Power* (New York: Basic Books, 2006), 43–44.

38. John Zogby, "Investors for Bush: How Social Security Reform Can Bring about a Republican Realignment," *Wall Street Journal* March 15, 2005.

39. Edsall, *Building Red America*, 44.

40. These rules had been increasingly circumvented in the surplus budgets of FY 1999–2001 to accommodate Clinton's domestic priorities and the congressional Republicans desire for bigger defense spending. See Congressional Budget Office, *The Budget and Economic Outlook: Fiscal Years 2003–2012* (Washington, D.C.: Congressional Budget Office, 2002), 71.

41. Stephen Slivinski, *Buck Wild: How Republicans Broke the Bank and Became the Party of Big Government* (Nashville, TN: Nelson Current, 2006); Richard A. Viguerie, *Conservatives Betrayed: How George W. Bush and Other Big Government Republicans Hijacked the Conservative Cause* (Los Angeles, CA: Bonus Books, 2006); Michael Tanner, *Leviathan on the Right: How Big-Government Conservatism Brought Down the Republican Revolution* (Washington, D.C.: Cato Institute, 2007).

42. Bartlett, *Impostor*, Chapter 7.

43. Ippolito, *Why Budgets Matter*, 299–300.

44. Dick Armey, "Where We Went Wrong," *Washington Post* October 29, 2006.

45. Slivinski, *Buck Wild*, 127–32; Tanner, *Leviathan on the Right*, 155–57.

46. Winslow Wheeler, *The Wastrels of Defense: How Congress Sabotages U.S. Security* (Washington, D.C.: Naval Institute Press, 2004), 37–38.

47. Slivinski, *Buck Wild*, 136–38. For a sympathetic assessment of earmarks, see John Cochran, "Budget Villain, Local Hero," *Congressional Quarterly Weekly* June 12, 2006, 1606–13.

48. Tanner, *Leviathan on the Right*, 168–69; Bartlett, *Impostor*, 131.

49. Mike Allen, "Bush Calls Farm Subsidies a National Security Issue," *Washington Post* February 9, 2004.

50. Slivinski, *Buck Wild*, 132–41 (quotation p. 141); Bartlett, *Impostor*, 64–81.

51. Martin Kady II, "Defense: A Deficit Driver," *Congressional Quarterly Weekly* January 17, 2004, 155.

52. Defense outlays were projected to reach $504.7 billion (FY 2000 dollars) in FY 2009, a real increase of nearly 70 percent since FY 2001, and 4.5 percent gross domestic product (GDP), a growth of half since Clinton's last budget. From FY 1982 to FY 1989, they grew from $282 billion to $399 billion, a real increase of 41.5 percent, and from 5.1 percent GDP to 5.6 percent GDP, a growth of under a tenth. Calculation based on data in Office of Management and Budget, *Budget of the United States Government Fiscal Year 2009: Historical Tables*.

53. Peter G. Peterson, *Running on Empty: How the Democratic and Republican Parties Are Bankrupting Our Future and What Americans Can Do About It* (New York: Farrar, Straus and Giroux, 2004), 84–85; Kady, "Defense: A Deficit Driver," 154; Dana Hedgpeth, "GAO Blasts Weapons Budget: Cost Overruns Hit $295 Billion," *Washington Post* April 1, 2008.

54. Bob Davis, "Bush Economic Aide Says Cost of Iraq War May Top $100 Billion," *Wall Street Journal* September 16, 2002; Jonathan Weisman, "Dropping Report's Chapter Was Unusual, Economists Say," *Washington Post* February 23, 2005.

55. John Cranford, "The Deficit's Hard Truths," *Congressional Quarterly Weekly* September 26, 2005, 2557.

56. Jonathan Weisman, "Congress Unlikely to Embrace Bush Wish List," *Washington Post* February 8, 2005.

57. Murray Weidenbaum, "How Much Defense Spending Can We Afford?" *The Public Interest* (Spring 2003): 52–61; Amy Belasco, "The Costs of Operations in Iraq, Afghanistan and Enhanced Security," *Congressional Research Service* February 9, 2005; Joseph Stiglitz and Linda Bilmes, *The Three Trillion Dollar War: The True Cost of the Iraq Conflict* (New York: Penguin Press, 2008), 59.

58. Stephen Moore, "Welcome to the GOP's New New Deal," *Wall Street Journal* September 19, 2005; Tanner, *Leviathan on the Right*, 160–62.

59. Shailagh Murray and Jim VandeHi, "Katrina's Costs May Test GOP Harmony," *Washington Post* September 21, 2005; Shailagh Murray, "Storm's Costs Threaten Hill Leaders' Pet Projects," *Washington Post* September 22, 2005.

60. Shailagh Murray, "Senate Passes $295 Billion Transportation Measure," *Washington Post* May 18, 2005; Carl Hulse, "Two 'Bridges to Nowhere' Tumble Down in Congress," *New York Times* November 17, 2005.

61. Christopher Cooper, "President Seeks Entitlement Cuts to Pay for Katrina," *Wall Street Journal* October 5, 2005; Jonathan Weisman, "Budget Cuts Pass By a Slim Margin: Poor, Elderly and Students Feel the Pinch," *Washington Post* February 2, 2006.

62. William A. Niskanen, "A Case for Divided Government," *Cato Institute Policy Report* (March–April 2003); Stephen Slivinski, "The Grand Old Spending Party: How Republicans Became Big Spenders," *Cato Institute Policy Analysis*, No. 543, May 3, 2005, available at www.cato.org/pub-display.php?pub-id=3750.

63. Lori Montgomery, "House Adopts Pay-as-You-Go Rules," *Washington Post* January 6, 2007; Lori Montgomery, "Democrats Plan to Restore Budget Discipline," *Washington Post* March 22, 2007; Lori Montgomery and Nell Henderson, "Burden Set to Shift on Balanced Budget: Bush Likely to Force Democrats' Hand," *Washington Post* January 16, 2007; Lori Montgomery and Christopher Lee, "Hill Democrats Critical of Bush's Budget Plan," *Washington Post* February 7, 2007.

64. Lori Montgomery, "Democrats Make Budget Proposal," *Washington Post*, May 17, 2007; Michael Abramowitz, "Bush Cautions Democrats on Spending," *Washington Post* June 17, 2007.

65. Carl Hulse, "Democrats Plan to Take Control of Iraq Spending," *New York Times* December 14, 2006; Michael Luo and Sheryl Gay Stolberg, "Bush and Congress Easing Tone of Debate on War Bill," *New York Times* April 28, 2007.

66. Lori Montgomery, "GOP Sees Tax Hikes in Budget Proposal," *Washington Post* March 15, 2007; Jonathan Weisman, "House Passes Bill to Ease Alternative Minimum Tax," *Washington Post* November 10, 2007.

67. Shailagh Murray, "Congress Passes Deadline-Free War Funding Bill," *Washington Post* May 25, 2007; Paul Kane and Jonathan Weisman, "Iraq Funds Approved in Senate Budget Bill," *Washington Post* December 19, 2007.

68. Jonathan Weisman, "House Approves Domestic Spending," *Washington Post* December 18, 2007; Jonathan Weisman and Paul Kane, "Key Setbacks Dim Luster of Democrats' Year," *Washington Post* December 20, 2007.

69. Michael Abramowitz and Jonathan Weisman, "Bush Vetoes Health Measure," *Washington Post* October 4, 2007; Peter Baker, "Bush Veto Sets Up Clash on the Budget," *Washington Post* November 14, 2007; Jonathan Weisman, "A Bush Veto Is Overridden for the First Time," *Washington Post* November 9, 2007.

70. Baker, "Bush Veto Sets Up Clash on Budget"; John Solomon and Jeffrey Birnbaum, "In the Democratic Congress, Pork Still Gets Served," *Washington Post* May 24, 2007; Paul Kane, "Candidates' Earmarks Worth Millions," *Washington Post* February 14, 2008.

71. Jonathan Weisman and Paul Kane, "Democrats Blaming Each Other for Failures," *Washington Post* December 13, 2007.

72. David Herszenhorn, "Bush and House in Accord for $150 Billion Stimulus," *New York Times* January 25, 2008; David Herszenhorn and David Stout, "$168 Billion Stimulus Plan Clears Congress," *New York Times* February 7, 2008.

73. Clive Crook, "Nationalization in All But Name," *Financial Times* September 8, 2008; David Teather, Larry Elliott, and Jill Treanor, "The Reckoning–Domino Effect That Reshaped Global Economy," *Guardian* September 20, 2008; "When Fortune Frowned: A Special Report on the World Wconomy," *Economist* October 11, 2008, 2–6.

74. "Spending and the Economy," *Economist* November 22, 2008, 53–54, and "Stimulus Packages," *Economist* November 22, 2008, 53–54.

75. "The President's Press Conference," January 12, 2009, *American Presidency Project* on www.presidency.uscb.edu; "The Frat Boy Ships Out," *Economist* January 17, 2009, 28.

76. *Economic Report of the President 2009*, 4, 285, 320, 328; Neil Irwin and Dan Eggen, "Economy Made Few Gains in Bush Years," *Washington Post* January 12, 2009.

77. George W. Bush, *Economic Report of the President 2009*, (Washington D.C.: Government Printing Office, 2009), 3–4.

78. George W. Bush, "The President's News Conference," February 9, 2009, *American Presidency Project* on www.presidency.ucsb.edu.

~

CHAPTER SIX

The Anatomy of a Divorce:
Conservatives versus
George W. Bush

Gleaves Whitney

In 2007, in the *Wall Street Journal*, former Ronald Reagan speechwriter Peggy Noonan opined that conservative supporters of George W. Bush had felt like battered wives for some time. If taxpayers did not like the dramatic increases in federal spending, too bad. If they did not like the intrusion of big government in their lives, deal with it. If they thought the war in Iraq was a mistake or has been mishandled, just trust the administration.[1] Noonan's words were an emperor-has-no-clothes moment for a number of conservatives who had been reluctant to criticize President Bush openly.

In this chapter I propose to look into why prominent conservative opinion leaders began distancing themselves from the 43rd president well before Election Day 2008, even before Election Day 2004. We will get to their divorce from Bush in a moment. The first order of business is to provide some context—both theoretical and historical—to explain how it happens in U.S. history that opinion leaders who are originally supportive of a president eventually break with him. There are at least four factors that can contribute to bringing about these messy divorces.

Context

First, there frequently arises a tension between the intellectual class and political class in Anglo American political culture. Sir Isaiah Berlin famously explored this point in his essays,[2] and in the tradition of Berlin, author Michael Ignatieff observed,

> [T]he trouble with academics and commentators is that they care more about whether ideas are interesting than whether they are true. Politicians live by ideas just as much as professional thinkers do, but they can't afford the luxury of entertaining ideas that are merely interesting. They have to work with the small number of ideas that happen to be true and the even smaller number that happen to be applicable to real life. In academic life, false ideas are merely false and useless ones can be fun to play with. In political life, false ideas can ruin the lives of millions and useless ones can waste precious resources. An intellectual's responsibility for his ideas is to follow their consequences wherever they may lead. A politician's responsibility is to master those consequences and prevent them from doing harm.[3]

Second, our winner-take-all system can aggravate this tension by the political necessity to compromise. We Americans are taught that we have a two-party system that tends to suppress third parties. In most elections people do not want to throw away their votes on a candidate who really does not have a chance to win. What has evolved over the past 100 years is a four-party system, and University of Louisville political scientist Gary Gregg explains how it works in the presidential primaries. In 1992, for example, the moderate Republican Party was represented by George H. W. Bush. The conservative Republican Party was represented by Pat Buchanan. The moderate Democratic Party was represented by Bill Clinton. The liberal Democratic Party was represented by Jerry Brown.

Now, the winner-take-all system established by the Electoral College encourages the moderates and true believers in the same party to merge in order to win elections. As we see repeatedly in U.S. history, ideas are moderated, compromised, and amended in this merging process. The merging often leads to dissatisfaction among the more ideological opinion leaders. And when the true believers among them become frustrated by the compromises of the president (or candidate), they face a tough choice: either stay at home and suffer, or get a divorce. At key turns in U.S. history, opinion leaders have served their president papers.[4]

A third contributing factor to political divorces is precedent. On numerous occasions, the true believers in a party have split with their president because there were too many compromises or too many violations of principle. Scholars have traced these breaks going back centuries.[5] Indeed, the Declaration of Independence can be viewed as the culmination of the "petitioning process" whose forerunners include the Magna Carta and the Petition of Right that Parliament presented to King Charles I in 1628.

In North America, in the aftermath of the French and Indian War, this "petition tradition" was carried forward by able lawyers and revolutionaries— James Otis, John Dickenson, Sam Adams, James Wilson, and Thomas Jefferson—all asserting the rights of British subjects in North America against the arbitrary rule of Parliament and King. U.S. writers and leaders had no trouble carrying on the tradition they inherited from Britain. Jefferson famously if surreptitiously broke with the indispensable man himself, George Washington, whom he had served as secretary of state. A few years later, High Federalists egged on by Alexander Hamilton broke with John Adams. This critical divorce occurred in the months leading up to the Election of 1800 when the nation was in the Quasi War with France. Arguably it is one of the factors that led to a change in the party occupying the White House.

During the Civil War, radical Republican opinion leaders expressed considerable unhappiness with the first Republican president, Abraham Lincoln, and outright disgust with Andrew Johnson, who assumed the presidency upon Lincoln's assassination. A half-century later, in the Ivy League election of 1912, progressive Republicans following Theodore Roosevelt abandoned William Howard Taft. That election was the only time in U.S. history when the third-party candidate—in this case, Roosevelt—humiliated the incumbent by receiving more votes than the president himself. Prominent Democrats began to abandon Woodrow Wilson after his uncompromising stance on the League of Nations, and this separation no doubt contributed to changing the party in the White House in 1921.

In the last half-century, the most famous divorce between the president and opinion leaders in his party occurred over the spring and summer of 1968, when prominent Democrats broke with Lyndon Johnson over the conduct of the Vietnam War. This split, too, contributed to changing the party headed for the White House later that year.

For a fourth factor that helps explain these divorces, it is useful to look at the nature of political movements: not one of them in our pluralistic society is monolithic—not greens, not progressives, not liberals, and certainly not conservatives. This last is a factious coalition, which makes the word *conservative* hard to define. Russell Kirk argued that classical conservatism is not an ideology, but a temperament. In the U.S. context, the conservative tries to carry forward the culture and institutions that maintain a justly ordered freedom. This traditionalist conception of conservatism has hardly anything in common with the libertarian emphasis on self-interested individuals in the free market or with the neoconservatives' ideological mission to expand the United States' power and freedom around the globe.[6]

In the post–World-War II United States, it took the tireless efforts of two great unifiers to turn conservatism into anything resembling a movement. Starting in 1955, William F. Buckley Jr. brought together anticommunists, libertarians, traditionalist Catholics, and Anglo-Catholics in the pages of *National Review*; while in 1980 Ronald Reagan added Protestant evangelicals and Jewish neoconservatives to make a potent political coalition.[7] Fractious though it was, this was the coalition that Bush inherited in 2000 when he was elected the 43rd president.

To sum up the argument thus far: At least four factors—the inherent tension between intellectuals and politicians, our winner-take-all Electoral College system, the Anglo American tradition of dissent, and factious movements—all provide the context to the high-profile divorce that took place between prominent conservative opinion leaders and President George W. Bush.

Conservatives versus George W. Bush

Before developing the argument further, I must say that many serious conservative scholars and opinion leaders remained supportive of President Bush until he left office on January 20, 2009. Not that they were uncritical, but overall, they supported the administration's policies and tone. Charles Krauthammer, Victor Davis Hanson, Bill Kristol, Max Boot, and Fred Barnes come to mind. Several prominent think tanks like the American Enterprise Institute, and leading conservative journals such as *The Weekly Standard* were also supportive.

Barnes, who is executive editor of *The Weekly Standard*, consistently portrayed the president in sympathetic terms: "Bush is a president who leads." He "has the temperament of a self-assured Texas male." He believes the role of a conservative president is "to be proactive, bold, energetic, and optimistic." "For Bush, clashes with conservatives are inevitable. . . . Given his rebel-in-chief style, President Bush is sometimes willing to take on fights with his conservative base, despite being a true (but unorthodox) conservative himself."[8]

Conservatives who continued to support Bush to the end believed that one of the reasons Barack Obama crushed John McCain in the 2008 election was that the administration was hurt by its own success. There were no significant terrorist attacks on U.S. soil after September 11, and the surge in Iraq worked—those dogs did not bark. Accordingly, when the economic crisis overwhelmed national security concerns in September 2008, a scant seven weeks before the election, Bush got the blame. It just was not the Republican Party's year. The 2008 election is typical of what happens to parties during recessions: they lose seats in Congress and often the White House.

But as I hope to show, numerous conservative opinion leaders turned on the Bush presidency *before* the recession and with a vengeance. They blamed the administration for deconstructing a coalition that was five decades in the building. To understand better how the divorce between these conservative opinion leaders and the president came about, I surveyed members of one of the nation's most prominent conservative organizations, the Philadelphia Society, and reviewed the books, articles, and op-eds that conservatives have generated during the past decade. A large majority of conservatives I surveyed and studied split with Bush administration policies, even if they liked Bush personally. Moreover, a surprising number of them spurned his successor, McCain and voted for Obama in 2008.

Courtship (1999–2000)

What a turnaround from 8 to 10 years before. Reviewing the way conservatives wooed Bush after he won re-election as Texas governor in 1998, few would have anticipated the ugly divorce to come. His record as governor with a conservative-pragmatic record had been impressive. In his bid for a second term, he gathered broad support from Democrats, including the Democratic lieutenant governor, and on Election Day carried 239 of Texas's 254 counties. He also appealed to Hispanics, winning almost 50 percent of their vote.[9] Conservatives observed that all of President Clinton's trips to Texas to support the Democratic challenger, a sacrificial lamb named Gary Mauro, had come to naught. Given who his father was, his record as governor, and his appeal to conservatives, Bush quickly became a serious contender for the White House.

I witnessed some of the courtship firsthand when Michigan governor John Engler, then head of the Republican Governors Association, got the nation's 30-odd Republican governors to back their colleague in Austin.[10]

Marriage

During the campaign, Governor Bush styled himself a "compassionate conservative." The marriage between Bush and movement conservatives occurred in August 2000 at the nominating convention in Philadelphia. His acceptance speech struck Burkean chords pleasing to conservative ears. The palace guard at *National Review* reported that "On the major issues, Bush was impeccably conservative."[11]

Although the election in 2000 was one of the most controversial in U.S. history, Bush received 10 million more votes than Bob Dole had in 1996.[12]

There was a genuine appeal to the conservative base of the Republican Party.

His first Inaugural Address struck numerous conservative themes, and his first weeks in office were full of symbolic and substantive acts that appealed to conservatives. For instance, on his first day in office, he restored the controversial Mexico City policy that outlaws using U.S. taxpayer funds to pay for abortions overseas. Soon after that, he established the Office of Faith-Based Initiatives.[13]

Bush would go on to experience two honeymoons in 2001. The first was rather modest, as Bush enjoyed approval ratings in the mid-50s among the general public (and higher approval ratings among conservatives). Then, just as his numbers were starting to sag, September 11 happened. This tragedy led to Bush's second honeymoon when his job approval ratings soared to 80 and 90 percent;[14] virtually all conservatives were backing him.

With the prodding of Karl Rove, the president threw red meat at conservatives by cutting taxes, invading Iraq, and intervening in the Terri Schiavo case. As the first post-September 11 president, Bush looked, acted, and talked like a philosophical conservative for the durable Republican majority to come.

End of the Honeymoon

And yet—and yet—between the two honeymoons were some grumblings of discontent. Just six months into the administration, libertarians criticized Bush's protectionist policies toward steel; small government conservatives criticized ongoing agriculture subsidies; cultural conservatives and national security types criticized immigration policy toward Latinos especially.[15]

As events unfolded, the cacophony of voices critical of Bush rose to ever higher decibels. People are well familiar with the litany: protests against the further federalization of education in No Child Left Behind, against the huge expansion of Medicare, against the misuse of intelligence in a fool's errand for weapons of mass destruction, against the prosecution of the war in Iraq, against parts of the Patriot Act, against the bungled response to Hurricane Katrina, against the attempt to nominate Harriet Miers to the U.S. Supreme Court, and against a vice president whose chief of staff acted above the law. The list goes on and on. As events unfolded, several major conservative responses took shape against the president. Let us look briefly into three of them.

Divorce by the Fiscal Conservatives

One of the earliest, most vociferous criticisms leveled against Bush came from the fiscal conservatives. Among their numbers were Dick Armey, Grover

Norquist, and Stephen Moore. Their standard bearer could be Bruce Bar-tlett. Bartlett is an economist with impeccable conservative credentials. An early supply-sider, he worked for Texas Congressman (and 2008 presidential candidate) Ron Paul. In 1981, he joined the Reagan administration and helped craft that year's famous tax cuts. Also during the first year of Reagan's presidency, he wrote a book, *Reaganomics*, one of the *Wall Street Journal's* best business books of the year.[16]

Fast forward two decades. Although he denies it now, Bartlett had high hopes for the Bush administration back in 2001 and in fact helped craft Bush's early tax cuts. But when the 43rd president tried to woo moderates by adopting parts of the liberal agenda, Bartlett quit the White House. More-over, in 2005 he lost his job at a free-market think tank for openly criticizing Bush. With some spare time on his hands, he penned a polemic published by Doubleday called *Imposter: How George W. Bush Bankrupted America and Betrayed the Reagan Legacy*. Chapter 1 starts, "I Know Conservatives, and George W. Bush Is No Conservative." "The purpose of this book," Bartlett wrote, "is to disabuse people of the idea that George W. Bush is a conserva-tive president who has relentlessly pursued a conservative agenda. Those in the conservative movement know better. They know that he is not a con-servative in any meaningful sense of the term philosophically. He is simply a partisan Republican."[17]

What angered Bartlett was Bush's willingness to expand, rather than cur-tail, Great Society programs. Exhibit "A" was the Medicare prescription ben-efit that the president rammed through Congress in November 2003. Lyndon Johnson could not have been prouder. Bush's fiscal recklessness caused both the annual deficit and national debt to balloon to all-time highs. The num-bers by Election Day 2008 were mind-numbing. "On the day President Bush took office, the national debt stood at $5.7 trillion. The latest number from the Treasury Department shows the national debt now stands at more than $9.8 trillion. That's a 71.9 percent increase on Mr. Bush's watch . . . the big-gest increase under any president in U.S. history."[18]

Divorce by the Anti-Imperialists

Bush was the longest-serving war-time commander in chief in U.S. history. He left office still fighting two unresolved wars and having lowered U.S. moral authority among nations around the world. That was bound to put strain on the conservative coalition. As the war in Iraq went south, a group of conservative critics emerged that included George Will, Brent Scowcroft, William F. Buckley Jr. and Jeffrey Hart. Variously called realists and anti-imperialists, these conservatives thoroughly reject Wilsonian idealism. In its place they counsel prudence, moderation, and restraint. They sound a bit like the William H. Taft conservatives of old or Burke in his *Reflections on the Revolution in France*, and sneer at the neoconservative, Ken Adelman, who infamously predicted: "Iraq will be a cakewalk."[19]

One of the standard bearers of the anti-imperialists is Andrew Bacevich. A self-described Catholic conservative, Bacevich is a West Point graduate, a colonel in the army, a Princeton Ph.D., a professor of international relations at Boston University, and a grieving father. He grieves because his 27-year-old son, his namesake, was killed by an improvised explosive device in Salah Ad Din Province in Iraq.[20]

Bacevich's books are hard-hitting critiques of neoconservative foreign policy. The titles are revealing. In 2002, he came out with *American Empire: The Realities and Consequences of U.S. Diplomacy*.[21] In 2006 came the publication of *The New American Militarism: How Americans Are Seduced by War*.[22] In 2007, there appeared *The Long War*,[23] and in 2008 came *The Limits of Power: The End of American Exceptionalism*.[24] Bacevich, notes the *Boston Globe*, has been "a persistent, vocal critic of the U.S. occupation of Iraq, calling the conflict a catastrophic failure."[25] In March 2007, he described Bush's endorsement of such "preventive wars" as "immoral, illicit, and imprudent."[26]

Underlying Bacevich's analysis is that Americans are more voracious, hedonistic consumers of resources than ever. But,

> [t]he collective capacity of our domestic political economy to satisfy those appetites has not kept pace with demand. As a result, sustaining our pursuit of life, liberty, and happiness at home requires increasingly that Americans look beyond our borders. Whether the issue at hand is oil, credit, or the availability of cheap consumer goods, we expect the world to accommodate the American way of life.
>
> The resulting sense of entitlement has great implications for foreign policy. Simply put, as the American appetite for freedom has grown, so too has our penchant for empire. The connection between these two tendencies is a causal one. In an earlier age, Americans saw empire as the antithesis of freedom. Today, as illustrated above all by the Bush administration's efforts to dominate the energy-rich Persian Gulf, empire has seemingly become a prerequisite of freedom.[27]

Divorce by the Cultural Conservatives

A third group of Bush critics are the cultural conservatives—among whom are Christopher Buckley, P. J. O'Rourk, Pat Buchanan, and Jeffrey Hart. Hart is particularly interesting. He taught English at Dartmouth for four decades. During that same period he was a regular contributor to *National Review* and at one point wrote speeches for Reagan. He characterizes himself as a Burkean. In fact, his brand of conservatism is "Burke updated." He recently quipped, "Many Republicans must feel like that legendary man at the bar on the *Titanic*. Watching the iceberg slide by outside a porthole, he remarked, 'I asked for ice. But this is too much.' Republicans voted for a Republican and got George W. Bush, but his Republican Party is unrecognizable as the party we have known."[28]

At the core of his criticism is Bush's use of evangelical piety to disguise a radical agenda. Hart wrote, "The Bush Presidency often is called conservative. This is a mistake. It is populist and radical, and its principal energies have roots in American history, and these roots are not conservative."[29] In an interview, the Dartmouth professor elaborated:

> Like the Whig gentry who were the Founders, I loathe populism. . . . Most especially in the form of populist religion, i.e., the current pestiferous bible-banging evangelicals, whom I regard as organized ignorance, a menace to public health, to science, to medicine, to serious Western religion, to intellect, and indeed to sanity. Evangelicalism, driven by emotion, and not creedal, is thoroughly erratic and by its nature cannot be conservative.[30]

Cultural conservatives mockingly prayed that Bush would be born again—this time as a true conservative![31]

Remarriage (Obamacans)

It is one thing to divorce. It is another to drive someone to marry a rival suitor. In our republican form of government, one principal way we ratify a president's leadership is to elect his successor. So, Truman ratified Franklin D. Roosevelt. Johnson ratified John F. Kennedy. George H. W. Bush ratified Ronald Reagan. In 2008, not only did John McCain not get elected, but he also did not even want to be considered Bush's successor, preferring instead to link himself to Reagan.

The prominent conservatives who threw their support to Obama include (as we have seen) Bruce Bartlett, Andrew Bacevich, Jeffrey Hart,[32] Douglas Kmiec, Andrew Sullivan, Ken Duberstein, Kathleen Parker, Antony Sullivan, and Christopher Buckley. With justification, some add to this list Bush's former secretary of state Colin Powell and the reformed neoconservative

Francis Fukuyama. The pedigree, influence, and intellectual firepower of the Obamacans suggest that Bush contributed mightily to deconstructing the edgy coalition that Buckley and Reagan had built up.

But there is nothing new or shocking in this turn of events. The conservatives who repudiated Bush and voted for Obama in 2008 were actually doing a very American thing, even a conservative thing. We forget that Russell Kirk backed Eugene McCarthy in 1968 and that *National Review* did not initially want to support Richard Nixon in 1960 and 1972. Then, as now, prominent conservatives were following a hallowed tradition going all the way back to the American Revolution: to divorce for the sake of principle rather than to suffer for the sake of politics.

Notes

1. Peggy Noonan, "Too Bad: President Bush Has Torn the Conservative Coalition Asunder," *Wall Street Journal* June 1, 2007.

2. See, for example, Isaiah Berlin, *The Crooked Timber of Humanity: Chapters in the History of Ideas*, edited by Henry Hardy (London: John Murray, 1990); and Berlin, *Against the Current: Essays in the History of Ideas*, edited by Henry Hardy (London: Pimlico, 1997).

3. Michael Ignatieff, "Getting Iraq Wrong," *New York Times Magazine* August 5, 2007. See also Ignatieff, *Isaiah Berlin: A Life* (New York: Holt, 1998).

4. Gary Gregg, in a formal debate with Burdett Loomis, "The Electoral College: An Election Year Debate," hosted by the Hauenstein Center for Presidential Studies, Grand Valley State University, April 24, 2008, available at http://main.gvsu.edu/hauenstein/?id=3060DE91-9E61-4CD5-A3EBDA15B36A62C0, accessed June 8, 2009.

5. See, for example, Joseph F. Kobylka's lectures titled "The Revolutionary Context," and "The Road to the Declaration of Independence," (Teaching Company: Chantilly, VA): 2007.

6. Russell Kirk, *The Conservative Mind: From Burke to Eliot*, 7th ed. (Chicago: Regnery, 1986), Introduction.

7. George Nash, *The Conservative Intellectual Movement in America Since 1945* (New York: Basic Books, Inc., 1976), xiii–xv.

8. Fred Barnes, *Rebel in Chief: Inside the Bold and Controversial Presidency of George W. Bush* (New York: Crown Forum, 2006), 16, 20, 21, 29.

9. "Race Summary Report: 1998 General Election," Texas Secretary of State, November 3, 1998, available at http://elections.sos.state.tx.us/elchist.exe, accessed October 16, 2008. See also Michael Janofsky, "Candidates Courting Hispanic Vote," *New York Times* June 25, 2000, available at www.nytimes.com/2000/06/25/

us/candidates-courting-hispanic-vote.html?sec=&spon=&pagewanted=all, accessed October 17, 2008.

10. Gleaves Whitney, *John Engler: The Man, the Leader, the Legacy* (Chelsea, MI: Sleeping Bear Press, 2002), 338–55.

11. "Philadelphia: The Big Speech," *National Review*, August 28, 2000.

12. In his 1996 campaign, Bob Dole received 39,198,755 or 40.7 percent of the popular vote. Four years later, George W. Bush received 50,456,002 or 47.9 percent of the popular vote. For more information, cf. University of Virginia Library's Geospacial and Statistical Data Center, "U.S. Presidential Election Maps," available at http://fisher.lib.virginia.edu/collections/stats/elections/maps/, accessed October 14, 2008.

13. See www.whitehouse.gov: The OFBCI was established by President George W. Bush through executive order on January 29, 2001.

14. Public Opinion Archives: Presidential Approval Ratings, Roper Center, University of Connecticut, available at www.ropercenter.uconn.edu/data_access/data/presidential_approval.html, accessed October 15, 2008.

15. Stephen Dinan, "Rumbling on the Hard-Line Right: Medicare Increase, Expanding Budget Irk Some Bush Supporters," *Washington Times*, December 30, 2003. Fred Barnes, "Hey Big Spenders! Under Bush, the Era of Small Government Is Over," *Weekly Standard* 9 (13), December 8, 2003.

16. Cf. Bruce Bartlett, *Reaganomics: Supply Side Economics in Action* (New York: Arlington House, Inc., 1981).

17. Bruce Bartlett, *Imposter: How George W. Bush Bankrupted America and Betrayed the Reagan Legacy* (New York: Doubleday, 2006), 16.

18. www.cbsnews.com/blogs/2008/09/29/couricandco/entry4486228.shtml, accessed November 12, 2008.

19. Ken Adelman, "Cake Walk in Iraq" *Washington Post*, February 13, 2002.

20. Andrew J. Bacevich, "I Lost My Son to a War I Oppose: We Were Both Doing Our Duty," *Washington Post*, May 27, 2007.

21. Andrew J. Bacevich, *American Empire: The Realities and Consequences of U.S. Diplomacy* (Boston, MA: Harvard University Press, 2002).

22. Andrew J. Bacevich, *American Militarism: How Americans Are Seduced by War* (New York: Oxford University Press, 2006).

23. Andrew J. Bacevich, *The Long War: A New History of U.S. National Security Policy since World War II* (New York: Columbia University Press, 2007).

24. Andrew J. Bacevich, *The Limits of American Power: The End of American Exceptionalism* (New York: Metropolitan Books, 2008).

25. Brian MacQuarrie, "Son of Professor Opposed to War Killed in Iraq," *Boston Globe*, May 15, 2007.

26. Andrew J. Bacevich, "Rescinding the Bush Doctrine," *Boston Globe*, March 1, 2007.

27. Bacevich, *The Limits of American Power*, 9.

28. www.amconmag.com/article/2006/nov/20/00013/, accessed November 13, 2008.

29. Jeffrey Hart, *The Making of the American Conservative Mind: National Review and Its Times* (Wilmington, DE: ISI Books, 2005).

30. James Panero, "How the Right Went Wrong: Professor Emeritus Jeffrey Hart '51 Doesn't Lack for Conservative Credentials, But He's Never Been on Board with the Bush Administration," *Dartmouth Alumni Magazine*, December 17, 2006.

31. www.gopusa.com/news/2006/february/0201_sotu_reaction.shtml, accessed November 13, 2008.

32. www.thedailybeast.com/blogs-and-stories/2008-10-31/obama-is-the-true-conservative/1/, accessed November 13, 2008.

PART TWO

PRESIDENTIAL POWERS
AND THE BUSH PRESIDENCY

CHAPTER SEVEN

~

War Powers in the
Bush Administration

John Yoo[1]

It is often said that George W. Bush advanced claims of executive authority farther than any other president. I believe this is an exaggeration. Presidents Thomas Jefferson, Abraham Lincoln, Franklin Roosevelt, Harry Truman, and Ronald Reagan all broadly exercised and expanded the constitutional powers of the office. Various Bush administration policies, including signing statements, executive privilege, and national security wiretaps, followed the precedents of its predecessors. Bush's exercises may have differed in number but not in kind.

This was the case with war powers. By war powers, I refer to the constitutional questions surrounding *jus ad bellum*, the right to go to war. I leave out of this chapter questions related to *jus in bello*, the rules about the conduct of hostilities once war had begun. I make this distinction for several reasons. The question whether the president or Congress has the constitutional power to decide whether to begin a war has been almost the exclusive focus of academic scholarship in this area since at least the late 1960s. Once war has begun, the constitutional balance of power would shift quite dramatically in the president's favor, or at least that appears to have been the historical practice. To understand the operation of war powers, we should examine that area—initiation of hostilities—where Congress's powers should be at their height. Finally, discussion of the powers of the president versus Congress over the conduct of war justifies an entire study of its own, one that goes well beyond the question of war initiation.

At first glance, the Bush administration did not provoke the constitutional questions that arose during previous presidencies. In both the 2001 war in Afghanistan and the 2003 invasion of Iraq, the executive branch sought and received legislation to authorize hostilities. Upon closer examination, however, the administration shared the same constitutional positions of its predecessors: the president has the constitutional authority to use force abroad to defend the security and interests of the United States. This stand was articulated in a September 25, 2001 memo that I signed while serving in the Office of Legal Counsel of the U.S. Department of Justice.[2] Justice asserted that the president had the authority to attack terrorists abroad, even before they launched an attack on the United States. This position was consistent with the views of presidents since Richard Nixon—all had refused to accept the legality of the War Powers Resolution (which prohibits presidents from deploying troops abroad for more than 60 days without congressional authorization)—and the original understanding of the Constitution itself.

This chapter will provide a more comprehensive explanation for presidential power over war. It will begin with a discussion of the state of the academic debate on war powers. It will then make the historical case against the common view that Congress must approve all wars ex ante. Instead, the Constitution allows a range of possible structures to govern war making. Then it will address functional considerations. It criticizes the assumption that congressional participation will improve decision making on war and argues that the costs of inaction can be just as great as mistakes toward war. Finally, I will argue that the changed conditions created by the September 11 terrorist attacks on the United States and the challenges posed by rogue nations and the proliferation of weapons of mass destruction further demand that our constitutional system recognize discretion on the part of the president to use force abroad.

Academic Debate over War Powers

By the time that the Bush administration took office in 2001, a conventional view on war powers had coalesced in the legal academy. Many of the nation's leading constitutional law scholars, including Bruce Ackerman, Walter Dellinger, John Hart Ely, Louis Henkin, Harold Koh, Charles Lofgren, and Laurence Tribe, among others, believe that only Congress can authorize the use of military force abroad. Wars waged by the president without congressional approval were unconstitutional. Arguing that the Framers "pursued a substantive end (the limitation of war to the absolutely necessary) by procedural means (requiring the concurrence of both houses of Congress as well as the president)" through the Declare War Clause, Ely proclaimed that wars like Korea violated the Framers' intent.[3] Louis Fisher argues that the "constitutional framework adopted by the Framers is clear in its basic principles. The authority to initiate war lay with Congress. The President could act unilaterally only in one area: to repel sudden attacks."[4]

These arguments crystallized in Ely's *War and Responsibility*, which I use as a foil here because it most clearly and simply states the consensus view. According to Ely, not only did the Constitution vest in Congress the power to declare war, but also "the [Framing] debates, and early practice, establish that this meant that all wars, big or small, 'declared' in so many words or not—most weren't, even then—had to be legislatively authorized."[5] Once Congress had given its approval for military hostilities, the president could conduct military operations. The only exception was in response to a direct attack on the United States. If presidents waged war without congressional approval, the Constitution required judicial intervention to stop them.

By requiring Congress to preapprove all wars, Ely believed, the Framers had used process to seek a substantive end. The Framers believed the executive most prone to military conflict. Introducing multiple institutions into the decision to make war would reduce the number of conflicts. If the president and Congress had to agree, Ely believed, conflicts would arise only after reason and deliberation. "The point was not to exclude the executive from the decision—if the President's not on board we're not going to have much of a war—but rather to 'clog' the road to combat by requiring the concurrence of a number of people of various points of view."[6] Deliberation would ensure not just fewer wars, but also that those wars that did occur would have broad popular support.

The pro-Congress view finds the original understanding so conclusive that it overlooks strong textual and structural clues to the contrary. These sources suggest that the Constitution does not impose a fixed method for going to war, but instead allows the political branches the flexibility to shape a variety of decision-making processes. First we turn to the constitutional text and structure. Ely bases his argument on a commonsense understanding of the power to "declare" war as the power to decide whether to start a war. The Constitution, however, does not consistently use the word *declare* to mean "begin" or "initiate." Article I, Section 10, for example, withdraws from states the power to "engage" in war; if *declare* meant "begin" or "make," the provision should have prohibited states from "declaring" war.[7] Article III defines treason as "levying War" against the United States.[8] Again, if *declare* had the clear meaning of "begin" or "wage," then Article III should have made treason the crime of "declaring war" against the United States. Eighteenth-century English speakers would have used *engage* and *levy* broadly to include beginning or waging warfare, but not *declare*, which carried the connotation of the recognition of a legal status, rather than of an authorization.

The structure of different constitutional provisions supports the notion that declaring war did not mean the same thing as beginning, conducting, or waging war. Article I, Section 10 allowed states to conduct hostilities only if Congress approved. "No State shall, without the Consent of Congress, . . . engage in War, unless actually invaded, or in such imminent Danger as will not admit of delay."[9] Here, in a nutshell, is a constitutional provision that creates the exact process that pro-Congress scholars want. It even contains the unwritten exception for unilateral responses to actual attack. If we assume that the Framers used words consistently throughout the Constitution, they should have written that "the President may not, without the Consent of Congress, engage in War, unless the United States is actually invaded, or in such imminent Danger as will not admit of delay."

We also should not overlook Article I, Section 8, Clause 11—the very provision that houses the Declare War Clause. In addition to the power to declare war, that provision also vests in Congress the power to grant letters of marque and reprisal and to make rules concerning captures.[10] Both are provisions recognizing a legal status. Rules on capture, for example, do not authorize captures in war time but only determine their ownership. Letters of marque and reprisal extend the benefits of combat immunity to private forces.[11] Reading the clauses to share a common nature suggests that the Declare War Clause similarly vested Congress with a power devoted to declarations of the international legal status of certain actions.

The Constitution makes very clear when the government must follow a specific process to take action. Article I establishes the system of bicameralism and presentment necessary to enact federal statutes.[12] Article II, Section 2 declares that presidents can make treaties subject to the advice and consent of two-thirds of the Senate, while appointments can be made subject to a majority of the Senate.[13] Both provisions establish a process, the order in which each institution acts, and the minimum votes required. In fact, the Treaty and Appointments Clauses divide power exactly as pro-Congress scholars wish. They give the president the initiative in deciding on treaties or appointments but prevent his action from becoming final until the Senate has approved. The Constitution could have easily included the power to initiate military hostilities in Article II, Section 2, too. There are no similarly defined steps for making war. Instead, the Constitution only distributes different war-related powers between the president and Congress. This suggests that the Constitution establishes no fixed procedure for war.

Looking to the broader historical context of the framing raises more doubt about the pro-Congress account. Pro-Congress scholars build their theory on the Framers' intent. While Ely acknowledged that "the 'original understanding' of the document's Framers and ratifiers can be obscure to the point of inscrutability," he flatly concluded that "[i]n this case, however, it isn't."[14] Ely relied on three pieces of evidence to support this conclusion. First, James Madison wrote that "the constitution supposes, what the History of all Governments demonstrates, that the Executive is the branch of power most interested in war, and most prone to it. It has accordingly with studied care, vested the question of war in the Legislature."[15] Second, James Wilson stated in the Pennsylvania ratifying convention that "[t]his system will not hurry us into war; it is calculated to guard against it. It will not be in the power of a single man, or a single body of men, to involve us in such distress" because the "important power of declaring war" is vested in Congress.[16] Third, Joseph Story observed that "the power of declaring war . . . is in its own nature and effects so critical and calamitous, that it requires the utmost deliberation, and the successive review of all the councils of the nation."[17]

Attention to the broader historical background, however, undermines this evidence. The quotations from Madison and Story are not directly relevant to the original understanding of those who drafted and ratified the Constitution. The former was made in a private letter to Thomas Jefferson in 1798, over a decade after the ratification and in the midst of a sharp partisan battle with the Federalists.[18] Story's comment is similarly out of time. It was made in 1833 (46 years after the federal convention) by a commentator who, no matter how astute, was only 8 years old at the time of the ratification of the Constitution. Justice Story had no personal experience that sheds light on the understanding of the document's Framers. Wilson's comments admittedly espouse a pro-Congress view of war powers. And Wilson himself was a prominent Federalist leader, perhaps second only to Madison in influence.[19] When placed in their broader historical context, however, Wilson's comments may be seen as less representative of what the framing generation would have thought on this question.

It is worth identifying briefly here a few elements of the historical context that point the story in a different direction.[20] First, the Framers would have understood the Constitution's distribution of war powers against the background of the British Constitution, which had supplied many of the legal concepts in the document. Under the British system, as described by Blackstone, the Crown exercised all of the war power. The declaration of war played the role of announcing to foreign enemies and domestic citizens a change in legal relations from peace time to war time.[21] Second, by the 18th century Parliament's control over funding became the primary legislative check over war making. In the century before the Revolution, Great Britain engaged in eight significant conflicts but declared war before the start of hostilities only once.[22]

Third, reading the Constitution to maintain the executive's ability to begin war bears more consistency with the general development of U.S. constitutional law during the framing. Under the British system, colonial governors had exercised unilateral control over the military under their command, subject to control by the assemblies over funding. State experiments in fragmenting the executive and frustration with the limited powers of the Continental Congress led nationalist reformers to seek the restoration of authority in a unified presidency.[23] Reading the Framers' treatment of war powers as vesting the power over war in Congress would run counter to this broader historical trend.[24] Fourth, details from the framing debates themselves provide evidence that some of the Constitution's supporters believed that it replicated the British system. When pressed during the Virginia ratifying convention, for example, with the charge that the President's powers could lead to a military dictatorship, Madison argued that Congress's control over funding would provide enough check to control the executive.[25]

This points the way toward a different model of war powers. A model similar to the 18th-century British Constitution suggests a more fluid, flexible approach. Rather than a strict process, like that of legislation or treaty making, war powers are exercised either through the cooperation or conflict of the president and Congress. They can work in concert, with congressional authorization and funding accompanying presidential military action. Or they can frustrate each other, with Congress cutting off funds for military hostilities or the president refusing to fight a war. This approach does not weight a process for or against war, but instead recognizes that the Constitution simply establishes no fixed, required process at all. Rather, it allows the political branches to shape the war-making process as they see fit.

Functional Considerations

Scholars of different interpretive stripes might agree that the Constitution does not mandate a single war-making process. Even those who maintain fidelity to the original meaning must admit that the historical evidence shows that there was no settled understanding in 1787–1788 on war powers. Those who have never been won over by appeals to the framing must recognize that the text and structure, standing alone, do not impose a defined decision-making process for entering into hostilities. If we admit that the Constitution does not demand a specific war-making process, then we must examine the instrumental goals of the "Congress-first" approach.

An obvious attraction of the Congress-first approach is its familiarity. It is identical to the enactment of legislation. Its effort to deploy that process to achieve deliberation, consensus, and clarity of legislative purpose builds upon the best ideals of the legal process school of the 1950s. It also has clear attraction to those working on the new legal process approaches that have so heavily influenced thinking about legislation and administrative law for the last 20 years.[26] Its reliance on the federal courts to ultimately referee the war-making process appeals to the confidence in judicial review on the part of most U.S. constitutional scholars. And lastly, its effort to reduce the amount of war itself draws upon deeply ingrained U.S. notions of our national exceptionalism.[27]

But first we must ask whether the pro-Congress approach produces the benefits it claims. It is difficult to judge with any confidence whether a Congress-first system indeed generates sufficient deliberation and consensus to ultimately result in good policy. History suggests that congressional participation does not necessarily lead to deliberation. The Mexican-American War, for example, did not result from extensive deliberation and consensus in Congress, but rather a rush to war after an alleged attack on U.S. forces along the border.[28] It resulted in the conquest of large amounts of territory that clearly benefited the United States in the long run, yet raised the divisive question of the extension of slavery to the territories.[29] Congress did not declare war against Spain in 1898 after long discussion and consultation, but rather after the destruction of the U.S.S. *Maine*.[30] Again, the conflict benefited the United States through the acquisition of an overseas empire and its emergence as a world power.[31] While World Wars I and II fit the pro-Congress model better, one wonders whether a declaration of war was necessary to achieve the consensus that prevailed in those conflicts, or whether—particularly in the case of World War II—the attack on the United States itself produced it. If Congress had simply participated in World Wars I and II by authorizing and funding the military needed to fight both conflicts, defeating Germany would still have been in the national interest.

It is also not obvious that congressional deliberation ensures consensus. Legislative authorization might reflect a bare majority of Congress or an unwillingness to challenge the president's institutional and political strengths. It is also no guarantee of consensus once combat begins. Thus, the Vietnam War, which many pro-Congress scholars admit satisfied their requirement for congressional approval, provoked some of the most divisive politics in U.S.

history.[32] It is also difficult to claim that the congressional authorizations to use force in Iraq, of either the 1991 or 2002 varieties, reflected a deep consensus over the merits of war there.[33] Indeed, the 1991 authorization barely survived the Senate, and the 2002 one received significant negative votes and has become an increasingly divisive issue in national politics.[34]

Conversely, the absence of congressional authorization does not necessarily result in less deliberation or more mistakes. Perhaps the most important example is the conflict between the United States and the Soviet Union from 1946 to 1992.[35] The United States waged war against Soviet proxies in Korea and Vietnam, the Soviet Union fought in Afghanistan, and the two almost came into direct conflict during the Cuban Missile Crisis. Yet the only war arguably authorized by Congress was Vietnam. There appeared to be a significant bipartisan consensus on the overall strategy (i.e., containment) and goal (i.e., defeat of the Soviet Union and protection of Europe and Japan). Congress consistently appropriated resources to the military to achieve them.[36] Different conflicts during this period that received no congressional authorization, such as Korea, Grenada, Panama, and Kosovo, did not suffer from a severe lack of consensus, at least at the outset. Korea initially received the support of the nation's political leadership; support declined only once battlefield losses had occurred.[37] Grenada, Panama, and Kosovo did not seem to suffer from any serious political resistance.[38]

The pro-Congress thesis is just as concerned with using constitutional process to stop "bad" wars as it is to promote political consensus for "good" ones. While trying to put aside the fortunes of war itself (a war may lead to defeat due to circumstances that could not be anticipated ex ante), we might say that a war results in bad policy when the expected costs of war outweigh its expected benefits. One can understand the pro-Congress camp as arguing that unilateral presidential war power, in which Congress does not approve hostilities ex ante, leads the nation into more military hostilities where the expected value of defeat exceeds the expected value of victory.[39] Some presidents may have higher discount rates than either Congress or the nation as a whole because of the desire for some type of historical legacy. Presidents may well be willing to engage the nation in unwise conflicts in which the expected costs might outweigh the expected benefits. Pro-Congress theorists assume that adding more institutional actors will lead to more accurate judgments about the variables involved in deciding between war and peace.

There are two reasons, however, why this assumption does not hold. First, it is not clear that more institutional deliberation produces better conflict selection. Most of the wars in the Cold War, including Kosovo, Panama, and Grenada, in addition to many of the smaller conflicts, were started by presidents unilaterally and ended successfully for the United States. To be sure, the Korean War did not. But even Korea may have succeeded in its objectives. Ex ante it appeared that U.S. intervention had every expectation of being successful, as U.S. forces (once they could reach the theater) outmatched those of North Korea.[40] The event that eventually led to the stalemate was the intervention by the People's Republic of China. U.S. leaders erred in estimating the chances that this would occur, but it does not appear that congressional involvement in the decision to go to war in Korea would have made any difference. We might even consider the possibility that the United States may have succeeded in its war aims at an acceptable cost. Although casualties were high, the United States prevented the conquest of South Korea, which has clearly benefited the Western economy, and contained Soviet and Chinese influence in East Asia. Historians will continue to argue about the merits of the Korean War, but it does not stand as an obvious example of presidential adventurism.

Second, it is not clear that congressional authorization would reduce the rate of mistakes. In regard to foreign affairs, Congress does not have independent sources of information but relies on information provided by the executive branch.[41] It is also not clear whether members of Congress will have a discount rate that more accurately represents the discount rate held by the U.S. people. While a Senator's 6-year term may give him a lower discount rate than a president, a representative might be expected to have higher discount rates due to his 2-year term. Neither, however, is elected by the nation as a whole as is the president and vice president. Collective action problems within the legislature may well prevent members of Congress from aggregating their individual preferences into one that represents the overall view of their nation.[42] Because of its election by the nation as a whole and its unitary organization under the Constitution, the presidency does not suffer from such problems.

Pro-Congress scholars focus on only one type of error. They are concerned that the president will lead the nation into a disastrous war. An error, however, can also run in the other direction: failure to enter a conflict that should be waged. Such actions could include launching a preemptive strike against a nation harboring a hostile terrorist group or entering a war to prevent the rise of a hostile power. The question is not whether the president has a higher discount rate than Congress (the president as military adventurer), but rather whether the president's discount rate more closely approximates that which is in the best interests of the nation.

In order to evaluate the Congress-first theory, it is also important to understand its potential costs. The costs may not be obvious, since grounding the use of force in ex ante congressional consent bears a close resemblance to the process for enacting legislation. The legislative process, however, increases the costs of government action. It is heavily slanted against the enactment of legislation, requiring the concurrence not just of the popularly elected House but also the state-representing Senate and the president.[43] This raises decision costs. The need for legislative concurrence creates delay, requires coordination between executive and legislature, and demands an open, public discussion of potentially sensitive information. Decision costs are found not only in the time-worn hypotheticals about whether the president can launch a preemptive strike before a nuclear attack. These costs also result from delay in using force that misses a window of opportunity, the possibility of legislative discussion alerting an enemy to a possible attack, or the uncertainty over whether congressional authorization will be forthcoming.

In the rules-standards debate, an increase in decision costs caused by placing an activity under a legal standard rather than a rule can be outweighed by a reduction in error costs.[44] A standard increases decision costs because it costs more in terms of process and it increases unpredictability and uncertainty ex ante, but it lowers error costs by allowing for the consideration of more information and shaping the decision to the facts of the case. It seems apparent that requiring congressional authorization for military hostilities would increase decision costs. On the other hand, it is not clear that there is any corresponding reduction in error costs. Error here is bringing the United States into a war where the costs outweigh the benefits, on an expected basis, or failing to wage a war where the opposite is true. My claim about the lack of a correlation between consensus and good policy, on the one hand, and ex ante legislative approval, on the other, is merely another way of saying that the Congress-first approach does not significantly reduce error costs, or that, if it does, the value of any such savings is uncertain. We simply do not know, judging from the historical record, whether ex ante legislative authorization leads to lower error costs.

The observation that a Congress-first approach is not functionally superior to the current system has important implications. If it is not clear which approach does a better job of managing error and decision costs, then the pro-executive model will perform better than the Congress-first process. It would only make sense to lock the nation into a single procedure for making war—one that could not be changed except through the supermajority vote required for a constitutional amendment—when the costs and benefits of the different possible processes are fully known and the procedure chosen maximizes the benefits. If the costs and benefits of different procedures are unclear, then the better option is to create a system with sufficient flexibility to allow the decision-making process to change in response to developments in the international system, the United States' position in the world, and the nature of warfare. This would especially be the case, it seems, if the international system and the challenges to U.S. national security themselves are undergoing rapid or significant change.

Rather than argue whether a specific war was constitutional, we should ask whether a certain war-making process instrumentally is more effective for the type of conflict when understood in its historical context. When the United States was more removed from great power conflict, as for much of the nineteenth century, a Congress-first approach was affordable. During this period, a conflict would not begin immediately, and the absence of a standing military meant that the nation required substantial time and resources to construct a fighting force before it could engage in significant military hostilities. When large-scale, total wars emerged in the first half of the 20th century, then a Congress-first system based on a declaration of war was also effective because it helped rally people and institutions to the political commitments necessary for widespread mobilization of the economy and society. At other times, such as the Cold War period, these purposes were not as important. During the Cold War, the United States maintained a permanent military establishment, pursued a long-term strategy against a persistent and capable opponent, and had consistent interests and involvement throughout the world. Rather than building political support for a rapid transformation from peace time to total war, the nation needed to conduct quick attacks or interventions with limited goals and restricted means. Congress provided continuing support by committing resources to the construction and maintenance of a standing military capable of acting swiftly and with global reach.

The pro-Congress approach calls upon the courts to adjudicate war powers disputes. An enlarged role for judicial review makes sense if the Constitution requires an exclusive method for making a decision. We should employ judicial review to police adherence to a process that we are certain that we wish to constitutionalize. But when we are unsure of the costs and benefits, embedding a single war-making process in the Constitution makes less sense. Judicial review should not be called for when several different processes are available and the costs and benefits of each are unclear due to changes in the international system and the security environment.

Many scholars have observed that courts work best at interpreting formal sources of law and applying that law to facts that are easily gathered and understood in the context of a bipolar dispute.[45] They do less well the more a dispute involves more actors, sources of law, and complicated social, economic, and political relationships. Choices by the two branches on the structure for going to war, or even a struggle between the branches over the issue, would entail calculation and comparison of costs and benefits that would be difficult, if not impossible, for courts to perform. It is hard to see how a court, in the context of a lawsuit, could accurately measure the costs and benefits to the nation of adopting a system for going to war. Indeed, no permanent rule makes sense, but rather the question depends on the security or historical context, which makes any judicial decision even more difficult.

In this sense, the debate over war powers bears a resemblance to arguments over the legitimacy of the administrative state. Pro-Congress scholars argue in favor of adherence to a single, formal process that requires congressional legislation under Article I, Section 8, followed by presidential implementation and judicial review. In this respect, they appeal to the same vision of lawmaking held by critics of the administrative state, who believe that all laws that affect private individuals must undergo bicameralism and presentment.[46] The approach presented here is similar to the arguments in favor of the administrative state. It is for the political branches to choose how to structure war decision making, just as in most areas of domestic regulation. The incentives for Congress to delegate authority in foreign and domestic areas are similar. Congress may not wish to take a stand on a war ex ante, just as it does not want to choose a particular regulatory standard because it does not have the technical expertise to make the right choice and it cannot predict whether the policy will be successful. Congress takes on less risk by allowing the executive branch to make the choice and bear the political costs.

In both contexts, the federal judiciary only polices the outer boundaries of the process. Anything more would require the courts to second-guess technical decisions or policy judgments for which they have little expertise or legitimacy, just as courts refrain from reviewing the substantive merits of administrative decision making.[47] One might respond, of course, that unlike the case of the administrative state, war powers do not involve a clear statutory delegation of congressional authority. That is true. On the other hand, unlike the administrative state, there is no clear constitutional text that delegates the war power directly to Congress rather than the president. And Congress has funded a military designed not just for homeland defense but for power projection abroad, which might be seen as an implicit delegation of authority.

Comparing the administrative state with the current war-making system also suggests that Congress has significant political controls over war making. Although Congress formally delegates broad authority to the administrative agencies, it also exercises many effective political and procedural checks on that power. If Congress disagrees with agency policy, for example, it can hold hearings to question the decision.[48] It can use funding to frustrate implementation of agency policies. It can restructure the agency or change agency jurisdictions, and it can refuse to approve nominations to agency positions. All of these tools remain available even in a system characterized by presidential initiative. If Congress disagrees with presidential war making, it can refuse to approve the funds necessary to wage the war (witness that in the Persian Gulf War and the conflicts in Kosovo, Afghanistan, and Iraq, the executive branch needed supplemental appropriations to conduct hostilities), it can refuse to approve the promotion or appointment of officers, or it can use hearings and negative publicity to force a change in policy. If it is distrustful of executive policy, Congress could even restructure the military to deny the president certain offensive weapons systems or large numbers of quickly deployable professional soldiers, as it did in the periods before World Wars I and II.

The point is not that the Constitution creates a war-making system that permits the president, in all cases, to decide whether to take the nation into war. Such an approach might lead to the unwarranted conclusion that Congress would be constitutionally required to fund these presidential war decisions or that Congress could not interfere with them.[49] Rather, the Constitution creates a system of war making with substantial flexibility provided to the political branches to shape a range of decision-making systems generated by the interaction of their plenary constitutional powers. Ultimately, this approach better explains the record of practice than does the pro-Congress thesis, which is forced to conclude that many of the nation's wars have been unconstitutional. It allows the federal government to adjust the costs and benefits of a particular decision-making system to the contemporary demands of the international system. The constitutional system permits a variety of different decision-making methods. We will see in the next part how the Constitution's war-making process might adapt to the world we live in today.

Less War, More Peace

This part addresses the broader substantive point made by pro-Congress scholars: increasing institutional participation and slowing down the decision-making process will lead to less war and more peace. They essentially believe that rendering the war-making process more difficult will produce benefits because inaction by the United States generally results in peace. This part argues that changes in the international system and the nature of new threats to the United States mean that the default state of the security environment may no longer favor inaction.

Pro-Congress scholars believe that the more institutions that participate in a decision and the slower their proceedings, the more likely that decision making will prove less emotional and more rational. But it would misunderstand the argument to assume that they are interested solely in more process for its own sake. Rather, layers of process would advance the substantive goal of promoting peace. More process will bias the government against making war. Government inaction would produce a steady state of peace. Ely, for example, believed that his methods and goals promoted the wishes of the Framers themselves. "The founders assumed that peace would (and should) be the customary state of the new republic—James Madison characterized war as 'among the greatest of national calamities'—and sought to arrange the Constitution so as to assure that expectation," he argued.[50]

This vision depends on a certain understanding of the costs of war. It assumes that war is a perilous undertaking that more likely than not will lead to disaster. Even if the nation is lucky enough to avoid disaster, war certainly will involve the loss of blood and treasure, often for little corresponding benefit. While war may be legal, pro-Congress scholars believe it should be rare. Because they view war as perhaps the greatest danger for the United States, it should only be entered into after careful deliberation by a number of different institutional actors. Slowing the process for war by creating more institutional obstacles will allow the necessary consideration and thought to occur. As Ely put it, "To invoke a more contemporary image, it takes more than one key to launch a missile: It should take quite a number to start a war."[51] War is the opposite of a public good, and the Constitution should discourage the government from creating more of it.

Pro-Congress scholars buttress their substantive argument with appeals to effectiveness. If we live in a world where war is going to occur, the United States should at least have a process that results in the optimal amount of war. Because executives, they fear, are prone to initiate unnecessary wars, a balanced institutional approach is more likely to result in the right amount of conflict. Congressional and judicial participation, they assume, will also make those few moments when the United States goes to war more likely to produce victory. If Congress is involved, it is more likely that the U.S. people as a whole will support the war. If Congress approves, it is also on record as supporting the war and less likely "later to undercut the effort."[52] Institutional participation and deliberation, under this line of thinking, more accurately reflect the wishes of the U.S. people than can the views of any single branch of government.

Significant changes in the international system and the national security interests of the United States have swept aside the assumptions that underpin these substantive goals. Ely, for example, wrote *War and Responsibility* in 1993. A number of the other major pro-Congress works also appeared around this time. Although the Cold War had recently ended, the nature of war continued to be thought of as occurring solely between nation-states. The Persian Gulf War had just witnessed a U.S.-led coalition's defeat of Iraq's grab for Kuwait—a traditional war over territory fought by the regular armed forces of nation-states. Nation-states are usually presumed to be both rational and susceptible to various levels of coercion, with force often being used only as a last resort.[53] Warfare, if it were to come, would take predictable forms with clearly identified armed forces seeking to take control over territory and civilian populations. The end of the Cold War and the Gulf War reaffirmed the centrality of the nation-state in world affairs and did nothing to dispel the prospect that any future threats to the United States would come solely from other nations. In 1993, the United States had begun to so outdistance its nearest nation-state competitors in terms of military strength and economic size that U.S. thinkers may well have assumed that there were no significant military threats on the horizon.

The disappearance of the threat of a war that could directly harm US. national security allowed policymakers and intellectuals the luxury to envision a future with far lower levels of armed conflict. The rest of the 1990s might have confirmed their hopes. There were wars, to be sure, but they were not the sort of conflicts generated by competition among the great powers. Rather, the need for the use of military force arose from the collapse of centralized authority within nation-states, or from ethnic or religious hatreds within nations, or from humanitarian disasters wrought by authoritarian regimes. Conflict in places such as Somalia, Haiti, and the former Yugoslavia allowed sufficient time for deliberation, did not raise direct threats to U.S. national security, and appeared to be undertaken more for humanitarian than security reasons.[54] They did not require the deployment of large units of the U.S. military, as did the wars in Korea and Vietnam, nor did they call for outright combat with the regular armed forces of another nation (except for Kosovo). Instead, they demanded smaller interventions with nation-building or peacekeeping goals. These wars were discretionary—the United States sent its troops out into the world to promote human rights or to bring stability to a region.

Involving more domestic institutions in the decision-making process would have made some sense. Without the demand for a rapid decision to respond to the threat of Soviet attack, the president and Congress had the time to consult and deliberate before undertaking these military actions. Because the balance between the costs and benefits of these types of military actions was more delicate, broader institutional perspectives and more time for deliberation might have produced better decision making. And the costs of inaction were low. If the humanitarian troubles in Somalia, Haiti, and Kosovo had been allowed to continue, global welfare as a whole would have dropped, but it is difficult to claim that continuing conflict in those areas would have directly harmed U.S. security. Indeed, the United States did not justify its intervention in any of these places as an exercise of self-defense.

With the Cold War over, a general presumption against war might have proved beneficial to the United States. Unlike the contest with the Soviet Union, the general costs of inaction to U.S. national security did not appear significant. It may have been terrible from a moral perspective, for example, that the United States did not send a small number of troops to Rwanda to stop genocide. But it is difficult to conclude that U.S. non-intervention had a negative impact on U.S. national security interests. Moreover, the benefits of military action for the United States were not as obvious or at least did not appear to clearly outweigh the costs. Bringing stability to parts of the world distant from core U.S. interests in Europe and East Asia did not seem to promise any great advantages. Humanitarian intervention has always been controversial in U.S. foreign policy circles, and the United States' hasty retreat in Somalia in 1993 suggests that U.S. policymakers at the time did not believe even those losses to be worth ending the humanitarian crisis there.[55] Declining to intervene in places such as Rwanda, Haiti, or Kosovo would not have allowed a rival nation-state to rise up and alter the distribution of power in the international system in a manner detrimental to the United States.

That world changed on September 11, 2001. It is no longer clear that the United States must seek to reduce the amount of war, and it is no longer clear that the constitutional system ought to be fixed so as to make it difficult to use force. Rather than disappearing from the world, the threat of war may well be increasing. Threats now come from at least three primary sources: the dissemination of weapons of mass destruction technology, rogue nations, and international terrorism.[56] Because of these developments, the optimal level of war for the United States may no longer be zero, but it may actually be dramatically higher than in the 1990s. In particular, the emergence of threats of a kind more difficult to detect and prevent may demand that the United States undertake preemptive military action to prevent these threats from coming to fruition. Further, it seems that the costs of inaction may be much higher than previously thought. In 1993, the costs to U.S. national security of refraining from the use of force in a Haiti or Kosovo would have appeared negligible. The September 11 terrorist attacks, however, demonstrate that the costs of inaction in a world of terrorist organizations, rogue nations, and more easily available weapons of mass destruction could be the possibility of a direct attack on the United States.

The Al Qaeda terrorist network poses a threat that, to be successfully defeated, may well require a resort to warfare on a more consistent and frequent basis than in the past. What makes the terrorism of September 11 different from previous examples is its reach and destructiveness—Al Qaeda can now launch attacks at the same level as some nation-states. Terrorist attacks are also more difficult to detect and prevent due to their unconventional nature. Al Qaeda terrorists, for example, blend into civilian populations, use the channels of open societies to transport personnel, material, and money, and target civilians with the object of causing massive casualties. Al Qaeda seeks to acquire weapons of mass destruction, is less reluctant than a nation-state to use them, and—since it has no population or territory to defend—seems immune to deterrence strategies.[57] Diplomacy and detection of an enemy's preparations for attack, which help address the threats posed by hostile nations, are of little use against terrorists who seek surprise attacks on civilians.

Terrorism may require the use of preemptive force well before an attack materializes. Temporal imminence finds little application here because, as September 11 showed, terrorist attacks can occur without warning because their unconventional nature allows their preparation to be concealed within the normal activities of civilian life.[58] The prospect of terrorists in possession of weapons of mass destruction only multiplies the possible magnitude of harm. To defend itself from such an enemy, the United States might need to use force earlier and more often than was the norm when nation-states generated the primary threats. It might also need to use force in different geographic locations in response to a stateless terrorist organization's dispersal of its own assets. The United States is currently fighting terrorists in Afghanistan, Yemen, Iraq, and the Philippines not because of hostility toward their governments but because Al Qaeda operates there.

In addition to the dispersed, camouflaged nature of terrorist groups, a second characteristic may render the use of force more necessary than in previous conflicts. Because Al Qaeda is not a nation, and has no territory or population, it may well be more difficult to defeat than a nation-state. Al Qaeda is similar to a traditional enemy in the resources it can command

and the damage it can inflict. It uses military force to achieve political, rather than financial, ends. But Al Qaeda is different in the sense that the traditional means of engaging in, let alone ending, a conflict do not seem to apply. Capture of a city or control over a population will not end the conflict with Al Qaeda. It is not clear whether Al Qaeda could sign a peace treaty, and even if leaders such as Osama bin Laden were caught and sought to enter into an agreement ending hostilities, it is unclear whether they could enforce it. Al Qaeda's decentralized structure may require a longer conflict than would be required against a nation-state because there is no clear way to prevail aside from defeating the organization in detail.

Rogue nations pose even more serious challenges. The Bush administration defines rogue nations as regimes that brutalize their citizens, exploit natural resources for the personal gains of their rulers, threaten their neighbors and disregard international law, seek to develop or possess weapons of mass destruction, sponsor terrorism, and "reject basic human values and hate the United States and everything for which it stands."[59] Both the Clinton and Bush administrations seemed to agree that nations such as Iran, Iraq, Libya, and North Korea qualify.[60] Putting the political rhetoric to one side, these nations share certain characteristics such as the development of weapons of mass destruction, repression of their civilian populations, and isolation from the international political and economic systems.

Rogue nations pose a special threat to U.S. national security interests not just because they seek to acquire weapons of mass destruction but because they take more risks in their foreign policy. Such nations might irrationally threaten to use weapons of mass destruction, or even spread weapons of mass destruction technology to other nations or to terrorist groups.[61] Before the proliferation of weapons of mass destruction and missile technology, rogue nations could not have posed a direct threat to the United States. Now, however, they can. Witness, for example, the looming threat of North Korean intercontinental ballistic missiles tipped with nuclear warheads, capable of reaching the United States, and the large expenditure of funds to construct a rudimentary missile defense system capable of countering them.[62]

As with terrorism, the threat posed by rogue nations may again require the United States to use force earlier and more often than in the past. Rogue nations may very well be resistant to pressure short of force. Rogue nations have isolated themselves from the international system, are less integrated into the international political economy, and repress their own populations. These facts make them less susceptible to diplomatic pressure or economic sanctions. Lack of concern for their own civilian populations renders the dictatorships that often govern rogue nations more resistant to deterrence.

North Korea, for example, appears to have continued its development of nuclear weapons despite years of diplomatic measures designed to change its course. International inspectors today are having trouble dealing with what appears to be Iran's clandestine nuclear weapons program. The United States has employed economic sanctions against both countries for decades. Suppose the United States were confronted with a North Korea armed with nuclear missiles and could only deploy a missile defense shield whose effectiveness was questionable. Given North Korea's bellicose threats against the United States and its refusal of diplomatic efforts, a resident might resort to force to prevent deployment.

Third, the nature of warfare against such unconventional enemies may well be different from the set-piece battlefield matches between nation-states. Gathering intelligence, from both electronic and human sources, about the future plans of terrorist groups may be the only way to prevent future September 11-style attacks. Covert action may prove to be the most effective tool for acting on that intelligence. Similarly, the least dangerous means for preventing rogue nations from acquiring weapons of mass destruction may depend on secret intelligence gathering and covert action, rather than open military intervention. A public revelation of the means of gathering intelligence, or discussion of the nature of covert actions taken to forestall the threat by terrorist organizations or rogue nations, could render the use of force ineffectual or sources of information useless. Suppose, for example, that U.S. intelligence agencies detected through intercepted phone calls that a terrorist group had built facilities in Yemen. A public discussion in Congress about a resolution to use force against Yemeni territory and how Yemen was identified could tip off the group, allowing terrorists to disperse and to prevent further interception of their communications.

These new threats to U.S. national security, driven by changes in the international environment, should change the way we think about the relationship between the process and substance of the war-making system. The nature and the level of threats are increasing, the magnitude of expected harm has risen dramatically, and military force unfortunately remains the most effective means for responding to those threats. It makes little sense to commit our political system to a single method for making war. At the very least we should not adopt a war-making process that contains a built-in presumption *against* using force abroad. Pro-Congress scholars use process to reach a desired substantive outcome. That outcome assumed that in the absence of government action, peace would generally be the default state. September 11 demonstrated that this assumption was unrealistic in light of the new threats to the United States.

Rather than the Congress-first approach, the constitutional system permits different war-making systems that might better address the new challenges of the post-September 11 world. One possible approach might be the one favored by the Bush administration, which sought and received a broad congressional authorization for the war against Al Qaeda.[63] While somewhat similar to the Congress-first approach, the resolution was different in important respects from previous enactments, which had authorized force in a certain place for certain goals.[64] The 2001 authorization was of broad scope and had no geographic or temporal limitation. It left to the president the choice where and when to use force and what type of action to undertake. Because it authorized force against a non-state actor, the 2001 congressional authorization conceivably permits military intervention from Afghanistan to East Africa to Indonesia. When it thought it might wish to use force against Iraq, the administration sought and received a country-specific authorization that bore closer similarities to resolutions in previous conflicts.[65] Such ex ante approval, however, could require extensive discussion of the sources of and methods for gathering intelligence, and the nature of any covert action to be used against the opponent. While it might play a useful part in mobilizing public opinion, especially as part of a series of escalating signals to a potential enemy, ex ante congressional approval might not make sense in the context of terrorist organizations or rogue nations already armed with weapons of mass destruction.

A different approach could look more like the system that had prevailed before the Bush administration. That system permitted presidents to initiate military hostilities abroad in places from Korea to Kosovo. Even if it were not involved ex ante, Congress still maintained a check on presidential initiative through its control over funding. This provides maximum flexibility to the executive branch to act with greater secrecy and expedition but potentially sacrifices public and congressional support should the intervention encounter difficulties. More consistent with a formalist approach to the separation of powers that views the branches as hermetically sealed rather than intertwined, this approach relies on the plebiscitary nature of the presidency for ex post accountability. If an open public discussion of intelligence gathering methods or covert action might cause more harm than good, then the electorate can voice its support or rejection of executive branch policies at the next presidential election.

Again, this is not to argue that a president-first approach is the only one. Rather, it is only to illustrate that different methods for deciding on war exist. It is not to deny that the joint agreement of the president and Congress can prove politically helpful even if not constitutionally necessary. Congressional approval not only can help to mobilize public opinion, but it can also lock Congress into long-term support for a conflict, thereby increasing the chances of success. Congressional resolutions may also prove more than just politically useful in the context of terrorism. September 11 wrought another significant change in the U.S. national security situation by blurring the line between war and the home front. Because of the United States' envious geographic position, wars traditionally had occurred abroad and hostilities never reached the homeland. It was this distinction that allowed the Court in the *Steel Seizure Case* to distinguish between the Commander-in-Chief's broad powers in a foreign theater of war and Congress's authority over domestic industrial regulation.[66] The struggle against Al Qaeda, however, does not follow those neat lines, as the September 11 attacks themselves demonstrated. Al Qaeda agents clearly have operated, and continue to seek to operate, within the United States itself, and the federal government correspondingly may need to take the rare step of conducting military operations domestically. Congressional authorization will bolster the legal and political authority of the executive branch for domestic operations.

Conclusion

Developments in the international system have rendered obsolete the goal of pro-Congress scholars to reduce the amount of conflict. They believed that war was a scourge and that our constitutional processes should be designed to discourage its use. Weapons of mass destruction proliferation, the rise of international terrorism, and the persistence of rogue states, however, have made the use of force more necessary and the prospects for a millennial peace less likely. At the same time, the demands of rapid strikes against international terrorists and rogue states may make ex ante consultation with Congress impractical if not self-defeating, although Congress would retain a substantial check on presidential war making through its ex post funding powers. Balanced institutional participation and greater deliberation may do a better job than sole presidential initiative in committing the nation to a war today that shows no sign of disappearing. We should understand, however, that the Constitution permits, but does not compel, this choice.

Notes

1. I am grateful for the comments of Jesse Choper, Dan Farber, Phil Frickey, Paul Mishkin, and Jide Nzelibe on a previous draft of this essay. Will Trachman provided excellent research assistance. I am grateful for the financial support of the Boalt Hall Fund.

2. Memorandum for the Deputy Council to the President, From: John C. Yoo, Deputy Assistant Attorney General, Office of Legal Counsel, U.S. Department of Justice, The President's Constitutional Authority to Conduct Military Operations Against Terrorists and Nations Supporting Them, (Sept. 25, 2001), available at www.usdoj .gov/olc/warpowers925.htm. Memorandum for the Deputy Council to the President, From: John C. Yoo, Deputy Assistant Attorney General, Office of Legal Counsel, U.S. Department of Justice, The President's Constitutional Authority to Conduct Military Operations Against Terrorists and Nations Supporting Them, (Sept. 25, 2001), available at www.usdoj.gov/olc/warpowers925.htm (accessed June 2, 2009). For my general approach to war powers, see John Yoo, *The Powers of War and Peace: The Constitution and Foreign Affairs after 9/11* (Chicago: Univ. of Chicago Press, 2005).

3. John Hart Ely, *War and Responsibility: Constitutional Lessons of Vietnam and its Aftermath* (Princeton: Princeton University Press, 1993).

4. Louis Fisher, *Presidential War Power* (Lawrence: University of Kansas Press, 1995). Recently, younger scholars, such as Saikrishna Prakash, Michael Ramsey, Jane Stromseth, and William Treanor, have agreed that the framing materials demonstrate that Congress must give its approval before the use of force abroad (except in cases of responding to a direct attack on the United States). See, for example, Saikrishna Prakash, "Unleashing the Dogs of War: What the Constitution Means by 'Declare War,'" 93 *Cornell Law Review* 45 (2007); Michael D. Ramsey, "Textualism and War Powers," 69 *University of Chicago Law Review* 1543 (2002); Jane E. Stromseth, "Rethinking War Powers: Congress, the President, and the United Nations," 81 *Georgia Law Journal* 597 (1993); William M. Treanor, "Fame, the Founding, and the Power to Declare War," 82 *Cornell Law Review* 695, 700 (1997). I have disagreed with these claims. See, for example, Robert J. Delahunty and John Yoo, "Making War," 93 *Cornell Law Review* 123 (2007); John Yoo, "War, Responsibility, and the Age of Terrorism," 57 *Stanford Law Review* 793 (2004); John Yoo, "War and the Constitutional Text," 69 *University Chicago Law Review* 1639 (2002).

5. Ely, *War and Responsibility*, *supra* note 2, at 3 (footnotes omitted).

6. Ely, *War and Responsibility*, *supra* note 2, at 4 (quotation and footnote omitted).

7. U.S. Constitution, Article I, § 10.

8. U.S. Constitution, Article III, § 3.

9. U.S. Constitution, Article I, § 10.

10. U.S. Constitution, Article 1, § 8.

11. See John C. Yoo, "The Continuation of Politics by Other Means: The Original Understanding of War Powers," 84 *Cal. L. Rev.* 167, 250–52 (1996).

12. U.S. Constitution, Article I, § 7. For a valuable discussion of this point, see Bradford R. Clark, "Separation of Powers as a Safeguard of Federalism," 79 *Texas Law Review* 1321 (2001).

13. U.S. Constitution, Article II, § 2.

14. Ely, *War and Responsibility*, *supra* note 2, at 3.

15. James Madison to Thomas Jefferson, Apr. 2, 1798, in *Writings of James Madison*, edited by Galliard Hunt (New York: Knickerbocker Press, 1906), 312–13.

16. "The Pennsylvania Convention, 20 November–15 December 1787," in *The Documentary History of the Ratification of the Constitution*, edited by Merill Jensen (Madison: WHS Press, 1976), 321, 583, statement by James Wilson to the ratifying convention on Dec. 11, 1787.

17. Joseph Story, *Commentaries on the Constitution of the United States*, edited by Ronald D. Rotunda and John E. Nowak (Durham: Carolina Academic Press, 1987), § 570.

18. Letter from James Madison to Thomas Jefferson (Apr. 2, 1798), in The *Writings of James Madison*, 312. For a discussion of the historical context of the letter, see Stanley Elkins and Eric McKitrick, *The Age of Federalism* (New York: Oxford University Press, 1993), 581–618; John C. Yoo, "Clio at War: The Misuse of History in the War Powers Debate," 70 *U. Colo. L. Rev.* 1169, 1183 (1999).

19. See, for example, Akhil Amar, "Of Sovereignty and Federalism," 97 *Yale Law Journal* 1425, 1439 n.57 (1987). "Although his name has unfortunately faded from American constitutional folklore, Wilson's role as a chief architect of the Constitution has long been recognized by historians.".

20. For a more complete account, see Yoo, *The Continuation of Politics, supra* note 7, at 196–290, *supra* note 7, at 1191–1208.

21. William Blackstone, *Commentaries* (Oxford: Clarendon Press, 1765–1769): 249–50, 254–58; see also Yoo, *The Continuation of Politics, supra* note 7, at 204–8.

22. Yoo, *The Continuation of Politics, supra* note 7, at 214–17.

23. Yoo, *The Continuation of Politics, supra* note 7, at 252–54.

24. Yoo, *The Continuation of Politics, supra* note 7, at 222–23, 228–34.

25. *The Virginia Convention, 2–27 June 1788* (Continued), in *The Documentary History of the Ratification of the Constitution*, volume 10, *supra* note 19, at 1179, 1282, statement of James Madison to the ratifying convention on June 14, 1788.

26. See William Eskridge, Jr., and Philip P. Frickey, *Publication Editors' Preface* to *The Legal Process: Basic Problems in the Making and Application of Law*, edited by Henry M. Hart, Jr., and Albert M. Sacks, (Eagan, MN: West Publishing Co., 1998), xi.

27. See, for example, Felix Gilbert, *To the Farewell Address: Ideas of Early American Foreign Policy* (Princeton: Princeton University Press, 1961), discussing the relationship between isolationism and idealism in early American foreign policy; Walter A. McDougall, *Promised Land, Crusader State: The American Encounter with the World since 1776* (Boston: Houghton Mifflin Harcourt, 1998), at 15–38, discussing the tradition of exceptionalism in U.S. foreign policy.

28. The events leading up to the Mexican-American War are detailed in David M. Pletcher, *The Diplomacy of Annexation: Texas, Oregon, and the Mexican War* (Columbia: University of Missouri Press, 1973).

29. See Jerald A. Combs, *American Diplomatic History: Two Centuries of Changing Interpretations* (Berkeley: University of California Press, 1983), 56–61,discussing accusations of slavery interests behind Mexican-American War.

30. The Spanish-American War and the events leading up to it are detailed in Ernest R. May, *Imperial Democracy: The Emergence of America as a Great Power* (New

York: Harcourt, 1961), 196–254; H. Wayne Morgan, *America's Road to Empire: The War with Spain and Overseas Expansion* (New York: Wiley, 1965).

31. McDougall, *Promised Land, Crusader State, supra* note 33 at 117–21, evaluating the significance of the Spanish-American War; see also Walter LaFeber, *The American Search for Opportunity, 1865–1913*, (New York: Cambridge University Press, 1993), 180; Akira Iriye, *The Globalizing of America, 1913–1945*, (New York: Cambridge University Press, 1993), 34–35, "[I]n the wake of the Spanish-American War, the nation had steadily extended its influence [in Central America and the Caribbean] through various means: annexation (Puerto Rico), a protectorate (Cuba), military occupation (the Canal Zone), customs receivership (Santo Domingo), and political intervention (Nicaragua)."

32. See, for example, Walter LaFeber, *The American Age: U.S. Foreign Policy at Home and Abroad, 1750 to the Present* (New York: Norton, 1994), 614–18, describing domestic opposition to Vietnam War.

33. The 1991 authorization to use force in the Persian Gulf barely passed. The Authorization for Use of Military Force against Iraq Resolution, Pub. L. No. 102-1, 105 Stat. 3 (1991), passed the House by 250 to 183 and in the Senate by 52 to 47. See Adam Clymer, "Confrontation in the Gulf—Congress Acts to Authorize War in Gulf," *New York Times* January 13, 1991.

34. H.R. 114, 107th Cong. (2002) became the Authorization for Use of Military Force against Iraq Resolution of 2002, Pub. L. No. 107-243, 116 Stat. 1498, passing by a vote of 296 to 133 in the House and 77 to 23 in the Senate. See Allison Mitchell and Carl Hulse, "Congress Authorizes Bush to Use Force against Iraq, Creating a Broad Mandate," *New York Times* October 11, 2002. The continuing controversy over the war in Iraq was perhaps most salient in the 2004 presidential campaign, in which John Kerry attacked the merits of the Bush administration's decision to go to war, and tracking polls the day before the election showed that Iraq was considered by a plurality of voters (26%) to be the most important issue in the election. "Charting the Campaign," November 1, 2004, available at www.washingtonpost.com/wp-srv/politics/elections/2004/charting.html, accessed June 2, 2009).

35. See generally John Lewis Gaddis, *The Long Peace: Inquiries into the History of the Cold War* (New York: Oxford University Press, 1987).

36. The strategy of containment and its demand for greater military resources is discussed in John Lewis Gaddis, *Strategies of Containment: A Critical Appraisal of Postwar American National Security Policy* (New York: Oxford University Press, 1982), 89–126, describing buildup in U.S. military required by NSC-68 and containment; Melvyn P. Leffler, *A Preponderance of Power: National Security, the Truman Administration, and the Cold War* (Stanford: Stanford University Press1992); McDougall, *Promised Land, Crusader State, supra* note 33, at 147–71; Daniel Yergin, *Shattered Peace: The Origins of the Cold War and the National Security State* (Boston: Houghton Mifflin, 1977).

37. See Yoo, *The Continuation of Politics, supra* note 7, at 178, describing widespread support for U.S. intervention at outset of Korean War and rising opposition to the war later.

38. See John C. Yoo, "Kosovo, War Powers, and the Multilateral Future," 148 *U. Pa. L. Rev.* 1673, 1879–1885 (2000), describing votes on authorizing and funding conflict.

39. In a related vein, William Treanor argues that the Framers believed that executives were more prone to military adventurism because of the pursuit of fame and glory. Treanor, "Fame, the Founding, and the Power to Declare War," *supra* note 3, at 695.

40. See Warren I. Cohen, *America in the Age of Soviet Power* (New York: Cambridge University Press, 1993), 68, describing reversal of North Korean gains upon arrival of U.S. forces. For more detailed historical discussion of the Korean War, see generally Bruce Cumings, *Origins of the Korean War* (2 vols.) (Princeton: Princeton University Press, 1981, 1990); Burton I. Kaufman, *The Korean War* (Philadelphia: Temple University Press, 1986); William Stueck, *Rethinking the Korean War: A New Diplomatic and Strategic History* (Princeton: Princeton University Press, 2002).

41. William G. Howell, *Power Without Persuasion: The Politics of Direct Presidential Action* (Princeton: Princeton University Press, 2003), 25–54, discussing Congress's structural disadvantages in informationally complex areas such as foreign affairs.

42. See generally David Epstein and Sharyn O'Halloran, *Delegating Powers: A Transaction Cost Politics Approach to Policy Making Under Separate Powers* (New York: Cambridge University Press, 1999), discussing transaction cost problems with the organization of Congress.

43. See Jesse H. Choper, *Judicial Review and the National Political Process: A Functional Reconsideration of the Role of the Supreme Court* (Chicago: University of Chicago Press, 1980), 23–25, discussing constitutional, procedural, and political obstacles to enactment of legislation.

44. See, for example, Richard A. Epstein, *Simple Rules for a Complex World* (Cambridge: Harvard University Press, 1995), 20–36; Louis Kaplow, "Rules Versus Standards: An Economic Analysis," 42 *Duke Law Journal* 557 (1992); Cass R. Sunstein, "Problems with Rules," 83 *California Law Review* 953 (1995); Adrian Vermeule, "Interpretive Choice," 75 *New York University Law Review* 74, 91 n.68 (2000).

45. See Lon L. Fuller, "The Forms and Limits of Adjudication," 92 *Harvard Law Review* 353 (1978); Paul Mishkin, "Federal Courts as State Reformers," 35 *Washington and Lee Law Review* 949 (1978). But see Owen Fiss, "The Charlotte-Mecklenburg Case: Its Significance for Northern School Desegregation," 38 *University of Chicago Law Review* 697 (1971); Judith Resnick, "Managerial Judges," 96 *Harvard Law Review* 374 (1982).

46. See, for example, Gary S. Lawson, "The Rise and Rise of the Administrative State," 107 *Harvard Law Review* 1231, 1237–41 (1994).

47. See, for example, *Chevron*, 467 U.S. at 843-44; see also Laurence H. Silberman, "Chevron—The Intersection of Law and Policy," 58 *George Washington Law Review* 821 (1990).

48. See generally Peter Strauss, "The Place of Agencies in the Government: Separation of Powers and the Fourth Branch," 84 *Columbia Law Review* 573 (1984).

49. See, for example, J. Gregory Sidak, "To Declare War," 41 *Duke L.J.* 27, 99 (1991).

50. Ely, *War and Responsibility, supra* note 2, at 3 (footnotes omitted). Madison's comment comes from *Records of the Federal Convention of 1787, supra* note 18, at 316.

51. Ely, *War and Responsibility, supra* note 2, at 4.

52. Ely, *War and Responsibility, supra* note 2, at 4.

53. See, for example, John J. Mearsheimer, *The False Promise of International Institutions,* 19 *Int'l Security* 5, 9–14 (1994–1995); *see generally* Kenneth N. Waltz, *A Theory of International Politics* (Reading, MA: Addison-Wesley, 1979).

54. See Yoo, *Kosovo, supra* note 7, at 1675–85, 1706–8, discussing these new conflicts.

55. See John Norton Moore, "Beyond the Democratic Peace: Solving the War Puzzle," 44 *Va. J. Int'l L.* 341, 400–401 (2004).

56. See John Yoo, "Using Force," 71 *University of Chicago Law Review* 729 (2004).

57. National Security Council, "The National Security Strategy of the United States of America," (2002), available at www.whitehouse.gov/nsc/nss.pdf, accessed June 2, 2009.

58. See Yoo, *Using Force, supra* note 68.

59. National Security Council, "The National Security Strategy," *supra* note 69, at 13–14.

60. These nations were listed as terrorist-sponsoring states long before President Bush took office. See Moore, *Beyond the Democratic Peace, supra* note 64.

61. National Security Council, "The National Security Strategy," *supra* note 69, at 13–16.

62. See John Yoo, "Politics as Law? The Anti-Ballistic Missile Treaty, the Separation of Powers, and Treaty Interpretation," 89 *California Law Review* 851, 901–14 (2001), discussing policy imperatives behind national missile defense program.

63. Authorization for Use of Military Force, Pub. L. No. 107-40, 115 Stat. 224 (2001).

64. See, for example, Authorization for Use of Military Force against Iraq Resolution, Pub. L. No. 102-1, 105 Stat. 3 (1991), authorizing use of force against Iraq to achieve specific United Nations Security Council resolutions calling on member nations to remove Iraq from Kuwait.

65. Authorization for Use of Military Force Against Iraq Resolution of 2002, Pub. L. No. 107-243, 116 Stat. 1498.

66. *Youngstown Sheet & Tube Co. v. Sawyer,* 343 U.S. 579, 642 (1952), J. Jackson concurring: "[N]o doctrine that the Court could promulgate would seem to me more sinister and alarming than that a President whose conduct of foreign affairs is so largely uncontrolled, and often even is unknown, can vastly enlarge his mastery over the internal affairs of the country by his own commitment of the Nation's armed forces to some foreign venture."

~

CHAPTER EIGHT

Bush and the War Power: A Critique from Outside

Louis Fisher

George W. Bush was not the first president to press the bounds of executive authority, engage in military operations not authorized by Congress, or exercise "inherent" powers not subject to the control of the legislative and judicial branches. But no president in U.S. history so consistently violated statutes and treaties by relying on confidential legal memos and secret policies. The damage he did to the office of the presidency, constitutional limits, individual rights, the U.S. economy, and the United States' standing in the world will be felt for many generations.

Precedents for Emergency Power

It is well established that executives in times of danger from abroad or within can take certain actions that lack legislative authority. Writing in 1690, John Locke understood that in some circumstances an executive must be left free to act in accordance with his perception of the public good. Legislatures could not anticipate and provide by laws everything needed to protect the community. In extraordinary conditions, an executive needed to act "for the good of the society" until lawmakers could assemble and pass remedial legislation. A strict and rigid observance of the laws, Locke said, might do more harm than temporarily vesting in the executive the duty to safeguard the community. The power to take action "according to discretion for the public good, without the prescription of the law and sometimes even against it, is that which is called prerogative." Locke placed certain limits on emergency power. It had to be invoked for the good of the people "and not manifestly against it." It was understood that the executive, after responding to a crisis, would come to the legislative branch, explain what had been done, and seek legislative approval.[1]

At the Philadelphia Convention, the Framers of the U.S. Constitution recognized that the president possessed an implied power to respond to emergencies. It was initially decided to give Congress the power to "make war," but Charles Pinckney objected that legislative proceedings "were too slow" for the country in the event of danger. Also, Congress might not be in session. James Madison and Elbridge Gerry moved to insert "declare" for make," thereby "leaving to the Executive the power to repel sudden attacks." Their motion carried.[2] This trust in executive judgment applied only to purely defensive actions in a time of emergency. Decisions to take the country from a state of peace to a state of war were left to the deliberative process of Congress.

In 1792, Congress debated legislation to establish a uniform militia drawn from the various states. The purpose of this military force was to suppress insurrections and repel invasions. To curb unwarranted use of the militia, lawmakers adopted language to require a state to request assistance in case of an insurrection. In addition, a Supreme Court Justice or district judge had to notify the president of the emergency conditions. President George Washington abided by this judicial check when he called out the militia to put down the Whiskey Rebellion in 1794.[3]

President Thomas Jefferson understood the difference between defensive and offensive actions. In 1801, he took certain defensive actions against the Barbary pirates in the Mediterranean but immediately came to Congress to request further authority. He said he was "unauthorized by the Constitution, without the sanctions of Congress, to go beyond the line of defense." It was up to Congress to authorize "measures of offense also."[4] Congress proceeded to pass at least 10 statutes explicitly authorizing military action against the Barbary pirates.[5] Later, Jefferson explained why it might be necessary for a president to act without specific legislative authority. After Congress had recessed in 1807, a British vessel fired on the U.S. ship *Chesapeake*. Responding to the emergency, Jefferson ordered military purchases but reported his actions to Congress after it convened. "To have awaited a previous and special sanction by law," he said, "would have lost occasions which might not be retrieved."[6]

In April 1861, with Congress in recess, President Abraham Lincoln invoked the Lockean prerogative by taking a number of extraordinary actions in the face of civil war. He issued proclamations calling forth state militias, suspending the writ of habeas corpus, withdrawing funds from the treasury without an appropriation, and placing a blockade on the rebellious states. Like Jefferson, he explained his actions to Congress when it convened. He said his actions, "whether strictly legal or not, were ventured upon under what appeared to be a popular demand and a public necessity, trusting then, as now, that Congress would readily ratify them."[7] In this manner he conceded that he lacked full constitutional authority to act as he did. Congress passed legislation retroactively approving his actions.[8]

In 1863, the Supreme Court upheld Lincoln's blockade. Justice Robert Grier, however, sharply limited presidential power to internal, defensive actions, noting that the president "has no power to initiate or declare a war against either a foreign nation or a domestic State."[9] The lawyer representing Lincoln in this case acknowledged that presidential actions during the Civil War had nothing to do with the right "to initiate a war, as a voluntary act of sovereignty. That is vested only in Congress."[10]

From 1789 to 1950, Congress either declared or authorized all major U.S. military actions. That pattern changed abruptly in June 1950 when President Harry Truman sent U.S. troops to Korea without ever coming to Congress for authority, either before or after. For "authority," he pointed to two resolutions passed by the United Nations (UN) Security Council. Nothing in the history of the UN Charter or in the Senate's debate on this treaty recognized any unilateral power of the president to engage in military action. In fact, Congress passed the UN Participation Act of 1945 explicitly requiring the president to seek congressional authority in advance of any military action through the UN machinery.[11] Congress, as an institution, never challenged this illegal action by Truman, preferring to form a common front against the possible spread of communism in Asia. Truman's initiative became a precedent for other presidents circumventing Congress, either by going to the UN Security Council for authority or to North Atlantic Treaty Organization (NATO) countries, as President Bill Clinton did in 1999 when he ordered military operations in Kosovo.[12]

Adding the Element of Secrecy

In these examples, presidents at times took the initiative in using military force but promptly presented their actions to Congress for legislative consideration and judgment. What the president did was public and could be debated by lawmakers and citizens. Democratic checks are not available when presidents act in secret. President Dwight D. Eisenhower was critical of Truman's action in Korea, for both political and constitutional reasons.

He wanted to restore executive-legislative coordination: "I deem it necessary to seek the cooperation of the Congress. Only with that cooperation can we give the reassurance needed to deter aggression."[13] Joint action by the president and Congress would send a strong signal both to allies and to enemies. At one meeting he reminded top congressional leaders that "the Constitution assumes that our two branches of government should get along together."[14]

Although Eisenhower pledged to work cooperatively with Congress in sharing military initiatives, he approved a number of covert operations without seeking legislative authority. In 1953, the Central Intelligence Agency (CIA) helped undermine the Mohammad Mossadegh regime in Iran and placed the Shah back on the throne. Through another CIA operation, the Eisenhower administration ousted the Jacobo Arbenz government in Guatemala in 1954.[15] Eisenhower and CIA advisers orchestrated the ill-conceived Bay of Pigs invasion of Cuba, conducted by President John F. Kennedy in 1961.[16]

The escalation of the Vietnam War began when President Lyndon B. Johnson came to Congress in August 1964 to request, and obtain, the Gulf of Tonkin Resolution. That part was in the open. Concealed, however, were funds and assistance given to the "Free World Forces" for contributing soldiers, engineers, and equipment to military action in Southeast Asia. Johnson praised such countries as the Philippines, Thailand, and South Korea for joining in the fight against communism. Congressional investigations later disclosed that the Johnson administration had been secretly subsidizing this help by providing funds, loans, and other inducements.[17]

During the early 1980s, the Ronald Reagan administration pursued a supposedly secret war by helping Contra rebels fight the Sandinistas in Nicaragua. The operation was too large to remain hidden. Newspapers and magazine articles publicly discussed the ongoing military operations. A May 1983 report by the House Intelligence Committee admitted: "This is no longer a covert operation. The public can read or hear about it daily. Anti-Sandinista leaders acknowledge U.S. aid."[18] Members of Congress introduced legislation to deny funds to the CIA and the Defense Department to furnish any military assistance to groups and individuals in Nicaragua.

In 1984, Congress enacted the Boland Amendment to delete all funds for the Contras. The statutory language was explicit: "During fiscal year 1985, no funds available to the Central Intelligence Agency, the Department of Defense, or any other agency or entity of the United States involved in intelligence activities may be obligated or expended for the purpose or which would have the effect of supporting, directly or indirectly, military or paramilitary operations in Nicaragua by any nation, group, organization, movement, or individual."[19]

Nonetheless, the Reagan administration took steps to circumvent the statutory prohibition. Executive branch officials actively solicited funds from private parties and foreign governments to assist the Contras. The illegalities first became public in November 1986, when details of what became known as the Iran-Contra Affair appeared in a newspaper in Beirut. The Reagan administration had sold arms to Iran (in violation of its publicly declared policy) and had sent weapons and aid to the Contras (violating the Boland Amendment). Investigation and prosecution by Independent Counsel Lawrence E. Walsh resulted in convictions and prison time for a number of federal officials and private citizens. More officials would have been indicted and convicted had President George H. W. Bush not pardoned six Iran-Contra figures, including three from the CIA, in December 1992.[20]

Military Tribunals and Enemy Combatants

In response to the terrorist attacks of September, the Bush administration initially acted publicly and worked jointly with Congress. President Bush twice came to Congress for statutory authority to commit U.S. troops to combat: in Afghanistan in 2001 and in Iraq the following year. The Authorization for Use of Military Force (AUMF) in 2001 passed the Senate 98 to 0 and the House 420 to 1. It authorized the president to use "all necessary and appropriate force against those nations, organizations, or persons he determines planned, authorized, committed, or aided" the September 11 attacks.[21] At the time of U.S. intervention in Afghanistan, the country was in the midst of a civil war, with the Northern Alliance (consisting primarily of Tajiks and Uzbeks) fighting against the Taliban. A team of CIA paramilitary officers carried cash to Afghanistan to enlist the support of members of the Northern Alliance. U.S. forces were on the ground to direct air strikes. Northern Alliance forces captured Kabul, the capital of Afghanistan, on November 12, 2001. Other regions of the country gradually fell, but Taliban and Al Qaeda forces continued to operate throughout Afghanistan and on the border with Pakistan.

On November 13, 2001, President Bush began the first of many unilateral actions, based on what he considered to be his exclusive powers under Article II of the Constitution. He issued a military order to authorize the creation of military tribunals to try any individual "not a United States citizen" (a population of about 18 million people inside U.S. borders) who provided assistance to the September 11 attacks. He acted without touching base with anyone in Congress, including the Judiciary and Armed Services Committees. Had he sought legislative authority, it is reasonably certain he would have obtained it, although perhaps at the cost of compromising on some language. In return for that accommodation, he would have had the legitimacy and credibility of statutory authority. But key figures within the administration were adamantly opposed to conceding any role for Congress. They insisted that President Bush possessed ample and unquestioned authority under his Article II powers as commander in chief.[22]

In addition to acting unilaterally against aliens, the Bush administration argued that it had authority to hold U.S. citizens indefinitely as "enemy combatants." The two citizens were Yaser Esam Hamdi and Jose Padilla. Hamdi was captured in Afghanistan, held at the U.S. naval base at Guantanamo Bay in Cuba, and moved to a naval brig at the Norfolk Naval Station and from there to a brig in Charleston, South Carolina. He was designated an enemy combatant but never charged with any crime or given access to an attorney. After years of litigation his case reached the Supreme Court in 2004. A plurality of four Justices decided that the AUMF constituted "explicit congressional authorization for the detention of individuals," even though it agreed that the AUMF never referred to detention.[23]

The plurality endorsed Hamdi's right to "a fair opportunity to rebut the Government's factual assertions before a neutral decisionmaker," drawing attention to previous rulings that due process requires a "neutral and detached judge."[24] It expressed satisfaction with some kind of review panel within the executive branch, perhaps even "an appropriately authorized and properly constituted military tribunal."[25] No review panel within the executive branch, much less within the military, could possibly possess the plurality's sought-for qualities of neutrality, detachment, independence, and impartiality in passing judgment on President Bush's designation of Hamdi as an enemy combatant.

Eight Justices rejected the administration's central proposition that Hamdi's detention was quintessentially a presidential decision and could not be reevaluated or overturned by the courts. They decided they had the institutional authority and competence to review and override presidential judgments in the field of national security. The plurality agreed on this core principle: "we necessarily reject the Government's assertion that separation of powers principles mandate a heavily circumscribed role for the courts in such circumstances. . . . Whatever power the United States envisions for the Executive in its exchanges with other nations or with enemy organizations in times of conflict, it most assuredly envisions a role for all three branches when individual liberties are at stake."[26] On that central value four other justices joined. Only Justice Clarence Thomas disagreed, holding that federal courts lack competence to decide such matters.

One problem with the treatment of Hamdi was the administration's dependence on the "Mobbs Declaration," a statement signed by Michael H. Mobbs, a Pentagon official. The declaration drew from intelligence sources and unnamed informants to justify the detention of Hamdi. Mobbs had no direct knowledge of Hamdi and remained at arm's length from evidence or the credibility of the informants. As one district judge remarked, the declaration by Mobbs was "little more than the government's 'say-so' regarding the validity of Hamdi's classification as an enemy combatant."[27] A dissent by an appellant judge described the Mobbs affidavit as purely a hearsay statement by "an unelected, otherwise unknown, government 'advisor.'" Mobbs did not claim "*any* personal knowledge of the facts surrounding Hamdi's capture and incarceration."[28]

Was Hamdi an enemy combatant or someone in the wrong place at the wrong time? Held incommunicado and never charged or brought to trial, he had no right to see the purported evidence against him or to know the names of the informants who supplied it. How credible was information furnished by members of the Northern Alliance? Did they have a financial incentive to identify individuals as Taliban or Al Qaeda? According to newspaper reports, Northern Alliance commanders expected to receive $5,000 when they designated someone as Taliban and $20,000 for individuals thought to be Al Qaeda fighters.[29]

After the Supreme Court's decision in the Hamdi case in 2004, the administration created combatant status review tribunals (CSRTs) to determine whether a detainee was an enemy combatant. Instead of deciding what kind of trial procedure should be used for Hamdi, the administration released him and sent him to Saudi Arabia. If there was credible evidence that he was a dangerous terrorist and a threat not merely to the United States but to civilized society, why did the administration set him free?

The treatment of the second U.S. citizen, Jose Padilla, raised additional questions about the administration's detention policy. Born in New York, Padilla was held by the military after September 11 as a suspect in a plot to detonate a radiological dispersal device (or "dirty bomb") in the United States. The Federal Bureau of Investigation (FBI) arrested him in Chicago on May 8, 2002, as a material witness to secure his testimony before a grand jury in New York City. During that period he was represented by counsel, but within a month he was designated an enemy combatant by President Bush, the material witness warrant was withdrawn, and the Defense Department moved him to a naval brig in Charleston, South Carolina. He was not charged, given counsel, or tried. Only after the Supreme Court on February 20, 2004, agreed to hear his case was he given limited rights to legal counsel.

As with Hamdi, the government prepared a "Mobbs Declaration" to make certain statements about Padilla, drawing on intelligence sources and confidential informants. The declaration raised substantial questions about the credibility and reliability of the sources.[30] A district court rejected the administration's position that a "some evidence" standard was sufficient to support the lawfulness of Padilla's detention. The record prepared by the executive branch consisted "solely of the government's evidence, to which the government's adversary has not been permitted to respond."[31] An appellate court held that the president lacked inherent constitutional authority as commander in chief to detain U.S. citizens on U.S. soil outside a zone of combat. It further held that the AUMF did not authorize Padilla's detention.[32]

When the Supreme Court held oral argument on April 28, 2004, much of the discussion centered on where the habeas petition challenging Padilla's confinement should be filed: in New York City or in South Carolina? Who was the custodian of Padilla? Neither the government's attorney nor the justices could find much legal clarity on this issue.[33] Nevertheless, the Supreme Court divided 5 to 4 in deciding that the petition should have been filed in South Carolina, thus sending the case back down to district court for another round of litigation.[34] The government prevailed in the Fourth Circuit, but may have concluded that five justices were prepared to rule against it. Padilla was removed from military custody, prosecuted in civil court, and found guilty of terrorism conspiracy charges. He was sentenced to 17 years in prison. In announcing the decision, the trial judge said that the government had offered no evidence linking Padilla to any specific terrorism act or engaging in any plot to overthrow the U.S. government.[35]

Guantanamo and Torture Memos

During military operations in Afghanistan in late 2001, U.S. forces captured several thousand individuals thought to be associated with the Taliban or Al Qaeda. Suspected terrorists were also captured in Pakistan, Bosnia, Gambia, and other countries. Hundreds were brought to the U.S. naval base at Guantanamo, Cuba. Over time, it was discovered that large numbers of detainees were innocent people erroneously swept up in military operations. Gradually they were released. Two legal issues preoccupied the administration. Did detainees at the naval base have access to federal courts? What methods of interrogation could be used to obtain needed information on the war against terrorism?

Military interrogators had long understood that persons being questioned were protected by the Geneva conventions and that coercive methods were prohibited. Acts in violation of those military regulations were criminal acts punishable under the Uniform Code of Military Justice.[36] Military interrogators learned that torture or abusive techniques were not necessary to gain necessary information, and that those techniques yielded unreliable results because individuals subjected to pain will say whatever they think the interrogator wants to hear. Furthermore, abusive interrogations would discredit the United States, undermine domestic and international support for military operations, and place Americans and allied troops in enemy hands at greater risk of abuse.[37]

After the September 11 attacks, executive officials in the Bush administration debated how to treat detainees at Guantanamo. Could CIA interrogators be given greater latitude in questioning detainees than permitted for military interrogators? The State Department decided that the Geneva Conventions applied to both Al Qaeda and the Taliban. Attorneys in the White House and the Justice Department were not willing to go that far. In a memo signed on February 7, 2002, President Bush accepted the Justice Department position that none of the Geneva provisions applied to Al Qaeda and that he had authority to suspend Geneva with regard to the Taliban if he so decided. Taliban detainees were "unlawful combatants" and did not qualify as prisoners of war. As a matter of policy (but not of law), detainees would be treated "humanely" by the United States.[38]

On August 1, 2002, in a legal memo that was highly confidential and did not leak to the public until 2004, the Justice Department analyzed federal statutes and treaties that prohibited torture. U.S. law regarded torture as any act that inflicted severe physical and mental pain or suffering, other than pain or suffering that resulted from lawful capture. The memo, designed to shield CIA employees who engaged in abusive interrogations, concluded that torture "must inflict pain that is difficult to endure" and that pain equivalent to torture "must be equivalent in intensity to the pain accompanying serious physical injury, such as organ failure, impairment of bodily function, or even death."[39] Moreover, the memo concluded that an interrogator would have to specifically intend to bring about organ failure, impairment of bodily functions, or death. If the specific intent was to obtain intelligence and the indirect result was permanent injury or death, the interrogator would not be guilty of torture and could not be prosecuted.[40]

The memo suggested other ways of limiting antitorture statutes and treaties. It argued that even if an interrogator arguably violated the torture statute, the statute would be unconstitutional "if it impermissibly encroached on the President's constitutional power to conduct a military campaign." As commander in chief under Article II of the Constitution, the president "has the constitutional authority to order interrogations of enemy combatants to gain intelligence information concerning the military plans of the enemy."[41] Through this interpretation, the Justice Department eliminated any statutory or treaty limitations on the president when discharging his functions as commander in chief.

These legal determinations heavily influenced Defense Department "working groups": officials from different agencies brought together to determine the administration's policy on interrogations. The end result supported "aggressive interrogations techniques" to obtain information from detainees and a decision that the torture statute and Geneva protections did not apply to detainees at the naval base. The final report of April 4, 2003, describes a number of interrogation techniques that would later appear in photos from Abu Ghraib, including hooding and nudity. Clothing could be removed, "to be done by military police if not agreed to by the subject." Nudity creates "a feeling of helplessness and dependence." Anxiety could be increased in various ways, such as the "simple presence of [a] dog without directly threatening action."[42]

In late April 2004, photos of U.S. abuse of detainees held at the Abu Ghraib prison in Iraq began circulating around the world. An investigation by Major General Antonio M. Taguba reported "numerous incidents of sadistic, blatant, and wanton criminal abuses" inflicted on detainees, referring to the abuses as "systemic and illegal." U.S. soldiers had committed "egregious acts and grave breaches of international law." His report revealed that a male military police officer had sex with a female detainee, unmuzzled dogs were used to intimidate and terrify detainees, and a detainee was sodomized with a chemical light and perhaps a broomstick.[43] Taguba concluded that the abusive interrogation methods used in Guantanamo had been transported to Iraq and that CIA personnel were involved.[44]

When the army manual was reissued in September 2006, it reflected the impact of Abu Ghraib and worldwide condemnation. Among the new prohibited actions: forcing a detainee to be naked, perform sexual acts, or pose in a sexual manner; placing hoods or sacks over the head of a detainee; using duct tape over the eyes; waterboarding (simulated drowning); and using "military working dogs."[45] Throughout U.S. history, beginning with the War of Independence, presidents and military leaders have understood that the abuse of detainees is not only wrong on humanitarian grounds but is injurious to military objectives.[46] In May 2007, when Army General David H. Petraeus learned that many U.S. troops in Iraq supported torture of suspects and were unwilling to report abuses by their colleagues, he posted an open letter on a military website with this instruction: "This fight depends on securing the population, which must understand that we—not our enemies—occupy the moral high ground." He rejected the position that torture is sometimes needed to quickly obtain military intelligence: "Beyond the basic fact that such actions are illegal, history shows that they also are frequently neither useful nor necessary."[47]

The second legal issue explored by the Justice Department was the status of the U.S. naval base at Guantanamo. Did detainees there have access to federal courts to file a habeas petition? The administration argued that the naval base was outside the United States and therefore beyond the jurisdiction of federal judges. In some lower court cases, the administration prevailed with that argument.[48] Other courts rejected the legal doctrine that the executive branch could put detainees in a black hole in Cuba outside the reach of courts. Although Cuba retained "sovereignty" over the naval base, for a century the United States had exercised sole jurisdiction and control.[49] The Supreme Court accepted the case and heard oral argument on April 20, 2004. A number of justices expressed skepticism when Solicitor General Ted Olson argued that the question of sovereignty and jurisdiction at the naval base was a "political decision" beyond the capacity of courts to decide.[50]

On June 28, 2004, in a 6-to-3 decision in *Rasul v. Bush*, the Supreme Court rejected the administration's position that the 1950 case of *Eisentrager* worked an automatic bar on detainee access to a habeas petition. The court pointed to key differences between the 1950 case and the detainees at the naval base. The prisoners at issue in 1950 were enemy aliens who had been charged, tried, convicted, and sentenced by a military tribunal. The detainees at the naval base were not nationals of countries at war with the United States and denied being engaged in or plotting acts of aggression against the United States. They had not been given access to any tribunal or even charged with or convicted of wrongdoing.[51] A concurrence by Justice Anthony Kennedy agreed that the naval base was "in every practical respect a United States territory" and expressed concern that the detainees were "being held indefinitely, and without benefit of any legal proceeding to determine their status."[52]

The Bush administration responded by establishing tribunals CSRTs to provide a hearing for each detainee, explaining the grounds for their detention and giving them an opportunity to challenge their designation as enemy combatant. The administration had no obligation to share with the detainee classified evidence used to make that designation. One of the status review panels involved Salim Ahmed Hamdan, whose case would wind through the federal judiciary and reach the Supreme Court in 2006. Before that occurred, Congress passed the Detainee Treatment Act (DTA) of 2005, providing that no individual in the custody of the U.S. government "regardless of nationality or physical location, shall be subject to cruel, inhuman, or degrading treatment or punishment."[53] In a sense, the statute merely restated what had been U.S. policy. It also placed some limits on detainee access to federal courts through habeas action and appeared to allow U.S. agencies to transfer detainees to other countries for cruel, inhuman, or degrading treatment if the individuals were not technically in U.S. custody.

In signing the bill, President Bush created doubt about his willingness to carry out the law. He said he would construe the statute "in a manner consistent with the constitutional authority of the President to supervise the unitary executive branch and as Commander in Chief and consistent with the constitutional limitations on the judicial power."[54] This language appeared to convert a statutory requirement to a mere advisory provision. With most signing statements, one can determine whether the president carries out the law as written. With interrogation, no one knows unless they are present in the room. Did the signing statement give Bush latitude to authorize abusive interrogations by the CIA?

The Supreme Court's decision in *Hamdan v. Rumsfeld* in 2006 expressly rejected the administration's position that President Bush possessed "inherent" power under Article II to create military commissions and did not need to come to Congress for statutory authority. The Justice Department argued that "throughout our Nation's history, Presidents have exercised their inherent commander-in-chief authority to establish military commissions without any specific authorization from Congress."[55] The administration indulged in false history by tracing independent presidential power to the military tribunal of British Major John André, who was tried in 1780 as a spy. The administration further argued that "there was no provision in the U.S. Articles of war providing for the jurisdiction in a court-martial to try an enemy for the offense of spying."[56] In fact, the Continental Congress has passed exactly that kind of legislation. Furthermore, it was a conceptual mistake for the Bush administration to search for presidential power in 1780. There was no president at that time. There was only one branch of government: the Continental Congress. No separate executive or judiciary existed.[57]

In *Hamdan*, the Court held that the type of military commission created by the administration was not authorized by Congress. Existing law, including Article 21 of the Uniform Code of Military Justice, did not permit the president to authorize any type of commission he decided was necessary, nor did the Supreme Court find anything in the text or legislative history of the AUMF that intended to alter the requirements of Article 21.[58] What the administration did was to risk concentrating in military hands "a degree of adjudicative and punitive power in excess of that contemplated either by statute or by the Constitution."[59]

The Supreme Court's decision forced the administration to seek statutory authority from Congress. Legislative history spotlighted the tension between civilian and military lawyers in the administration. To John D. Hutson, the Navy's top uniformed lawyer from 1997 to 2000, the administration's proposed rules for military commissions allowed the government to tell a detainee: "We know you're guilty. We can't tell you why, but there's a guy, we can't tell you who, who told us something. We can't tell you what, but you're guilty."[60] One of the prosecutors assigned to the commission charged with trying Salim Ahmed Hamdan called the system "a half hearted and disorganized effort by a skeleton group of inexperienced attorneys to prosecute fairly low-level accused in a process that appeared to be rigged."[61]

Some lawmakers initially challenged the administration's bill, but in the end the administration got pretty much what it wanted. The bill became the Military Commissions Act (MCA) of 2006. The statute placed restrictions on habeas petitions and established the procedures to be followed by the commissions. The accused would be permitted to present evidence at his trial, cross-examine witnesses who testify against him, and examine evidence admitted against him. Yet those procedural guarantees were undermined by the use of classified information. If the government deleted the name of an informer, the accused would have no right of confrontation and no right to meaningfully examine evidence presented against him. It was not even clear if the accused's attorney would have access to classified information. It appeared also that evidence gained by coercion could be admitted at trial.[62]

Passage of the DTA and the MCA sparked a new round of litigation. Did the DTA serve to insulate what the administration did at the naval base? Were the CSRTs adequate in protecting basic procedural rights of the detainees? On February 20, 2007, the D.C. circuit court held that the MCA denied jurisdiction to federal courts to consider the habeas petitions filed by detainees at Guantanamo previous to the date of the statute. The decision revived the issue whether the naval base was "sovereign" U.S. territory or merely under the "jurisdiction" of the United States. A lengthy dissent by one judge concluded that the MCA offended the constitutional language that habeas may be suspended only in cases of "Rebellion or Invasion." Moreover, nothing in the Suspension Clause distinguished between the rights of citizens and noncitizens. Because the MCA was void by violating the Constitution, the dissent said the statute did not deprive federal courts of jurisdiction.[63]

Those issues were decided by the Supreme Court on June 12, 2008 in the case of *Boumediene v. Bush*. A 5-to-4 Supreme Court held that the statutes passed by Congress (DTA and MCA) gave insufficient procedural safeguards to the detainees held at Guantanamo. Those statutes, said the court, amounted to an unconstitutional suspension of the writ of habeas corpus. The detainees, many held for more than 6 years at the naval base, were entitled to file a habeas petition with a federal district court. Habeas, for both citizens and noncitizens, was an essential procedure for protecting individual rights and curbing executive abuse: "The Framers viewed freedom from unlawful restraint as a fundamental precept of liberty, and they understood the writ of habeas corpus as a vital instrument to secure that freedom."[64]

Neither the opinion for the majority by Justice Kennedy nor the separate dissents by Chief Justice John Roberts and Justice Antonin Scalia deserve high marks for coherent legal reasoning. The majority decided that "[i]n every practical sense Guantanamo is not abroad; it is within the constant jurisdiction of the United States."[65] That issue had been previously addressed in *Rasul*. If Congress wanted to deny the detainees the privilege of habeas corpus, it "must act in accordance with the requirements of the Suspension Clause."[66] The majority opinion concluded: "The laws and Constitution are designed to survive, and remain in force, in extraordinary times. Liberty and security can be reconciled; and in our system they are reconciled within the framework of the law."[67]

A long list of key issues, left unresolved by the Supreme Court, went back to Congress and the executive branch to be addressed by new legislation and administrative regulations. All three branches were once again struggling to adopt policies that would protect the detainees from arbitrary and unlawful restraint. At each step of this litigation the court rejected claims of inherent presidential power in the field of national security. Congress, seemingly unaware of its separate and coequal powers and responsibilities under the Constitution, rarely exercised independent judgment. Many assertions of inherent executive power, as with warrantless surveillance by the National Security Agency and the practice of transporting suspected terrorists to other countries for interrogation and torture (extraordinary rendition), met little resistance from the courts or from Congress.[68]

Secret Legal Opinions

One of the controversies during the Bush administration was the pattern of deciding legal and constitutional issues by secret memos. Some of those surfaced in 2004, as with the "torture memos" written by attorneys in the Office of Legal Counsel (OLC), but others remained classified and unavailable to Congress or the public. Classification procedures were often ignored. On March 14, 2003, John Yoo of OLC wrote a memo explaining the legal principles for interrogating suspected terrorists. It was declassified and publicly released on March 31, 2008. If it consisted of legal reasoning alone, why was it classified? A society cannot remain faithful to the rule of law if governed by secret legal memos, especially those that promote broad and unchecked presidential power.

Yoo's memo is titled "Military Interrogation of Alien Unlawful Combatants Held Outside the United States." At the bottom of the first page appears this notation: "Declassify under authority of Executive Order 1958 by Acting General Counsel, Department of Defense by Daniel J. Dell'Orto, 31 March 2008." What is "Executive Order 1958"? The series of numbered executive orders currently exceeds 13,000. Is 1958 a date? A typo? Was it supposed to be 12958, the executive order that covers classified national security information? The notation is remarkably casual and slapdash.

Who originally classified the memo and why? Without the name of the classifier there is no accountability. Executive Order 12958, as amended, states that part of the steps in classifying a document is to provide "a concise reason for classification that, at a minimum, cites the applicable classification categories" identified in the order.[69] Was that ever done? If so, who did it?

For classification, the agency originating the document "shall, by marking or other means, indicate which portions are classified, with the applicable classification level, and which portions are unclassified." Nothing in the Yoo memo indicates compliance with that requirement. The Director of the Information Security Oversight Office (ISOO) "may grant waivers of this requirement." Was there a waiver? Did the director even know of the Yoo memo? Decisions to classify and declassify require accountability and thus far we have no evidence of how or why the Yoo memo was classified.

The executive order explains when it is improper to classify a document. In no case shall information be classified in order to "conceal violations of law, inefficiency, or administrative error." The Yoo memo encouraged and sanctioned violations of statutes and treaties. No information shall be classified to "prevent embarrassment to a person, organization, or agency." The

Yoo memo might have been classified to avoid embarrassment to the CIA and the Bush administration. The executive order states that no information shall be classified to "prevent or delay the release of information that does not require protection in the interest of the national security." Nothing in the Yoo memo appears to be anything other than legal reasoning. No reference is made to anything that looks like sources or methods, the standard justification for classification. If such material existed, it could have been blackened out and the balance of the memo made public.

At a hearing on April 30, 2008, before the Senate Judiciary Committee, several experts testified on the scope and purpose of secret law and the harm it inflicts on constitutional government. J. William Leonard, former ISOO director, told the committee that the declassified Yoo memo "represents one of the worse abuses of the classification process" that he had seen during his 30-year federal career. He made these points about the memo: "(1) it was 'purely legal analysis—it is not operational in nature,' and therefore there was no basis to have it classified; (2) whoever classified the memo 'had either profound ignorance or deep contempt for the process' set forth in executive orders; (3) the memo did not contain the identity of the official who classified it; (4) the person who classified it did not indicate which portions are classified and which are not; and (5) 'it is exceedingly irregular' that this memorandum was declassified by the Defense Department even though it was written 'and presumably classified' by the Justice Department."[70]

Legal memos are legitimately held secret when needed to protect national security interests, such as identifying a covert agent. Those memos can be easily made public after redacting names and sensitive references. No plausible case can be made for withholding legal reasoning. Certainly OLC did not hesitate to issue its January 19, 2006, defense of the highly sensitive and controversial National Security Agency (NSA) surveillance program, which the administration continues to regard as such a covert operation that it treats the program as a "state secret" and seeks to block any information from being disclosed in current litigation.[71]

Secret legal memos are particularly damaging to the rule of law when they build on untested theoretical definitions of presidential power. At various places in his memo, Yoo championed broad and inherent executive prerogatives in foreign affairs and war. Such a reading undermines constitutional limits because it encourages the view that when the president acts under Article II and invokes inherent powers, conflicting statutes and treaties may be ignored. The rule of law is further weakened when legal memos remain secret without the opportunity for colleagues in the executive branch to determine compliance with legal and constitutional standards. Secrecy makes vetting within the administration minimal.

Under Yoo's interpretation, there is no rule of law. Government functions by fiat. The dominant force is not law or statute or treaty. It is executive will over democracy and representative government. Over the years, unchecked presidential power has regularly weakened, not strengthened, national security. The public and executive agencies cannot comply with law if it is hidden and unknown.

Notes

1. John Locke, *Second Treatise on Civil Government* (London: J.M. Dent & Sons), ch. 14.

2. Max Farrand, ed., *The Records of the Federal Convention of 1787* (New Haven, CT: Yale University Press, 1937), 2: 318–19.

3. Louis Fisher, *The Constitution and 9/11: Recurring Threats to America's Freedoms* (Lawrence: University of Kansas Press, 2008), 63–64, 65–66.

4. James D. Richardson, ed., *A Compilation of the Messages and Papers of the Presidents* (New York: Bureau of National Literature, 1897–1925), 1: 315.

5. Louis Fisher, *Presidential War Power* (Lawrence: University Press of Kansas, 2nd ed., 2004), 35–37.

6. Richardson, *A Compilation of the Messages*, 1: 416.

7. Richardson, *A Compilation of the Messages*, 7: 3225.

8. 12 Stat. 326 (1861).

9. The Prize Cases, 2 Black 635, 668 (1863).

10. The Prize Cases, 2 Black 635, 660 (emphasis in original).

11. Fisher, *Presidential War Power*, 81–104.

12. Fisher, *Presidential War Power*, 105–111, 198–201.

13. *Public Papers of the Presidents*, 1957, 11 (Washington, D.C.: Government Printing Office).

14. Dwight D. Eisenhower, *Waging Peace* (Garden City, NY: Doubleday, 1965), 179.

15. Stephen Kinzer, *All the Shah's Men: An American Coup and the Roots of Middle East Terror* (Hoboken, NJ: John Wiley & Sons, 2008); John Prados, *Safe for Democracy: The Secret Wars of the CIA* (Chicago: I. R. Dee, 2006); John Prados, *President's Secret Wars: CIA and Pentagon Covert Operations from World Word II through the Persian Gulf* (Chicago: I. R. Dee, 1996).

16. Peter Wyden, *The Bay of Pigs* (New York: Simon & Schuster, 1980).

17. Fisher, *Presidential War Power*, 135–37.

18. H. Rept. No. 122 (Part 1), 98th Cong., 1st Sess. (1983), 12.

19. 98 Stat. 1935, sec. 8066(a) (1984).

20. Lawrence E. Walsh, *Firewall: The Iran-Contra Conspiracy and Cover-up* (New York: Norton, 1997).

21. 115 Stat. 224 (2001).

22. Jack Goldsmith, *The Terror Presidency: Law and Judgment Inside the Bush Administration* (New York: W. W. Norton, 2007), 109, 121–26.

23. *Hamdi v. Rumsfeld*, 542 U.S. 507, 517–19 (2004).

24. *Hamdi v. Rumsfeld*, 553.

25. *Hamdi v. Rumsfeld*, 538.

26. *Hamdi v. Rumsfeld*, 535–36.

27. *Hamdi v. Rumsfeld*, Civil Action No. 2:02cv439 (E.D. Va. 2002), at 14.

28. *Hamdi v. Rumseld*, 337 F.3d 335, 368, 373, 4th Cir. 2003, Motz, J., dissenting; emphasis in original.

29. Petition for Writ of Certiorari, *Hamdi v. Rumsfeld*, No. 03-7338, U.S. Supreme Court, 9, note 8.

30. Fisher, *The Constitution and 9/11*, 198–99.

31. *Padilla ex rel. Newman v. Rumsfeld*, 243 F.Supp.2d 42, 56 (S.D. N.Y. 2003).

32. *Padilla v. Rumsfeld*, 352 F.3d 695 (2d Cir. 2003).

33. Fisher, *The Constitution and 9/11*, 201–2.

34. *Rumsfeld v. Padilla*, 542 U.S. 426 (2004).

35. Kirk Semple, "Padilla Gets 17-Year Term for Role in Conspiracy," *New York Times* January 23, 2008. See Fisher, *The Constitution and 9/11*, 197–209.

36. U.S. Department of the Army, *FM 34-52 Intelligence Interrogation*, September 28, 1992, at 1–7 and 1–8.

37. U.S. Department of the Army, *FM 34-52 Intelligence Interrogation*, 1–8.

38. Fisher, *The Constitution and 9/11*, 216–18.

39. Memorandum from Jay Bybee, Office of Legal Counsel, U.S. Department of Justice, to Alberto Gonzales, White House Counsel, "Re: Standards of Conduct for Interrogation under 18 U.S.C. 2340-2340A," August 1, 2001.

40. Memorandum from Jay Bybee to Alberto Gonzales, 3–6.

41. Memorandum from Jay Bybee to Alberto Gonzales, 31.

42. "Working Group Report on Detainee Interrogations in the Global War on Terrorism: Assessment of Legal, Historical, Policy, and Operational Considerations," April 4, 2003 (Final Report), 64–65.

43. Article 15-16 Investigation of the 800th Military Police Brigade, 16–17, 50.

44. Seymour M. Hersh, "The General's Report," *New Yorker* June 24, 2007, 63–65.

45. U.S. Department of the Army, *FM 2-22-3 (FM 34-52), Human Intelligence Collector Operations*, September 2006, 5–21 (para. 5–75).

46. Fisher, *The Constitution and 9/11*, 214.

47. Thomas E. Ricks, "Gen. Petraeus Warns against Using Torture," *Washington Post* May 11, 2007.

48. *Rasul v. Bush*, 215 F.Supp.2d 55 (D.D.C. 2002); *Al Odah v. United States*, 321 F.3d 1134 (D.C. Cir. 2003).

49. *Gheribi v. Bush*, 352 F.3d 1278, 1283 (9th Cir. 2003).

50. Fisher, *The Constitution and 9/11*, 232–33.

51. *Rasul v. Bush*, 542 U.S. 466 (2004).

52. *Rasul v. Bush*, 542 U.S., 487–88.

53. 119 Stat. 2739, sec. 1003(a) (2005).

54. *Weekly Compilation of Presidential Documents*, 41: 1919 (2005).

55. Brief for Respondents, *Hamdan v. Rumsfeld*, No. 05-184, Supreme Court of the United States, February 23, 2006, at 21–22.

56. Brief for Appellants, *Hamdan v. Rumsfeld*, No. 04-5393 (D.C. Cir. December 8, 2004), 58.

57. Fisher, *The Constitution and 9/11*, 172–74.

58. *Hamdan v. Rumsfeld*, 126 S. Ct. 2749, 2775 (2006).

59. *Hamdan v. Rumsfeld*, 126 S.Ct. 2749, 2780.

60. R. Jeffrey Smith, "White House Proposal Would Expand Authority of Military Courts," *Washington Post* August 2, 2006.

61. "The Supreme Court's Decision in *Hamdan v. Rumsfeld*," hearings before the Senate Committee on the Judiciary, 109th Cong. (2006), statement by Lt. Com. Charles D. Swift, JAGC. U.S. Navy. The prosecutor was Air Force Captain John Carr.

62. Fisher, *The Constitution and 9/11*, 243.

63. *Boumediene v. Bush*, 476 F.3d 981 (D.C. Cir. 2007).

64. *Boumediene v. Bush*, majority decision for the Supreme Court, case op. at 9 (June 12, 2008).

65. *Boumediene v. Bush*, majority decision for the Supreme Court, case op. at 39.

66. *Boumediene v. Bush*, majority decision for the Supreme Court, case op. at 41.

67. *Boumediene v. Bush*, majority decision for the Supreme Court, case op. at 70.

68. Fisher, *The Constitution and 9/11*, chapters 9 and 10.

69. For Executive Order 13292, amending Executive Order 12958, available at www.whitehouse.gov/news/releases/2003/03/print/20030325-11.html, accessed on June 3, 2008.

70. J. William Leonard, Former Director, Information Security Oversight Office, statement before the Subcommittee on the Constitution, Senate Committee on the Judiciary, "Secret Law and the Threat to Democratic and Accountable Government," April 30, 2008, 3.

71. Fisher, *The Constitution and 9/11*, chapters 8 and 9.

CHAPTER NINE

~

George Bush as Commander in Chief

Dale R. Herspring

In a now-classic study of president management styles, Alexander George and Eric Stern argued that presidential leadership style has a major impact on the way "high-level foreign policymaking" is made.[1] As they put it, "all presidents have found it necessary to impose mechanisms for control and coordination of policy analysis and implementation from above."[2] In the process, they have all adopted a different approach for dealing with policy. For some it was highly personalistic, while in other cases it is more collegial. Then there have been cases in which the president has relied on competition between his subordinates. There have also been instances where the president has relied on a more formal bureaucratic model to run the country.

The approach to leadership adopted by a president has an especially important impact on civil-military relations. The president's personality, his approach to dealing with the military, and the kind of individuals he assigns to run the Pentagon and his attitude toward the military plays a big role in how the Pentagon works and how the military relates to civilian leaders and their policies. This is an approach I used as a starting point in a study I did of U.S. presidents and their relations with the Pentagon several years ago.[3] This study was updated in a more recent study of civil-military relations in the George W. Bush administration.[4]

Bush's approach to dealing with the bureaucracy as a whole, and the Pentagon in particular, was different from his predecessors. The reason was simple, Bush was the first president with a background as a chief executive officer (CEO). He tried to run the U.S. government as if it was a corporation, and in appointing Donald Rumsfeld to oversee the Department of Defense, he selected a person who had been a CEO and who did his best to run the Pentagon as if he were still in charge of the Searle Corporation.

For Bush, this meant he stayed above the policy-making process when it involved purely military issues such as weapons procurement and modernization or structural modifications. Bush was involved only insofar as he provided public support for his secretary of defense. He would repeatedly praise Rumsfeld, but he did not normally intervene in the decision-making process. It was up to Rumsfeld to deal with the military, and Bush paid little or no attention to how Rumsfeld ran the Pentagon. How he ran things was his business.

The situation was somewhat different when major foreign policy issues were involved. For example, when it came to the wars in Afghanistan and Iraq, the president expected the Pentagon to brief him. In these meetings he would ask questions, receive explanations, and make suggestions. However, here too, the president left the management of the process to the secretary of defense. It was up to him to oversee the military and decide what the president should see and who should speak with him, and what they should say—and that included the Chairman of the Joint Chiefs of Staff who in accordance with the Goldwater-Nichols act of 1986 is the president's primary military advisor. Thus, when Bush would honestly say that he depended on the views of the generals on the ground, what he more often than not received, was Rumsfeld's views. The latter went out of his way to select senior officers who he could control. As retired Army General Barry McCaffrey put it, "The man is capable of raking down all opposition, and has an astonishing ability not to listen to experts."[5]

The decision-making process changed somewhat after Rumsfeld's ouster in late 2006, with the appointment of Robert Gates as Secretary of Defense. The basic difference between Rumsfeld and Gates was that the latter was not a CEO. Gates was more transparent and collegial in the formulation and implementation of national security policy. Gates was also far more open to the military brass and their views on topics such as the wars in Iraq and Afghanistan. For his part, Bush would become more involved in decision making, but Gates and his military colleagues remained the critical part of the process.

Military Transformation

If the issue of military transformation demonstrated anything it was how aloof Bush was from a critical military policy. The key issue was how to move the U.S. military from the 20th century to the 20th *while jumping a whole generation of weapons!* Bush provided rhetorical support throughout the process—he, too, wanted a more modern military and he expected his secre-tary of defense to create one. Unfortunately, Bush's delegation of authority to Rumsfeld had very negative consequences. It meant a serious downturn in civil-military relations as the arrogant and demanding Rumsfeld openly ig-nored the generals and admirals, those individuals who had spent more than 30 years in uniform and were the experts in the management of violence. The long-term result was to slow down the process of military transformation as Rumsfeld spent most of his time fighting with the military and especially with the Army headed by General Eric Shinseki.

It is clear that Bush supported the idea of military transformation even prior to his inauguration as president. As he put it in a speech at the Citadel in 1999, "Our military is still organized more for Cold War threats than the challenges of the twenty-first century—for industrial age operations, rather than information battles."[6] He reiterated his support for a more modern mili-tary during his 2000 election campaign when he suggested that he would put more money into the military than Clinton had with the comment, "Help is on the way!"[7] Bush said that meant replacing "existing programs with new technologies and strategies" that would skip forward to a new "generation of technology."[8]

In working to transform the military, Rumsfeld almost destroyed civil-military relations. He did not care whether the military (and especially the Army) liked his approach or not. He believed he knew what the president wanted and he was determined to achieve that goal.

Rumsfeld Clashes with the Army

Rumsfeld began his time in the Pentagon by making it clear that he had no intention of working with the military on transformation. To begin with, he set up a number of committees to work on transforming the military—but did not include a single active senior military officer on them. That was an unfortunate decision because individuals like Army Chief of Staff Shinseki had begun efforts to transform the Army as early as 1999.[9] Shinseki realized that the Army had to do something or it would be left behind. It was too big and heavy. The other services were transforming and if the Army wanted to remain relevant, it had to become lighter and more flexible.

Rumsfeld, however, had no intention of working with Shinseki. The sec-retary wanted to cut two divisions from the Army and use the money saved to pay for high tech weapons programs. Needless to say, senior officers like Shinseki were opposed. In fact, the latter believed he needed two more divi-sions just to carry out the tasks already assigned to him.[10]

Bush came to Rumsfeld's defense in May when, in an address to the graduating class of the U.S. Naval Academy, he called for more creativity in military thinking. He called on graduating seniors to help "change the course of a mighty ship." He continued, "I'm committed to building a future force that is defined less by size and more by stealth, precision weaponry and information technologies." Finally, he turned to downsizing the military, "suggesting the active force could shrink. At 1.4 million, it is 33% below the level of 2.1 million in uniform near the end of the Cold War."[11]

Bush's rhetorical support for Rumsfeld had little impact on the military. By mid-July, the two sides were deadlocked. Rumsfeld's arrogance and refusal to listen to senior officers had alienated them. Not only the military but also the Hill. The generals and admirals had learned years ago that one of the most effective devices for dealing with what they considered a hostile administration was to enlist their friends on the Hill and in the media.

In fact, the mood between the military and Rumsfeld and his civilian entourage was so bad that one unidentified general commented that Rumsfeld had privately told the chiefs and other senior officials that "we have a problem." He stated that "Things are on hold until the Joint Staff and [Rumsfeld's aides] figure out the way ahead. . . . There is a huge rift between the Joint Staff and [Rumsfeld's aides] over this"[12] To make things worse, civilians on Rumsfeld's staff seemed to do everything possible to alienate the military further. For example, Steven Cambone, who was Rumsfeld's point man on transformation at that time, walked into a room full of "three stars" a half-hour late on a Saturday morning to discuss transformation. . . . He began the meeting by saying, "So guys, . . . what's transformation?" He walked around the table asking each officer what he thought—in a military context—treating them "like morons." When they met a week later, they all refused to say anything—instead remaining mute. Furious, Cambone left. One three star was so infuriated by Cambone's disdainful behavior that he reportedly said, "If I were being overrun by the enemy and I had one round left, I'd save it for Steven Cambone."[13]

On August 4, Rumsfeld met with the service secretaries and four-star generals. He quickly discovered that the military and the secretaries were standing together shoulder-to-shoulder. They opposed a further reduction in active-duty personnel and dug in their heels on other issues. The meeting was contentious, or as one Army officer put it, "It did not go well, and it ended early."[14]

Faced with this standoff, by the middle of August, Rumsfeld decided to let the services themselves decide which weapons system to cancel or field. He would limit himself to describing "only missions, military requirements, and budget items, and leave to the services the hard and contentious task of deciding how many people to put into uniform, how many weapons to field, and what kind of weapons these should be."[15] Rumsfeld had backed down. Bush remained aloof from the struggle.

It was at this time that Rumsfeld faced another major decision—who to appoint as Chairman of the Joint Chiefs. Hugh Shelton's tour was up, and the secretary had no intention of reappointing an Army general who had made it clear that he was prepared to go directly to the president as was his right under Goldwater-Nichols. After interviewing a number of four-star generals, Rumsfeld settled on General Richard Myers. The latter had been vice chief of staff and he had commanded the North American Aerospace Defense Command and the Space Command for four years. As a result, he was very familiar with the high tech items that were of concern to the secretary. Myers was also a team player; he let himself be overruled on issues such as picking his own staffers for the Joint Staff. "Inside the military, he was widely regarded as the best kind of uniformed—yes-man—smart, hardworking, but wary of independent thought."[16]

By the beginning of September, there was talk that Rumsfeld would be replaced in spite of his apparent support from Bush—Senator Richard Lugar's name was floated. However, September 11 changed everything. Not only was Rumsfeld pictured on the evening news helping to save those injured at the Pentagon, but defense also became a matter of major concern to the country, and the idea of firing Bush's secretary of defense at such a critical time became unthinkable.

Meanwhile, Bush again came to Rumsfeld's aide on the issue of transformation on December 11, 2001. Bush told cadets at the Citadel that the 6-week-old war in Afghanistan had shown the need for military transformation. As he put it, "Afghanistan has been a proving ground for this new approach."[17] Few military officers believed him. Meanwhile, Bush also went to the Hill in an effort to get more money for the Pentagon. Following September 11, he had asked for the biggest military budget increase since Ronald Reagan's first term—$43 billion in 2003.[18] This included a permanent increase of $38 billion to cover pay raises, operations, and procurement, as well as money to support the transformation effort.

Bush continued to remain aloof when Rumsfeld took on the Army and the Hill. A key issue was the Crusader artillery weapons system. The Crusader was a 15.5 millimeter, self-propelled howitzer. It could be driven into battle, not towed, and it could fire 10 to 12 rounds per minute. The Army believed it was necessary to replace the aging Paladin. Rumsfeld, however, wanted to cancel it, thereby saving an estimated $9 billion.[19] In the end, Rumsfeld not only cancelled the Crusader, but he also did so in a manner guaranteed to alienate the Army. Paul Wolfowitz, the deputy secretary, told the Army it could have an additional 30 days to make its case for the weapon, only to have Rumsfeld unceremoniously cancel it 3 days later.

Bush's continued support for Rumsfeld was obvious on June 10, 2002, when he delivered a speech to cadets at West Point. In it he announced that the United States was moving away from its Cold War doctrine of deterrence and containment toward one that permitted preemptive action against states of terrorist groups if they were developing chemical, biological, or nuclear weapons.[20] Bush argued that the United States had the right to preempt; that is, to use force if it had good reason to believe that the other side was planning to attack it—another argument in favor of the high tech world of transformation.

Unfortunately, from the president's and Rumsfeld's standpoint, the wars in Afghanistan, and especially the conflict in Iraq, made it increasingly difficult for Rumsfeld to implement Bush's policy of transformation. The wars continued to take more and more of the money Rumsfeld wanted to spend on transformation, while opposition on the part of the military and Congress to Rumsfeld's arrogance in this and other matters further slowed the process. By 2006, Rumsfeld was finding it increasingly difficult to get rid of some weapons favored by the military and championed by members of Congress. To cite only one example, Rumsfeld had done everything possible to get rid of the Air Force's F-22 Raptor from the time he became secretary of defense. He believed the program's budgeted $68 billion could be spent better on transformational systems. He repeatedly tried to cancel the plane only to have Congress put it back in the budget.

By the time he left office in 2006, Rumsfeld's impact on transformation was more negative than positive. His attempt, supported by Bush, to jump a whole generation of weapons made no sense. Such a project would work only if the United States could be certain there would not be any need for weapons to protect its national interest. Obviously, that did not happen. The United States had to use the weapons on hand. As a consequence, the administration's idea of cutting forces while spending more and more on advanced weapons systems became increasingly unrealistic.

Bush, Rumsfeld, and the War in Iraq

If Bush remained above the fray when it came to transformation, that was not the case when it came to the wars in Afghanistan. He expected to be consulted and briefed on what and how the Pentagon's (and other agencies including the Central Intelligence Agency [CIA]) planned to carry out military operations. The factor that stands out in a review of Bush's dealings with both of these wars was how dependent he would again be on Rumsfeld. He would ask questions, and he would push for explanations, but in most cases, he permitted Rumsfeld to determine how, when, and where the military was to use its forces, and in the end, was one of the main reasons for the Republican defeat in the 2006 Congressional elections.

Those working around the president immediately after September 11 felt the event had a profound impact on him. "It transformed him in ways I don't think any of us could have fully predicted," said former CIA director George Tenet.[21] Bush ordered Colin Powell and the State Department to issue an ultimatum to the Taliban, ordering them to turn over Osama bin Laden or "We'll attack them."[22] He was serious, in charge, and wanted to know what the Pentagon was prepared to do to punish the Taliban if military force became necessary.

On September 12, a National Security Council (NSC) meeting was held to discuss the U.S. response to the attacks of September 11. Rumsfeld raised the issue of Iraq, suggesting that the United States should attack Iraq as well as Al Qaeda in Afghanistan. It would be an opportunity to kill two birds with one stone. Powell strongly disagreed, as did Vice President Richard Cheney and General Shelton.[23] Bush also made clear he did not think that this was the time to resolve the Iraq issue. The president's primary concern was to see a military plan that would inflict "real pain and destruction on the terrorists" in Afghanistan.[24]

Unfortunately, for Rumsfeld, who wanted the Pentagon to be the lead agency, it did not have an actionable plan to move ground troops into Afghanistan. As a result, the CIA, that did have agents ready to deploy to Afghanistan, was told to come up with a war plan at the September 12 NSC meeting. Meanwhile, a frustrated Rumsfeld was pushing the military hard for military options for Afghanistan. Central command (CENTCOM) began to work around the clock to draw up plans while moving ships, planes, and troops so they would be in a position to attack when the order was given.

Bush met with his senior advisors at Camp David on September 15. He remained determined to act and act decisively. Tenet updated the president on the CIA's plan, which provided immediate assistance to the Northern Alliance and sped up contacts with southern leaders. The group reconvened on September 17. Bush announced that the government would move ahead with Tenet's plan. "Start now," he said.[25] Tenet assured the president that the CIA teams would be in Afghanistan in eight days. Bush then asked what kind of targets the Pentagon was prepared to hit, how soon it planned to hit them, and what allies would support the United States. Meanwhile, with Iraq very much in mind, Bush told Condoleezza Rice that he wanted contingency plans drawn up if it turned out Iraq was implicated in the September 11 attacks.

Rumsfeld insisted on being directly involved in military planning. For example, in the aftermath of the September 11 attacks, he, General Peter Pace, General Myers, Paul Wolfowitz, and Douglas Feith would spend hours going over intelligence reports. As he would when it came to Iraq, Rumsfeld took great delight vetoing plans prepared by the generals as "unimaginative."[26] General Tommy Franks was sent back several time to come up with plans more in line with Rumsfeld's thinking.

On September 15, Franks briefed Bush on the upcoming air war. When Bush asked if the air war could begin the first week in October, General Shelton told him that the United States could not begin air operations with tactical aircraft until combat search and rescue helicopters were in place—in case a plane was shot down. Since that was not the case, Bush was informed that B-2 planes stationed in Missouri would carry the load, and they began operations on October 7. By the end of November 2001, the Taliban had been removed from power.

The War in Iraq

On November 26, Rumsfeld flew to see General Franks at CENTCOM's headquarters in Tampa, Florida. As soon as they were together privately, Rumsfeld noted that while the president had not yet decided to use force against Iraq, he wanted to see his options. As Franks recounted the conversation, Rusmfeld told him, "General Franks, the President wants us to look at options for Iraq. What is the status of planning?"[27] The only plan available was OPLAN 1003-98 which had been prepared by Franks' predecessor, General Anthony Zinni; one that called for 500,000 troops.

Rumsfeld immediately made it clear to Franks that he had no intention of approving a plan involving 500,000 troops. It would go against his idea of military transformation—small, flexible units able to hit hard and destroy an enemy before he knew what hit him. Furthermore, Franks was forbidden to speak with Zinni because of the latter's criticism of the Bush administration. Franks originally tried to buy off Rumsfeld with 385,000 troops—the number Zinni considered to be the minimum required. Rumsfeld would have none of it. He told Franks to come up with another plan involving fewer troops. Indeed, throughout the coming months, Rumsfeld would repeatedly badger Franks into cutting back on the number of troops needed for the Iraqi invasion.

During mid-December, Rumsfeld informed Franks that he would be fly-
ing to Bush's ranch in Crawford, Texas, to brief the president on the Iraqi
invasion plan. Franks informed Bush that he and Rumsfeld had decided that
the existing plan drawn up by Zinni was "outdated." He went on to inform
Bush that the war would be divided into four parts, including phase IV—
post-combat period—which he admitted could be a problem. His most significant point—one taken from Rumsfeld—was that "force could be applied
selectively and carefully across different points."[28] He also impressed on the
president the need to have international support.

Lest the reader get the wrong impression, Franks was not alone in briefing
the president. To ensure that he stayed on target, Rumsfeld participated by
teleconference. For example, when Franks mentioned 275,000 as the number of troops that might be needed for the invasion, Rumsfeld interrupted
to say, "We are still working through the numbers. The number Tom is
giving you is soft."[29] He then added that "Tom and I will talk about these
things."[30] Bush appeared pleased by the briefing, did not seem bothered by
the prominent role Rumsfeld played, or the number of troops that would be
involved. He suggested that it was time for the government to begin doing
some of things mentioned by Franks. On September 29, 2001, Feith claims
that Rumsfeld, "asked General Meyers . . . to begin preparing military options for Iraq."[31]

Bush had September 11 very much in mind in his now "infamous" "Axis
of Evil" speech. It would outline his strategy for the future. He was convinced that September 11 was not an isolated event. "The president was not
just talking about opposing threats, he was talking about a reorientation of
American foreign and domestic policy."[32] He decided to take on terrorism
directly. As he noted, "states like these and their terrorist allies constitute an
axis of evil, arming to threaten the peace of the world." He also said that the
United States would "deliberate," but he made it clear that time was not on
the United States' side. "I will not wait on events while dangers gather. I will
not stand by as peril draws closer and closer. The United States of America
will not permit the world's most dangerous regimes to threaten us with the
world's most destructive weapon."[33]

On January 30, 2002, there was another meeting at the White House to
discuss Iraq. Bush was most interested in the combat component of military
operations. The service chiefs, who were in attendance, approved the plan.
Also in January, at a NSC meeting Bush asked Franks about post-combat
operations. Franks reportedly responded, "Don't worry. . . . We've got that
covered." Unfortunately, Franks' response was complete nonsense. Nothing
had been done about planning for the post-combat period. In Bush's defense,

he had every reason to believe that the military brass was fully on board—after all, they had told him they were.

On February 7, 2002, Franks presented his plan for an invasion of Iraq to the NSC. Bush was in attendance. This was the first time Bush would actually see such a plan that he could order the military to carry out. Franks told the president that the operation would take 90 days of preparation and force movement, then 45 days of heavy bombing prior to inserting ground forces. Rumsfeld, however, said they were working on another plan which he dubbed, "shock and awe."

Interestingly, Lieutenant General Ricardo Sanchez who would go on to command U.S. troops in Iraq complained that Rumsfeld's constant interference and micro-management of the process made planning almost impossible. As Sanchez put it,

> But the Secretary and his staff got so involved, and were so intrusive in the planning stages, that they ended up completely disrupting the process. Constant changes were made to the operation's plans of the warfighting forces. The most devastating impact of Rumsfeld's micromanagement was that warfighting commanders, all the way down to the division level, were never able to plan beyond the basic mission of defeating Saddam Hussein's military.[34]

During August 2002, Secretary of State Powell had his now well-known discussion with Bush about the implications of invading Iraq. Powell used the opportunity to point out to the president (and NSC advisor Rice) the implications of the actions he was considering taking. He also noted that senior military officers shared his views even if the civilians at the Pentagon did not.[35] He pointed out that an invasion of Iraq could destabilize the entire region and could drive up the price of oil. It would also take attention away from the war on terror and become the dominant foreign policy issue. In the end, Bush agreed to take the issue to the United Nations (UN) as Powell requested.[36]

Vice President Cheney was to play a major, if unexpected, role in the push toward an invasion of Iraq. Indeed, Cheney's role was unusual for a vice president. Instead of adopting a laid back position as Al Gore did on most issues—then telling the president what he thought in the privacy of the Oval Office, Cheney was actively engaged, and in most cases sided with Rumsfeld against Powell. He even went so far as to make policy on his own. For example, on August 26, 2002, he spoke to the Veterans of Foreign Wars. He stated, "There is no doubt" that Baghdad had weapons of mass destruction. He called for war. "The risks of inaction are far greater than the risks of action."[37] The impact of Cheney's speech was to box Powell in a corner.

No loyal official wanted to openly contradict the vice president. Why Bush permitted him to play such a role is unclear.

Bush moved to shore up congressional support when he invited senior members of the House and Senate to the White House on September 4. He made it clear that he was ready to work with them, but in return he wanted a quick vote on a resolution giving him the authority to take on Saddam Hussein. He received it on October 10.

On September 12, Bush spoke to the UN. Bush's key point was that he hoped the UN would act against Iraq. If it did not, he left no doubt that the United States was prepared to act on its own. His efforts led to a Security Council resolution calling on Iraq to make a full statement of all its chemical, biological, and nuclear weapons programs to the Council. Bush continued his verbal assault on Hussein in a speech on October 7. He stated that Iraq presented a clear and present danger to the United States and reiterated the claim that Baghdad was working with Al Qaeda. Then on November 8, the Security Council voted 15 to 0 in favor of a resolution demanding that Iraq prove that there were no weapons of mass destruction in the country or face "serious consequences." Finally, on January 28, 2003, Bush delivered his State of the Union Speech in which he made it clear that the United States wanted UN support, but that it was prepared to use military force if necessary.

Meanwhile, attention focused on Powell's UN speech. Preparations for it involved a major bureaucratic battle. Cheney's office prepared a draft speech by putting together whatever supported the U.S. case. It made little difference whether or not U.S. intelligence backed up the assertions. The Pentagon and the vice president's office were working together. Powell took one look at the proposed speech, and said, "This is bullshit."[38] Had the administration, including the vice president's office, listened to the intelligence specialists, they could have avoided a major U.S. embarrassment.

As far as war planning was concerned, Rumsfeld continued to dominate it. For example, during a February meeting with the president, Bush turned to General Myers and asked "How long will the war last?" Before Myers could respond, Rumsfeld put a hand on his arm and said, "Now, Dick, you don't want to answer that."[39] Rumsfeld had just prevented the Chairman of the Joint Chiefs of Staff from answering a direct question from the commander in chief—and Bush did not object! The next month, shortly prior to the invasion, there was a meeting between Bush and his top aides in the Situation Room. One of the main issues was what to do with former Baath Party members or "de-Baathification" as it was often called. The president noted that one of his top priorities was getting the Iraqis to take charge as soon as possible, while a senior Pentagon official assured the president that the United States wanted to keep the Iraqi military in tact. In any case, according to Scott McClellan, the president "and his leadership team believed that victory in Iraq could be achieved swiftly and decisively, and that the Iraqi people would then welcome and embrace freedom."[40] In fact, Bush was ignoring Iraq's very different political culture and the fact that it had lived under Hussein's tyrannical rule for many years. To paraphrase one of Joseph Stalin's comments about Poland, introducing democracy into Iraq immediately after the invasion was like putting a saddle on a cow.

The Invasion Begins

On March 17, the president delivered an ultimatum to Hussein—telling him and his sons to leave the country. Two days later the invasion began with a U.S. ground force of only 145,000—far below what General Zinni had recommended. Then to make matters worse, General Franks permitted Rumsfeld to once again override his better judgment by not bringing the First Cavalry Division (17,500 troops) into Iraq. The latter would have helped significantly in dealing with Phase IV problems.

By April 14, U.S. troops were in Baghdad and the war was over—or so Rumsfeld and his civilian assistants thought. In fact, because of the low number of troops, U.S. forces were unable to deal with the looting; Iraqis begged U.S. troops to help them, but there were not enough soldiers or Marines in Baghdad or in any other part of the country to ensure security.[41] General Sanchez probably put it best when he observed that "There was chaos everywhere." However, this did not stop Franks from suggesting to Bush that he should declare the war over. On May 1, Bush traveled to the USS *Abraham Lincoln*, where with much fanfare and many television cameras, he declared the end of the Iraq War. After all, armed resistance by organized military units had long since ended. Now it was time to begin to withdraw U.S. troops, but that was not to be—an insurgency soon emerged.

In deciding how to deal with post-invasion Iraq, Bush made an important, yet tragic decision. Overall responsibility was given to Rumsfeld. This meant that major decisions were made in the Pentagon. For example, L. Paul "Jerry" Bremer was sent to Iraq to bring order to an increasingly out of control country. This meant that Bremer worked directly for Rumsfeld or in some cases the president. Bremer would take two decisions that had been approved by Rumsfeld; decisions that played a major role in the collapse of the Iraqi bureaucracy. First, he issued a "de-Baathification" order—one that forced thousands of otherwise apolitical bureaucrats, including physicians, engineers, teachers, and such out of work because they had been members of the Baath Party. If that were not enough, Bremer disbanded the Iraqi Army, thereby putting close to 400,000 men on the streets with no job.[42] Key players like Powell, Rice, and even General Myers were circumvented! Sanchez called this decision "devastating."[43] He was right. The immediate result was an intensified insurgency.

Rumsfeld was widely criticized on the Hill and in the media because of continuing problems in Iraq. He was blasted for not having "a coherent plan" to stabilize Baghdad. "The lack of stability concerns me," said Senator Peter Domenici (R-NM).[44] Senator Robert Byrd (D-WV) criticized Rumsfeld for the same reason. Rumsfeld, however, was unmoved. On May 27, he gave what was to become his standard answer to such questions. "Just as it took time and patience, trial and error, and years of hard work before the founders got it right, so too it will take time, and patience, and trial and error, and hard work for the Iraqi people to overcome the challenges they face."[45] Others were not so optimistic. General John Abizaid and Bremer both expressed concern over events in Iraq. The bottom line was simple: Coalition forces were taking growing numbers of casualties in places like Fallujah and Ramadi, as well as in Baghdad. All Rumsfeld could think of was to draw down troops in the face of a growing insurgency! The bottom line was that the United States did not have enough troops to do the job in Iraq. As General Sanchez commented, "I continued my requests for manning. I asked the Joint Staff for expertise in intel, operations, strategy, policy, planning, detention and legal affairs."[46] However, with Rumsfeld refusing to accept the idea of more troops, the normal bureaucratic obstructionism from the different services meant that nothing happened.

Rumsfeld's behavior led Bremer to reportedly comment during a visit to Washington in late July, "'Rumsfeld's impossible to deal with,' Bremer told a colleague. He was really steamed. . . . Rumsfeld was throwing his weight around, and the rest of the NSC was just too weak to do anything about it."[47]

What was even worse, almost everyone involved on the ground in Iraq agreed that Rumsfeld either did not want to understand what was happening or could not. For example, during the third week of September, Bremer had a teleconference call with Rumsfeld, Wolfowitz, and Abizaid. Rumsfeld suggested that Iraqi forces replace coalition forces. Bremer responded, "Mr. Secretary . . . we have to be realistic. . . . I got the impression that nobody in the conference wanted to hear this assessment."[48] Unfortunately, Rumsfeld would continue with this optimistic tone regardless of what he was told by those on the ground in Iraq.

Concerned about the criticism the administration was receiving, on October 6, 2003, Bush gave Rice more authority to deal with Iraq. She set up four groups to deal with events in that country. While some in the Defense Department tried to downplay the importance of this interagency group, Rumsfeld was concerned enough to give an interview in Europe in which he "showed disdain for the White House power grab quite clearly. . . . He said he had known nothing of the reorganization until he read about it in the news."[49]

The president was concerned enough about Rumsfeld's behavior that he asked to meet with Bremer during one of his trips to Washington. Bush inquired about working with Rumsfeld. Bremer responded that he was a micro-manager, but he said that he found ways to work with him. For his part, Rumsfeld was furious when he learned about the private meeting. He told Andrew Card, Jr., the president's chief of staff, "He works for me!" "No," Card responded, "He's the presidential envoy."[50]

The organizational chaos that resulted from the appointment of Bremer in charge of the Coalition Provisional Authority and General Ricardo Sanchez as commander of U.S. ground forces was legendary. Bremer was convinced he was in charge—that Sanchez worked for him. Sanchez believed he worked for Rumsfeld. In fact, the two did not get along and both reported directly through Rumsfeld, who was determined to keep the State Department out of the action. This led to a constant war between Bremer and Sanchez. For example, on March 24, 2004, the Marine Corps took control of Fallujah, a city only 43 miles west of Baghdad. On May 4, four security officers working for the Blackwater firm took a wrong turn in Fallujah and were killed and mutilated.

Rumsfeld, together with General Abizaid, met with the president on April 1, 2004. What was most interesting in terms of Bush's leadership style was that Rumsfeld felt comfortable in refusing to share the views of the general on the spot. In spite of General James Conway's warnings, Rumsfeld told the president that an attack on Fallujah "was something they could do with a relatively low level of casualties."[51] This was a clear case of deceiving the president. So the Marines were ordered to attack on April 4. The bottom line was that while the attack was succeeding, the Iraqi Governing Council was fuming—upset that this attack took place without its approval. Bremer, too, seemed left out of the loop. The attack was called off, much to the chagrin of the Marines. They got even when on November 7 some 6,500 Marines, 1,500 soldiers with tanks along with two Iraqi units with a total of 2,000 troops attacked. The battle was soon over,[52] but the problems involved in coordinating civilian and military activities in Iraq continued as long as Bremer was in the country.

Meanwhile, there was a fundamental difference between Rumsfeld and Rice, who had replaced Powell as Secretary of State. Rumsfeld was convinced that the right way to handle Iraq was to give its leaders a chance to fail. Rice, however, had come to the conclusion that the United States could not simply pack up and leave. There was a real danger of a civil war if that happened. She favored a counter-insurgency strategy; one of "take, clear, build." Rice made that point when she testified to Congress on October 19, 2005. Rumsfeld was furious, but there was little he could do, Rice was gradually winning the battle for control over Iraq policy.

On March 19, 2006, Major General Paul Eaton, a retired army general, wrote an op-ed in the *New York Times*, calling Rumsfeld "incompetent" and a "bully."[53] This was followed in quick succession by similar articles by a number of other generals. Indeed, such an outpouring of criticism by retired generals had not been seen since the days of Robert McNamara. While other generals came to his aid, it was clear that Rumsfeld was becoming an ever bigger problem for Bush. Bush, however, continued to support him, stating that "he has my full support and deepest appreciation."[54]

Finally, on November 6, 2006, there was an editorial in the *Army, Navy, Air Force, and Marine Times*. It was one thing when a majority of Americans believed Rumsfeld had failed. "But when the nation's current military leaders break publicly with their defense secretary, then it is clear that he is losing control of the institution he heads," and it called on him to step down.[55] On November 5, one day prior to the off-year election, Rumsfeld submitted his letter of resignation. The president realized he had no choice but to fire his old friend.

Enter Gates

Bush did not change his approach to dealing with Iraq when he asked Robert Gates to become secretary of defense. Instead, he appears to have been lucky to get someone who had not been a CEO, but instead had worked for years in the CIA and understood how complex bureaucracies work and how to make them work for his benefit. His problems were great. How to devise a new strategy to win the war in Iraq as well as finding a way to reopen communications between the secretary and the uniformed military?

For his part, Gates made it clear in his hearings on the Hill, that he intended to work for close relations with the Hill, that he intended to take the counsel of the military professionals under his command, and that he understood the need for teamwork in working with other parts of the government.[56]

The key question facing the Bush administration at this point was whether the addition of thousands of more U.S. troops (the "surge") would or could turn things around in Iraq. Most senior officers had advised against it. However, Bush had met with several experts, including retired Army General Jack Keane, who argued that more troops were needed to ensure security in Iraq. Bush was determined to take hold of U.S. policy, and he was convinced that a surge offered the only way to begin to turn things around in Iraq. One of the first hints that Bush was leaning in that direction was the announcement that he was appointing General David Petraeus as commander of U.S. forces in Iraq. Petraeus holds a Ph.D. from Princeton and was the author of the Army's manual on counter-insurgency. Bush admitted that the United States had made mistakes in Iraq and announced that the United States would introduce an additional 20,500 (later increased to 30,000) troops in a TV address on January 10, 2007. He said the plan to secure Baghdad has "failed for two principal reasons: There were not enough Iraqi and American troops available to secure neighborhoods that had been cleared of terrorists," and he said that de-Baathification had gone too far.[57] Democrats in Congress tried to stop Bush by refusing to fund the additional troops but were unsuccessful, and Petraeus took command of coalition troops on February 10, 2007.

Gates also reversed the procedure for briefing the president on an issue like Iraq. Instead of speaking on behalf of the generals or bringing along generals who would meekly support his position, Gates encouraged the generals to give Bush their honest opinions. And they did.[58] For example, General Petraeus and Admiral William Fallon openly disagreed on U.S. strategy for Iraq in a meeting with Bush. Petraeus argued in favor of the surge, while Admiral Fallon "argued for accepting more risks in Iraq. . . . In order to have enough forces available to confront other potential threats in the region."[59] Gates also went out of his way to rebuild the Pentagon's relations with Congress and did something Rumsfeld avoided: he told the truth about the situation in Iraq. On August 2, 2007, for example, he stated openly that "I think the developments on the political side are somewhat discouraging at the national level."[60] Petraeus agreed with Gates in his September appearance before Congress.

It was not long before Petraeus' new strategy began to work. Casualties, on both the U.S. and Iraqi side went down. For example, U.S. military deaths were down from 101 in June to 39 in October. Iraqi civilian deaths were also down sharply from 1,791 in August to 750 in October.[61] Meanwhile, Anbar Province, previously an insurgent stronghold, turned on Al Qaeda and began to work with the Marines to stabilize matters in the province.

Gates decided not to renew General Peter Pace as Chairman of the Joint Chiefs, supposedly because of Congressional concerns because he had been a part of the invasion of Iraq.

Conclusion

If a review of Bush's role as commander in chief tells us anything, it is how important leadership style can be. Bush's approach to dealing with the Pentagon meant that he would be dependent on whomever he appointed to be secretary of defense. His appointment of Rumsfeld was a disaster. Bush paid no attention to a topic like transformation choosing to believe whatever Rumsfeld told him while issuing statements of support as needed.

The situation was even worse when it came to the invasion of Iraq. Bush may well have thought he was getting the generals' views prior to and after the invasion, but everything was filtered through Rumsfeld. Even when the combatant commander spoke to the president, Rumsfeld was there and corrected him. He also saw to it that all of the officers appointed to senior positions during his tenure were prepared to support him or they were individuals he believed he could control. Rumsfeld continually called the Iraqi adventure a success, even when it was clear to the generals on the ground that it was not. Indeed, it was very surprising to see six retired generals come out publicly against him, calling him "incompetent" and arguing that he should be fired. This was something almost unheard of in the U.S. annals of civil-military relations. Eventually, Bush felt he had no option but to fire him.

Gates was a completely different type of individual. He was close to Rice—where Rumsfeld had done his best to exclude State from involvement in Iraq—and he made it clear to the military that he expected them to speak up when asked by the president for their opinion. Indeed, the selection of Admiral Mike Mullen as chairman was a clear sign that he did not want a senior officer he could control. Rather, he wanted a competent officer who "would tell it like it is."

Gates' more open approach to national security decision making was obvious in the discussions that were held in the White House and on the Hill in the lead up to the surge and the shift toward a policy of counter-insurgency in Iraq. Indeed, the appointment of two senior officers (Petreaus and Fallon) was a strong indication of Gates' willingness to put up with different points of view. Fallon would eventually be removed because of an interview he gave to *Esquire* magazine in which he publicly criticized U.S. policy in the Middle East.[62]

The bottom line in following a leadership approach such as that adopted by Bush is that he is almost totally dependent on the quality of the person he picks to run the Pentagon. Unfortunately, there is no bottom line such as corporate profit to tell the president if that person is doing a good or bad job. Bush's total support for Rumsfeld, while admirable in a leader, made the situation worse. That is not to suggest that he should have tried to micro-manage the Pentagon from the White House. However, he was told more than once by people such as Card, not to mention to members of Congress that Rumsfeld was a disaster and that he should be removed. He refused and the United States paid the price.

In the end, he was lucky to pick someone as open and collegial as Gates for the last two years of his administration. Indeed, if U.S. policy succeeds in Iraq, and that is still open to question, it will be because Gates made sure that the president heard all sides of the story—and not just his own views.

Notes

1. Alexander L. George and Eric Stern, "Presidential Management Styles and Models," in *Presidential Personality and Performance*, edited by Alexander George and Buliette George (Boulder, CO: Westview Press, 1998), 199–280.

2. George and Stern, "Presidential Management Style," 200.

3. Dale R. Herspring, *The Pentagon and the Presidency: Civil-Military Relations from FDR to George W. Bush* (Lawrence: University Press of Kansas, 2005).

4. Dale R. Herspring, *Rumsfeld's Wars: The Arrogance of Power* (Lawrence: University Press of Kansas, 2008). For those interested in a comparative study, this author expanded the previous book to include the Russian experience. See Dale R. Herspring, *The Kremlin and the High Command: Presidential Impact on the Russian Military from Gorbachev to Putin* (Lawrence: University Press of Kansas, 2006).

5. As quoted in Robert Kaplan, "What Rumsfeld Got Right," *Atlantic* July/August 2008, 66.

6. Thomas Mahnken and James R. Fitzsimmonds, "Tread-Heads or Technophiles? Army Officer Attitudes toward Transformation," *Parameters* (Summer 2004): 60

7. Michael Duffy, "Rumsfeld: Older but Wiser?" *Time* August 27, 2001, 22–27.

8. As quoted in Andrew Cockburn, *Rumsfeld: His Rise, Fall and Catastrophic Legacy* (New York: Scribner, 2007), 99.

9. Robert R. Tomes, U.S. *Defense Strategy from Vietnam to Operation Iraqi Freedom* (New York: Routledge, 2006), 136.

10. Rowan Scarborough, "Troops-cut Plan Faces Wide Opposition: Civilian Secretaries, Joint Officers to Argue against Reduction in Forces," *Washington Times* August 13, 2001.

11. James Gerstenzang and Paul Richter, "Bush Appeals for More Agility, 'Forward Thinking' by Military," *Los Angeles Times* May 26, 2001.

12. Thomas E. Ricks, "For Military, 'Change is Hard': Rumsfeld Indicates His Review Is Running into Resistance," *Washington Post* July 19, 2001.

13. Cockburn, *Rumsfeld*, 114.

14. Rowan Scarborough, "Troops-cut Plan Faces Wide Opposition," Civilian Secretaries, Joint Officers Argue against Reduction in Forces," *Washington Times* August 9, 2001.

15. Thom Shanker, "Defense Chief May Leave Size of Field Forces Up to Services," *New York Times* August 17, 2001.

16. Thomas Ricks, *Fiasco: The American Military Adventure in Iraq* (New York: Penguin, 2006), 89.

17. "President Speaks on War Effort to Citadel Cadres," White House Press Release, December 11, 2001.

18. Mike Allen and Thomas E. Ricks, "Bush Seeks Major Defense Boost," *Washington Post* January 24, 2002.

19. Warren Vieth, "Rumsfeld Army Chief at Odds on Weapons System," *Los Angeles Times* May 17, 2002.

20. Cockburn, *Rumsfeld*, 156–57.

21. George Tenet, *At the Center of the Storm: My Years in the CIA* (New York: HarperCollins, 2007), 171.

22. Bob Woodward, *Plan of Attack* (New York: Vintage, 2006), 98.

23. Stephen F. Hayes, *Cheney: The Untold Story of America's Most Powerful and Controversial Vice President* (New York: HarperCollins, 2007), 352.

24. Woodward, *Bush at War*, 49.

25. Woodward, *Bush at War*, 99.

26. Tommy Franks, *American Soldier* (New York: Regan Books, 2004), 232.

27. Franks, *American Soldier*, 315.

28. Woodward, *Plan of Attack*, 57.

29. Michael Gordon and Bernard Trainor, *Cobra II: The Inside Story of the Invasion and Occupation of Iraq* (New York: Pantheon, 2006), 58.

30. Woodward, *Plan of Attack*, 63.

31. Douglas J. Feith, *War and Decision: Inside the Pentagon at the Dawn of the War on Terrorism* (New York: Harper, 2008), 218.

32. Feith, *War and Decision*, 85–86.

33. Ricks, *Fiasco*, 35.

34. Ricardo S. Sanchez, *Wiser in Battle* (New York: HarperCollins, 2008), 146.

35. Dana Milbank and Thomas E. Ricks, "Powell and Joint Chiefs Nudged Bush Toward UN," *Washington Post* September 4, 2003.

36. In a very unconvincing discussion of the role played by Powell and Armitage, Feith claims they were the ones primarily guilty of sabotaging the Pentagon's efforts to plan for a successful invasion of Iraq by using the interagency process to undermine the Pentagon's efforts to go to war "through passivity and delaying tactics," Feith, *War and Decision*, 250. Scott McClellan confirmed in his book that Powell was "the only advisor who even tried to raise doubts about the wisdom of war." Scott McClellan,

What Happened: Inside the Bush White House and Washington's Culture of Deception (New York: PublicAffairs, 2008), 144.

37. Michael Isikoff and David Corn, *Hubris: The Inside Story of Spin, Scandal, and the Selling of the Iraq War* (New York: Crown, 2006), 29.

38. Isikoff and Corn, *Hubris*, 181.

39. Thom Shanker and Eric Schmitt, "Rumsfeld Seeks Consensus through Jousting," *New York Times* March 19, 2003.

40. McClellan, *What Happened*, 129.

41. In his effort to place the blame the failures on the Iraqi invasion—including the failure to plan for Phase 4, or post-combat operations, Fieth argued once again that it was State and the CIA and to a lesser degree, General Tommy Franks, which worked overtime to sabotage Feith's, efforts to ensure that the post-combat period would develop in a positive manner. See Feith, *War and Decision*, 266–98, 361, 364.

42. Feith lays the blame for both orders on Bremer, Feith, *War and Decision*, 366–72, 428–34, 440–41, 446–49. Indeed, throughout his book, Feith blames everyone except Rumsfeld and Feith for the mistakes made in handling the postwar period in Iraq.

43. Sanchez, *Wiser in Battle*, 184.

44. Esther Schrader, "Senators Criticize Rumsfeld Over Instability Plaguing Iraq," *Los Angeles Times* May 15, 2003.

45. "Remarks by Secretary of Defense Donald Rumsfeld," Transcript of Meeting at Council on Foreign Relations, New York, May 27, 2003, available at www.cfr.org/publications/5998/remarks_by_secretary_of_defense_donald_h_rumsfeld.html.

46. Sanchez, *Wiser in Battle*, 208.

47. Bob Woodward, *State of Denial* (New York: Simon & Shuster, 2006), 234.

48. L. Paul Bremer, *My Year in Iraq: The Struggle to Build a Future of Hope* (New York: Simon and Schuster, 2006), 169.

49. "No More Secretary Nice Guy," *New York Times* October 9, 2003.

50. Woodward, *State of Denial*, 263.

51. Rajiv Chandrasekaran, *Imperial Life in the Emerald City: Inside Iraq's Green Zone* (New York: Knopf, 2006), 274.

52. Ricks, *Fiasco*, 399.

53. Cockburn, *Rumsfeld*, 214.

54. Mark Mazzetti and Jim Rutenberg, "Pentagon Memo Aims to Counter Rumsfeld's Cuts," *New York Times* April 16, 2006.

55. "Military Papers: 'Rumsfeld Must Go,'" MSNBC.com, November 3, 2006, available at http://www.msnbc.msn.com/id/15552211/from/ET/.

56. "Rumsfeld Leaves His Successor in a Difficult Position," GOVEXEC.com, December 18, 2006, available at http://www.govexec.com/dailyfed/1206/121806nj1.htm.

57. Peter Baker, "As He Touts a 'Way Forward,' Bush Admits Errors of the Past," *Washington Post* January 11, 2007.

58. Thom Shanker, "Gates Seeks Troop Estimates," *New York Times* January 18, 2007.

59. Peter Baker, Karen DeYoung, Thomas E. Ricks, Ann Scott Tyson, Jody Warrick, and Robin Wright, "Among Top Officials, 'Surge' Has Sparked Dissent, Infighting," *Washington Post* September 9, 2007.

60. David Cloud, "Gates Offers Blunt Review of Progress in Iraq," *New York Times* 2007, accessed November 3, 2008.

61. David Sands and Sharon Behn, "Are We Winning the War?" *Washington Times* November 14, 2007.

62. Thomas Barnett, "The Man between War and Peace," *Esquire* March 11, 2008.

CHAPTER TEN

~

Executive Privilege:
The Bush Record and Legacy

Mark J. Rozell and Mitchel A. Sollenberger

President George W. Bush engaged in a number of battles over executive privilege—the constitutional principle that recognizes the right of presidents and high-level staff to withhold information from Congress, the courts, and ultimately the public. Presidents going back to the earliest years of the republic have asserted the right to conceal various forms of information. The phrase *executive privilege* itself was never used by any presidential administration until the 1950s, but the same power effectively has existed since the George Washington administration.

Executive privilege became highly contentious during the Richard Nixon presidency primarily because of the Watergate scandal. Nixon's efforts to use the privilege to conceal evidence of White House crimes fueled a negative perceptive of that presidential power. The phrase *executive privilege* seemed forever linked to Watergate and the abuse of presidential power. One consequence of this development was that Nixon's immediate successors were reluctant to claim executive privilege. Presidents Gerald Ford and Jimmy Carter generally avoided using executive privilege, and Presidents Ronald Reagan and George H. W. Bush also made sparing use of this power. It was not until the presidency of Bill Clinton that a post-Watergate administration showed little or no embarrassment about claiming executive privilege. The trouble was Clinton's best-known use of that power was in a personal scandal that did not provide for the type of circumstance to create a favorable view of executive privilege.

President Bush adopted an expansive view of presidential powers. Many attribute his aggressive use of his powers to the tragedy of September 11 and to the subsequent Global War on Terror (Crotty 2003; Yoo 2005; Suskind 2006). Advocates of Bush's broad exercises of authority maintain that his actions were driven by necessity. Nonetheless, Bush's efforts to enlarge the powers of the presidency predated September 11, and he clearly had an agenda to regain what he considered lost or declining powers of the presidency.

Given this context, it is not surprising that Bush tried to defend and expand executive privilege. Whether Democrats or Republicans controlled Congress, the president put aside conciliation and compromise in favor of pushing battles to the brink in order to win favorable outcomes for the executive branch. This approach did little to reestablish the stature of executive privilege, and it probably did further harm to the future standing of this principle.

In this chapter we describe and analyze the major executive privilege controversies during the Bush presidency. These incidents range from the White House refusal to disclose decades old Department of Justice (DOJ) material to withholding of testimony regarding the firing of several U.S. attorneys. Although there were a number of lesser battles and threats of executive privilege, the controversies addressed here offer a comprehensive overview of the Bush administration's major uses of this power.

Department of Justice Documents and Congressional Oversight

On December 12, 2001, President Bush made his first formal claim of executive privilege in response to a congressional subpoena for prosecutorial records from the DOJ. The House Government Reform Committee, then chaired by Representative Dan Burton, was investigating two separate matters that concerned DOJ decision making: First, the decision by former attorney general Janet Reno, who refused to appoint an independent counsel to investigate allegations of campaign finance abuses in the 1996 Bill Clinton-Al Gore campaign; second, allegations of Federal Bureau of Investigation (FBI) corruption in its Boston office handling of organized crime in the 1960s and 1970s. The committee made it clear that it was not requesting DOJ documents or other materials pertaining to any ongoing criminal investigations.

At the core of this battle was a dispute over whether an administration could withhold documents that involve prosecutorial matters, even if those matters are officially closed. Burton and other members of the committee challenged the Bush administration's effort to expand the scope of its authority to withhold information from Congress by refusing documents from terminated DOJ investigations. They were also troubled with the DOJ decision to declare that the unfinished investigation of the 1996 campaign finance controversy would be closed. Burton penned a strongly worded letter to Attorney General John Ashcroft protesting the administration's "inflexible adherence to the position" that all deliberative materials from the DOJ be routinely withheld from Congress. Burton said that the administration had not made a valid claim of executive privilege and therefore had no right to withhold the documents (Burton 2001a).

White House Counsel Alberto R. Gonzales recommended that the president needed to assert executive privilege in response to any congressional subpoena for the documents or if Ashcroft appeared before the committee. The committee subpoenaed the documents and called Ashcroft to appear at a hearing on September 13, 2001. Because of the terrorist attacks two days before the scheduled hearing, Ashcroft's appearance was delayed. A new hearing was scheduled for December 13, 2001. Bush instructed Attorney General Ashcroft not to comply with the congressional request for any deliberative documents from DOJ (Bush 2001a).

At the hearing (Ashcroft was not present), the DOJ Criminal Division Chief of Staff issued the administration's statement before the committee. The statement claimed that revealing information about DOJ investigations would have a "chilling effect" on department deliberations in the future. Nonetheless, during the hearing the witness, Michael Horowitz, allowed that although the administration had adopted the policy that Congress should never receive access to deliberative documents, in the future the DOJ could conduct a case-by-case analysis of the validity of congressional requests for such documents (U.S. House 2001a). This statement indicated for the first time that there was some flexibility on the administration's part with regard to the principle of withholding deliberative materials.

DOJ followed with a letter to Burton that emphasized the president's assertion of executive privilege over the subpoenaed documents and expressed a desire to reach some accommodation. Assistant Attorney General Daniel Bryant announced the unwillingness of the DOJ to release certain memoranda that pertained to former Attorney General Reno's decision not to appoint a Special Counsel to investigate allegations of campaign improprieties. Regarding the investigation of allegations of FBI corruption, he expressed DOJ's willingness to "work together" with the committee to provide "additional information without compromising the principles maintained by the executive branch" (Bryant 2001). Burton responded that this offer was meaningless because ultimately the administration remained unwilling to allow the committee to review the most crucial documents (Burton 2001b). Gonzales followed that the administration did not have a "bright-line policy" of withholding all deliberative documents from Congress. Yet he asserted that "the Executive Branch has traditionally protected those highly sensitive deliberative documents against public and congressional disclosure," a characterization that Burton strongly rejected (Gonzales 2001a; Burton 2001c).

It seems puzzling that President Bush took his first executive privilege stand over materials concerning closed DOJ investigations if one does not keep in mind that he entered office intending to regain the lost ground of executive privilege after the years of Clinton scandals and misuses of that power. Yet he chose to take his stand in a circumstance in which there appeared little justification for the exercise of that power. There were no national security implications or any public interest at stake; and the claim of privilege did not even fall into the category of protecting the integrity of an ongoing criminal investigation.

The dispute between the branches became especially heated when news stories reported that the FBI had abused its authority when it investigated organized crime in the 1960s and 1970s. There was credible evidence that the FBI had caused the wrongful imprisonment of at least one person while it protected a government witness who committed multiple murders even while he was in protection. Burton demanded access to 10 key DOJ documents, which were on average 22 years old, in order to investigate the allegations of wrongful conduct by the FBI (Burton 2002). The administration refused to turn over these documents and Burton threatened to take this controversy to the courts.

Burton had the complete support of the committee, as evidenced by a February 6, 2002, hearing at which all the members, Republican and Democrat alike, joined in lambasting the administration's actions and declared their intention to carry the fight for the documents as far as necessary (U.S. House 2002).The unanimity of the committee was remarkable, especially given that the administration—during a period of war and with extraordinary high levels of public approval—had made direct appeals for support to Republican Party members on the eve of the hearing.

The administration witness at the hearing, Bryant, an assistant attorney general in the Office of Legislative Affairs of the Department of Justice, asserted the position that all prosecutorial documents are "presumptively privileged" and never available for congressional inspection. This claim ran counter to a long history of congressional access to DOJ prosecutorial documents, especially in cases of closed investigations where the need for secrecy has disappeared. It also appeared to run counter to previous administration policy clarifications that there was no blanket policy of withholding such materials from Congress. Bryant stated that the administration was willing to give an oral presentation about the general contents of the disputed documents to members of the committee but not to allow the members to actually see the documents. This offer only brought more comments of disdain from committee members.

On March 1, 2002, the two sides reached an accommodation in which the committee would be permitted to openly view 6 of the 10 disputed documents. Both sides declared victory. The committee claimed that it had won the right to access to the most important documents that were necessary for its investigation of the Boston FBI office scandal. The administration took the view that it had allowed access only to a narrow category of documents—in this case, those that concerned an indicted FBI agent were considered necessary to Congress's oversight function. The administration continued to insist that it did not have to give Congress access to deliberative documents. The committee accepted this agreement because of a lack of a consensus that members should instead continue to push for all 10 documents.

The Presidential Records Act of 1978 and Executive Order 13223

The next effort by the Bush administration to invoke executive privilege stemmed from the Presidential Records Act, which Congress passed in 1978 to establish procedures for the public release of the papers of presidential administrations. Initially the act allowed for the public release of presidential papers 12 years after an administration had left office. The principle was that these presidential records ultimately belong to the public and should be made available for inspection within a reasonable period of time. Section 2206 of the act gave responsibility for implementing this principle to the National Archives and Records Administration (NARA). The act retained the public disclosure exemptions of the Freedom of Information Act that required certain materials involving national security or state secrets could be withheld from public view for longer than the 12-year period.

The only major change from 1978 until the Bush administration occurred on January 18, 1989, when President Ronald Reagan issued Executive Order 12267 that expanded certain implementation regulations of NARA. The executive order identified three areas in which records could be withheld: national security, law enforcement, and the deliberative process privilege of the executive branch (Section 1g). In addition, it gave a sitting president primary authority to assert privilege over the records of a former president. Although the executive order recognized that a former president has the right to claim executive privilege over his administration's papers, the archivist of the United States did not have to abide by his claim. The incumbent president could override the archivist with his own assertion of executive privilege, but that had to occur within a period of 30 days after the decision of the archivist. After that period, absent a formal claim of executive privilege, the documents were to be automatically released.

On November 1, 2001, President Bush issued Executive Order 13223 to override portions of Reagan's 1989 order and to vastly expand the scope of privileges available to current and former presidents. Bush's executive order dropped the law enforcement category and added two others: the presidential communications privilege and the attorney-client or attorney work product privileges. Under the new executive order, former presidents may assert executive privilege over their own papers, even if the incumbent president disagrees. Indeed, Bush's executive order also gives a sitting president the power to assert executive privilege over a past administration's papers, even if the former president disagrees. The Bush standard therefore allows any claim of privilege over old documents by an incumbent or past president to stand (Gonzales 2001b). Furthermore, the order requires anyone seeking to overcome constitutionally based privileges to have a "demonstrated, specific need" for presidential records (Section 2c). The Presidential Records Act of 1978 did not contain such a high obstacle for those seeking access to presidential documents to overcome. Thus, under Bush's executive order, the presumption always is in favor of secrecy, whereas previously the general presumption was in favor of openness.

President Bush's action set off challenges by public advocacy groups, academic professional organizations, press groups, and some members of Congress. All were concerned that his executive order vastly expanded the scope of governmental secrecy in a way that was damaging to democratic institutions. Several groups, including the American Historical Association, the Organization of American Historians, American Political Science Association, and Public Citizen, initiated a lawsuit to have it overturned. In October 2007, the D.C. district court struck down the provision of Bush's executive order that had allowed a former president indefinitely to withhold the release of records from his administration (*American Historical Association v. National Archives and Records Administration* 2007). Although the administration did not challenge this ruling, it is clear that Bush's executive order improperly trenched on an act of Congress and attempted to expand executive privilege far beyond the traditional standards for the exercise of that power. A number of problems with the executive order stand out.

First, governance of presidential papers should be handled by statute, not executive order. Presidential papers are public documents that are part of our national records and are paid for by public funds. These materials should not be treated merely as private papers that any president or former president can order hidden from congressional and public view. Ultimately they provide detail and understanding into important events in our nation's history.

Second, there is precedent for allowing an ex-president to assert executive privilege (Exec. Order No. 12,267, 54 Fed. Reg. 3,403 [Jan. 18, 1989]). Yet the standard for allowing such a claim is very high and executive privilege cannot stand merely because an ex-president has some personal or political interest in preserving secrecy. A former president's interest in maintaining confidentiality begins to erode substantially from the day he leaves office and it continues to erode even further over time. Bush's executive order does not acknowledge any such limitation on a former president's interest in confidentiality.

Third, the executive order makes it easy for such claims by former presidents to stand and almost impossible for those challenging the claims to get information in a timely and useful way. The legal constraints will effectively delay requests for information for years as these matters are fought out in the courts. These obstacles alone will settle the issue in favor of former presidents because many with an interest in access to information will conclude that they do not have the ability or the resources to stake a viable challenge. The burden shifts then from those who must justify withholding information to those who have made a claim for access to information.

Fourth, executive privilege may actually be frivolous in this case because there are already other secrecy protections in place for national security purposes. For instance, sensitive Central Intelligence Agency (CIA) information is not only protected by certain exemptions in the Freedom of Information Act but also by other statutes that shield "intelligence sources and methods" from disclose (50 U.S.C. § 403(d)(3) [2006]). Furthermore, a general interest in confidentiality is not enough to sustain a claim of executive privilege over old documents that may go back as far as 20 years (U.S. House 2001b).

The Energy Task Force Controversy

The Bush administration was also aggressive in its efforts to defend and expand what it considered constitutionally based presidential prerogatives through judicial rulings. A primary advocate for an expanded view of presidential power was Vice President Richard Cheney who, with the backing of the president, led an effort to protect, and even enhance, executive powers in a controversy over internal discussions of national energy policy that resulted in an expansive view of presidential independence by the Supreme Court.

A few weeks into his first term, President Bush announced the creation of the National Energy Policy Development Group (NEPDG), better known as the energy task force, which was charged with developing a national energy policy (Bush 2001b, 236–37; Government Accountability Office [GAO] 2001). Bush appointed various federal officials to the task force with Vice President Cheney as chairman (GAO 2001, 8). The task force held a total of 10 sessions between January and May of 2001, with group members and staff conducting numerous supplemental meetings "to collect individual views" for future energy policy decision making (GAO 2001, 9; Addington 2001a). These meetings included "nonfederal energy stakeholders, principally petroleum, coal, nuclear, natural gas, and electricity industry representatives and lobbyists" and, to "a more limited degree . . . academic experts, policy organizations, environmental advocacy groups, and private citizens" (GAO 2001, 5). The task force issued its final report on May 16, 2001 and the group formally disbanded on September 30, 2001 (Bush 2001c; Department of Energy 2005).

From the beginning the Bush administration resisted efforts by members of Congress and outside interest groups to reveal information about the task force meetings. This struggle developed into a full-blown legal controversy and ultimately a Supreme Court decision that addressed broader issues pertaining to presidential secrecy, protecting internal deliberations in an administration, and separation of powers. Congressional challenges to task force secrecy focused on obtaining documents and records through the Federal Advisory Committee Act (FACA), which mandates that executive branch advisory committees adhere to various openness requirements such as making available to the public their minutes, records, reports, and other documents (5 U.S.C.A. app. § 2 [2006]). The administration denied these requests and declared that "the FACA does not apply to" the task force because section 3(2) of the act exempts "any committee that is composed wholly of" federal employees (Dingell and Waxman 2001; Addington 2001a).

The GAO, at the urging of Democratic members of Congress, also tried unsuccessfully to obtain task force documents through its investigatory powers and even sued in federal court (Addington 2001b, c; *Walker v. Cheney* 2002). Soon after, Judicial Watch, Inc., and the Sierra Club filed separate suits, later consolidated, against the energy task force (*Judicial Watch, Inc. v.*

Nat'l Energy Pol'y Dev. Group 2002a, 25–27). The two groups alleged that the task force gave significant roles to private individuals, which resulted in FACA violations (5 U.S.C.A. app. 2 § 1 [2006]). They sought the release of documents relating to task force meetings to determine the extent of the allegedly illegal nature of the group.

In July 2002, D.C. district court Judge Emmet G. Sullivan granted the groups' request for discovery arguing that the terms of FACA create "substantive requirements to which the government must adhere" (*Judicial Watch, Inc. v. Nat'l Energy Pol'y Dev. Group* 2002a, 30, 56–57). Judge Sullivan did not address the administration's separation of powers argument that asserted that the application of FACA in this circumstance "interferes with the President's constitutionally protected ability to receive confidential advice from his advisors, even when those advisors include private individuals." The court merely noted that a resolution to this question was "premature" (*Judicial Watch, Inc. v. Nat'l Energy Pol'y Dev. Group* 2002a, 44–45). After the court denied the administration's request for a stay of the proceedings (*Judicial Watch, Inc. v. Nat'l Energy Pol'y Dev. Group* 2002b, 15), Cheney filed an interlocutory appeal in which he asked for review of the complex and serious constitutional issues raised. Both the D.C. district court and circuit court dismissed the appeal. However, the Supreme Court granted certiorari to decide whether the discovery was constitutional and if the appeals court had the power to stop it (*Judicial Watch, Inc. v. Nat'l Energy Pol'y Dev. Group* 2002c, 23; *In re Cheney* 2003, 1101; *Cheney v. U.S. Dist. Court for Dist. of Columbia* 2003).

The Supreme Court vacated the judgment of the D.C. appeals court and remanded the case for rehearing (*Cheney v. U.S. Dist. Court for Dist. of Columbia* 2004, 378). Speaking for the Court, Justice Anthony Kennedy declared that the lower courts must "give recognition to the paramount necessity of protecting the Executive Branch from vexatious litigation that might distract it from the energetic performance of its constitutional duties" (382). The Supreme Court held these concerns are even greater when considering civil litigation. Rejecting the appeals court's claim that *U.S. v. Nixon* (1974) stood as an absolute barrier against discovery protection, Kennedy asserted that the need for information in civil cases "does not share the urgency or significance of" a criminal subpoena request (384). The failure to disclose information in a civil case, he reasoned, "does not hamper another branch's ability to perform its 'essential functions' in quite the same way" (384). Addressing the application of FACA to the White House, Kennedy argued that even if the Court declared that the Act "embodie[d] important congressional objectives, the only consequence from respondents' inability to obtain the discovery they seek is that it would be more difficult for private complainants to vindicate Congress policy objectives under FACA" (384–85).

Kennedy then turned to executive privilege and held that due to "the breadth of the discovery requests in this case compared to the narrow subpoena orders in *United States v. Nixon* (1974), our precedent provides no support for the proposition that the Executive Branch 'shall bear the burden' of invoking executive privilege with sufficient specificity and of making particularized objections" (388). The fact is that "*Nixon* does not leave them the sole option of inviting the Executive Branch to invoke executive privilege while remaining otherwise powerless to modify a party's overly broad discovery requests." Once executive privilege is invoked, the judicial branch "is forced into the difficult task of balancing the need for information in a judicial proceeding and the Executive's Article II prerogatives. This inquiry places courts in the awkward position of evaluating the Executive's claims of confidentiality and autonomy" (389). Kennedy thus ordered the appeals court to give due consideration to "the weighty separation-of-powers objections" when reconsidering the appeal and addressing the discovery issue (391).

Not only had most of the lower courts' arguments been refuted, but the High Court had also handed a significant victory to the administration. The Supreme Court accepted the administration's assertion that forcing disclosure would have a negative impact on the president's ability to carry out his responsibilities under Article II of the Constitution. As such, the decision established a rather high standard of judicial deference to executive authority.

Acting on the Supreme Court's clarifications the D.C. appeals court had no other choice but to rule for Cheney and issue a writ of mandamus ordering the district court to dismiss the Judicial Watch and Sierra Club's complaints (*In re Cheney* 2005, 731). Circuit Judge A. Raymond Randolph wrote that FACA must be interpreted "strictly" in light of the "severe" separation of powers concerns. He reasoned that Congress could not have intended FACA coverage to include presidential advisory committees (which are normally exempt from FACA if comprised of federal employees) when private citizens merely participate in "meetings or activities." Raymond stated that although a private citizen might influence a committee's decisions, "having neither a vote nor a veto over the advice the committee renders to the President, he is no more a member of the committee than the aides who accompany Congressmen or cabinet officers to committee meetings." Raymond concluded that "[s]eparation-of-powers concerns strongly support this interpretation of FACA." Therefore, in "making decisions on personnel and policy, and in formulating legislative proposals, the President must be free to seek confidential information from many sources, both inside the government and outside" (*In re Cheney* 2005, 728).

The appeals court's decision largely sided with Cheney's argument by enhancing the administration's ability to block the disclosure of information. The Supreme Court's opinion validated the White House's argument that it had the right to withhold from the public and the Congress information dealing with public policy discussions with private parties. No doubt the Court is correct that one should be mindful of the vexing constitutional issues at stake. However, there are also important tradeoffs between transparency and secrecy that must be considered and resolved. The disclosure of information is one of the primary ways to combat fraud and abuse in government. On the other hand, there needs to be some level of confidentiality at the executive level where a president has the ability to discuss public policy matters in confidence. Such conflicts thus involve a balancing test to determine under the circumstances which branch's interests are more compelling. Here the Supreme Court appears to have gone out of its way to protect the executive branch in a dispute where it was capable of defending itself.

The problem with the judiciary's answer to this controversy is that it provided far too much protection to the executive branch at the cost of openness and accountability. The solution, in essence, offset the balance of power between the president and Congress. What the judiciary ended up endorsing was immunity from disclosure for the White House, which precludes any type of nuanced approach that could recognize tradeoffs and political accommodations that seek to balance the interests of the two branches.

The U.S. Attorneys Firings

The Bush administration pushed the bounds of secrecy in another major controversy where multiple claims of executive privilege were made to conceal White House documents and to prevent current and former presidential aides from testifying before Congress about the contentious decision to force the resignations of a number of U.S. attorneys. White House stonewalling led to Congress issuing several subpoenas; a contempt resolution; and, finally a lawsuit to force the executive branch to comply with a committee investigation.

Discussion of removing U.S. attorneys and appointing those who would better serve the president's agenda began early in Bush's second term. Nearly two years later, after extensive deliberations between the DOJ and White House, the administration decided to remove seven U.S. attorneys on December 7,

2006. Although the formal list of dismissals only included these seven, the DOJ had removed several other individuals (Rozell and Sollenberger 2008, 319–20).

The House and Senate Judiciary Committees launched investigations. In early 2007, the White House and DOJ failed to turn over a number of documents to the committees and several White House officials refused to testify about the U.S. attorney controversy (Rozell and Sollenberger 2008, 320–21). In March 2007, after repeated requests for documents and testimony, the House and Senate Judiciary Committees approved, but did not issue, subpoenas for White House Deputy Chief of Staff Karl Rove, DOJ Chief of Staff D. Kyle Sampson, White House Counsel Harriet Miers, Deputy White House Counsel William Kelley, and special assistant to the president in the Office of Public Affairs J. Scott Jennings (Hulse 2007, A1). The next month, the House Judiciary Committee served the first subpoena for documents and ordered that Gonzales turn over all information relating to the removals of U.S. attorneys (Eggen 2007, A1). In May the Senate Judiciary Committee as well subpoenaed Gonzales and demanded that he turn over all the relevant e-mails (Leahy 2007).

In June, the Senate and House Judiciary Committees issued subpoenas to Miers and the former deputy assistant to the president and director of political affairs Sara Taylor. White House Counsel Fred Fielding responded by claiming executive privilege on the request to handover additional documents (Fielding 2007a). Less than two weeks later Fielding again wrote Conyers and Leahy and this time asserted executive privilege regarding the testimony of Miers and Taylor. He claimed that the White House had acted "to protect a fundamental interest of the Presidency" by not revealing internal decision-making processes (Fielding 2007b).

At a July 11 Senate Judiciary Committee oversight hearing Taylor testified but refused to answer questions that she considered protected by executive privilege. Miers followed Bush's request and did not to appear before the committee. In an Office of Legal Counsel memorandum issued July 10, the administration argued that Miers "is immune from compelled congressional testimony about matters that arose during her tenure as Counsel to the President . . . and is not required to appear in response to a subpoena to testify about such matters" (Bradbury 2007). Because of this open defiance of a request for testimony and the White House Chief of Staff Joshua Bolten's failure to produce documents, the House Judiciary Committee voted 22 to 17 on July 25, 2007 to cite Miers and Bolten for contempt of Congress (Lewis 2007, A13).

The following day Leahy issued subpoenas for Rove and Jennings to appear before the Senate Judiciary Committee at an August 2 hearing. On August 1, Bush invoked executive privilege for a third time in this controversy within a month, this time to prevent Rove from testifying. In December 2007, the Senate Judiciary Committee voted to hold Bolten and Rove in contempt of Congress (Rozell and Sollenberger 2008, 324).

Nearly a month into the second session of the 110th Congress, the House voted 223 to 32 to issue contempt citations against Bolten and Miers (Kane 2008, A4). The White House again stood its ground and responded: "This action is unprecedented, and it is outrageous. . . . It is also an incredible waste of time—time the House should spend doing the American people's legislative business" (Schmitt 2008, A13). The resolution calls on the U.S. attorney for the District of Columbia to enforce the contempt charges. However, if no action is forthcoming then the chairman of the Judiciary Committee can seek in federal court a declaratory judgment "affirming the duty of any individual to comply with any subpoena" of the House (H. Res. 980 [2008]). Soon after issuing the contempt resolution, Attorney General Mukasey said that Miers and Bolton's noncompliance to the subpoenas does "not constitute a crime" and as such the DOJ "will not bring the congressional contempt citations before a grand jury or take any other action" (Mukasey 2008a). House Democrats disagreed. "There is no authority," House Speaker Nancy Pelosi declared "by which persons may wholly ignore a subpoena and fail to appear as directed because a President unilaterally instructs them to do so" (Pelosi 2008).

On March 10, the House Judiciary Committee filed suit in the D.C. district court against Miers and Bolten (*Committee on the Judiciary v. Miers et al.* 2008).[1] The suit requested the court to declare that Miers is not immune from testifying before a congressional committee and also sought the disclosure of documents not produced by Miers and Bolten during prior congressional subpoenas. At the heart of this suit was the claim of absolute immunity that was articulated by Principal Deputy Assistant Attorney General Stephen Bradbury in his OLC July 10 memorandum. He declared that "Since at least the 1940s, Administrations of both political parties have taken the position that 'the President and his immediate advisers are absolutely immune from testimonial compulsion by a Congressional committee'" which "'may not be overborne by competing congressional interests'" (Bradbury 2007). Continuing, Bradbury articulated the rationale that the "separation of powers principle" not only makes the president himself immune to testimony, but it also applies "to senior presidential advisers." Bradbury even broadened the absolute immunity claim to include former presidential aides such as Miers: "Separation of powers principle dictate that former Presidents and former senior presidential advisers remain immune from compelled congressional testimony about official matters that occurred during their time as President or senior presidential advisers" (Bradbury 2007).

The memorandum thus offered a broadly expansive rationale for executive branch immunity to congressional testimony that contradicted constitutional principles and history. A president's independence from Congress is not threatened by having cabinet members or White House officials testify. Similar arguments were used in Miers' memorandum to the D.C. court (Defendant's Memorandum 2008, 47). The separation of powers principle was never intended to inoculate executive branch officials from congressional oversight. In *U.S. v. Nixon*, the Supreme Court refuted such an argument: "neither the doctrine of separation of powers, nor the need for confidentiality of high level communications, without more, can sustain an absolute, unqualified Presidential privilege of immunity from judicial process under all circumstances" (*United States v. Nixon* 1974, 706).

As for additional support for his executive branch immunity assertion Bradbury cites Attorney General Janet Reno's 1999 memorandum on executive privilege. Reno largely provides the same legal rationale as Bradbury but also claims that the courts would gladly defer to the president over Congress in a subpoena conflict: "[g]iven the close working relationship that the President must have with his immediate advisors as he discharges his constitutionally assigned duties, I believe that a court would recognize that the immunity such advisers enjoy from testimonial compulsion by a congressional committee is absolute and may not be overborne by competing congressional interests" (Reno 1999). Of course the congressional interest in pursing its legislative and oversight functions has traditionally meant that executive branch officials testify on policies and projects passed by Congress. In the context of the U.S. attorneys' firings, congressional oversight presents a "demonstrated, specific need for evidence . . ." (*United States v. Nixon* 1974, 713). In addition, the D.C. circuit court recognized "where there is reason to believe the documents sought may shed light on government misconduct, the privilege is routinely denied on the grounds that shielding internal government deliberations in this context does not serve 'the public interest in honest, effective government'" (*In re Sealed Case* 1997, 737–38).

Aside from relying on misguided constitutional principles Bradbury's memorandum was also limited by the history behind it. For example, Reno's 1999 opinion argued in favor of President Clinton's executive privilege claim on documents and testimony that were sought by a congressional committee as part of its investigation into offers of clemency to members of a terror-ist group known as the Armed Forces of Puerto Rican National Liberation (FALN). Although Clinton claimed executive privilege, the administration was not immune from congressional pressure for documents and testimony. As Louis Fisher noted "Congress conducted considerable oversight . . . and received thousands of pages of documents related to the decision. Several senior administration officials testified, including Deputy Attorney General [Eric] Holder and Pardon Attorney [Roger] Adams" (Fisher 2004, 216).

Bradbury's memorandum asserted that administrations since "at least the 1940s" have claimed an absolute immunity to congressional testimony. This statement falsely implied that administrations have successfully defended against congressional pressure for testimony and documents even in the face of subpoenas. As the House Judiciary Committee noted: "White House aides, in the past, have appeared before congressional committees in overwhelm-ing numbers—both voluntarily and pursuant to subpoenas. Since World War II, close presidential advisers—including former Counsels and Special Assistants—have appeared before congressional committees to offer their testimony on more than *seventy* occasions" (Plaintiff's Motion 2008, 32).

Miers' memorandum also failed to grasp the historical novelty of the cur-rent controversy by remarking that no one has identified a single case in U.S. history "in which a senior presidential adviser has been forced to testify as the result of a congressional subpoena by an Article III court" (Defendant's Memorandum 2008, 54). A better point to make is that no administration pushed a congressional investigation so far. History has shown that the ex-ecutive and legislative branches have usually reached an accommodation and thus prevented a standoff of this magnitude. The problem was not the lack of evidence, but the efforts of a White House to heavily tilt the balance of powers to instill greater institutional strength in one branch.

On July 31, 2008, the U.S. District Court for the District of Columbia thoroughly rejected the administration's position that presidential aides have absolute immunity. Judge John D. Bates left no doubt of the legal weakness of the administration's argument: "The Executive's current claim of absolute immunity from compelled congressional process for senior presidential aides is without any support in the case law" (*Committee on the Judiciary v. Har-riet Miers, et al.* 2008, 3). In fact, Bates pointed out that even the president himself "may not be absolutely immune from compulsory process" (84). On August 26, Bates rejected a White House request to delay testimony by Miers and the House Judiciary Committee reacted by scheduling a hearing. The DOJ responded to this second legal rebuke by petitioning the D.C. Court of Appeals for a stay of testimony (Eggen 2008, A11). The Court granted a stay but did not mandate an expedited hearing in the hope that a new Congress and new Administration would eventually weigh in.

Executive Privilege and the Bush Legacy

The Bush presidency sparked substantial debate over the limits of executive power and the proper balance between accountability and secrecy. The president advanced an expansive view of executive powers that greatly impacted our governing order and will comprise a key part of his legacy. Bush perceived his actions as necessary to restore what he considered to be the proper balance between the presidency and Congress, but, by and large, he pushed the boundaries of executive privilege too far. His claims have been inherently flawed and have likely contributed to a further downgrading of the stature of this constitutional principle. Thus, Bush's actions may make it politically difficult for his successors to claim executive privilege and some legal rebukes of his administration's actions may also dissuade future presidents from posing legal challenges to protect the principle.

Late in the second term, Bush claimed executive privilege on documents relating to a House Oversight and Government Reform Committee investigation into the Environmental Protection Agency's (EPA) decision to deny the state of California the authorization to regulate the greenhouse gas emissions of vehicles (Bliley 2008). In a letter to Chairman Henry Waxman, Associate Administrator Christopher P. Bliley remarked that "The documents or portions of documents over which the President is asserting executive privilege identify communications or meetings between senior EPA staff and White House personnel, or otherwise evidence information solicited or received by senior White House advisors" (Bliley 2008).

Attorney General Michael Mukasey supplied the legal justifications for this claim of privilege. Citing *In re Sealed Case*, Reno's 1999 OLC opinion, and *United States v. Nixon*, Mukasey declared that the "[d]ocuments generated for the purpose of assisting the President in making a decision are protected by the doctrine of executive privilege." Continuing, the "doctrine of executive privilege also encompasses Executive Branch deliberative communications that do not implicate presidential decisionmaking." The privilege therefore can "protect Executive Branch deliberations against congressional subpoenas." Mukasey finally reasoned that the "subpoenaed [EPA] documents implicate both the presidential communications and deliberative process components of executive privilege" (Mukasey 2008b).

The reasons given by the administration to claim executive privilege followed similar patterns as previous incidents. President Bush was willing to make a privilege claim that went far beyond the deliberation process between himself and his immediate staff. Besides the dubious notion that there is now an absolute immunity for former presidential staff the administration moved executive privilege protection to include "deliberative communications that do not implicate presidential decisionmaking." In addition, the administration was able to close off FACA challenges to its executive branch deliberations with the assistance of the Supreme Court.

Not surprisingly the administration used the Supreme Court's *Cheney* decision to bolster the claim of absolute immunity in the Miers case. Referencing Kennedy's opinion Miers' brief announces that "repeated invocations of Executive Privilege signals the presence, not the absence, of acute separation-of-powers concerns." Therefore "serious concerns" are raised if a committee is permitted to compel senior officials to testify even if they can assert executive privilege "on a question-by-question basis" (Defendant's Memorandum 2008, 55). Although Kennedy appears to give Miers support in her immunity contention, there is an important distinction between the two cases. In *Cheney*, the Supreme Court was dealing with a lawsuit brought by several interest groups, not another branch of government.

There are many dangers of allowing the executive branch to make unreasonable arguments to expand the use of executive privilege based on separation of powers and other constitutional principles. To be sure, executive privilege has already suffered a bad reputation due to the misuse of that power by previous presidents. Presidents need to be cautious in claiming executive privilege by making clear and limited justifications for its use. The problem is that Bush's use of executive privilege did not rise to the level of protecting some broad national interest. Many of his claims appeared to be attempts to conceal department and agency decision-making processes, not high-level presidential deliberations on issues of national importance. This executive privilege claim had little direct connection to the president since the EPA decision in question rested with the administrator of that agency.

One should be mindful not to leave the executive branch unprotected by weakening executive privilege to the point where all presidential deliberations become public almost instantly. Still executive privilege, when taken too far, can hinder congressional investigations into policy-making endeavors, corruption cases, and other important matters. By expanding executive privilege into all White House, departmental, and agency affairs presidents do great harm to one of the most fundamental aspects of our government—the need for proper checks and balances. Throughout Bush's presidency the executive branch prevented Congress from viewing documents and material that related to key aspects of the interworkings of government. Ensuring that public officials are not corrupted and finding a workable national energy policy are not just the goals of the executive branch. These concerns should be primarily initiated by Congress, which has the responsibilities of oversight and passing laws. Creating a closed door policy where the executive branch alone decides these important issues removes Congress from the process and does much to encumber our constitutional form of government.

Addendum

In early 2009, as this book was being prepared to print, President Barack Obama made some significant decisions on government transparency including an executive order that overturned the Bush executive order on presidential records.

Note

1. Rozell and Sollenberger filed an amicus brief in the case of *Committee on the Judiciary v. Harriet Miers, et al.* with Thomas E. Mann and Norman J. Ornstein arguing against the absolute immunity claim for Miers.

References

Addington, David S. 2001a. Letter to W. J. "Billy" Tauzin, Dan Burton, John Dingell, and Henry Waxman, May 4. Available at http://oversight.house.gov/ Documents/20040831095650-29059.pdf, accessed July 9, 2008.
———. 2001b. Letter to Anthony Gamboa, May 16. Available at http://oversight .house.gov/Documents/20040831095214-51332.pdf, accessed July 9, 2008.
———. 2001c. Letter to Anthony Gamboa, June 7. Available at http://oversight. house.gov/Documents/20040831010840-55687.pdf, accessed July 9, 2008.
American Historical Association v. National Archives and Records Administration. 2007. 516 F.2d 90 (D.D.C.).
Bliley, Christopher P. 2008. Letter to Henry A. Waxman, June 20. Available at http:// oversight.house.gov/documents/20080620114653.pdf, accessed July 6, 2008.
Bradbury, Stephen G. 2007. "Immunity of Former Counsel to the President from Compelled Congressional Testimony." Office of Legal Counsel, July 10. Available at www.usdoj.gov/olc/2007/miers-immunity-Opinion071007.pdf, accessed July 9, 2008.
Bryant, Daniel J. 2001. Letter to Dan Burton, Dec. 19, on file with Mark J. Rozell.
Burton, Dan. 2001a. Letter to John Ashcroft, Aug. 29, on file with Mark J. Rozell.
———. 2001b. Letter to John Ashcroft, Jan. 3, on file with Mark J. Rozell.
———. 2001c. Letter to Alberto R. Gonzales, Jan. 11, on file with Mark J. Rozell.
———. 2002. Letter to John Ashcroft, Feb. 4, on file with Mark J. Rozell.

Bush, George W. 2001a. "Memorandum on the Congressional Subpoena for Executive Branch Documents." *Weekly Compilation of Presidential Documents*, vol. 37, Dec. 12.

———. 2001b. "Remarks Prior to a Meeting with the Energy Policy Development Group and an Exchange with Reporters." *Weekly Compilation of Presidential Documents*, vol. 37, Jan. 29.

———. 2001c. Report of the National Energy Policy Development Group. "National Energy Policy." Available at www.whitehouse.gov/energy/National-Energy-Policy .pdf, accessed July 9, 2008.

Cheney v. U.S. Dist. Court for Dist. of Columbia. 2003. 540 U.S. 1088.

———. 2004. 542 U.S. 367.

Committee on the Judiciary v. Miers et al. 2008, Civil No. 1:08-cv-00409 (D.D.C.).

Crotty, William. 2003. "Presidential Policymaking in Crisis Situations: 9/11 and Its Aftermath." *Policy Studies Journal* 31: 451–64.

Defendant's Memorandum. 2008. *Committee on the Judiciary v. Miers et al.* 2008, Civil No. 1:08-cv-00409 (D.D.C.).

Department of Energy. 2005. "National Energy Policy Status Report on Implementation of NEP Recommendations." Available at www.energy.gov/media/NEP_ Implementation_Report.pdf, accessed July 9, 2008.

Dingell, John, and Henry Waxman. 2001. Letter to Andrew Lundquist, April 19. Available at http://oversight.house.gov/Documents/20040831095838-21952.pdf, accessed July 9, 2008.

Eggen, Dan. 2007. "House Panel Issues First Subpoena Over Firings." *Washington Post* April 11.

———. 2008. "The Answer's Still No," *Washington Post* September 1.

Fielding, Fred F. 2007a. Letter to John Conyers and Patrick Leahy. June 28, Available at www.whitehouse.gov/news/releases/2007/06/LetterfromCounseltothe President06282007.pdf, accessed July 9, 2008.

———. 2007b. Letter to John Conyers and Patrick Leahy. July 9. Available at www .whitehouse.gov/news/releases/2007/07/Memo_070907.pdf, accessed July 9, 2008.

Fisher, Louis. 2004. *The Politics of Executive Privilege.* Durham, NC: Carolina Academic Press.

Gonzales, Alberto R. 2001a. Letter to Dan Burton. Jan. 10, on file with Mark J. Rozell.

———. 2001b. Letter to Stephen Horn. Nov. 2, on file with Mark J. Rozell.

Government Accountability Office. 2001. "Energy Task Force: Process Used to Develop the National Energy Policy." GAO-03-894. Available at www.gao.gov/new .items/d03894.pdf, accessed July 9, 2008.

Hulse, Carl. 2007. "Panel Approves Rove Subpoena on Prosecutors." *New York Times* March 22.

In re Cheney. 2003. 334 F.3d 1096 (D.C. Cir.).

———. 2005. 406 F.3d 723 (D.C. Cir.).

In re Sealed Case. 1997. 121 F.3d 729 (D.C. Cir.).

Judicial Watch, Inc. v. Nat'l Energy Pol'y Dev. Group. 2002a. 219 F.2d 20 (D.D.C.).

———. 2002b. 230 F.Supp.2d 12 (D.D.C.).

———. 2002c. 233 F.Supp.2d 16 (D.D.C.).

Kane, Paul. 2008. "West Wing Aides Cited for Contempt." *Washington Post* February 15.

Leahy, Patrick. 2007. "Chairman Leahy Issues Subpoena for 'Lost' Karl Rove E-Mails," May 2. Available at http://leahy.senate.gov/press/200705/050207.html#Letter, accessed July 9, 2008.

Lewis, Neil A. 2007. "Panel Votes to Hold Two in Contempt of Congress." *New York Times* July 25.

Mukasey, Michael B. 2008a. Letter to Nancy Pelosi, Feb. 29. Available at http://judiciary.house.gov/Media/PDFS/Mukasey080229.pdf, accessed July 6, 2008.

———. 2008b. Letter to George W. Bush, June 19. Available at http://oversight.house.gov/documents/20080620114653.pdf, accessed July 6, 2008

Pelosi, Nancy. 2008. Letter to Michael B. Mukasey, Feb. 28. Available at www.house.gov/pelosi/press/releases/Feb08/mukasey.html, accessed July 6, 2008.

Plaintiff's Motion for Partial Summary Judgment [Plaintiff's Motion]. 2008. *Committee on the Judiciary v. Miers, et al.* 2008, Civil No. 1:08-cv-00409 (D.D.C.).

Reno, Janet. 1999. "Assertion of Executive Privilege with Respect to Clemency Decision." Office of Legal Counsel, Sept. 16. Available at www.usdoj.gov/olc/falnpotus.htm, accessed July 5, 2008.

Rozell, Mark J., and Mitchel A. Sollenberger. 2008. "Executive Privilege and the U.S. Attorneys Firings." *Presidential Studies Quarterly* 32: 315–28.

Schmitt, Richard B. 2008. "House OKs Contempt Citations for Bush Aides." *Los Angeles Times* February 15.

Suskind, Ron. 2006. *The One Percent Doctrine: Deep Inside America's Pursuit of Its Enemies Since 9/11*. New York: Simon & Schuster.

U.S. House. Committee on Government Reform. 2001a. *Investigation into Allegations of Justice Department Misconduct in New England: Hearings before the H. Comm. on Gov't Reform*. 107th Cong., 1st sess., H. Rept. 383.

U.S. House. Subcommittee on Government Efficiency, Financial Management and Intergovernmental Relations of the House Committee on Government Reform. 2001b. *Hearings on the Presidential Records Act*, 107th Cong., 1st sess.

U.S. House. Committee on Government Reform and Oversight. 2002. *The History of Congressional Access to Deliberative Justice Department Documents*, 107th Cong., 2nd sess.

United States v. Nixon. 1974. 418 U.S. 683.

Walker v. Cheney. 2002. 230 F.2d 51 (D.D.C.).

Yoo, John. 2005. *The Powers of War and Peace: The Constitution and Foreign Affairs after 9/11*. Chicago: University of Chicago Press.

~

CHAPTER ELEVEN

Bush's Greatest Legacy?
The Federal Courts and the
Republican Regime

Thomas M. Keck[1]

As Andrew Busch and Gleaves Whitney make clear in chapters 3 and 6, respectively, conservatives have been of mixed opinion about the presidency of George W. Bush. This relationship represents a classic example of the leadership dilemma faced by presidents elected to fulfill the long-standing ambitions of a reigning regime. As with Lyndon Johnson before him, Bush's accomplishments did not match these ambitions, and his failures and compromises sparked repeated charges of apostasy.[2] In this chapter, I assess President Bush's judicial appointments, and it is fair to say that most conservatives have been pleased with his major decisions in this regard. Even here, though, he strayed from the path with his selection of Harriet Miers for the Supreme Court, sparking a conservative rebellion that handed him the literally unprecedented fate of having a high court nomination defeated by the president's own party. Conservatives have been far happier with the president's other two nominees for the high court—John Roberts and Samuel Alito—and with most of his nominees for the lower federal courts as well, but when they look back on the Bush era some years from now, they are likely to see it as an example of promise unfulfilled.

As court scholars have long noted, presidents regularly seek to advance the ideological and partisan interests of their electoral coalition by delegating certain legal and political conflicts to their life-tenured allies on the federal courts.[3] Aggressively employing his powers to nominate federal judges and to direct the litigation efforts of the Department of Justice, Bush sought to construct a reliable institutional ally that would facilitate his policy and political goals in the short term and would remain in place long after he had left the White House himself. Having successfully appointed more than 60 federal appellate judges, including 2 members of the Supreme Court, Bush clearly made a lasting mark. But given the scope of Republican ambitions in this context—a true remaking of the third branch—his efforts ultimately fell short.

Conservative legal elites of the Reagan/Bush era—and dating even to President Richard Nixon—have tried mightily to reshape the federal courts in their own image. They have succeeded in many ways, but a variety of political and institutional barriers have made it difficult for them to consolidate their control. In particular, Republican presidents have regularly been preoccupied by commitments other than staffing the federal courts, and even when focused on the task at hand, they have regularly faced divided government or narrow congressional majorities that limit their options. Once having placed their partisan allies on the bench, moreover, Republican presidents have sometimes been frustrated by those judges' independent behavior.

During Bush's two terms in office, Democratic senators consistently played hardball on this issue, using what powers they had to block some of his most conservative nominees even at the height of his political authority. This obstructionist task was a difficult one, and if Bush had been succeeded by John McCain, the Republican Party may well have consolidated its hold on the courts for a generation. But the electoral repudiation of Bush's presidency in November 2008 stopped the conservative judicial revolution in its tracks. Barack Obama's victory, coupled with an expanded Democratic majority in the Senate, dramatically shifted the playing field of judicial politics, and by the end of his first term, President Obama is likely to have moved the federal courts back into a state of partisan balance. If he serves a second term—and particularly if his presidency develops into a reconstructive one, ushering in a new era of Democratic Party governance—then we will look back on 2008 as the peak of the Republican Party's control of the judicial branch, after which it suffered a long slow decline.

Bush's Judges

From the opening months of his tenure, President Bush sought to revive the long-standing Republican effort to remake the federal courts, an effort that had been reduced to a defensive strategy of obstruction and delay for the 8 years of Bill Clinton's presidency. In fact, Bush signaled his aggressive judicial strategy even before taking the oath of office, announcing in late December 2000 that lame-duck Senator John Ashcroft would be his nominee for

Attorney General. Ashcroft had a long record of social conservatism dating to his years as governor of Missouri, and more recently, he had been a leader of the Republican Senate's efforts to obstruct some of President Clinton's judicial nominations. When Bush nominated Theodore Olson as Solicitor General in February, the signal seemed clear, and when he announced in March that he was suspending the 50-year-old practice of allowing the American Bar Association (ABA) to prescreen judicial candidates before the White House publicly announced their nominations, it seemed clearer still.[4] Olson had long been a pillar of the conservative legal establishment—most recently, Bush had tapped him to lead his legal team in the 2000 election controversy—and the ABA's role in judicial nominations had long been a sore point for conservatives.

When the president announced his first judicial nominees in early May, some observers read the list as a more conciliatory gesture.[5] It excluded several rumored nominees whom Democratic senators had publicly opposed, and it included two former Clinton appointees (Barrington Parker and Roger Gregory), three women (Edith Clement, Priscilla Owen, and Deborah Cook), and three people of color (Parker, Gregory, and Miguel Estrada). Then again, the list also included the favorite academic constitutional scholar of the religious right (Michael McConnell), a past president of the Mississippi Baptist Convention and one-time segregationist (Charles Pickering), former staffers for Senators Jesse Helms and Strom Thurmond (Terrence Boyle and Dennis Shedd), a D.C. lawyer with long-standing ties to Republican administrations (John Roberts), two men whom President Bush's father had unsuccessfully nominated to the federal bench a decade previously (Boyle and Roberts), and a member of the Texas Supreme Court whom White House Counsel Alberto Gonzales had once accused of reading her pro-life views into state law (Owen).

By this time, moreover, the Democratic leadership in the Senate had already determined to push back aggressively. In April, most of the caucus attended a weekend retreat at which two liberal constitutional scholars and a leading women's rights litigator "urged the senators to oppose even nominees with strong credentials and no embarrassing flaws, simply because the White House was trying to push the courts in a conservative direction."[6] When Vermont Senator Jim Jeffords quit the Republican Party in May, handing control of the chamber to the opposition, the new Democratic leadership of the Judiciary Committee quickly objected to several of the president's nominees, with Senator Charles Schumer publicly calling for an open and forthright consideration of their ideology prior to confirmation. Noting that President Bush seemed determined to push the courts sharply to the right, despite having been "elected by the narrowest of margins," Schumer signaled his willingness to block judicial nominees who were "outside the mainstream."[7]

Following this strategy, Schumer and his Democratic allies confirmed most of Bush's judges, but sought to rally their base by blocking—and publicly criticizing—the ones they considered most controversial. They selected Pickering as their first target, with the Senate Judiciary Committee rejecting his nomination on a party line vote in March 2002. Six months later, the committee did the same with Owen. All told, the Democratic Senate confirmed 17 nominees for appellate judgeships in 2001 and 2002, but blocked or failed to act on 15 others.

Republican senators had taken a similar approach toward President Clinton's judicial nominees, but they nonetheless complained bitterly about these tactics, and when they regained control of the Senate following the 2002 mid-term elections, they pushed forward aggressively.[8] President Bush renominated 14 of the 15 candidates whose appellate nominations had failed in the previous Congress, and the newly Republican Senate quickly confirmed 5 of them (including Roberts), along with a number of new nominees submitted by the president. But the Democratic minority filibustered the nominations of Pickering, Owen, and Estrada, and this stalemate persisted throughout 2003.

Estrada withdrew his name in September of that year, but early in 2004, the president sought to bypass the Senate by installing two controversial nominees via recess appointment: Pickering on the 5th Circuit and Alabama Attorney General William Pryor on the 11th. The use of recess appointments to name Article III judges was once quite common, but the practice had fallen into disfavor since the John Kennedy administration, in part because some leaders of the bench and bar consider it a dangerous threat to judicial independence.[9] The original Constitution allowed the president temporarily to fill vacancies in federal government offices while Congress was not in session, but the justification for doing so in the case of federal judges is generally quite weak. (How urgently does a single vacancy on the 11th Circuit need to be filled before Congress reconvenes?) Moreover, the judge who sits via recess appointment is empowered to decide federal legal controversies without the protections of life tenure. If he or she hopes to be renominated (and confirmed) for a regular appointment, he or she might be tempted to tailor his or her decisions to satisfy the president (and the Senate).

Whether constitutionally legitimate or not, these recess appointments marked an escalation of Bush's efforts to stack the courts with known conservatives and to rally his base by picking a fight with liberal Democrats. Pickering's nomination had been stalled for almost three years and had failed to survive a cloture vote in October 2003. Pryor's had emerged more recently, but had sparked one of the sharpest conflicts of all, with Democratic senators opposing him on the grounds of his outspoken conservative positions on abortion, gay rights, and school prayer, and some Republican senators responding by accusing the Democrats of anti-Catholic bias.[10] Senate Democrats responded to the Pickering and Pryor appointments by refusing to allow votes on any pending nominees, and the president eventually backed down, agreeing not to make any more recess appointments for the remainder of his term in exchange for a Democratic promise to allow votes on 25 pending nominees.[11] Only 5 of these pending nominations were for the appellate courts, and those 5 were the only appellate nominees confirmed all year.

Democratic senators continued to block action on Boyle, Owen, and three others whose confirmations had been stalled since 2001, as well as a number who had been nominated more recently. Along with Pryor, the most controversial of Bush's 2003 and 2004 nominees were Brett Kavanaugh, a 38-year-old White House lawyer and former member of Independent Counsel Kenneth Starr's staff; William J. Haynes, whose tenure as General Counsel of the Department of Defense was marked by several controversial legal opinions regarding presidential authority in the war on terror; William Myers, a former lobbyist for the timber and mining industries; and Janice Rogers Brown, a California Supreme Court Justice who had regularly and publicly expressed intemperate and extreme legal views. All told, Democratic senators prevented confirmation of 13 pending appellate nominees in 2004, hoping to have these vacancies filled by a victorious John Kerry after the November elections.

This strategy did not work out, and Bush's re-election dramatically strengthened the Republicans' hand. Not only did the voters provide a significant public endorsement of Bush's first term—one that was widely interpreted as a bigger mandate for conservative change than his narrow and disputed election four years previously—but the national media tended to credit the outcome to the sizeable turnout among religious conservatives. Postelection coverage highlighted the national exit polls reporting that 22 percent of voters indicated "moral values" as the most important issue facing the country and that 80 percent of them voted for Bush. Whether accurate or not—a number of leading political scientists challenged this reading of the results—religious conservatives claimed credit for Bush's victory and demanded repayment in the form of conservative judges. And with the Republicans also picking up 4 Senate seats, increasing their caucus to 55, they were ever less tolerant of the Democrats' obstructionist tactics. Bush began his second term by resubmitting almost all of the nominations that the Senate had refused to act on prior to the election, including Boyle, Owen, Kavanaugh, Haynes, Myers, and Brown. Around the same time, Senate Majority Leader Bill Frist—who harbored presidential aspirations of his own—signaled his willingness to force through a rules change prohibiting filibusters of judicial nominations.

Even at this moment of Republican strength, however, obstacles remained. The president's attention and priorities were largely elsewhere, with the administration unveiling bold plans for privatizing Social Security and reforming the federal tax code, and with the ongoing Iraq War proving ever more unpopular. In this context, the Democratic minority in the Senate was able to throw up some road blocks. Even with only 44 members (plus one independent who caucused with them), a unified Democratic caucus could still block judicial confirmations by voting against cloture. Frist's proposal—which came to be known as the "nuclear option"—was an effort to undermine this Democratic tactic, but Democrats responded by threatening to obstruct all further Senate business, and some members of Frist's own caucus were not fully on board. In the wake of the November elections, Republican Senator Arlen Specter had noted that fervently antiabortion judges might not be confirmable. He almost lost the chairmanship of the Judiciary Committee as a result, but the institution's seniority norms prevailed. In May 2005, Specter joined McCain and five other Republican Senators in striking a deal with seven of their Democratic colleagues. The Republican senators agreed not to support the nuclear option—thus depriving Frist of a working majority on this issue—and in return, the Democratic senators agreed not to support filibusters of future Bush nominees except in "extraordinary circumstances." The Democrats also agreed to allow floor votes on three of Bush's pending nominees (Brown, Owen, and Pryor), but expressly reserved such a commitment for two others (Myers and 6th Circuit nominee Henry Saad) and left the fate of other nominees unmentioned (including Boyle and Haynes).

In the midst of this partisan combat, Justice Sandra Day O'Connor announced her retirement from the Supreme Court. A task force led by Vice President Richard Cheney selected five candidates for O'Connor's seat, all of them white, male, appellate judges who had been appointed by Ronald Reagan, Bush's father, or Bush himself. Bush interviewed all five and quickly settled on Roberts, who had by this time served just over two years on the D.C. Circuit. When Chief Justice William Rehnquist died two months later, Bush renominated Roberts for Chief Justice instead. The confirmation hearings in September went smoothly, in part because of Roberts's stellar credentials, in part because he was now replacing Rehnquist and hence could not (from the Democrats' perspective) make things any worse, and in part because he persuasively reassured the Senate of his own modest judicial vision. Perhaps his most memorable line from the confirmation hearings was his comparison of judges to umpires, whose duty is merely to call balls and strikes, not to influence the outcome of the game.

Bush's second nomination to replace O'Connor proved far less successful. According to Jan Crawford Greenburg's account, Bush was determined to name either a woman or a Latino, but was also determined to avoid his father's "Souter mistake." Given these constraints, he settled on his own White House Counsel and longtime adviser, Harriet Miers. Because he had known Miers so well and for so long, he was confident that her conservatism would not waver over time. It was this confidence that he signaled when announcing her nomination on the first Monday in October: "I've known Harriet for more than a decade. I know her heart. I know her character."[12] But Miers's qualifications were thin, and to those who did not know her personally, her conservatism was suspect. The president's announcement sparked immediate conservative opposition, and just three weeks later, Bush dispatched Chief of Staff Andrew Card, Jr., to instruct Miers to withdraw.

Quickly regrouping, the president's advisers returned to their original list and selected the man who had been a close second to Roberts previously in the year. While Roberts's confirmation had been quite smooth, Alito's proved somewhat rockier—in part because he would be replacing the Court's swing justice rather than a fellow conservative and in part because opponents found clearer written evidence of ideological conservatism in his professional career. Roberts and Alito both served in the Reagan Justice Department, but only in the latter's case did opponents turn up a 1985 job application indicating enthusiastic support for that department's opposition to abortion and affirmative action. They had both served with distinction on the federal bench as well, but Alito's much longer service revealed a pattern of judicial votes that some observers characterized as unduly ideological. The ABA's interviews with those who had worked with Judge Alito revealed an almost universal sense that he was open-minded, collegial, and a careful legal craftsman, and the association rated him "well qualified" on that basis, but its committees of legal scholars and practitioners who studied his 15 years of appellate opinions raised a concern that "the results of [his] judicial decision-making tend to favor identifiable categories of litigants and reflect a particular bias."[13] This concern was publicly echoed by at least one prominent constitutional scholar and one Democratic senator, but with all members of the "Gang of 14" voting for cloture, Alito's opponents lacked the votes to derail the nomination.[14]

Following Alito's confirmation in January 2006, Democratic senators continued to object to some of the president's appellate court nominees. The president withdrew Saad's nomination to the 6th Circuit in March, but he continued to press for confirmation of Boyle, Kavanaugh, Haynes, and Myers. Kavanaugh was confirmed by a vote of 57 to 36 in May, but the Senate failed to act on Boyle, Haynes, and Myers before its August recess. Bush renominated each of them in September, but the Senate again took no action, and in November, the Democrats recaptured both houses of Congress. Bush renominated each of them yet again after the election, but Senator Specter announced that he would not consider them during the lame duck session. Once the Democrats took control in January 2007, Bush withdrew their nominations.

By this time, Bush's window of opportunity for capturing the federal courts had closed. The Democratic Senate confirmed only 10 appellate nominees in 2007–2008, and one of those was a former Clinton nominee, confirmed over Republican opposition.[15] This confirmation rate was significantly lower than the 17 appellate judges confirmed by the Democratic Senate in 2001–2002 and the 18 and 16 confirmed by the two Republican Senates that followed. Bush complained about the Senate's slowdown in February 2008—and McCain echoed this complaint in May—but with Democrats hoping to capture the White House and pick up several additional Senate seats in November, they had little incentive to accommodate him.[16]

Still, the president had already accomplished much. At the close of his second term, he had appointed almost 38 percent of active federal judges. Together with the remaining judges appointed by his father and President Reagan (and a couple holdovers from Nixon and Ford), Republican appointees made up 59 percent of the federal bench. At the appellate level, where most federal legal questions are settled, the numbers were 34 and 60 percent, respectively. With life tenure, many of these Bush appointees will be in a position to shape federal law long after Bush himself had left office. Roberts and Alito are each in their 50s, and some of Bush's appellate nominees, including Kavanaugh and Pryor, are still in their 40s.

Moreover, every major faction in Bush's electoral coalition supported Roberts and Alito, and each of these factions can find a number of Bush judges on the appellate courts to its liking as well. Social conservatives are surely pleased with Kavanaugh, who had been the principal author of Starr's report detailing Clinton's affair with Monica Lewinsky, and Pryor, who had an aggressively antiabortion and pro-Christian litigation record as Alabama Attorney General. Likewise for Michael McConnell, who had been a leading scholarly critic of the high court's abortion rights and establishment clause jurisprudence; Owen, whose antiabortion opinions on the Texas Supreme Court had gone too far for her colleague, Gonzales; Lavenski Smith, who had been an antiabortion litigator in Arkansas; and Timothy Tymkovich, who had vigorously led Colorado's unsuccessful defense of its 1992 anti-gay constitutional amendment in *Romer v. Evans*. Tymkovich's aggressive support of "states rights" limitations on federal regulatory authority were appealing to business conservatives as well, and this segment of Bush's base was surely also pleased with Jeffrey Sutton, the lead litigator in the Rehnquist Court's federalism revolution; Deborah Cook, an Ohio Supreme Court Justice with a sharply pro-corporate voting record; and Brown, who had repeatedly proclaimed key legislative accomplishments of the New Deal to be unconstitutional. Foreign policy conservatives generally pay less attention to judicial nominations, but if they were watching, they were probably happy with Jay Bybee, who directed the Office of Legal Counsel during Bush's first term and authored some of the key Justice Department legal opinions supporting an expansion of presidential power during the war on terrorism.

From the Democrats' perspective, however, things could have been worse. Democratic senators played a significant role in constraining Bush's choices for the intermediate appellate courts, successfully blocking more than 20 of his nominees, confirming 3 who had first been nominated by Clinton, and compelling the president to cease issuing recess appointments. The list of rejected Bush nominees included social conservatives like Claude Allen and Caroline Kuhl, business conservatives like William Myers, and foreign policy conservatives like William Haynes. In at least one instance, moreover, threatened obstruction led Bush to refrain from nominating his initial choice for a particular judgeship.[17] Perhaps most significantly, the slowdown by Senate democrats in 2007 and 2008 preserved 16 appellate vacancies to be filled by President Obama, and with solid Democratic control of both houses in 2009–2010, they may well enact legislation authorizing a number of additional judgeships as well.

Bush's Law

Of course, what matters to supporters of Presidents Bush and Obama alike is not who our federal judges are but what those judges do with their judicial power. In other words, Bush's impact on the third branch should be measured not just by counting seats but also by assessing the degree to which his judicial appointees have pushed the law in a conservative direction. In some instances, such legal shifts can be traced specifically and directly to the president's appointment decisions.

Consider the case of *Hudson v. Michigan* (2006), a dispute that began with police officers failing to follow the Supreme Court's so-called knock-and-announce rule when searching a private home. The officers had a warrant to search the home for drugs, but they did not knock on the door, announce their presence, and wait a reasonable time before entering, as the Supreme Court has held the Fourth Amendment requires. When the case was first argued, Roberts had already replaced Rehnquist, but Alito had not yet been confirmed, so O'Connor was still on the Court. Justice Breyer drafted a majority opinion holding that the evidence was illegally obtained and hence must be excluded from trial. Justice Antonin Scalia drafted a dissent that endorsed the Bush administration's position that the Fourth Amendment exclusionary rule does not apply to violations of the knock-and-announce rule and went even further than the administration by suggesting that the rule may no longer be necessary at all. Before the decision was issued, Alito's confirmation went through, and O'Connor stepped down. With the other eight justices evenly divided, standard procedure dictated that the case be reargued with the new justice participating. On this second go-around, Alito reversed O'Connor's vote, turning Scalia's dissent into a majority.

Scalia's opinion would have marked a sea change in the law, reversing a landmark Warren court precedent from the early 1960s. But Justice Anthony Kennedy refused to go along with that sea change. In a separate concurring opinion, he wrote that "the continued operation of the exclusionary rule, as settled and defined by our precedents, is not in doubt." Since Kennedy's vote was necessary to the five-justice majority, his limiting construction was controlling. In sum, Bush's replacement of O'Connor with Alito directly reversed the outcome in the case and nearly produced a sweeping conservative change in constitutional law. Nearly but not quite.

Even when the shift did not occur within the context of a single case, the impact of Bush's appointments was sometimes plain to see. In the context of campaign finance regulation, for example, Roberts and Alito joined their conservative colleagues to unsettle a doctrinal compromise that had been forged in large part by Justice O'Connor. Before the Bush appointees joined the Supreme Court, O'Connor cast a deciding vote with the liberal justices in *McConnell v. FEC* (2003), upholding the McCain-Feingold Act's ban on "soft money" contributions to political parties and its tight regulation of so-called issue ads that seek to influence election outcomes while posing as mere legislative advocacy. The *McConnell* decision sparked sharp dissents from Scalia, Clarence Thomas, and Kennedy—along with Rehnquist—and once they were joined by Roberts and Alito, the Supreme Court appeared to switch course. The first sign of this shift came in *Randall v. Sorrell* (2006), a

6-to-3 decision (with Breyer joining the conservatives) in which the court struck down both the contribution and expenditure limits in Vermont's campaign finance law. The decision to strike the expenditure limits was consistent with 30 years of case law, but the invalidation of the contribution limits marked a significant departure and seemed to call into question O'Connor's recent effort to settle the issue. When McCain-Feingold's regulation of issue ads returned to the court the following year, Scalia, Thomas, and Kennedy reiterated their arguments from 2003 and called for *McConnell* to be overruled. The Bush appointees would not go that far, but they agreed that the act was unconstitutional as applied in this case, *FEC v. Wisconsin Right to Life* (2007). President Bush had signed the McCain-Feingold Act into law, and his Office of the Solicitor General (OSG) had dutifully defended it in court, but the administration's support for the law had always been lukewarm, and the White House expressed no signs of displeasure with the court's decision to narrow its reach. This dynamic was repeated the following year, when OSG defended another provision of McCain-Feingold, but urged the court to dismiss the challenge on jurisdictional grounds and duck the substantive issue. Instead, the court struck the provision down, and the White House did not complain.[18]

This same general pattern of incremental but significant conservative shifts characterized much of what the Roberts court did in its first three terms. In broad strokes, at least, it captures the dynamics of constitutional change on the lower federal courts as well. In the pages that follow, I offer a provisional assessment of the key legal victories and defeats, traceable to Bush's judicial appointments, for the three principal components of the Republican electoral coalition: social, economic, and foreign policy conservatives.

Social Conservatives

From the beginning, the modern social conservative movement has been defined in large part as an effort to reverse objectionable Supreme Court decisions, with *Roe v. Wade* the prime target. Over time, the movement has developed an increasingly sophisticated litigation network to pursue this effort, and this network of social conservative lawyers, both inside and outside the administration, has won several notable legal victories that can be traced to President Bush's judicial appointments.

Consider the issue of what pro-life advocates call partial birth abortion. In the mid-1990s, the Republican Congress voted twice to outlaw the practice, but President Clinton vetoed each of these bills, and in June 2000, the Supreme Court held that a similar bill enacted by Nebraska was unconstitutional.

Despite this holding, Congress tried again, and in 2003, President Bush signed the federal ban into law. By failing to provide an exception for maternal health, Bush and the Republican Congress offered a direct challenge to the Supreme Court, which had held in the Nebraska case that such an exception was constitutionally required. Relying on this recent precedent, 11 of the 12 lower court judges who considered the constitutionality of the federal ban voted to strike it down. But when *Gonzales v. Carhart* (2007) reached the high court, the Bush appointees joined Scalia, Thomas, and Kennedy to uphold it. Kennedy's opinion for the Supreme Court did not call *Roe* or any of the court's other abortion precedents into question, but it evinced a clear determination to read those precedents narrowly. And with the Roberts court leading the way, Bush appointees on the lower courts have pushed the law in this direction as well. In June 2008, for example, six judges appointed by President Bush joined one appointed by his father in lifting a preliminary injunction and allowing South Dakota to begin enforcing a 2005 statutory requirement that abortion providers give their clients a written statement indicating that "the abortion will terminate the life of a whole, separate, unique living human being."[19]

A similar dynamic has unfolded in the gay rights context, where the Roberts court has not yet intervened directly, but where Bush appointees on the lower courts have at times joined their Republican colleagues to advance a narrow reading of the high court's existing liberal precedents.[20] In July 2004, for example, the 11th Circuit refused to rehear a previous decision by one of its three-judge panels to uphold Florida's statutory ban on adoption by homosexuals, the only such state law in the country at the time.[21] Six of the circuit's judges—three appointed by Clinton, and one each by Carter, the first President Bush, and Ford—argued that the panel decision was inconsistent with the Supreme Court's landmark 2003 decision invalidating criminal sodomy laws, *Lawrence v. Texas*. But six other judges—including William Pryor, then serving on the controversial recess appointment from President Bush—voted to let the panel decision stand. If Pryor's seat had still been vacant, the court's 6-to-5 vote would have resulted in rehearing and probably reversing the panel's decision. But with Pryor participating, the tie vote produced a denial of the request for rehearing.

On the issue of racial equality—as with abortion and campaign finance regulation—Roberts and Alito quickly unsettled a doctrinal compromise recently negotiated by Justice O'Connor. In two landmark 2003 decisions involving the University of Michigan, O'Connor had led the court in reaffirming its long-standing holding that race-conscious university admissions policies were constitutionally permissible so long as they did not go too far in the direction of a strict racial quota. But in *Parents Involved in Community Schools v. Seattle School District* (2007), Roberts wrote for a five-justice conservative majority in striking down the race-conscious school assignment policies that were key components of the long-standing effort to integrate the public schools in Seattle, Washington (and, in a companion case, Louisville, Kentucky as well). As in the partial birth abortion case, the conservative majority adopted a position that was supported by the Bush administration but had been rejected almost unanimously by federal judges before reaching the high court.

The high court's reversal of a distinct pattern of lower court holdings signaled a significant legal shift in each of these cases, but the biggest legal shift authored by the Roberts court to date came in its widely noted 2008 decision in *District of Columbia v. Heller* (2008). In yet another decision issued by a bare conservative majority, the court invalidated an unusually strict local ban on the private possession of handguns. Writing for the court, Justice Scalia held that the Second Amendment guarantees an individual right to bear arms in defense of one's home and that the federal courts are duty bound to enforce this right against contrary legislative regulations. This reading of the amendment may or may not be persuasive—it has been the subject of intense scholarly controversy since the early 1990s—but it clearly marked a significant legal shift. In the amendment's 217-year history, the court had never before issued such a holding.

In sum, the Roberts court's decisions on gun rights, school desegregation, and abortion were all issued by five-justice conservative majorities, and they all marked a clear rightward shift in the law. But while the Bush administration helped conservative litigators win these individual victories in the culture wars, the judicial revolution sought by these culture warriors has not yet come. None of the landmark liberal precedents from the Warren and Burger court eras have been reversed, and social conservatives have continued to suffer judicial defeats at key moments.

In 2005, for example, Bush and the Republican Congress were unable to pressure the federal courts to intervene in a long-standing state-law dispute regarding Terri Schiavo, who was in a persistent vegetative state and whose family was divided over whether to keep her alive with artificial feeding and hydration. Despite an unusual bill signed by President Bush, extending federal jurisdiction to hear a suit by Schiavo's parents alleging violations of her constitutional rights, 10 judges on the 11th Circuit (including Pryor and five other Republican appointees) declined to order the reinsertion of her feeding tube, and the Supreme Court then refused to hear the case.[22]

In an unrelated case the following year, the high court definitively rejected the administration's position regarding the only state law in the country authorizing physician-assisted suicide. Adopted by Oregon voters in 1994, the Oregon Death with Dignity Act had long been a target of the religious right. After the failure of a 1997 repeal initiative—with the state's voters endorsing the statute a second time—Senator Orrin Hatch and Representative Henry Hyde urged the federal Drug Enforcement Agency to prosecute (or otherwise sanction) Oregon physicians who assist patients in committing suicide. The Clinton administration denied this request, but Attorney General Ashcroft reversed course in 2001, announcing a new interpretation of the federal Controlled Substances Act, under which doctors and pharmacists would be prohibited from prescribing or dispensing controlled substances to assist with suicide, notwithstanding Oregon law. The state challenged the attorney general's interpretation, and in *Gonzales v. Oregon* (2006), the court sided with the state. Two years later, Washington became the second state to legalize assisted suicide.

In addition to suffering such defeats, social conservatives have regularly been disappointed in the incremental scope of their judicial victories. In the partial birth abortion decision, Kennedy clearly shifted the law rightward, but he went out of his way to characterize the shift as a small step with limited practical effect. In the school desegregation case, Roberts tried to make a more dramatic shift toward the color-blind Constitution that conservatives had long called for, but Kennedy refused to join him, writing a separate opinion that effectively narrowed Roberts's holding. The most far-reaching victory for social conservatives was the gun rights case, which reversed a 70-year-old precedent, unsettled a legal understanding that dated back 200 years, and did so to adopt a reading of the Second Amendment that had been a key theme in the contemporary culture wars.[23] But even here, it is too soon to say how far this change will go. Scalia took pains to indicate that the District of Columbia's handgun ban was unusually strict and that most existing gun control measures probably remained constitutional. In sum, social conservatives have had a number of successes that are traceable to President Bush's judicial strategies, but they have not yet achieved their transformative goals of making the court and the Constitution anew.

Economic Conservatives

A long line of argument—dating back to the Reagan years—suggests that Republican elites have exploited the votes of working class social conservatives to win office but have then used their power almost exclusively to enact a conservative economic agenda.[24] Along these lines, some early analyses of the Roberts court suggested that its key accomplishments were legal victories for the chamber of commerce.[25] These cases tend to get somewhat less attention than the polarizing culture war conflicts, but their practical impact is no less significant.

The most widely known such decision from the early years of the Roberts court was *Ledbetter v. Goodyear Tire & Rubber Co.* Writing for a five-justice conservative majority in 2007, Alito dismissed Lilly Ledbetter's pay equity suit because she had waited too long to file the challenge against her employer. Overturning the long-standing position of the Equal Employment Opportunity Commission (EEOC), Alito held that such challenges must be filed within six months of the initial discriminatory salary determination, even if—as is often the case—the female employee is unaware that her male colleagues are being paid more than she is. The EEOC had long held that Title VII's 6-month statute of limitations was renewed with each discriminatory paycheck, but Alito disagreed, emphasizing that the stricter "filing deadline protect[s] employers from the burden of defending claims arising from employment decisions that are long past."[26] In a sharp dissenting opinion, Justice Ruth Bader Ginsburg noted that eight federal circuits had endorsed the EEOC's interpretation of the statute and complained that in reaching a contrary result, Alito had relied heavily on a 1989 high court precedent that had subsequently been reversed by Congress. She concluded by noting that "[o]nce again, the ball is in Congress' court."[27]

Ledbetter has been widely cited in federal court decisions dismissing civil rights claims, and it was just one of a number of decisions in which the Roberts court sought to shield U.S. corporations (and their executives and directors) from legal liability.[28] The court repeatedly did so in the context of securities litigation, strictly construing a number of statutes enacted by the post-1994 Republican Congress that tightened requirements on when investors can file shareholder suits alleging Enron-type accounting and securities fraud.[29] It did so in the area of antitrust law as well, reversing a 96-year-old precedent to adopt a newly narrow construction of the Sherman Antitrust Act.[30] In addition, the Roberts court dismissed a massive class action against the nation's four leading providers of local telephone service, held that federal law preempts state tort suits challenging the safety or effectiveness of a medical device that had been approved by the Food and Drug Administration, and vacated the punitive damage awards levied in the *Exxon Valdez* case and a leading antitobacco suit.[31] When the Oregon courts responded to the latter decision by reinstating the punitive damages award against Phillip Morris that the high court had vacated, the high court announced that it would review the case once again, hearing arguments in December 2008.

These cases involve a wide variety of legal claims, but the practical result of all of them has been to protect corporate defendants against lawsuits filed by aggrieved workers, consumers, or investors.

As with the legal victories of social conservatives, however, one should not overstate the reach of this conservative shift. Ginsburg's *Ledbetter* dissent drew the attention of congressional Democrats, who had recently retaken control of both houses of Congress, and before the year was out, the House had passed a bill to reverse the decision. Senate Republicans successfully filibustered the bill in April 2008, but Obama continued to press the issue on the campaign trail, and in late January 2009, he signed a bill reversing the court's decision. Even before the conservative justices had been reversed, moreover, they seemed to back down in the face of this reaction. From October 2007 through June 2008, the court heard five cases involving claims of employment discrimination under federal civil rights law, and it sided with the employee plaintiff in all five.[32] The chamber of commerce's litigation record no longer looked so impressive.[33]

Consider also the Roberts court's two leading decisions on federal environmental law: a widely noted, though partial, victory for the chamber of commerce in 2006, followed by a stinging defeat the following year. After the Environmental Protection Agency (EPA) and the Army Corps of Engineers accused developer John Rapanos of unlawfully destroying more than 50 acres of wetlands, libertarian lawyers adopted his case to argue that the federal government could not constitutionally regulate wetlands that did not abut navigable waters—the theory being that such wetlands are merely local, and hence beyond the reach of federal commerce power. The Supreme Court avoided this broad constitutional issue in *Rapanos v. U.S.* (2006), but held that the agencies had relied on an unreasonable construction of the Clean Water Act. Opening with a sweeping denunciation of the irrationally expansive regulations issued by the "enlightened despot[s]" at the EPA and the Army Corps, Scalia argued that their "interpretation stretches the outer limits of Congress's commerce power and raises difficult questions about the ultimate scope of that power." Interpreting the act with these constitutional limits in mind, Scalia held that it did not extend federal regulatory authority to wetlands unless those wetlands had a "continuous surface connection" to "a relatively permanent body of water connected to traditional interstate navigable waters."[34] As in the school desegregation case, however, Kennedy wrote a separate opinion that limited the reach of this conservative holding, a limit that may help explain the muted congressional response to the decision.[35]

In the court's next major environmental case, Kennedy jumped ship altogether, joining the liberals to reject the Bush administration's argument that EPA lacks authority under the Clean Air Act to regulate automobile emissions that contribute to global climate change. On this highly salient public issue, in a case where the administration's lawyers aggressively defended the actions of an executive agency, actions that themselves represented a direct expression of clear administration policy, the court rebuked the administration on every front. To note just one example, writing for the court, Justice John Paul Stevens responded to EPA's argument that "climate change raises important foreign policy issues, and it is the President's prerogative to address them" by noting that "the President has broad authority in foreign affairs, [but] that authority does not extend to the refusal to execute domestic laws."[36] In so holding, Stevens alluded to the ongoing constitutional controversy regarding the administration's repeated assertions of unilateral executive authority in the context of the post-September 11 war on terrorism. These assertions have represented the top constitutional priority of the Bush administration, but after an initial period of judicial deference in the immediate aftermath of September 11, the federal courts have regularly stepped in to reject these expansive claims.

Foreign Policy Conservatives
In fact, the record of foreign policy conservatives before the Roberts court has been significantly worse than that of social and economic conservatives. I do not mean to suggest that the court fundamentally thwarted the key priorities of Bush administration foreign policy. In this context, the court tends to get involved only at the margins. But where it has intervened—in the context of the administration's detention and trial policies for captured enemy combatants—it has sharply and repeatedly rejected the administration's central constitutional commitments.

At least since the Reagan-era Iran-Contra controversy, leading Republican elites have called for sweeping judicial and congressional deference to the president in matters of foreign affairs. Led by the office of Vice President Cheney, the Bush administration pressed these arguments even further than its predecessors, and led by a number of prominent Reagan-Bush appointees, the federal courts at first seemed willing to go along. For example, when Yaser Hamdi, a U.S. citizen captured in Afghanistan, challenged his ongoing detention without trial, Reagan-appointee J. Harvie Wilkinson wrote for a 4th Circuit panel in 2003, rejecting Hamdi's challenge and emphasizing the vital necessity of judicial deference to the executive branch during war time.[37] And when Salim Hamdan challenged the legality of the system of military tribunals created by the Bush administration to try noncitizen enemy combatants, Bush appointee John Roberts joined a D.C. Circuit panel in 2005 rejecting his challenge as well.[38]

But by this point, the Supreme Court had already reversed the Hamdi decision, and in June 2006—with Roberts and Alito now on the Court—it held that "the rules specified for Hamdan's trial are illegal."[39] Those rules had been established by a November 2001 executive order from President Bush, but the court found that order inconsistent with both the Geneva Conventions and the federal statute establishing the Uniform Code of Military Justice (UCMJ). Writing for the court in *Hamdan v. Rumsfeld* (2006), Stevens first rejected the administration's contention that the Detainee Treatment Act, enacted by the Republican Congress and signed by President Bush in 2005, had withdrawn the court's jurisdiction over Hamdan's then-pending case. He then noted that Article 21 of the UCMJ authorizes the use of military tribunals under certain conditions to try people for violations of the law of war, but that the statute requires these tribunals to conform as much as possible to the procedures used for military courts-martial. The UCMJ also requires military commissions to comply with international law, including the four Geneva Conventions signed in 1949. These conventions guarantee an extensive set of rights to prisoners of war (POW) and a lesser set of rights—some basic minimum protections—to other combatants who do not qualify as POW. These lesser rights, spelled out in Common Article III, include protection against cruel and inhumane treatment, including outrages upon personal dignity, and a prohibition on "the passing of sentences and the carrying out of executions without previous judgment pronounced by a regularly constituted court affording all the judicial guarantees which are recognized as indispensable by civilized peoples." The Supreme Court held that these provisions apply to captured members of Al Qaeda, and that they require such members to be tried by the courts-martial established by congressional statute unless some demonstrated practical need explains deviations from that practice.

Because Roberts had joined the D.C. Circuit decision dismissing Hamdan's suit in 2005, he recused himself from hearing the case again when it reached the high court. In his absence, Alito, Scalia, and Thomas each advanced a spirited defense of the administration's position, but Kennedy cast his deciding vote with Stevens. Roberts and his fellow conservatives have sometimes voiced a concern with unchecked executive power as well, but they have generally done so in a way that does not unduly constrain the administration. Writing for a five-justice conservative majority in *Medellin v. Texas*

(2008), for example, the chief justice flatly rebuked the administration's assertion that a presidential memorandum had created a binding federal rule requiring Texas courts to reopen a capital case, but on an important question of international law that intersected this issue of executive power, Roberts sided with the administration. The administration may not have been happy with Roberts's observation that "[t]he President has an array of political and diplomatic means available to enforce international obligations, but unilaterally converting a nonself-executing treaty into a self-executing one is not among them," but it would have been even less happy with the dissenting justices' proposed holding that a decision of the International Court of Justice interpreting the Vienna Convention on Consular Relations was directly enforceable in U.S. courts.[40]

One implication of Stevens' argument in *Hamdan*, emphasized by Justice Breyer in a separate opinion, was that if anyone has the authority to create a new kind of court to try enemy combatants, it is Congress, not the president. A few months after the decision, in one of its last significant acts before the 2006 elections, the Republican Congress passed a law authorizing the trial of enemy combatants in military commissions. In addition to authorizing such tribunals, the Military Commissions Act of 2006 also severely limited the jurisdiction of the civilian federal courts to hear challenges "relating to any aspect of the detention, transfer, treatment, trial, or conditions of confinement of an alien who is or was detained by the United States" as an enemy combatant. With Kennedy casting the deciding vote once again, the court declared this provision unconstitutional in *Boumediene v. Bush* (2008), emphasizing the "principles [of] freedom from arbitrary and unlawful restraint and the personal liberty that is secured by adherence to the separation of powers"—principles that the administration's war-time policies had repeatedly failed to honor.

Bush's Legacy and the Third Branch

As with *Massachusetts v. EPA*, the Roberts court's rejection of the administration's position in *Hamdan* and *Boumediene* was both broad and deep. In each case, the administration's lawyers advanced multiple arguments, each of which would have been sufficient to support the administration's preferred policy. In each case, the court rejected all of these arguments, and it did so explicitly and pointedly. But each decision was determined by a single judicial vote, and each left a number of questions unanswered. As such, the legal fate of the Republican coalition's environmental and war-time detention policies remained uncertain as the November 2008 election approached. If

Senator McCain had won, he would have been likely to replace at least one of the court's liberals—Justice Stevens was, on the day of the election, 88 years old—and hence could have moved the court significantly to the right. Every five-justice liberal victory from the court's recent years would have been suddenly vulnerable. But with any retiring liberal justices to be replaced by President Obama, those liberal victories are, for now, secure.

The conservatives' recent judicial victories are more secure because the conservative justices are younger than their liberal colleagues and because none of them will voluntarily retire during Obama's presidency. As I have emphasized in this chapter, however, all of these conservative victories— with the possible exception of the gun rights decision—have been incremental rather than sweeping in scope. There has been a significant rightward shift across many areas of the law, but with Obama's victory, the conservative judicial revolution fell once again short of the mountaintop, topping out at four solid votes and one occasional one. These five conservative justices will stick together often enough, and they can be expected to impose some constitutional limits on the policy agenda of the new Democratic governing coalition, but the engine of constitutional change will shift from the Court to the White House.

Notes

1. I would like to thank Julie Gozan for helpful comments, Richard Price for valuable research assistance, and the American Philosophical Society for fellowship support that aided my completion of this chapter. In addition, some of the ideas advanced here were developed in the course of coauthorship (of another piece) with Kevin J. McMahon.

2. I build here on Stephen Skowronek's account of presidential leadership in political time. For Skowronek's account of the Bush presidency, see *Presidential Leadership in Political Time: Reprise and Reappraisal* (Lawrence: University Press of Kansas, 2008), 117–66.

3. This literature dates at least to an influential 1957 article by Robert A. Dahl, "Decision-Making in a Democracy: The Supreme Court as a National Policy Maker," *Journal of Public Law* 6 (Fall 1957): 279–95. For more recent examinations that focus explicitly on the implications of Skowronek's thesis for judicial politics, see Keith E. Whittington, *Political Foundations of Judicial Supremacy: The Presidency, the Supreme Court, and Constitutional Leadership in U.S. History* (Princeton, NJ: Princeton University Press, 2008); and Kevin J. McMahon, "Presidents, Political Regimes, and Contentious Supreme Court Nominations: A Historical Institutional Model," *Law and Social Inquiry* 32 (Fall 2007): 919–54. Following Dahl, while also elaborating and complicating his account in a number of ways, Whittington and McMahon are

among a growing group of contemporary scholars associated with a "regime politics" approach to the courts. For a survey of this literature, see Thomas M. Keck, "Party Politics or Judicial Independence: The Regime Politics Literature Hits the Law Schools," *Law and Social Inquiry* 32 (Spring 2007): 511–44.

4. Neil A. Lewis, "White House Ends Bar Association's Role in Screening Federal Judges," *New York Times* March 23, 2001.

5. Neil A. Lewis, "Bush Appeals for Peace on His Picks for the Bench," *New York Times* May 10, 2001.

6. Neil A. Lewis, "Mixed Results for Bush in Battles Over Judges," *New York Times* October 22, 2004. See also Neil A. Lewis, "Democrats Readying for Judicial Fight," *New York Times* May 1, 2001.

7. Charles E. Schumer, "Judging by Ideology," *New York Times* June 26, 2001.

8. On Republican obstruction of President Clinton's judicial nominees, see Nancy Scherer, *Scoring Points: Politicians, Activists, and the Lower Federal Court Appointment Process* (Palo Alto, CA: Stanford University Press, 2005): 136–39, 144–45, 149–50.

9. Scott E. Graves and Robert M. Howard, "Ignoring Advice and Consent? The Uses of Judicial Recess Appointments," *Political Research Quarterly*, available at http://prq.sagepub.com/cgi/rapidpdf/1065912909333129v1.

10. Neil A. Lewis, "Bypassing Senate for Second Time, Bush Seats Judge," *New York Times* February 21, 2004.

11. Neil A. Lewis, "Deal Ends Impasse Over Judicial Nominees," *New York Times* May 19, 2004.

12. Jan Crawford Greenburg, *Supreme Conflict: The Inside Story of the Struggle for Control of the United States Supreme Court* (New York: Penguin Press, 2007), 245–66.

13. Stephen L. Tober, Chair, Standing Committee on the Federal Judiciary, American Bar Association, Letter to Senator Arlen Specter (January 9, 2006): 10–11.

14. When Senator Edward Kennedy delivered his opening statement on Alito's confirmation, he released the results of a preliminary study, conducted by University of Chicago Professor Cass Sunstein at Kennedy's request, finding that 84 percent of Judge Alito's dissenting opinions urged his colleagues to rule against a claim of individual rights. Senator Kennedy's statement and Professor Sunstein's study are available at http://democrats.senate.gov/judiciarycommitteesupremecourt/kennedy -commitment.cfm (accessed June 1, 2009).

15. The former Clinton nominee was Helene White, first nominated for the 6th Circuit in 1997. The Republican Senate had refused to act on her nomination in the late 1990s, and Michigan's Democratic Senators had, in turn, blocked action on several of President Bush's nominees to that court, including Henry Saad. In April 2008, Bush withdrew Stephen Murphy's nomination to the 6th Circuit and replaced it with White, in exchange for the Democratic leadership's agreement to act on his other pending nominee to that court, Raymond Kethledge, and on Murphy's new nomination for the federal district court seat in Michigan's Eastern District.

16. "President Bush Discusses Pending Presidential Nominations, Urges Senate Confirmation," February 7, 2008, available at http://georgewbush-whitehouse.archives.gov/news/releases/2008/02/20080207-8.html (accessed June 1, 2009); Remarks prepared for delivery by John McCain at Wake Forest University, Winston-Salem, NC, May 6, 2008, available at http://i.usatoday.net/news/memmottpdf/mccain-on-judges-may-6-2008.pdf (accessed June 1, 2009).

17. Scherer, Scoring Points, 146.

18. The provision was the so-called millionaire's amendment, which lifted the contribution limits for certain candidates when their opponent contributed more than $350,000 in personal funds to her own campaign. The conservative justices invalidated this provision in Davis v. FEC (2008).

19. Planned Parenthood v. Rounds, 530 F.3d 724 (8th Cir. 2008).

20. The Roberts Court has issued one decision that indirectly implicated gay rights, unanimously rejecting a First Amendment challenge to the Solomon Amendment, a federal statute specifying that colleges and universities would forfeit certain federal funds if they denied military recruiters access equal information to that provided other employers. A number of law schools had refused to provide such access because the military's exclusion of gays and lesbians from service was inconsistent with their own antidiscrimination policies, and they unsuccessfully challenged the statute in court.

21. Lofton v. Secretary of the Department of Children and Family Services, rehearing denied, 377 F.3d 1275 (2004).

22. Schiavo ex rel. Schindler v. Schiavo, 403 F.3d 1261 (11th Cir. 2005).

23. See Reva B. Siegel, "Dead or Alive: Originalism as Popular Constitutionalism in Heller," Harvard Law Review 122 (November 2008): 191–245.

24. See, for example, Thomas Frank, What's the Matter with Kansas? How Conservatives Won the Heart of America (New York: Owl Books, 2005).

25. Jeffrey Rosen, "Supreme Court Inc.," New York Times March 16, 2008.

26. Ledbetter v. Goodyear Tire & Rubber Co., 127 S. Ct. 2162, 2170 (2007).

27. 127 S. Ct. 2162, 2188 (2007).

28. See, for example, Garcia v. Brockway, 526 F.3d 456 (9th Cir. 2008), in which two Bush appointees (among others) joined an opinion by Ninth Circuit Judge Alex Kozinski (a Reagan appointee) dismissing a housing discrimination claim under the Americans with Disabilities Act on the grounds that it had been filed too late.

29. Note, for example, Stoneridge Investment Partners v. Scientific-Atlanta (2008), which held that even intentionally fraudulent transactions designed to inflate a company's stock price were immune from liability so long as the defendants' acts or statements had not been relied on by investors.

30. Leegin Creative Leather Products v. PSKS (2007). Note also Credit Suisse v. Billing, 127 S. Ct. 2383, 2396-7 (2007), in which the Court dismissed a shareholder suit alleging antitrust violations, holding "that the securities laws are 'clearly incompatible' with the application of the antitrust laws in this context." In so holding, the Supreme Court took note of the fact that "Congress, in an effort to weed out unmeri-

torious securities lawsuits, has recently tightened the procedural requirements that plaintiffs must satisfy when they file those suits. To permit an antitrust lawsuit risks circumventing these requirements by permitting plaintiffs to dress what is essentially a securities complaint in antitrust clothing."

31. *Bell Atlantic v. Twombly* (2007), *Riegel v. Medtronic* (2008), *Exxon Shipping Company v. Baker* (2008), and *Phillip Morris v. Williams* (2007).

32. Alito joined all five of these liberal decisions, and Roberts joined four of them. See *Sprint/United Management Company v. Mendelsohn* (2008), *Federal Express Corporation v. Holowecki* (2008), *Gomez-Perez v. Potter* (2008), *CBOCS West v. Humphries* (2008), and *Meacham v. Knolls Atomic Power Laboratory* (2008).

33. For an example of the sort of sweeping pro-corporate interpretations of federal civil rights law that the Supreme Court was now starting to reject, see the Brief Amicus Curiae of the Chamber of Commerce of the United States of America, *Sprint/United Management Company v. Mendelsohn*, Docket No. 06-1221, filed August 20, 2007.

34. 547 U.S. 715, 742 (2006).

35. Democratic Senator Russ Feingold introduced the Clean Water Restoration Act in July 2007, but unlike the Lilly Ledbetter Fair Pay Act, this bill did not make it out of committee.

36. 127 S. Ct. 1438, 1462-3 (2007).

37. *Hamdi v. Rumsfeld*, 316 F.3d 450 (4th Cir. 2003).

38. *Hamdan v. Rumsfeld*, 415 F.3d 33 (D.C. Cir. 2005).

39. 126 S. Ct. 2749, 2793 (2006). For more on the Rehnquist Court's rejection of the administration's executive power claims in *Hamdi v. Rumsfeld* and related cases, see Thomas M. Keck, "The Neoconservative Assault on the Courts: How Worried Should We Be?" in *Confronting the New Conservatism: The Rise of the Right in America*, edited by Michael Thompson (New York: New York University Press, 2007): 164–93.

40. 128 S. Ct. 1346, 1368-70 (2008). Roberts and his conservative colleagues gave the administration another split decision in *Munaf v. Geren* (2008), rebuking the administration to hold that the federal courts did indeed have jurisdiction to hear habeas petitions from persons detained by U.S. forces in Iraq, but siding with the administration in holding that the courts lacked authority to enjoin U.S. forces from transferring the detainees to the Iraqi government for criminal prosecution.

CHAPTER TWELVE

~

George W. Bush and the Imperial Presidency

Andrew Rudalevige

Arthur Schlesinger's 1973 book *The Imperial Presidency* quickly brought its title into the lexicon as the standard shorthand for describing the strength of the executive office. Presidents were, or were not, "imperial"—and George W. Bush, some argued, was not likely to be. In December 2000, for instance, historian Michael Beschloss argued that "Election 2000 marks the end of . . . the 'imperial presidency,'" and labeled Bush the "first truly post-imperial president."[1]

But as Bush's defense secretary Donald Rumsfeld famously put it, "stuff happens." And on September 20, 2001, with Bush fresh from a powerful speech to a joint session of Congress, Beschloss himself announced that "the imperial presidency is back!"[2]

By the time Bush left office, the phrase had proven to be pure catnip for commentators of all stripes. One could find *The New Imperial Presidency* and *Takeover: The Return of the Imperial Presidency* on the bookshelves and trace in editorial pages the ups and downs of the administration: from "The Imperial Presidency at Work," to "the downfall of Bush's imperial presidency" (after the 2006 mid-terms) to—just a couple of months later—a rebooted "Imperial Presidency 2.0." In keeping with that upgrade, a Google search yielded more than 150,000 web references to "Bush 'imperial presidency'" by the start of 2009.[3]

For the most part, these references were not complimentary. Their focus was on the Bush administration's aggressive efforts to claim unilateral presidential authority at the cost of democratic values and civil liberties—on how, in the bleak words of one subtitle, "the imperial presidency hijacked the Constitution."[4]

But with the end of the Bush administration, we should unpack the phrase—and use it to explain rather than to simply denounce. Indeed, while Schlesinger certainly wanted to warn against the abuses of the Vietnam-era presidents, his choice of terms served two other substantive purposes as well.

First, it aimed to lift his argument above partisan polemic and nestle it into the oldest of disputes about the potentially worrisome scope of presidential power: both at the Constitutional convention and during the ratification debates critics prophesied of the literal transformation of president into emperor. "Your posterity," warned the pseudonymous Cato in 1787, may well find "a Caesar, Caligula, Nero, and Domitian in America. . . ."[5]

Second, the phrase captured nicely a sense of borders crossed, of extra-territorial expanses conquered and annexed. Here those borders were between the branches and those annexations of governmental authority. Thus, imperial presidents sought to enhance their influence over governmental outcomes in the long-standing "invitation to struggle" with other political actors over those actions.[6]

As this suggests, presidential "imperialism" speaks to the timeless tension between a Constitution that makes limited and vague assignations of power and the press of threatening events that riddle real-world politics. How do we maneuver between the effective and the ideal? How do our troubled times weigh in on the difficult dilemma that Supreme Court Justice Robert Jackson raised in his famous *Youngstown* concurrence: that "comprehensive and undefined presidential powers hold both practical advantages and grave dangers for the country"?[7]

The end of the Bush administration[8] is certainly an appropriate time for such an exercise. President Bush sought to expand presidential authority across previous lines of demarcation. He also sought to claim sole responsibility for surveying and settling those boundaries. The latter may be the key issue raised since 2001—it was present across policy arenas and before September 11. And it makes the study of an "imperial" presidency all the more apt. What did that mean for governance in the Bush years? And what will it mean for the future?

This chapter thus seeks to assess both president and precedent. It suggests that the rise of the "unitary executive" as a justification for unilateral action without admitting the constraint of the other branches of government achieved impressive short-term results. Having entered the Oval Office determined to strengthen its autonomy vis-à-vis legislative constraints—and crucially, to extend its control over the behavior of the executive branch more generally—President Bush bequeaths to his successors a stronger office in institutional terms. At the same time, though, his insistence on unilateralism, and on its infallibility, forfeited much of the consensus and credibility that makes those institutions function smoothly. Thus, and rather ironically given his attitude toward his immediate predecessor, Bush weakened the moral authority of the presidency and invited a congressional backlash. An open question is which of these outcomes will prove to be the graver danger.

"The Executive Power Is Vested": The "Old" Imperial Presidency

Article II of the Constitution begins with what seems to be an unusually unhampered assignment of authority: "the executive Power," it says, "shall be vested in a President of the United States of America." Such a delegation "does not mean *some* of the executive power," Supreme Court Justice Antonin Scalia would write 200 years later, "but *all* of it." Or, as a court majority put it in 1959, discoursing on the reach of legislative oversight, Congress cannot "supplant the Executive in what exclusively belongs to the Executive."[9]

Such is the concise heart of the theory of the "unitary executive," which beat strong and steady throughout the Bush administration. At the outset, it is important to note that the theory does not in itself designate *which* powers belong exclusively to the president. The executive power is vested in the president; but what is the executive power? The Constitution does not define it.[10] Its meaning has thus been left to be worked out in practice through interbranch contestation. Scalia's comments came in just such a context, dissenting from a decision that held that the independent counsel's office set up by Congress to police executive ethics after Watergate was a pragmatic compromise that did *not* violate the separation of powers.

Opponents of the Constitution were fearful of this ambiguity from the start. Cato wrote that with the nation's "political compact inexplicit," presidents had room to maneuver toward monarchical control. But Alexander Hamilton complained in the *Federalist* about the "unfairness of [such] representations," responding that the president—unlike the kings of England or the emperors of Rome—would be hemmed in by a long list of checks, from veto overrides to treaty ratification to impeachment and removal from office. Even the commander-in-chief power was downplayed in favor of the powers over warfare that were vested in Congress.[11] Indeed, the presidential office, as strictly defined by the Constitution, is obstructed, rather than omnipotent; "presidential weakness," as Richard Neustadt observed in his classic book, is "the underlying theme of *Presidential Power*."[12]

Yet (as Neustadt recognized) presidents have long sought to creatively leverage both historical context and their vantage points within the government to overcome the limitations on their authority. Hamilton himself, as a key figure in George Washington's administration, almost immediately took a more expansive view of the matter. The "executive power" granted by the vesting clause, he wrote in 1793, was limited only by "the exceptions and qualifications, which are expressed in the instrument." In short—as the argument was developed by later presidents like Theodore Roosevelt—presidents were not limited to the specific powers affirmatively listed in the Constitution or granted in statute but could take whatever actions they deemed in the public interest so long as those actions were not actually prohibited. This prerogative-heavy formulation was not universally accepted—not by Hamilton's old writing partner James Madison, nor by Theodore Roosevelt's protégé, William Howard Taft, nor by most scholars of the Constitutional convention.[13] But it has won more ground than it has lost over time, the argument settled less by philosophy than pragmatics, notably the explosion of the size and scope of government in the 20th century, and cemented by the expansive national security apparatus built during World War II. By the time Franklin D. Roosevelt's "modern presidency" was institutionalized by his Cold War successors, presidents had acquired many tools to work around their constitutional weakness. They used their formal powers strategically, building on their structural advantage as a unitary actor to move quickly and decisively. They constructed a large presidential staff to oversee an executive branch shaped (they hoped) in their own image. And they continually and creatively interpreted constitutional vagueness in their favor to reshape the policy landscape, relying on an increasingly direct connection with the public to legitimize their actions. Arguably, a new framework for U.S. government was created along the way.[14]

This development was largely accepted, even lauded, by scholars and the public. Into the 1960s, indeed, many were more worried about a fragmented Congress apparently unable to meet the challenges of the post-war era. If, as Edward Corwin concluded long before Watergate, "the history of the presidency has been a history of aggrandizement," such aggrandizement got good reviews.[15]

But Vietnam and Watergate showed the dark side of unchecked presidential activism. Schlesinger's iconic book focused mostly on the war powers: "the rise of presidential war," sometimes in secret and anyway independent of congressional authorization. But he also excoriated efforts to centralize administrative powers and impound appropriated funds, to build up a large, politicized staff, to expand the "secrecy system," and broaden the notion of executive privilege.[16] Some of the president's actions were justified by appealing to war-time (and antiwar movement) threats to the national security; but others were designed to enhance presidential control of a reluctant bureaucracy. The "wars of Watergate" were only partly fought, then, over the crimes committed by "all the president's men," and by the president.[17] They were also fueled by fierce debate over the appropriate roles of the branches of government and the scope of presidential power itself.

During the 1970s, Congress responded with a "resurgence regime" of interlaced statutes and procedures designed to strengthen its authority in interbranch relations. A truncated list of relevant enactments is sufficient to give a sense of congressional ambition during the decade: the Anti-Detention Act, the War Powers Resolution, the amendments to the Freedom of Information Act (FOIA), the Congressional Budget and Impoundment Control Act, the Presidential Records Act, the Ethics in Government Act, the Foreign Intelligence Surveillance Act (FISA), the Case Act, the Intelligence Oversight Act. In areas ranging from using force to forcing executive transparency, legislators sought to reshape key policy processes and rein in presidential discretion.[18]

For observers like Vice President Richard Cheney, who entered public life as an aide to Richard Nixon and became Gerald Ford's chief of staff, these "concerted efforts to place limits and restrictions on presidential authority" were "misguided" even at the time. "For the 35 years that I've been in this town, there's been a constant, steady erosion of the prerogatives and the powers of the president of the United States, and I don't want to be a part of that," he told an interviewer in 2002.[19] Thus, attention to the strength of the executive office would be key to the Bush-Cheney administration, even before the brutal catalyst of the September 11 terrorist attacks.

But Cheney's timeline was somewhat off. Presidents pushed back almost immediately against the "resurgence" framework and often found surprisingly little resistance. In some cases, ironically, efforts to set legal limits had given statutory sanction to presidential powers exercised only informally; in others Congress itself backed away from using the processes it had created to challenge the president, or could not make them work. The shortcomings of the War Powers Resolution (WPR), and the Congressional Budget Act, for instance, have received bountiful scholarly attention. By the WPR's 25th anniversary in 1998 even observers sympathetic to its efforts to control the president's unilateral use of force argued it had failed miserably in this regard. In 2002, the budget act was declared "dead" by the very director of the Congressional Budget Office it had created. The beneficiary, he argued, was the president, for "without this kind of process . . . the Congress is going to be dominated by any President." [20] Even in the decade following Nixon's resignation, then, the presidential office retained a solid base of authority, utilizing the same structural advantages that marked the modern presidency: setting the public agenda; emphasizing the commander-in-chief power; bargaining via veto; and shaping policy implementation through administrative orders and executive appointments.

Not every piece of the regime crumbled at once or forever: Bill Clinton's impeachment hardly smacks of legislative deference. Still, that very process helped to discredit its use and killed the 1978 independent counsel statute. It is worth remembering that President Clinton was able to order airstrikes that summer on Sudan and Afghanistan even as House members debated his alleged "high crimes and misdemeanors." As one 1998 headline put it, by then Clinton had perfected "the Art of Go-Alone Governing." [21]

Such governing relied in part on what Richard Nathan dubbed "the administrative presidency," tracing to Nixon's efforts to gain control over what he saw (perhaps for good reason) as a recalcitrant permanent bureaucracy. The strategy included building a "counterbureaucracy" in the White House so as to lengthen the president's reach into different policy arenas. Nixon also attempted to centralize regulatory review in the Executive Office of the President (EOP); to direct implementation through such tools as signing statements and fiscal impoundment; and to make careful selection of political appointees to ensure responsiveness from the departments and agencies. [22] From Nixon's perspective bureaucratic control was a right grounded in the vesting clause; and "the manner in which the president exercises his assigned executive powers," he said, "is not subject to questioning by another branch of the government." [23]

Nathan summed this up as a "plot that failed," but later presidents would help the plot thicken. Ronald Reagan, for instance, successfully institutionalized centralized review of agency regulations in the Office of Management and Budget (OMB), which Nixon had created out of the older Bureau of the Budget, and his successors have continued to utilize this management tool. [24] Reagan also learned from Nixon's belated efforts at coordinating executive branch appointments, adopting early the credo "personnel is policy" and stressing the need for "ideological fortitude" in dealing with departmental inertia. [25] Where Nixon had occasionally issued administrative orders attempting to ensure statutes were implemented in a manner congenial to presidential preferences, Reagan and his successors did so far more systematically, grounded in the doctrine of the unitary executive that became what one participant called "the gospel according to OLC."[26] The idea was to enforce against what one Office of Legal Counsel (OLC) opinion in the first Bush administration termed "common legislative encroachments on executive authority"; the battle over the legislative veto in 1983 which led to *INS v. Chadha* was one example. Clinton's OLC likewise urged upon general counsels throughout the government the "obligation" of the executive branch to highlight and fight back against separation of powers issues arising from legislative "micromanagement . . . in as forceful and principled a way as possible."[27]

Bush was to escalate both principle and force. And he inherited a well-stocked arsenal with which to do so.

The New Imperial Presidency: Zones of Autonomy

"The President and Vice President always made clear that a central administration priority was to maintain and expand the President's formal legal powers," wrote Jack Goldsmith, who headed the Bush OLC in 2003–2004. As the president himself put it in early 2002, "I'm not going to let Congress erode the power of the executive branch. I have a duty to protect the executive branch from legislative encroachment. I have an obligation to make sure that the Presidency remains robust."[28]

Again, Bush was not the first to feel this way; and again, the capacity for presidential imperialism had been largely rebuilt before he took office. But the clarity and scope of the Bush administration's claims and capacities on this score were new, and they occurred across the spectrum of governance. Their consistency was such that despite the obvious importance of the September 11 terrorist attacks, those attacks are a part of the story rather than the whole of it. It seems odd, perhaps, to frame a discussion of the Bush administration with environmental regulatory policy rather than terrorism, with appointments to OMB rather than with Iraq or Guantanamo Bay. But in fact all of these, at least insofar as they reflect an approach to the use of presidential power and the place of the presidential office in the constitutional structure, are very much of a piece. As Nathan pointed out long ago, "much of what we would define as policymaking is done through the execution of laws in the management process."[29] And the most salient actions of the Bush presidency are basically administrative in nature, from the response to Hurricane Katrina, to the planning for the war (and postwar) in Iraq, to the alleged politicization of various departments, to the implementation of the terrorist detention regime. Here the doctrine of the unitary executive merges with another age-old question—"who controls the bureaucracy?"—and answers it.

The Unitary Executive in Practice

It could do so because as the Bush administration proceeded that doctrine was reinforced in important ways by its legal theorists.

Recall that unitary executive theory, most basically, posits that the executive power vested in the president cannot be infringed upon by other political actors. The implications that flow from this, however, depend on how one defines the executive power. For example, the pardon power is clearly a pure executive function in the Constitution. And since the president is enabled to judge which measures he deems "necessary and expedient" for recommendation to Congress, he might well argue he cannot be forced in statute to submit legislation.

Despite the president's role as chief executive, though, the scope of his control over the executive bureaucracy is complicated enough that it "has haunted the relationship between the president and Congress from the very beginning of their history together."[30] In a series of important articles, law professor Steven Calabresi and his coauthors added to the substance of the unitary executive by concluding that the executive power must mean "that the president retains supervisory control over all officers exercising executive power." This could mean that large swaths of the regulatory state (which is, after all, populated by independent agencies whose decisions are often intentionally insulated from presidential influence) are constitutionally problematic.[31] On the other hand, such a conclusion went against Supreme Court cases that allowed for pragmatic ambiguity in such structural arrangements.[32] How far did supervisory control have to extend? Could it overturn a reporting requirement? Could it overturn statutory directive? After all, the bureaucracy was created by Congress in the first place, and its basic missions are written into the law, subject to legislative overseers and their funding decisions; the Constitution in turn demands that the president "take care that the laws be faithfully executed."

And so key questions remained about the nuances of that fidelity. For one, as a 1986 memo by Samuel Alito, then at OLC, asked but did not answer: "what happens when there is a clear conflict between the congressional and presidential understanding? Whose intent controls?"[33]

The Reagan administration never quite addressed that question head on, but the second Bush administration did not hesitate. Its affirmation was laid out in a now-famous wave of substantive signing statements, appended to bills newly signed into law by the president, which challenged 1,168 provisions in 171 statutes.[34] They provided a new boilerplate of bureaucratic control, repeated so frequently as to become routine; the legalistic, even formulaic, nature of the language used in asserting executive claims tended to conceal the breadth of their avowal. But across every substantive realm, Congress only "purported" to act; the president had, as a matter of fact, "Constitutional authority to supervise the unitary executive branch." What that meant was not formulaic: it meant centralized direction of what the departments and agencies did, what qualifications their personnel held, what information they released, and with whom they communicated. And presidential preferences in these regards were intended to override the language of the law he had just signed. As Bush staffer Brad Berenson observed, referring to powerful Cheney aide David Addington and his role in systematizing signing statements, such efforts served to "unite two of Addington's passions. One is executive power. And the other is the inner alleyways of bureaucratic combat. It's a way to advance executive power through those inner alleyways."[35]

The entry to those alleyways was constricted by another swelling of the unitary executive theory: a new stress on exclusivity. To the notion that the executive power was the indivisible purview of the president was appended the assertion that the scope of that executive power was also defined entirely by the president. This gave new resonance to the established claim that Congress could not infringe legislatively on the president's constitutional authority.

Such sweeping claims combined an expansive view of the executive power itself with Justice Scalia's argument previously cited, which held that any statute that constrained the president's "exclusive control" over a "purely executive" power must be invalid. But recall that this view, when applied to the independent counsel statute, received only Scalia's own endorsement on the Supreme Court. As such its elevation to administration doctrine disturbed even oft-sympathetic scholars like the OLC's Goldsmith, who would later write that "when one concludes that Congress is disabled from controlling the President . . . respect for separation of powers demands a full consideration of competing congressional and judicial prerogatives" which did not always occur.[36]

It is important not to read too much into signing statements alone. After all, in themselves they are a claim, not a final outcome. They do have important political impact, and a Government Accountability Office (GAO) examination of the fiscal 2006 appropriations bills also found they affected the manner in which at least some statutory provisions were implemented. Still, how much systematic impact they have on bureaucratic behavior in practice, future study must reveal.[37]

But this was only a small segment of the overall administrative strategy. Complementary methods also aimed to ensure bureaucratic responsiveness, as the Bush team showed great skill and discipline in upgrading the managerial resources its predecessors had bequeathed.

From the outset, great care was taken to install presidential loyalists across and deep within, the executive branch; when senators (relatively rarely) objected to a given appointment, a recess appointment was often utilized to by-pass the confirmation process.[38] In short, the president sought with some success to (in one White House staffer's phrase) "implant his DNA throughout the government."[39]

This extended even to the General Services Administration—the normally nonpartisan agency that deals with cleaning federal buildings and the motor pool—whose head would attract unwelcome public attention after asking the White House what the organization could do "to help our candidates."[40] Reporter Charlie Savage has detailed the more systematic genetic modification of the Civil Rights Division within the Department of Justice, perceived as a bastion of liberal careerists: first, changing hiring procedures to shut out civil service input, then restoring that influence once the makeup (and thus the preferences) of the civil service itself had been shifted.[41] In another wing of Justice controversy erupted over the dismissal of a number of U.S. Attorneys alleged to be "underperforming," instead of being "loyal Bushies." When Congress sought to investigate, the White House refused to allow officials to testify on the matter. When lawmakers threatened charges of contempt, the administration replied that since prosecutors reported hierarchically to the president, he could mandate they not pursue such charges, and the attorney general declined to do so. The claim rested on a Reagan-era Justice Department opinion; but the closer parallel was 1974's *U.S. v. Nixon*, where the president argued he could not be pursued by a subordinate prosecutor who could, after all, be ordered not to pursue him.[42]

Government officials, however loyal, were overseen by a new President's Management Initiative housed in the OMB, which developed a ratings tool for assessing the worth of individual programs. OMB's regulatory review function, charged with newly skeptical analysis of what constituted the costs and benefits of agency action, was also made a top priority (in 2007, the head of this office was installed by recess appointment) and given additional heft. This was bolstered again when in his second term the president issued an executive order adding internal "guidance documents" to the regulatory materials requiring centralized review and required a new political appointee to sign off on anything included in an agency's annual rulemaking plan.[43]

In so doing the White House hoped to stem agency activism before it made its way up Pennsylvania Avenue. As a backstop, though, presidential staffers energetically involved themselves in a wide range of agency activities that threatened to prescribe policy divergent from presidential preferences. A variety of scientific groups charged that ideology trumped research in areas ranging from climate change to workplace safety standards to the evaluation of toxic chemicals. One Environmental Protection Agency (EPA) regional administrator was apparently ousted in 2008 for her aggressive enforcement of dioxin cleanup laws. EOP staff even weighed in on a Commerce Department measure seeking to lower maritime speed limits in shipping lanes populated by right whales.[44] A flood of new regulations were issued as the administration prepared to leave office in early 2009. In short, Bush officials aggressively combined centralization and politicization in a way that extended control of bureaucratic outputs and denied the validity of extra-executive inputs.

Indeed, the administration's efforts to control the flow of information within and between the branches went far beyond the regulatory arena. Decision making was tightly held within the administration, eliminating layers of potential dissent. And externally, from the outset, the White House staked out aggressive ground on issues of executive privilege, refusing to release records pertaining to Vice President Cheney's energy task force to the GAO and issuing administrative orders that would both restrict access to federal documents requested through the Freedom of Information Act and those governed by the Presidential Records Act.[45] The energy task force court case provided a telling summary of the administration's attitude toward the other branches of government. The efforts of Congress and the courts to gather information on White House proceedings, argued the solicitor general, amounted to "unwarranted intrusion" into "vital Executive Branch functions." Instead, the Constitution allowed the president "a zone of autonomy"[46]—a zone whose boundaries would be determined by the president himself, but which clearly lay in newly occupied interbranch territory.

Commander in Chief

The same logic applied in the national security sphere after the shock of September 11. The basic issue remained one of boundaries, enhanced by the exigencies of the battlefield—which, in the war on terror, might be anywhere, for any length of time. This greatly broadened the potential reach of the president's "zone of autonomy." There is no need to project malicious motivations onto the administration, as many critics have done, to recognize that the aftermath of the attacks opened up new and newly credible claims for executive authority, nor that a preference to act on those claims unilaterally rather than in consultation fit comfortably with the president's default predilections.

Almost immediately after the attacks, OLC was asked to explicate the legal scope of presidential war powers. Much of the debate over those powers is captured by the Fisher and Yoo chapters in this book and will not be replicated here. It is worth noting the OLC's response of September 25, 2001, though, since it clearly highlights both the breadth of powers that might be asserted and the claim of exclusivity over the definition of those powers. Congress, of course, had passed a sweeping Authorization for the Use of Military Force (AUMF) on September 14, 2001. This delegated to the president the power both to identify the attacks' perpetrators and to take action not only to punish them (and those who harbored them) but also to forestall future attacks. The Justice Department said that the AUMF was nice, but unnecessary:

> It is clear that Congress's power to declare war does not constrain the President's independent and plenary constitutional authority over the use of military force. . . . [W]e think it beyond question that the President has the plenary constitutional power to take such military actions as he deems necessary and appropriate to respond to the terrorist attacks upon the United States on September 11, 2001. Force can be used both to retaliate for those attacks, and to prevent and deter future assaults on the Nation. Military actions need not be limited to those individuals, groups, or states that participated in the attacks on the World Trade Center and the Pentagon.[47]

Such a determination imposed few limits on the presidential use of force, especially when combined with the new national security strategy issued in 2002 that disavowed the need for an imminent threat to justify military action.[48] And in keeping with its logic, in short order the president unilaterally approved a wiretapping program that by-passed the warrant requirements of the 1978 FISA; designated and detained a large number of "unlawful enemy combatants," including U.S. citizens arrested within the United States; issued orders limiting the applicability of the Geneva Conventions and setting up a system of military tribunals; and at least tacitly approved widely applied interrogation techniques that many thought constituted torture prohibited both by treaty obligation and U.S. law. In each case, the action was justified as flowing from the executive power itself. The Justice Department, for example, claimed in a lengthy justification of the warrantless surveillance program, run by the National Security Agency (NSA), that it was "supported by the President's well-recognized inherent constitutional authority of Commander in Chief."[49] Similarly, the administration declared, "Congress can no more interfere with the President's conduct of the interrogation of enemy combatants than it can dictate strategic or tactical decisions on the battlefield." Indeed, "in order to respect the president's inherent constitutional authority to manage a military campaign, 18 U.S.C. § 2340A [the prohibition against torture] as well as any other potentially applicable statute must be construed as inapplicable to interrogations undertaken pursuant to his Commander-in-Chief authority."[50]

Thus, when Congress passed an amendment banning torture in the course of such interrogations, President Bush appended a signing statement to the statute. The administration would enforce the law, it implied, only to the extent it was "consistent with the constitutional authority of the President to oversee the unitary executive branch and as Commander in Chief." Much debate over what constituted torture resulted in little movement on this score. In 2008, the president vetoed legislation restricting Central Intelligence Agency (CIA) operatives' interrogation techniques, and the Justice Department continued to argue that violating antitorture statutes and treaties might still be justified.[51]

Congress was often itself willing to expand presidential power. But even when Congress did so—with the AUMF, for instance, or in authorizing the use of force in Iraq—the president did not argue he needed legislative approval. He assumed he did not. Many in the White House inner circle believed that the very act of asking for legislative authorization would imply that the president could not act on his own. And there were practical considerations, too. As a senior administration attorney noted, taking the congressional route meant "you will never get everything that you want. So, why wait weeks and get eighty-five percent of what you want, if you can get a hundred percent of what you want, and get it immediately, by doing it on your own?"[52] Into 2008, the administration insisted that a long-term "status of forces agreement" dictating a continuing U.S. troop presence in Iraq could be approved administratively without negotiating a treaty that would require Senate ratification.[53] There thus seems some merit, as well as sour grapes, in one senior Democrat's bitter complaint that "this administration thinks that Article I of the Constitution was a fundamental mistake."[54]

But Article III fared little better. The courts, too, were expected to defer to administration determinations of evidence and relevance. "The court may not second-guess the military's enemy combatant determination, and therefore no evidentiary proceedings concerning such determination are necessary," the administration told a circuit court in 2002 in the *Hamdi* case.

"Going beyond that determination would require the courts to enter an area in which they have no competence, much less institutional expertise, and intrude upon the Constitutional prerogative of the Commander in Chief." At most, judges could decide whether there was a factual basis for the determination that an individual was an enemy combatant—but not the merits of those facts or that determination. Such claims continued to the end of the administration in arguments over the case of Ali al-Marri—a U.S. resident alien moved from the civilian courts to military detention in 2003 and thus, by the end of 2008, held for more than 5 years without charges having been brought against him.[55]

In many other cases, the administration argued that the "state secrets" doctrine prevented them from being tried at all—that doing so would result in the release of information critical to national security. "Bush has asserted the state secrets privilege more times than any president in history," concluded Robert Pallitto and William Weaver, "and . . . he has prevailed in virtually all of these assertions." Such claims could result in something of a catch-22. At times, information already in the public domain was deemed inadmissible as evidence. Or when litigation over the wiretapping program was dismissed in July 2007, judges ruled that plaintiffs had no standing to sue since they could not prove they had been harmed by the wiretapping. But that they could not do so was because the names of those wiretapped was a secret that the administration could not reveal.[56]

Resurgence Redux?

It is important to remember that the constitutional structure does not lend itself to an imperial presidency. Congress is, and remains, the first branch of government. Yet it seems likely that the Bush years will be remembered for a Congress that largely empowered, rather than checked, executive expansionism. From the use of force, to the authorization and renewal of the Patriot Act, to the determination of enemy combatants and suspension of habeas corpus, legislators proved willing to delegate authority to the president in critical ways. Even when congressional offers to legalize the NSA surveillance program were rejected as superfluous, legislators did so anyway, at least temporarily—despite the return to divided government in 2007.[57] As deficits rose, the legislative response was not to raise taxes (and certainly not to cut spending) but to seek to expand the president's rescission authority through some form of a line-item veto.

For much of his administration, President Bush had the luxury of unified government—the first time since the 1950s for a Republican president.

This meant, naturally enough, that Republican legislators were reluctant to oppose presidential priorities for fear of weakening the party brand. But too often the president's copartisans saw themselves as working for the president rather than with him, cheerleaders for whatever actions he chose to take. When the NSA surveillance program was criticized by congressional Democrats (and a few Republicans), for instance, Senate Majority Leader Bill Frist (R-TN) warned of the dangers of sending signals that "there is in any way a lack of support for our commander in chief, who is leading us with a bold vision in a way that is making our homeland safer."[58]

The 2006 and 2008 elections suggested that such lockstep allegiance did not ultimately help the Republican cause. Still, even in the president's last year in office, as his approval ratings stagnated in the 30-percent range, legislators proved unable to formulate strategies for Iraq that would override the unilaterally imposed "surge" of U.S. troops to Baghdad—or check threatened unilateral military action against Iran. Overall, President Bush did not did not find it necessary to veto a single congressional enactment for nearly five and one-half years, until July 2006. The Democratic majority in 2007–2008 prompted additional vetoes but succeeded only in overriding those that threatened to prevent the provision of localized benefits such as water projects or agricultural subsidies. The structure of the office, it seemed, could withstand the sustained unpopularity of its occupant. Congress, on the other hand, looked like "the broken branch."[59] Oversight hearings increased in the 110th Congress, to be sure, but rarely led to effective checks on presidential action.

Despite the administration's efforts to limit judicial intrusion, the courts were at times more willing to check executive authority. In the *Hamdan* decision, for instance, the Supreme Court struck down the administration's unilateral efforts to curtail due process guarantees in the military tribunal process and scolded Congress for its lack of attention to the detention regime.[60] Even so, Bush won judicial victories on issues ranging from enemy combatants to the rendition of detainees to executive privilege. More broadly, the courts have been rightly reluctant to step into interbranch disputes, especially when Congress has not taken a clear legislative stand. In the *Hamdi* case, the Supreme Court held that the wide legislative delegation of powers granted by Congress in the AUMF allowed the president to name and detain U.S. citizens as enemy combatants. Some lawmakers said they had not meant to do so; but Congress never clarified its intent. In sum, they often allowed President Bush the leeway to say (as in 2004), "I did it on my own."[61]

Practical Advantages and Grave Dangers

Yet doing it "on my own" rests uneasily with our political tradition. It is certainly not a conservative viewpoint;[62] for despite the doctrine of "unitarianism," the Constitution is devoutly trinitarian. In this context, then, it is worth returning to Justice Jackson's dilemma, the tension between the "practical advantages and grave dangers" that flow from presidential imperialism.

Both advantages and dangers seem salient at the close of the Bush years. On the one hand, the growth of executive responsibility is in some ways a natural and even laudable development. One cannot provide direction to an enormous nation, with an enormous national executive establishment, with enormous public expectations, while denying the authority necessary to meet those needs. Congress is much better at stopping things than at running them. And a nation cannot meet crises, or even the day-to-day needs of governing, with 535 chief executives or commanders in chief. As Alexander Hamilton long ago foresaw, unity would create "energy" in the executive: a leader thus endowed can make quick decisions, in secrecy if necessary, and put them into action with dispatch.[63] In Hamilton's day the administrative problems that arose during the Articles of Confederation period—in a much smaller country, with a much smaller Congress, in what seemed a much larger world—were sufficient to drive the Framers to overcome their fear of monarchy and empower a single person as president. These days a globalized, polarized, terrorized world seems to call out for endowing leadership sufficient to match its powers to the tasks at hand.

The Bush administration made strong claims. Still, with the "vision thing" in overabundance it could make a coherent case that carrying out that vision required careful discipline. Its centralized management presupposed suspicion for its agenda by the risk-averse experts in the departments and sought to overcome the usual bureaucratic recalcitrance by blunt force. Bureaucratic pushback—by the EPA, or the military Judge Advocate General's (JAG) corps dealing with Guantanamo detainees, or (eventually) the Justice Department—merely reinforced the Oval Office view that outside actors could not be trusted unless controlled. The *presidential* branch had to extend its reach not just over legislative territory but that of the separate *executive* branch as well.[64] Thus, the Bush administration and its legal craftsmen pushed forth their theories of executive power in good faith: they felt that only by enhancing energy in the executive could the nation meet the threats it faced.

Yet their good faith did not lead to good works. Indeed, if one argument for executive strength is simply that of governmental efficiency—making the trains run on time—the Bush administration too often undercut that advantage. Its failures were not of imagination but of implementation. Post-war Iraq, contractor spending, the bank bailout, and the response to Hurricane Katrina seized the headlines, but the footnotes are just as telling: "On September 11th, there were only eight fluent Arabic-speaking agents in the FBI," Lawrence Wright observed in early 2008; "now there are nine."[65]

There is a broader danger, though. Efficiency, however attractive, is only one interest among many others, including transparency, inclusion, and the protection of civil liberties. No single branch can dictate the proper balance between those goods. In *Federalist #49*, James Madison addressed the issue of interbranch interaction head on in observing that "The several departments being perfectly co-ordinate by the terms of their common commission, none of them, it is evident, can pretend to an exclusive or superior right of settling the boundaries between their respective powers."[66] Presidential direction, then, is not by definition virtuous, if it does violence to constitutional tenets, and through them, to well-considered policy; an expansive executive becomes dangerous if it does not feel compelled to publicly justify its aims, seeing their merits as self-evident. Speaking of his legacy in May 2008, President Bush said he would be remembered as "a guy who clearly saw the world the way it is."[67] Clear goals have real value to leadership; but clarity alone does not make a goal worthy of pursuit; and clarity can be confused with correctness. Congress has many faults, but deliberation, debate—and even delay—do tend to unearth cautionary arguments and sift competing priorities against the national interest.

Even congressional gridlock does not necessarily suggest a need for presidential action but may instead indicate a lack of the national consensus our system of separated institutions requires for dramatic action. Unilateral override of that system is possible, and sometimes even desirable (Lincoln's example comes to mind). But it is not systematically legitimate.

A Justice Department attorney summed up a crucial presupposition of the imperial presidency in 2006 Senate testimony about the military tribunal process: "The President," he noted, quite seriously, "is always right." Unfortunately democracy—as E. E. Schattschneider pointed out long ago—"is a political system for people who are not too sure they are right."[68]

The Next Imperial Presidency

Under President Bush's direction, the Constitution's executive power was defined broadly—and the need for that power to be regulated by the iterative interaction of the president with other political actors was defined away.

Some observers suggest that the very reach of its unilateralism may have jeopardized future presidents' ability to utilize similar strategies. OLC head Goldsmith concluded ruefully that Bush "has been almost entirely inattentive to the soft factors of legitimation . . . [and] instead relied on the hard power of prerogative. And he has seen his hard power diminished in many ways because he has failed to take the softer aspects of power seriously." One is reminded more broadly of the historian Paul Kennedy's comments on the "imperial overstretch" that led to the inexorable collapse of empires over the centuries.[69] Might the Bush years have set such a phenomenon in motion? Certainly it seems unlikely that the president will leave office on a wave of popular acclaim that would embolden future chief executives to follow his example.

But if future presidents will not always be right, they will likely be imperial, in important ways. For one thing, President Bush leaves behind him an array of institutional controls over the dissemination of information and a Supreme Court ruling—in the Cheney energy commission case—that gives the president wider deference, even shy of formal claims of executive privilege. The case may join the famous *Curtiss-Wright* decision as favored bedtime reading in the White House. And as to future cases, the administration has reshaped the federal judiciary with the appointment of more than 300 new members. The most prominent, of course, are Chief Justice John Roberts and Associate Justice Samuel Alito on the Supreme Court, both of whom served in the Reagan administration and have shown themselves generous interpreters of the executive power. One recent study concluded that this is the key thread connecting the Bush appointees.[70]

Further, any sort of imperial collapse will have to be precipitated by a Congress newly willing to utilize its own authority. Yet both structural and political considerations mitigate against a full-blown legislative resurgence in this regard. In times of crisis—and not coincidentally as the administrative response to crisis itself institutionalizes—legislators are naturally and sorely tempted to shift the burden of action from the Congress to the executive. It is, frankly, easier for legislators (and voters) to delegate powers to the president than to deliberate on their proper scope. John Owens has gone so far as to predict a "new constitutional equilibrium" based on heightened legislative deference inculcated by the "security culture" of a potentially permanent war on terror and the "new function of 'defender of the homeland'" it has added to the presidential portfolio.[71] Congress *can* act, and decisively, to regain lost ground—but when it does not, the default position between the branches has moved toward the presidential end of Pennsylvania Avenue.

Indeed, as noted, even a Congress in opposition hands has difficulty re-shaping a policy landscape groomed by executive action. The supermajoritarian procedures of the veto override and of the Senate more generally lessen legislative leeway, a result only reinforced by the sort of partisan polarization that led then-Republican senator Arlen Specter to score the Military Commissions Act of 2006 as "patently unconstitutional on its face"—and then vote for it anyway.[72]

The 111th Congress instead presents an expanded Democratic majority and a popular Democratic president. Will majority legislators be any more eager than they were during the Bush administration to rein in a president of their own party? Will that president renounce expansive authority? Recent campaigns suggest the question is one of position rather than personality. In 2004 the Democratic nominee, Senator John Kerry, went so far as to argue that the congressional resolution approving the use of force in Iraq was actually superfluous: "we did not give the president any authority that the president of the United States didn't [already] have." The 2008 candidates ducked the rare questions they received regarding executive authority. All promised to avoid the overt confrontations of the Bush years. But as Clinton chief of staff—and Obama CIA director—Leon Panetta recently observed, "I don't think any president walks into their job and starts thinking about how they can minimize their authority."[73]

The most likely result moving forward, then, is a less aggressive, less public, but hardly less potent, set of executive claims. That is not to say that symbolic changes—closing the prison at Guantanamo Bay, for example, or making bold promises of transparency—are not important. But even criticized precedents accrete for presidential use: as Justice Jackson wrote in another famous case assessing executive power, a principle once established "lies about like a loaded weapon ready for the hand of any authority that can bring forward a plausible claim of urgent need."[74] Reworking a famous comment by Justice Holmes, a Reagan staffer confirmed the enduring value of unilateral action: "a page of history," he wrote, "is worth a volume of political rhetoric."[75]

Future presidents will take note of what has been authored since Watergate and since 2001. Even as the most extreme claims made by the Bush administration are curtailed, the administrative strategies of his presidency, building as they do on established pages of history, are likely to remain useful tools for his successors. Presidents, in short, will continue to seek control where they can find it. And the "imperial presidency" will continue to be a phrase in demand.

Notes

1. Arthur M. Schlesinger, Jr., *The Imperial Presidency* (Boston: Houghton Mifflin, 1973); Michael Beschloss, "The End of the Imperial Presidency," *New York Times* December 18, 2000.

2. Rumsfeld press briefing of April 11, 2003, available at www.defenselink.mil/transcripts/transcript.aspx?transcriptid=2367, accessed February 10, 2009; Beschloss quoted in Tom Shales, "From President Bush, a Speech Filled with Assurance and Reassurance," *Washington Post* September 21, 2001.

3. Andrew Rudalevige, *The New Imperial Presidency: The Resurgence of Presidential Power after Watergate* (Ann Arbor: University of Michigan Press, 2005); Charlie Savage, *Takeover: The Return of the Imperial Presidency and the Subversion of American Democracy* (Boston: Little, Brown, 2007); "The Imperial Presidency at Work," *New York Times* January 15, 2006; William Rees-Mogg, "The Downfall of Bush's Imperial Presidency," *London Mail on Sunday* November 16, 2006; "The Imperial Presidency 2.0," *New York Times* January 7, 2007. The Google search was conducted on February 10, 2009.

4. Peter Irons, *War Powers: How the Imperial Presidency Hijacked the Constitution* (New York: Metropolitan Books, 2005).

5. "Cato," Letter V, originally published in the *New York Journal* (November 22, 1787 and available at www.constitution.org/afp/cato_05.htm, accessed February 10, 2009.

6. The phrase is Edward Corwin's—see, for example, Edward Corwin, Randall W. Bland, Theodore Hindson, and Jack Peltason, eds., *The President: Office and Powers*, 5th rev. ed. (New York: New York University Press, 1984), 201.

7. *Youngstown Sheet & Tube v. Sawyer*, 343 U.S. 579 (1952).

8. Please note that unless otherwise specified, in this essay "the Bush administration" should be taken to mean that of George W. Bush and not his father.

9. Scalia, dissenting opinion in *Morrison v. Olson*, 487 U.S. 654 (1988), emphasis added; *Barenblatt v. United States*, 360 U.S. 109 (1959)

10. Indeed, as Edward Corwin lamented, Article II is "the most loosely drawn chapter" in that notably vague document. Corwin et al., *The President*, 3.

11. "Cato," Letter V; Hamilton, Federalist #69, available at www.foundingfathers.info/federalistpapers/fed69.htm, accessed May 1, 2008.

12. Richard E. Neustadt, *Presidential Power and the Modern Presidents* (New York: Free Press, 1990), ix

13. For additional discussion, and further cites, see Rudalevige, *New Imperial Presidency*, 26–29.

14. On this point see Fred I. Greenstein, ed., *Leadership in the Modern Presidency* (Cambridge, MA: Harvard University Press, 1988), and Jeffrey K. Tulis' discussion of a "second constitution" in *The Rhetorical Presidency* (Princeton, NJ: Princeton University Press, 1987).

15. Corwin et al., *The President*, 4.

16. Schlesinger, *Imperial Presidency*, 252.

17. Stanley Kutler, *The Wars of Watergate* (New York: Knopf, 1990); Carl Bernstein and Bob Woodward, *All the President's Men* (New York: Simon & Schuster, 1974).

18. Rudalevige, *New Imperial Presidency*, ch. 4; James Sundquist, *The Decline and Resurgence of Congress* (Washington, D.C.: Brookings Institution, 1981).

19. James Taranto, "The Weekend Interview with Dick Cheney: A Strong Executive," *Wall Street Journal* January 28, 2006; January 2002 NBC interview quoted in John W. Dean, "More Than Just His Location Remains Undisclosed," *Findlaw.com* (May 24, 2002), available at http://writ.news.findlaw.com/dean /20020524.html, accessed June 1, 2009.

20. Louis Fisher and David Gray Adler, "The War Powers Resolution: Time to Say Goodbye," *Political Science Quarterly* 113 (Spring 1998), 1; Dan L. Crippen, "Observations on the Current State of the Federal Budget Process," Address at the Fall Symposium of the American Association for Budget and Program Analysis, November 22, 2002.

21. Francine Kiefer, "Clinton Perfects the Art of Go-Alone Governing," *Christian Science Monitor* (July 24, 1998), 3; see also David Gray Adler, "Clinton in Context," in *The Presidency and the Law: The Clinton Legacy*, edited by David Gray Adler and Michael A. Genovese (Lawrence: University Press of Kansas, 2002).

22. Richard Nathan, *The Administrative Presidency* (New York: Macmillan, 1983), and Richard Nathan, *The Plot that Failed* (New York: Wiley, 1975); on the Nixon-era bureaucracy, see Joel D. Aberbach and Bert A. Rockman, "Clashing Beliefs within the Executive Branch," *American Political Science Review* 80 (June 1976): 456–68. See also Andrew Rudalevige, "The Plot That Thickened," paper presented to the annual meeting of the American Political Science Association, August 2006.

23. Nixon, "Statement on Executive Privilege," *Public Papers of the President* (March 12, 1973).

24. Nathan, *Plot That Failed*; William F. West, "The Institutionalization of Regulatory Review: Organizational Stability and Neutral Competence at OIRA," *Presidential Studies Quarterly* 35 (March 2005): 76–93.

25. Thomas J. Weko, *The Politicizing Presidency* (Lawrence: University Press of Kansas, 1994), 89; Don Moran to Ed Harper, no title, 26 December 1981, National Archives II, Record Group 51 (Office of Management and Budget Files), Deputy Director's Subject Files: Ed Harper, 1981–1982 (FRC 51-82-50), Box 3, "Reorganization." See also Martin Anderson, *Revolution: The Reagan Legacy*, expanded ed. (Stanford, CA: Hoover Institution Press, 1990), 193–205.

26. Supreme Court Justice Samuel Alito—a lawyer in Office in Legal Counsel during the Reagan years—quoted in Jess Bravin, "Judge Alito's View of the Presidency: Expansive Powers," *Wall Street Journal* January 5, 2006. For a discussion of signing statements in this period and in general, see Savage, *Takeover*, ch. 10; Charles Tiefer, *The Semi-Sovereign Presidency: The Bush Administration's Strategy for Governing without Congress* (Boulder, CO: Westview Press, 1994)

27. *Common Legislative Encroachments on Executive Branch Authority*, 13 Op. Off. Legal Counsel 248 (1989); *The Constitutional Separation of Powers between the*

President and Congress, 20 Op. Office of Legal Counsel 124 (1996). The legislative veto was termed by Attorney General William French Smith, pre-*Chadha*, a "major danger to the independence and authority of the Executive branch." See Rudalevige, "The Plot That Thickened," 15–16.

28. "President Bush Holds Press Conference," *Weekly Compilation of Presidential Documents* (March 13, 2002), 411; Jack Goldsmith, *The Terror Presidency: Law and Judgment Inside the Bush Administration* (New York: W. W. Norton, 2007), 132.

29. Nathan, *The Administrative Presidency*, 82.

30. Francis E. Rourke, 1993. "Whose Bureaucracy Is This, Anyway?" *PS: Political Science and Politics* 26 (December), 687.

31. Steven G. Calabresi and Kevin H. Rhodes, "The Structural Constitution: Unitary Executive, Plural Judiciary," *Harvard Law Review* 105 (1992), 1215; Jeffrey Rosen, "Power of One," *New Republic* July 24, 2006. See, more generally, Steven G. Calabresi and Christopher S. Yoo, *A History of the Unitary Executive* (New Haven, CT: Yale University Press, 2008).

32. See, for example, *Morrison v. Olson*; *Humphrey's Executor v. United States*, 295 U.S. 602 (1935)

33. Samuel A. Alito, Jr., to Litigation Strategy Working Group, "Using Presidential Signing Statement to Make Fuller Use of the President's Constitutionally Assigned Role in the Process of Enacting Law." National Archives II, Record Group 60, Files of Stephen Galebach, Accession 060-89-269, Box 6, "SG/Litigation Strategy Working Group."

34. These figures—nearly twice as many as all of Bush's predecessors combined—were correct as of October 15, 2008. Thanks to Prof. Christopher Kelley for updating them on his website, available at www.users.muohio.edu/kelleycs/, accessed February 10, 2009. See also Joel Aberbach, "Supplying the Defect of Better Motives? The Bush II Administration and the Constitutional System," in *The George W. Bush Legacy*, edited by Colin Campbell, Bert A. Rockman, and Andrew Rudalevige (Washington, D.C.: CQ Press, 2007), 116–20; Savage, *Takeover*, ch. 10.

35. Quoted in Savage, *Takeover*, 236. It is worth noting that the Reagan staff thinking about this issue did anticipate the potential for a broader impact. Ralph Tarr, acting head of Office of Legal Counsel, suggested in 1985 that signing statements were "presently underutilized and could become far more important as a tool of Presidential management of the agencies. . . ." See Savage, *Takeover*, 233.

36. Francis E. Rourke, "Whose Bureaucracy Is This, Anyway," 687; Goldsmith, *The Terror Presidency*, 149.

37. "Presidential Signing Statements Accompanying the Fiscal Year 2006 Appropriations Acts," letter from Gary L. Kepplinger, General Counsel to Government Accountability Office, to Rep. John Conyers and Sen. Robert Byrd, reference B-308603, June 18, 2007.

38. On staffing strategies, see Hult and Walcott, "The Bush Staff and Cabinet System," in this book; Andrew Rudalevige, "'The Decider': Issue Management and the Bush White House," in *The George W. Bush Legacy*, edited by Colin Campbell,

Bert A. Rockman, and Andrew Rudalevige (Washington, D.C.: CQ Press, 2007). On recess appointments, see Henry B. Hogue and Maureen Bearden, *Recess Appointments Made by President George W. Bush, January 20, 2001–January 31, 2008,* Report RL33310, Congressional Research Service, 2008. Through early 2008, Bush made 171 such appointments—more than Bill Clinton, but fewer than Ronald Reagan, reflecting once again the ongoing nature of administrative strategies. Still, the strategy sufficiently angered Senate Majority Leader Harry Reid that he kept the Senate in continuous pro forma sessions over the Thanksgiving holiday in 2007 in order to prevent recess appointments.

39. Quoted in Rudalevige, "'The Decider,'" 140.

40. Robert O'Harrow, Jr., and Scott Higham, "Doan Ends Her Stormy Tenure as GSA Chief," *Washington Post* May 1, 2008.

41. Savage, *Takeover,* 294–300. The idea, as one careerist who left in 2005 said, was "to leave behind a bureaucracy that approached civil rights the same way the political appointees did" (300).

42. Dan Eggen and Paul Kane, "Justice Department Would Have Kept 'Loyal' Prosecutors," *Washington Post* March 16, 2007; Dan Eggen and Amy Goldstein, "Broader Privilege Claimed in Firings," *Washington Post* July 20, 2007; U.S. Office of Legal Counsel, "Prosecution for Contempt of Congress of an Executive Branch Official Who Has Asserted a Claim of Executive Privilege," 8 U.S. Opinions of the Office of Legal Counsel 101, 1984 WL 178358; *U.S. v. Nixon,* 418 U.S. 683 (1974).

43. Rudalevige, "'The Decider,'" 139–45; Al Kamen, "Recess Appointments Granted to 'Swift Boat' Donor, Two Other Nominees," *Washington Post* April 5, 2007; Curtis Copeland, "Executive Order 13422: An Expansion of Presidential Influence in the Rulemaking Process," *Presidential Studies Quarterly* 37 (September 2007): 531–44.

44. "Toxic Chemicals," testimony of John Stephenson of the Governmental Accountability Agency before the Senate Committee on Environment and Public Works, April 29, 2008, available at www.gao.gov/new.items/d08743t.pdf, accessed May 9, 2008; Michael Hawthorne, "EPA Official Ousted While Fighting Dow," *Chicago Tribune* May 2, 2008; documents posted by Rep. Henry Waxman, Chair of the House Oversight Committee, on the committee website—for example, "Responses to 16 November Questions from White House on Right Whale Ship Strike Reduction Final Rule," available at http://oversight.house.gov/documents/20080430104534.pdf, accessed May 9, 2008. More generally, see Christopher Lee, "Scientists Report Political Interference," *Washington Post* April 24, 2008.

45. At one stage the vice president sought to shift records from the first category to the (more restrictive) second, arguing that the visitor logs to his residence should be considered presidential, rather than Secret Service, records, and thus immune from Freedom of Information Act. A federal judge rejected this argument in late 2007.

46. Theodore B. Olson, et al., Brief for the Petitioners, *Cheney v. U.S. District Court for the District of Columbia,* U.S. Supreme Court case 03-475, April 2004, pp.

12–13. For a summary see Linda Greenhouse, "Administration Says 'Zone of Autonomy' Justifies Its Secrecy on Energy Task Force," *New York Times* April 25, 2004.

47. P.L. 107-40; Office of Legal Counsel, "The President's Constitutional Authority to Conduct Military Operations Against Terrorists and Nations Supporting Them," September 25, 2001, available at www.usdoj.gov/olc/warpowers925.htm, accessed February 9, 2009.

48. National Security Council, *National Security Strategy of the United States of America*, September 2002, 15, available at http://ics.leeds.ac.uk/papers/pmt/exhibits/378/NSS.pdf.

49. U.S. Department of Justice, *Legal Authorities Supporting the Activities of the National Security Agency Described by the President* (January 19, 2006); and see the President's press conference of December 19, 2005. Intriguingly, while Foreign Intelligence Surveillance Act (FISA) says that it is the "exclusive" means of gaining authority to wiretap for foreign intelligence purposes, an Office of Legal Counsel memo in 2001 argued that Congress would have had to specifically ban the procedures contemplated by the president for *legislative* exclusivity to hold. See Robert Barnes, "Sentence in Memo Discounted FISA," *Washington Post* May 23, 2008.

50. U.S. Department of Justice, "Re: Standards of Conduct for Interrogation under 18 U.S.C. §§2340-2340A," Office of Legal Counsel, August 1, 2002; U.S. Department of Defense, Working Group Report on Detainee Interrogations in the Global War on Terrorism: Assessment of Legal, Historical, Policy, and Operational Considerations, April 4, 2003, p. 21 and Section III generally. A useful compilation of these and similar memos is Karen Greenberg and Joshua Dratel, eds., *The Torture Memos* (New York: Cambridge University Press, 2005).

51. "President's Statement on Signing of H.R. 2863," Office of the White House Press Secretary, December 30, 2005; Mark Mazzetti, "Letters Give CIA Tactics a Legal Rationale," *New York Times* April 27, 2008.

52. As David Addington asked, "Why are you trying to give away the President's power?" Goldsmith, *The Terror Presidency*, 124; attorney quoted in Savage, *Takeover*, 131.

53. This was completed in November 2008. However, previous efforts to include security guarantees to Iraq in such an agreement were dropped. Karen DeYoung and Thomas Ricks, "Frustrated Senators See No Exit Signs," *Washington Post* April 9, 2008; Karen DeYoung, "Iraq Wants U.S. to Compromise More on Security Deals," *Washington Post* April 22, 2008.

54. Rep. David Obey, quoted in Lisa Caruso, "You've Got to Know When to Hold 'Em," *National Journal* July 12, 2003, 2258.

55. Paul J. McNulty, et al., "Brief for Respondents-Appellants," *Hamdi v. Rumsfeld* (4th Circuit Court of Appeals, June 19, 2002); Adam Liptak, "Judges Say U.S. Can't Hold Man as 'Combatant,'" *New York Times* June 12, 2007. The three judge panel of the 4th Circuit Court of Appeals ruling in June 2007 in favor of al-Marri was overturned by a 5-to-4 ruling by the full circuit in July 2008. In the spring of 2009,

however, the Obama administration moved al-Marri to the civilian court system, where he pled guilty to a charge of criminal conspiracy.

56. See Louis Fisher, "The State Secrets Privilege: Relying on Reynolds," *Political Science Quarterly* 122 (Fall 2007): 385–408; Robert M. Pallitto and William G. Weaver, *Presidential Secrecy and the Law* (Baltimore: Johns Hopkins University Press, 2007), 117 and chapter 3; Amy Goldstein, "Lawsuit against Wiretaps Rejected," *Washington Post* July 7, 2007.

57. See the "Protect America Act" of 2007, Public Law 110-55.

58. Douglass K. Daniel, "Senator Pushes to Censure Bush for U.S. Eavesdropping," *Boston Globe* March 13, 2006.

59. Thomas Mann and Norman Ornstein, *The Broken Branch* (New York: Oxford University Press, 2006); and see the Broken Branch Project updates published on the Brookings Institution website.

60. *Hamdan v. Rumsfeld*, 548 U.S. 557 (2006)

61. "President's Remarks at Faith-Based and Community Initiatives Conference," Office of the White House Press Secretary, March 3, 2004.

62. George Will, "Questions for John McCain," *Washington Post* February 17, 2008; Bruce Bartlett, *Imposter* (New York: Doubleday, 2006)

63. Hamilton, *Federalist #70*.

64. See John Hart, *The Presidential Branch*, 2nd ed. (Chatham, NJ: Chatham House, 1995). The relationship led to (but also perhaps stemmed from) an insular decision-making process that marginalized dissent. See Rudalevige, "'The Decider'"; Savage, *Takeover*, 181 and ch. 12. Foreign policy analyst Kenneth Pollack would note, vis-à-vis Iraq, that the administration's marginalization of bureaucratic expertise aimed to "dismantle the existing filtering process that for 50 years had been preventing the policymakers from getting bad information." Quoted in Seymour Hersh, "The Stovepipe," *New Yorker* October 27, 2003.

65. Lawrence Wright, "The Spymaster: Can Mike McConnell Fix America's Intelligence Community?" *New Yorker* January 21, 2008, 56.

66. And, notwithstanding Alexander Hamilton's role as patron saint of executive Unitarians, see his very similar conclusions in *Federalist #66*.

67. From an interview with the Israeli media, May 12, 2008, available at www.haaretz.com/hasen/spages/982914.html, accessed February 10, 2009.

68. Quoted in Dana Milbank, "It's Bush's Way or the Highway on Guantanamo Bay," *Washington Post* July 12, 2006; E. E. Schattschneider, *Two Hundred Million Americans in Search of a Government* (New York: Holt, Rinehart, and Winston, 1969), 53.

69. Goldsmith, *The Terror Presidency*, 215; Paul Kennedy, *The Rise and Fall of the Great Powers* (New York: Random House, 1987), 515.

70. See David Yaloff, "In Search of a Means to an End: George W. Bush and the Federal Judiciary," in *The George W. Bush Legacy*, edited by Colin Campbell, Bert A. Rockman, and Andrew Rudalevige (Washington, D.C.: CQ Press, 2007).

71. John E. Owens, "George W. Bush, The 'War on Terror,' and the New Constitutional Equilibrium," in *L'empire de l'executif*, edited by Pierre Lagayette (Paris: PUPS, 2007), 170–71.

72. Specter quoted in Charles Babington and Jonathan Weisman, "Senate Approves Detainee Bill Backed by Bush," *Washington Post* September 29, 2006. For a more systematic survey of the partisan divide in this area, see Joel D. Aberbach, Mark A. Peterson, and Paul J. Quirk, "Who Wants Presidential Supremacy? Findings from the Institutions of American Democracy Project," *Presidential Studies Quarterly* 37 (September 2007): 515–30.

73. Panetta quoted in David Nather, "New Handshake, Same Grip," *CQ Weekly* (December 17, 2007), 3702; Kerry, Democratic primary debate of February 27, 2004, partial transcript, available at http://transcripts.cnn.com/TRANSCRIPTS/0402/27/ltm.04.html, accessed February 10, 2009; Keith Perine, "Detainee Rights Pose a Question for '08 Hopefuls," *CQ Weekly* (December 10, 2007), 3636.

74. *Korematsu v. U.S.* 323 U.S. 214 (1944)

75. Peter J. Rusthoven to John Peterson, "Recess Appointments during Temporary Senate Recesses," July 26, 1984, Ronald Reagan Library, John Roberts Papers: Series I: Subject Files, Box 47, Folder titled *JGR/Recess Appointments (3)*. Holmes's actual aphorism, which is also apt, ends: "worth a volume of *logic*." See *New York Trust Co. v. Eisner*, 256 US 345 (1921).

Index

Abizaid, John, 189, 190
abortion, 8, 9, 14, 48, 54–55, 63, 64, 66, 122, 223–27, 229–32
Abu Ghraib. See Iraq
Adams, John Quincy, 15
Addington, David, 32–33, 206, 251
Afghanistan: war with, 80, 84, 92, 102–3, 143, 150, 164, 181, 235; and the constitutionality of the war, 132; and enemy combatants, 162; and the Northern Alliance, 161, 163; and the Soviet invasion in 1979, 138; and the Taliban, 76, 78, 85, 163, 164, 165, 183, 184; and transformation of the American military, 182; and the U.S. led invasion, 8, 10–11, 78
Africa, x, 79, 150
AIDS, x
Air Force, United States, 182, 191
Alito, Samuel, 15, 219, 225–26, 228, 230, 233, 236, 250, 260
Al Marri, Ali, 256
Al Qaeda, 8, 10, 18, 36, 79, 82, 85, 146–47, 147–48 150–51, 161, 163, 164, 165, 183, 187, 192, 236

Alternative Minimum Tax (AMT), 58, 98, 99, 105, 106
American Association of Retired Persons (AARP), 58
American International Group, Inc. (AIG), 107
Americans for Tax Reform, 99
Anti-Ballistic Missile (ABM) Treaty, 78
Anti-Detention Act, 247
Arctic National Wildlife Refuge (ANWR), 51, 63
Armey, Dick, 101, 122
Armitage, Richard, 20n14, 195
Ashcroft, John, 6, 8, 34, 37, 201, 220, 221, 232
Authorization for the Use of Military Force (AUMF), 161, 162, 164, 254, 255, 257
Aviation security, 9
"Axis of Evil," 77, 185

"bailout." See Wall Street
Baker, James, 31
Balanced budget Act of 1997, 96, 100

Bartlett, Dan, 8, 12
Baucus, Max, 97
Bayh, Evan, 106
Bin Laden, Osama, 76, 78, 148, 183
Boehner, John, 105–6
Bolten, Joshua, 12, 16, 38, 210, 211
border security. See immigration
Breaux, John, 56–57, 58, 59, 63
Bremer, Paul "Jerry," 188–89, 190
Breyer, Steven, 228–29, 237"Bridge to
    Nowhere," 104Brownback, Sam, 64
Buchanan, Pat, 118, 124
Buckley Jr., William F., 120, 123
Budget and Accounting Act of 1921, 94
Budget Enforcement Act, 100Bush
    Doctrine. See George W. BushBush,
    George H. W., 24, 32, 75, 93,
    118, 125, 161, 199; and the Iran-
    Contra Affair, 161; and moderate
    Republicanism, 118; and the
    judiciary, 220; and the Persian Gulf
    War, 75; and the transition of, 5; and
    political honeymoon of, 6, 48, 122
Bush, George W.: and the 2000
    election, 45, 47–48, 74; and the
    2001 inauguration, 80; and the
    2004 State of the Union, 55; and
    the 2005 inauguration, 80; and the
    2005 State of the Union, 57; and
    the 2008 State of the Union, 58;
    and Afghanistan, war with, 8, 10,
    80, 161, 254–56; and agenda of, 5,
    6, 7, 10, 13, 14, 15–16; and approval
    ratings, 13; and the bailout of banks
    and financial institutions, 19; and
    budget deficits, 91–94, 107–9; and
    the "Bush Doctrine," 77–82, 84;
    and cabinet of, 5, 6, 8, 12; and
    civil-military relations, 177–79,
    180–84, 191–93; and conservatives,
    117, 120–25, 229–37; as decision
    maker, 4, 8, 9, 10–11, 14, 16–19;
    and the Democratic Congress,
    104–7; and domestic policy agenda,
    62–67; and Economic Growth and
    Tax Relief Reconciliation Act, 49,
    63; and economy, 18–19, 81; and
    education reform, 66; and election
    to governor in Texas, 46; and
    embryonic stem cell research policy,
    63; and enemy combatants, 167–68;
    and energy policy, 50, 205–9;
    and the environment, 253; and
    executive authority, 157, 161–62,
    168, 171–72, 201, 245–49, 252;
    and executive orders, 7, 203–205;
    and executive privilege, 199–200,
    202–25, 214–16; and the farm bill,
    53; and the federal budget deficit,
    91–92, 107–9, 237–38; and the
    federal courts, 219–21, 224; and the
    Federal Reserve, 93; and the firing of
    several U.S. attorneys, 209–14, 252;
    and his first one hundred days, 34;
    and foreign policy, 73–80; and the
    "Freedom Agenda," 84–85; and the
    Global War on Terror (GWOT).
    See also Global War on Terror
    (GWOT), 36–38, 92; as governor
    of Texas, 45–47; and health care
    policy, 51; and the "honeymoon,"
    48–51; and Hurricane Katrina. See
    also Hurricane Katrina, 259; and
    ideology, 27; and the "imperial
    presidency," 243–45, 249–50,
    259–61; and the inauguration speech
    in January 2001, 48, 80; and the war
    with Iraq, 8, 10–11, 17–18, 38–39,
    57, 77–80, 82–84, 85, 102–3, 105–6,
    117, 120, 122, 123–25, 132, 161,
    182–88, 192–94, 224, 249, 255–56.
    See also Iraq; and his legacy, 237–38,
    259; and the McCain-Feingold Act,
    229; and the Mexico City Policy,
    122; and military tribunals, 15; and
    the nomination of Supreme Court

justices, 225–26; and organization of his administration, 23, 25–26, 40; and political honeymoon of, 6, 48, 122; and political partisanship, 13; and preemptive war, 140; and reelection, 56, 223; and the Republican nomination to president in 2000, 47, 121; and his appointment of Donlad Rumsfeld, 193; and same-sex marriage, 55; and second term of, 12–16, 29; and September 11, 2001, 35–36, 51–53, 92; and Social Security reform, 56; and his speech before Congress on Sept. 20, 2001, 243; and spending programs, 100-104; and Supreme Court nominations, x, 14–15, 122, 210, 219, 225–27, 228; and tax cuts, 38, 47–50, 52–54, 56, 61–62, 64, 66, 74, 95–100; and "torture memos," 171–73; and the troop "surge" in Iraq, 192; and vetoes, 14, 15, 257; and Vice President Richard Cheney, 32–33; and war powers, 131–32, 148, 150, 157; and warrantless wiretaps, 15; and White House staff of, 5, 6, 7, 12, 14, 29–31
Byrd, Robert, 189

campaign finance reform, 67
Canada, 76
Card Jr., Andrew, 5, 6, 12, 30–31, 190, 194, 225
Carter, James, 4, 5, 61, 199, 230
Central Command (CENTCOM), 183, 184
Central Intelligence Agency (CIA), 8, 36, 49, 160, 166, 168, 183, 191, 205, 255; and the overthrow of Mohammad Mossadegh, 160; and paramilitary officers in Afghanistan, 161; and the torture memos, 165; and the Valerie Plame scandal, 39

Cheney, Richard, xi, xiv, 6, 10, 11, 29, 30, 32–33, 34, 36–38, 40, 50, 54, 94, 206, 207, 224, 235, 247, 251; and the administration's energy policy, 50, 254, 260; and Colin Powell's speech at the UN, 187; and the D.C. Court of Appeals case, 208–9; and the decision to go to war with Iraq, 183, 186; and the federal budget deficit, 94; and the Supreme Court, 215
Chertoff, Michael, 36
China, 74, 75, 76, 80, 139
Churchill, Winston, 17
Chrysler Corp., 19
Citizens for Tax Justice, 97
Clean Water Act, 234, 235
Clinton, William J., xi, 5, 6, 15, 16, 24, 25, 26, 28, 32, 47, 54, 62, 64–65, 67, 93, 94, 118, 121, 148, 159, 179, 199, 202, 200, 212-13, 232, 248, 249, 261; and the Armed Forces of Puerto Rican National Liberation (FALN), 213; and disorganization of the administration, 29–30; and the economy, 108; and executive privilege, 199; and the federal budget, 91, 100, 102, 103, 104; and foreign policy, 73-74, 79; and health care, 58; and impeachment, 248; and the judiciary, 220, 221, 222, 227, 229, 230; and military operations in Kosovo, 159; and the Monica Lewinsky scandal, 4, 46; and the "New Democrats," 64; and reducing the size of the federal bureaucracy, 28; and the Republican Congress, 46; and tax policy, 93; and the White House staff, 34
Coalition Provisional Authority (CPA). See Iraq
Commerce, Department of, 29, 46, 253
Cold War, 75, 79, 103, 138–39, 141, 145, 146, 179, 180, 182, 246

compassionate conservatism. *See* conservatism

Congress, U.S., 5, 6, 7, 9–10, 15, 16, 19n11, 26, 27, 34, 36, 39, 46, 52, 60, 65, 66, 76, 79, 90, 92, 95, 96, 103–6, 121, 158-62, 168–71, 182, 191, 192, 209, 211, 216, 222, 229, 230, 233–37, 243, 245–49, 250-59, 260–61; and the Anti-Ballistic Missile (ABM) Treaty, 78; and campaign finance reform, 67; and the Clinton administration, 46, 101, 213; and the economic stimulus package, 61; and executive privilege, 199–206, 208, 212; and the Federal Marriage Amendment, 55; and George W. Bush's first term, 104; and George W. Bush's second term, 13–15; and the Medicare prescription drug benefit legislation, 123; and mid-term elections, 9, 15, 53, 226; and presidential elections, 21n25; and September 11, aftermath of, 8, 51, 77; and Social Security, 58; and war powers, 131–51, 157; and welfare reform, 59

Congressional Budget Office (CBO), 91, 93, 97, 98, 102

Congressional Research Service (CRS), 28, 103

conservatism, 28, 66, 67, 80, 101, 120, 125; and "big government" conservatives, 62, 100; and classical conservatism, 119; and "compassionate conservatism," ix, 46–47, 49, 55, 59, 62, 64, 67, 121; and cultural conservatives, 124–25; and economic conservatives, 232–35; and foreign policy conservatives, 235–37; and the judiciary, 219–20, 236, 238; and libertarians, 120, 122; and limited government and federalism, 45, 47; and neoconservatives, xii, 120, 123, 125, 183–84; and "Obamacons," 125–26; and social conservatives, 47, 51, 55, 64–65, 221, 229–32; and southern "blue dog" democrats, 96; and the traditionalist conception of conservatism, 199–120; and William F. Buckley and the *National Review*, 120

Council of Economic Advisors (CEA), 103

Cuba, 4, 21, 160, 162, 164, 167

Cutler, Robert 17

Daniels, Mitch, 94, 95

Daschle, Tom, 49

Deaver, Michael, 31

Defense, Department of (DoD), xiii, 28, 34, 36, 37, 76, 82, 160, 166, 170, 177, 188, 194, 223; and defense spending, 100, 101, 102–3; and the Iraq War, 190; and transformation, 182

Deficit Reduction Act of 2005, 104

DeLay, Tom, 98

Democrats, 6, 9, 10, 27, 30, 34, 59, 50, 52–62, 65, 67, 96, 97, 99, 101, 105-7, 121, 192, 200, 211, 222, 223–25, 227, 234, 257; in 111th Congress, 104–7; Blue Dog conservatives, 96, 106; and the Bush honeymoon, 48; and tax cuts, 96–97; and spending, 101–2; Detainee Treatment Act (DTA), 168, 236

DiIulio, John, 7, 63

Domenici, Peter, 189

Domestic Policy Council (DPC), 25

Dow Jones Industrial Average (Dow), 18

Dubai ports deal, 14

earmarks, 61, 101, 104–6

Economic Growth and Tax Relief Reconciliation Act (EGTRRA), 49, 63, 97–98, 99

economic stimulus, x, 18, 49, 61, 63, 66, 98, 106, 107; and the global economic crisis, 80, 81

Education, Department of, 47, 67, 101

Eisenhower, Dwight D., 4, 5, 7, 15, 16, 17, 56, 104, 159, 160

Electoral College, 6, 120

embryonic stem cell research, 51, 63, 65

Energy Independence and Security Act of 2007 (EISA), 60

Enron scandal, 52, 67, 233

Environmental Protection Agency (EPA), 28, 67, 214, 215, 234, 253, 258

Executive Office of the President (EOP), 24, 26, 248

"Faith-Based" initiatives, 5, 7, 39, 47, 51, 53, 55, 59, 62–63, 122

Fallon, William, 192, 193

Fanny May, 107

Farm Security Act of 2002, 53, 101–2

Federal Advisory Committee Act (FACA), 206

Federal Bureau of Investigation (FBI), 8, 36, 163, 200, 202–3

Federal Emergency Management Agency (FEMA). See Hurricane Katrina

Federal Marriage Amendment, 55, 63, 64

Federal Reserve Board, 51, 93–94

Feith, Douglas, 184, 185

financial crisis of 2008, 61–62, 64, 66–67, 80, 107

Food and Drug Administration (FDA), 233

Ford, Gerald, 30, 76, 199, 226, 247

Foreign Intelligence Surveillance Act (FISA), 61, 247, 254

Foster, Richard, 28

Frank, Barney, 106

Franks, Tommy, 184, 185, 186, 188

Freddie Mac, 107

Freedom of Information Act (FOIA), 205, 247, 253

Frist, Bill, 224, 257

Frum, David, 7, 8

Gates, Robert, xiii, 37, 38, 178, 191–93, 194

gay marriage. See same-sex marriage

General Motors, 19

Geneva Convention, 165, 236, 254

Gerson, Michael, 62

Gingrich, Newt, 46

Ginsburg, Ruth Bader, 233, 234

Global War on Terror, ix, xi, xiv, 4, 8, 36–38, 77, 79, 80, 84, 85, 92, 147–49, 186, 200, 223, 227, 235, 253, 260. See also George W. Bush and the Global War on Terror.

Goldwater-Nichols Act of 1986, 178, 181

Gonzales, Alberto, 32–33, 201, 210, 221, 227

Gore, Albert, ix, 5–6, 28, 32, 48, 74–75, 95, 96, 186, 200

Government Accountability Office (GAO), 34, 206, 251; and President Cheney's energy task force, 253, 260

Grassley, Charles, 97

Great Britain, 136

Great Depression, x, 18, 104

Great Society. See Johnson, Lyndon B.

Green, Joshua, 13

Greenspan, Alan, 93

Grossman, Michael, 13

Guantanamo Bay Detention Camp (Gitmo), 33, 162, 164–70, 249, 258, 261

Hacker, Jacob, 94, 99
Hadley, Stephen, 6, 16, 18, 29
Haiti, 73, 145, 146, 147
Hamdan, Salim Ahmed, 168–69, 236, 237
Hamdi, Yaser Esam, 162–64, 235
Hamilton, Alexander, 119, 245, 246, 258
Hayes, Rutherford B., 5, 48
HIV. See AIDS
health care, 33, 51, 54, 56, 58, 61, 105. See also Medicare, Medicaid; and Health Savings Accounts (HSAs), 54, 61, 63; and State Children's Health Plan (SCHIP), 61
Health and Human Services, Department of (HHS), 28
Highway Act of 2005, 104
Hispanics, 47, 59, 64, 121
Homeland Security, Department of, 63, 64, 65, 66; and the creation of, 9, 35–36; and homeland security, 8, 40, 52–53, 67, 84, 92, 100, 142, 151, 257, 260; and the Transportation Security Administration (TSA), 52
Huckabee, Mike, 64
Hughes, Karen, 6, 7, 12, 31–32
Hurricane Katrina, ix, x, 14, 16, 24, 58–59, 62, 64, 92, 103–4, 122, 249, 259; and conservative criticism of the response to, 122; and the Federal Emergency Management Agency (FEMA), 14, 24, 36, 166, 233
Hussein, Saddam, 10, 33, 38, 78, 79, 83, 186, 187, 188
Hutto, F. Chase, 29

immigration, 33, 47, 51, 57, 59–60, 61, 62, 64, 66, 122; and border security, 60, 63; and (comprehensive) immigration reform, 13, 63, 66
Iran, 77, 148, 149, 161, 257; and the 1953 CIA aided overthrow of

Mohammad Mossadegh, 160; and the Iranian hostage crisis, 4; and their nuclear weapons program, 149
Iraq, 18–19, 33, 35, 38, 56–57, 60–61, 65, 77, 80, 84, 92, 102–3, 105, 107, 122, 138, 143, 145, 147, 148, 178, 182, 183, 249, 255, 257, 259, 261. See also George W. Bush and Iraq; and Abu Ghraib, 166; and the Baker-Hamilton Commission, 19; and the beginning of the 2003 U.S. led invasion, 78, 188–91; and the Coalition Provisional Authority (CPA), 190; and conservatism criticism of the war, 123–24; and the constitutionality of the war, 132; and counter-insurgency strategy, 191; and "de-Baathification," 187; and the disbanded Iraqi military, 189; and the battle for Fallujah, 190; and General David Petraeus, see Petraeus, General David; and the planning of the U.S. invasion, 184; and "shock and awe," 186; and the "Sunni Awakening," 18; and the troop "surge," 18, 120, 192, 193, 257; and transformation of the American military, 182; and the war, 8–11, 12, 15, 16, 17-18, 37, 57, 65, 78, 82, 98, 132, 161, 178, 182–90, 193, 224; and "yellow cake" uranium in Niger, 10

Jefferson, Thomas, 119, 131, 135, 158–59
Jeffords, James, 7, 34, 50, 221
Job Creation and Worker Assistance Act, 52, 53, 63
Job Growth and Tax Relief Reconciliation Act (JGTRRA), 98
Johnson, Andrew, 119
Johnson, Lyndon B., 50, 85, 119, 125, 219; and the Great Society, 25,

102, 123; and the Gulf of Tonkin
Resolution, 160
Joint Chiefs of Staff, 11, 37–38, 75,
178, 180, 187, 193
Joint Committee on Taxation, 92
Justice, Department of, 165, 166, 167,
168, 200, 201, 209, 211, 214, 255,
258; and the 2004 torture memos,
171–72; and the Civil Rights
Division of, 252; and the Office of
Legal Counsel, 37, 132, 171, 202,
227, 249, 250;

Keane, Jack, 192
Kennedy, Anthony, 167, 170, 207–8,
215, 228, 230, 232, 234, 235, 236, 237
Kennedy, Edward, 49–50
Kennedy, John F., 4, 125, 138, 160
Kerry, John F., 12, 99, 223, 261
Korean War. See Truman, Harry S.
Krugman, Paul, 94, 99
Kumar, Martha Joynt, 13

"lame duck" presidency, 4, 15
Lewis, Jerry, 102
Lieberman, Joseph, 35, 58
Lincoln, Abraham, 119, 131, 158, 159,
259
Lindsay, Lawrence, 39, 103
Locke, John, 157, 158

Mack, Connie, 56, 58
Madison, James, 135, 136, 144, 158,
246; and Federalist 49, 259
Mankiw, Gregory, 102
Marshall, George, 75
McCain-Feingold Act, 228–29
McCain, John, 64, 108, 120, 121, 125,
220, 238
McClellan, Scott, 31, 188
McCrery, Jim, 99
McKinley, William, 5
McNamara, Robert, 191

Medicaid, 104
Medicare, 5, 9, 28, 47, 48, 49–50,
52–53, 62, 64, 66, 74, 95, 102, 104;
and conservative criticism, 122, 123;
and Medicare Part D (prescription
drug benefit for seniors), 8, 54, 58,
62, 63, 66, 102
Meese, Edwin, 31
Mexico, 76
Meyers, Richard, 181, 185
midterm election; 1994, 46; 2002, 52,
101–2, 222; 2006, 12, 183, 191, 237,
257
Miers, Harriet, x, 14, 122, 210–13, 215,
219, 225
Military Commission Act (MCA) of
2006, 169, 170, 237, 261
Mineta, Norman, 34, 49
missile defense system, 47, 74, 75, 76,
78, 148–49
Mondale, Walter, 32
Moynihan, Daniel Patrick, 58, 91
Mukasey, Michael B., 211, 214
Mullen, Mike, 193

NASDAQ, 18
National Archives and Records
Administration (NARA), 203–4
National Economic Council (NEC), 25,
38, 103, 107
National Endowment for Democracy, 83
National Energy Policy Development
Group (NEPDG), 206
National Oceanic and Atmospheric
Administration (NOAA), 26
National Review, 120, 121, 125, 126
National Security Agency (NSA), 29,
30, 31, 34, 35, 170, 172, 254–55; and
the domestic surveillance program,
256–57
National Security Council (NSC), 6, 8,
16, 17, 18, 25, 37, 183; and the plan
for the Iraq War, 186, 189

"National Security Strategy of the
United States," 78
neoconservatism. *see* conservatism
New York City, 35, 51, 92, 163, 164
Nixon, Richard M., 4, 13, 24, 25, 26,
67, 76, 126, 132, 199, 207, 220, 247,
248, 252; and the judiciary, 220,
226; and the War Powers Resolution,
132, 247; and Watergate, xiv, 4, 199,
245, 246, 247
No Child Left Behind, xi, 7, 13, 14, 26,
29, 34, 39, 49–50, 52–53, 62, 63, 64,
66, 101, 122, 132; and conservative
criticism of, 122; and the No Child
Left Behind Act of 2002, 101
North American Aerospace Defense
Command, 181
North Atlantic Treaty Organization
(NATO), 78, 159
Northern Alliance. *See* Afghanistan
North Korea, 77, 83, 139, 148–49

Obama, Barack H., x, 18, 62, 73, 81,
82, 83, 84, 107, 120, 121, 125–26,
220, 227, 234, 238
Obey, David, 105
O'Connor, Sandra Day, 15, 224, 225,
228, 229, 230
Office of Legal Counsel. *See*
Department of Justice
Office of Management and Budget
(OMB), 12, 23, 38, 94, 248, 252;
and the Office of Information and
Regulatory Affairs (OIRA), 26
Olasky, Marvin, 47
Omnibus Budget Reconciliation Act of
1990, 100
O'Neil, Paul, 30, 34, 38–39, 94
"Ownership Society," 55–57, 62

Pace, Peter, 184, 193
Padilla, Jose, 162, 163, 164

Pakistan, 81, 84, 161, 164
Panetta, Leon, 261
Partial Birth Abortion Ban Act, 54
Patriot Act. *See* USA Patriot Act
Paul, Ron, 123
Paulson, Henry, 39, 61, 106
Pelosi, Nancy, 106–7, 211
Pentagon. *See* Department of Defense
(DoD)
Persian Gulf War, 75, 124, 143, 145
Petraeus, General David, 18, 167, 192,
193
Pfiffner, James A., 8
Pierson, Paul, 99
Plame, Valerie. *See* Central Intelligence
Agency (CIA)
political polarization, 45–46, 53–54, 58,
65–66
Pork Barrel Reduction Act of 2006, 101
Powell, Colin, 6, 10–11, 29, 31, 34, 37,
38, 75, 125, 183, 189, 191; and his
reservations over the Iraq War, 186;
and his speech before the U.N. on
Iraq, 187
presidential elections: 1800, 119; 1912,
119; 2000, 5, 33, 48, 73–74, 95, 121–
22, 179, 221, 243; 2004, x, 11–12,
56, 65, 119, 223; 2008, 73, 82, 107,
117, 119, 120, 121, 123, 228, 257
Putin, Vladimir, 80

Quayle, Dan, 32

Reagan, Ronald, xi, 5, 6, 12, 15, 16,
24, 30, 45, 49, 56, 61, 66–67, 75,
85, 91, 92, 96, 99, 100, 102, 108,
109, 160–61, 199, 226, 232, 248–49,
250, 252, 260; and conservatism,
120, 123, 125; and the creation of
the National Archives and Records
Administration (NARA), 203–4;
and the economy, 108; and the

federal budget deficit, 94; and the Iran-Contra Affair, 161, 235; and the judiciary, 220, 225, 232, 235; and the military budget, 181; and support of the Contra rebels, 160; and tax policy, 93, 95; and war powers, 131

recession of 2001, 49, 51–52

Rehnquist, William, 14, 224, 227, 228

Reid, Harry, 58

religious right, xii, 221, 232

Reno, Janet, 200, 201, 212

Republican party, 34, 45–48, 50, 53–55, 57–62, 64–65, 74, 96, 99–100, 118, 121–22, 125, 202, 221; in 111th congress, 104–107; and realignment of, 5; Republican Study Group within, 104; and spending, 100–104; and tax cuts, 96–99

Rice, Condoleezza, 6, 8, 9–11, 29, 31, 37, 38, 75, 77, 184, 186, 189–90, 191, 193

Ridge, Tom, 35–36

Risen, James, 11

Roberts, John, x, 14, 15, 170, 219, 221–22, 224, 225, 226, 228–37, 260

Rockefeller, Nelson, 32

Roosevelt, Franklin D., 9, 13, 125, 131, 246

Roosevelt, Theodore, 119, 246

Rove, Karl, ix, 5–7, 9, 12, 13, 31, 39, 40, 122, 200, 210

Rumsfeld, Donald, xiii, 6, 10, 11, 12, 30, 31, 33, 34, 36, 37, 38, 75–76, 101, 181–83, 193–94, 243; and his "CEO style" management style, 178–81; and congressional criticism, 189–90; and the decision to go to war with Iraq, 183, 185, 187–89; and differences with Rice over Iraq, 191; and his relationship with the Army, 181–82; and his relationship

with Paul Bremer, 188; and his relationship with Richard Cheney, 38, 186

Russia, 75, 80, 137, 139, 146

same-sex marriage, 55, 64, 66

Sanchez, Ricardo, 186, 188–90

Saudi Arabia, 83, 163

Scalia, Anthony, 170, 228, 229, 230, 234, 245, 251

Schiavo, Terri, 65–66, 122, 231

Schumer, Charles, 221, 222

Scully, Thomas A., 28

Sarbanes-Oxley Act, 52, 63, 66, 67

Senate Banking Committee, 93

Senate Finance Committee, 96–97

September 11, 2001, 4, 8–10, 11, 16, 24, 33–38, 40, 51–53, 55, 59, 64, 73, 76–77, 80, 92, 94, 100, 120, 122, 132, 146, 147, 149, 150–51, 161, 163, 165, 181, 183–85, 200, 235, 244, 247, 249, 253–54, 259; and Bush's "Axis of Evil" speech, 185; and its immediate impact, 77; and national security decision making, 38; and the perpetrators of the terrorist attacks, 36

Serbia, 73

Shinseki, Eric, 179

"shock and awe." See Iraq

Sierra Club, 208

Skowronek, Stephen,

Small Business Association, 28

Snow, John, 3, 39

Social Security, 5, 7, 13, 14, 33, 48, 51, 56, 57–58, 62, 74, 95, 99, 100, 107, 224; and reform, 56–58, 63, 65, 66, 99–100

Somalia, 73, 145–46

South Korea, 4, 139, 160

Soviet Union. See Russia

Specter, Arlen, 224, 226, 261

Starr, Kenneth, 223, 226
State Children's Health Plan (SCHIP), 61
State, Department of, 34, 37, 38, 83, 165, 183, 190
State of the Union. See Bush, George W.
steel tariffs, 53, 122, 151
Stevens, John Paul, 235, 236, 237, 238
Summers, Lawrence, 107
Supreme Court, xiv, 14–15, 54, 122, 158–59, 162–64, 167–69, 170, 206–9, 212, 215, 219, 220, 224, 228, 229–31, 234, 236, 244–45, 250–51, 257, 260; and Boumediene v. Bush, 170, 237; and District of Columbia v. Heller (2007), 231; and Gonzales v. Carhard (2007), 230; and Hamdan v. Rumsfeld (2006), 168–69, 237, 257; and Hamdi v. Rumsfeld (2004), 257; and Hudson v. Michigan (2006), 228; and INS v. Chadha, 249; and Lawrence v. Texas, 230; and Ledbetter v. Goodyear Tire & Rubber Co. (2007), 233–34; and Massachusetts v. EPA, 237; and McConnel v. FEC (2003), 228; and Medellin v. Texas (2008), 236–37; and Parents Involved in Community Schools v. Seattle School District (2007), 231; and Randall v. Sorrell (2006), 228; and Rapanos v. U.S. (2006), 234; and Rasul v. Bush, 167, 170; and U.S. v. Nixon (1974), 207–8, 214, 252

Taft, William H., 119, 124, 246
Taliban. See Afghanistan
Tax Rebate Act of 2008, 106–7
Tenet, George, 49, 183
Thomas, Clarence, 163, 228, 230, 236
Tilden, Samuel, 5
tort reform, 53

torture, 37, 164–67, 170–71, 254–55
Transportation, Department of, 34
Transportation Security Administration (TSA). See Homeland Security
Treasury, Department of the, 30, 34, 93, 103, 123
Troubled Asset Recovery Program of 2008 (TARP), 107
Truman, Harry S., 4, 12, 85, 125; and the Korean War, 138, 139, 145, 159; and the "Truman Doctrine," 81; and war powers, 131

Uniform Code of Military Justice (UCMJ), 165, 169, 236
unitary executive theory, 250–58
United Nations (UN), 79, 159, 186–87
USA Patriot Act, ix, xi, 9, 52, 63, 66; 122, 256

Vietnam, xiv, 74, 75, 119, 137, 138, 145, 160, 244, 246
Voinovich, George, 53

Wall Street, ix, 61, 105–8
War on Terror. See Global War on Terror
warrantless wiretapping, 15, 61, 254, 256
Washington, George, 119, 158, 199, 246
waterboarding, 166
Watergate. See Nixon, Richard M.
weapons of mass destruction (WMDs), xii, 75, 78, 122, 132, 187
Weekly Standard, 120
welfare reform, 36, 59, 63, 74, 104
West Point, 124, 182
White House Office of Faith-Based and Community Initiatives, 63
Wolfowitz, Paul, 182, 184, 189
Woodward, Bob, 9, 10, 11, 20n14

Working Families Tax Relief Act
(WFTRA), 98, 99
World War I, 137
World War II, 16, 25, 73, 84, 120, 137,
143, 213, 246

Yoo, John, 37, 171–73, 200

Zandi, Mark, 108
Zinni, Anthony, 184–85, 188
Zogby, John, 99

About the Authors

Ryan J. Barilleaux is professor of political science, Miami University. He is the author or editor of seven books on the presidency and American politics, and has published dozens of scholarly articles as well. His latest book, *The Unitary Executive and the Modern Presidency*, will be published in 2010. He received a B.A., *summa cum laude*, from the University of Louisiana at Lafayette (1979), and an M.A. (1980) and Ph.D. (1983) from the University of Texas at Austin. Earlier in his career, he served as a staff aide in the U.S. Senate.

John P. Burke specializes in U.S. politics, the U.S. presidency, ethics, and public affairs. He has published numerous articles and eight books. Currently in press publication is a new study of the president's national security advisor: *Honest Broker? The National Security Advisor and Presidential Decision Making*. Another area of his recent and ongoing research is on presidential transitions to office. Burke has published a number of articles on presidential transitions and two books: *Becoming President: The Bush Transition 2000–2003* and *Presidential Transitions: From Politics to Practice*, which focuses on the Carter, Reagan, Bush Sr., and Clinton transitions and early presidencies. He has served on the editorial board of *Public Administration Review* and as a member of the executive committee of the Presidency Research Group of the American Political Science Association. From 1991 to 1995, he was the chairperson of the political science department at University of Vermont. He received his A.B. from Stanford University (1975) and his M.A. and Ph.D. (1982) degrees from Princeton University. He is a member of Phi Beta Kappa.

Andrew Busch is a professor of government at Claremont McKenna College. He is the author or co-author of eleven books on American government, his most recent being Epic Journey: The 2008 Elections and American Politics. In 2007, Dr. Busch received a Fulbright Teaching Fellowship for the Diplomatic Academy of Ukraine, and he was recently named the Ann and Herbert W. Vaughan Visiting Fellow in the James Madison Program in American Ideals and Institutions at Princeton University in 2009–2010. Prior to his career at Claremont McKenna College, Dr. Busch held a teaching position at the University of Denver. Dr. Busch received a B.A. from the University of Colorado and a M.A. and Ph.D. in Government from the University of Virginia.

Louis Fisher is a constitutional law specialist with the Law Library at the Library of Congress. Prior to this post, he worked for more than 30 years at the Congressional Research Service, serving as research director of the House Iran-Contra Committee in 1987, writing major sections of the final report. Dr. Fisher also frequents the halls of Congress, testifying on various issues from war powers, covert spending, and Central Intelligence Agency whistle blowing. He is also the author of books including, his most resent work, *The Constitution and 9/11: Recurring Threats to America's Freedoms*. Dr. Fisher has taught at a number of different universities around the country including: Georgetown University, American University, and Johns Hopkins University. He received his Ph.D. in political science from the New School for Social Research. The views expressed in his article are personal, not institutional.

Dale Herspring is a university distinguished professor in the Political Science Department at Kansas State University. He is also a visiting professor to the University of Kansas. Dr. Herspring has published numerous books including most recently *Rumsfeld's Wars: The Arrogance of Power* (2008). Dr. Herspring created the Political, Military and Diplomatic Lecture Series at Kansas State University, bringing over 130 senior academics, retired military, and diplomatic officials to campus providing graduate students with an opportunity to meet and discuss key problems in international relations. He has taught at various institutions, including the National War College, Georgetown University, and University of Maryland. Dr. Herspring received his A.B. from Stanford University and a M.A. from Georgetown University. He did his Ph.D. work at the University of Southern California.

Karen Hult is a professor of political science at Virginia Tech University. Her research interests include researching and publishing on the U.S.

presidency, executive branch bureaucracy, and the judiciary. Dr. Hult is the author of four books, including her most recent work titled *Empowering the White House: Governance under Nixon, Ford, and Carter*, coauthored with her colleague Charles Walcott. She is also a book review editor for the *Presidential Studies Quarterly*. Prior to arriving at Virginia Tech University, Dr. Hult taught at Pomona College and the Claremont Graduate School. She received her B.A. sum cum laude at Creighton University, did graduate work at Harvard University, and a Ph.D. in political science from the University of Minnesota.

Thomas M. Keck holds the Michael O. Sawyer Chair of Constitutional Law and Politics in the Maxwell School of Citizenship and Public Affairs at Syracuse University. He is the author of *The Most Activist Supreme Court in History: The Road to Modern Judicial Conservatism*, and with support from the American Philosophical Society, is currently writing a book on the courts and the culture wars during the Clinton and Bush eras. His research has also appeared in the *Law and Society Review* and *American Political Science Review*, with his 2007 article in the latter journal receiving the Houghton Mifflin Award for the best journal article on law and courts published by a political scientist that year. Dr. Keck received his B.A. in politics from Oberlin College, and his M.A. and Ph.D. in political science from Rutgers University.

Iwan Morgan is professor of U.S. studies and head of U.S. programs at the Institute for the Study of the Americas, University of London. A specialist on U.S. economic and budgetary policy, his publications include *Eisenhower versus the Spenders: The Eisenhower Administration, the Democrats and the budget, 1953–1960*; *Deficit Government: Taxing and Spending in Modern America*; and *Nixon*. His newest study, *The Age of Deficits: Presidents and Unbalanced Budgets from Jimmy Carter to George W. Bush*, is to be published in 2009.

Mark J. Rozell is a professor of public policy at George Mason University in Arlington, Virginia. He has written extensively on the presidency and has a variety of other research interests, including publishing works on religion and politics and the influence of the media on the political process. Dr. Rozell's most recent work is titled *Interest Groups in American Campaigns: The New Face of Electioneering*. He has also given congressional testimony in the U.S. House of Representatives on executive privilege issues, as well as making appearances on major national news programs. Prior to his arrival at George Mason University, Dr. Rozell has held a teaching post at Catholic University, where he was the chair of the Department of Politics.

He did his undergraduate work at Eisenhower College and earned his M.A. in Public Administration and Ph.D. in U.S. Government at the University of Virginia.

Andrew Rudalevige is Walter E. Beach '56 chair of political science at Dickinson College. Most recently the co-editor of *The George W. Bush Legacy* (2008), he is author of various essays and books on interbranch relations, including *Managing the President's Program*, which won the Richard E. Neustadt Prize, and *The New Imperial Presidency: Renewing Presidential Power after Watergate*. He has served as director of the Dickinson Humanities Program at the University of East Anglia, Norwich, England, and as a visiting scholar at the Center for the Study of Democratic Politics at Princeton University. In a prior life he was a staffer in the Massachusetts State Senate and an elected city councilor in his hometown of Watertown, Mass.

Mitchel Sollenberger is an assistant professor in the Political Science Department at the University of Michigan in Dearborn. He has recently authored a work on congressional power and the presidency titled *The President Shall Nominate: How Congress Trumps Executive Power*. Dr. Sollenberger has also served as an analyst in American National Government for the Congressional Research Service in the Library of Congress. In additional, he is a member of the American Political Science Association and a Reviewer for the *Political Science Quarterly*. Prior to arriving at the University of Michigan in Dearborn, he accepted teaching positions George Mason University and Bowling Green State University. Dr. Sollenberger did his undergraduate work at Fairfield University, majoring in Politics. He received his M.A. and Ph.D. in Politics from the Catholic University.

Charles Walcott is professor in the Political Science Department at Virginia Tech University, where he has been teaching since 1989. He has written or edited five books, including most recently, *Empowering the White House: Nixon, Ford and Carter*, co-authored with Karen M. Hult. Since July 2001, Professor Walcott has been an editor of *Congress and the Presidency*, an interdisciplinary journal of research in political science and history. Professor Walcott has also won several awards for teaching excellence, including a Certificate of Teaching Excellence from the Virginia Tech College of Arts and Sciences in 2003. Before coming to Virginia Tech, Dr. Walcott had a distinguished teaching career at the University of Minnesota. He is a graduate of Occidental College and received his M.A. and Ph.D. at the University of California at Santa Barbara.

Gleaves Whitney became the first full-time director of the Hauenstein Center in 2003. During his tenure he has been the architect of more than150 public programs and launched a website which has reached more than 17 million hits since its inception. Prior to his arrival at Grand Valley, Gleaves worked 11 years in Michigan Governor John Engler's administration, serving as senior writer, chief speechwriter, and historian. Gleaves graduated with honors from Colorado State University (1980) was a Fulbright scholar in Germany (1984–1985). He received his MA and doctoral candidacy at the University of Michigan, where he was a Richard M. Weaver fellow (1987–1988) and an H. B. Earhart Fellow (1988–1991). In 2006, he received the honorary Doctor of Humane Letters from the Graduate Theological Union in Berkeley, California.

John Yoo received his B.A., summa cum laude, in American history from Harvard University. Between college and law school, he worked as a newspaper reporter in Washington, D.C. He received his J.D. from Yale Law School, where he was an articles editor of the Yale Law Journal. He then clerked for Judge Laurence H. Silberman of the U.S. Court of Appeals of the D.C. Circuit.

Professor Yoo joined the faculty of the Berkeley School of Law in 1993, and then clerked for Justice Clarence Thomas of the U.S. Supreme Court. He served as general counsel of the U.S. Senate Judiciary Committee from 1995–1996. From 2001 to 2003, he served as a deputy assistant attorney general in the Office of Legal Counsel at the U.S. Department of Justice, where he worked on issues involving foreign affairs, national security and the separation of powers. Professor Yoo is the author of *The Powers of War* and *Peace: The Constitution and Foreign Affairs after 9/11* (University of Chicago Press, 2005), and *War by Other Means: An Insider's Account of the War on Terror* (Grove/Atlantic 2006).

David Zellers is a research associate with Susquehanna Polling and Research in Harrisburg, Pennsylvania. He is a graduate of York College (Pennsylvania) and received an M.A. in political science from Miami University, Oxford, Ohio. He was an intern with the Pennsylvania Department of State's Bureau of Commissions, Elections, and Legislation, and conducted research for the Center for Public Management and Regional Affairs at Miami University.